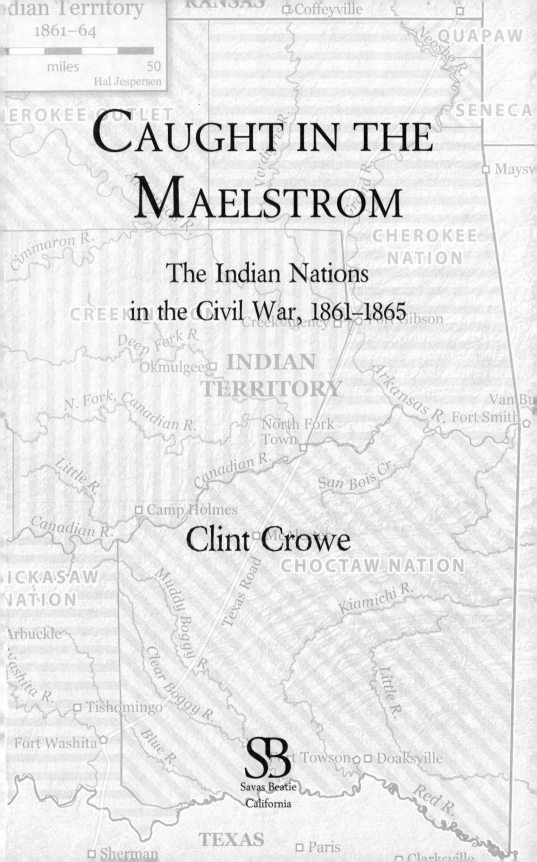

CAUGHT IN THE MAELSTROM

The Indian Nations
in the Civil War, 1861–1865

Clint Crowe

SB

Savas Beatie

California

Library of Congress Cataloging-in-Publication Data

Names: Crowe, Clint, author.
Title: Caught in the Maelstrom: The Indian Nations in the Civil War, 1861-1865 / by Clint Crowe.
Description: First edition. | El Dorado Hills, California: Savas Beatie, [2019] | Includes bibliographical references and index.
Identifiers: LCCN 2019005197| ISBN 9781611213362 (hardcover: alk. paper) | ISBN 9781940669687 (ebk)
Subjects: LCSH: Indians of North America—History—Civil War, 1861-1865. | United States—History—Civil War, 1861-1865—Participation, Indian.
Classification: LCC E540.I3 C76 2019 | DDC 973.70897--dc23
LC record available at https://lccn.loc.gov/2019005197

First edition, first printing

SB

Savas Beatie
989 Governor Drive, Suite 102
El Dorado Hills, CA 95762
Phone: 916-941-6896
(web) www.savasbeatie.com
(E-mail) sales@savasbeatie.com

Our titles are available at special discounts for bulk purchases. For more details, contact us at sales@savasbeatie.com.

Proudly printed in the United States of America.

Maps by Hal Jespersen

For Mother and Father

Table of Contents

Introduction   vii

Acknowledgments   x

1. The Division Over Removal   1

2. The Knights of the Golden Circle and the Keetoowah Society   10

3. Alliance with the Confederacy   25

4. Opothleyahola's Revolt   44

5. Pea Ridge   59

6. John Ross Throws in with the Union   75

7. Facing Artillery   86

8. The War for the Nations   93

9. Southern Refugees   109

10. Intervention   124

11. The Travails of General Blunt   135

12. Fort Gibson   151

13. The Rebellion Continued   162

14. The War Ends   202

15. Reconstruction in the Nations   218

16. Washington   230

Bibliography   244

Index   254

Author bio   262

List of Maps

Indian Territory   40

Battle of Chusto-Talasah   53

Battle of Chustenahlah   55

Battle of Pea Ridge   65

Battle of Newtonia   89

Battle of Old Fort Wayne   95

First Battle of Cabin Creek   100

Battle of Honey Springs   105

Colonel Phillips' Raid   168

Battle of Poison Spring   176

Demonstration on Fort Smith   188

Gano's and Watie's Raid   196

List of Illustrations

Stand Watie   14

John Ross   17

Albert Pike   33

Ben McCulloch   35

Rose Cottage   43

Opothleyahola   45

Maj. Gen. Earl Van Dorn   61

General Samuel Curtis   64

Senator James Lane   76

General James G. Blunt   103

Colonel William Penn Adair   169

Confederate Cherokee Delegation   235

Introduction

The Choctaws, Chickasaws, Seminoles, Creeks, and Cherokees resisted removal from the southeast to west of the Mississippi in modern day eastern Oklahoma. When the mixed blood leadership signed removal treaties, the result, particularly in the Creek and Cherokee Nations, was violence and separation that continued for years after removal. The mixed blood, English-speaking, slaveholding factions and the full-blood, native-speaking communities lived apart within their new nations in the westernmost reaches of the South. When the Civil War approached, the five nations officially aligned with the Confederacy, the division over removal returned, and the full bloods aligned with the Union. The result was a civil war within the Civil War.

The division in the Cherokee Nation manifested itself in the growth of secret societies. The full bloods mobilized the Keetoowah Society, which maintained ties to traditional culture while maintaining a close relationship with abolitionist Baptist missionaries Evan and John Jones. The mixed blood English speakers were active in the Knights of the Golden Circle. This pro-slavery organization formed the nucleus of many early Confederate military units across the South. In the Indian Nations, its leaders maintained close relationships with secessionist politicians in the adjoining Southern states.

Arkansas and Texas leaders lobbied their slaveholding neighbors to join them in the secessionist movement. Understanding that his full-blood political base opposed the alliance with the Confederacy, Cherokee Chief John Ross resisted. Stand Watie led the Rebel Cherokees. Eventually Ross was forced to accept a Confederate alliance to keep the nation united and his power intact, while gambling that the full bloods would remain loyal to his leadership. Arkansas lawyer Albert

Pike, who had successfully represented the Choctaws and Creeks over Congressional compensation for land concessions, negotiated treaties of alliance with the Confederacy.[1]

Creek and Cherokee full bloods resisted the Confederate alliances from the beginning. While full blood Cherokees bided their time within the Keetoowah Society, full blood Creeks openly opposed the alliance with the Confederacy. Chief Opothleyahola was the leader of the Creek opposition. He let the opposition believe that he was taking his people west to the Southern Plains. Instead, he used this deception to lead his people northeast into the Cherokee Nation. There members of the Keetoowah Society joined Opothleyahola, who had been promised military assistance by Union authorities in Kansas. In the process, Opothleyahola's forces won two engagements against their Confederate pursuers, but, when Federal support failed to materialize, Texas cavalry defeated and drove the refugees north into Kansas during a deadly snow storm. The young men among them became the nucleus of the Union Indian Brigade under the command of Col. William Phillips.

Two Cherokee regiments were at the battle of Pea Ridge in March of 1862, but their performance has been misinterpreted. The mixed blood Cherokee regiment enthusiastically supported the Confederacy. The full blood Keetoowah regiment was not motivated to fight for the Rebels, but when it was later allied with the Union, it served bravely. When federal forces reoccupied the Cherokee Nation, the remaining full bloods aligned with the Union, and to the end of the war both Creek and Cherokee full bloods made valuable contributions to Union victories.

In 1862 and 1863, Union and Confederate forces contended for control of the Indian Nations. The Union army occupied Fort Gibson and, following a series of battles that culminated in a Union victory at the battle of Honey Springs, took possession of Fort Smith. The result created refugees on both sides. Confederate-aligned families from the Cherokee and Creek Nations, numbering around 14,000, fled south to tributaries of the Red River, and Union-aligned families, numbering some 16,000, fled first to Kansas and then moved to Fort Gibson, where they remained to the end of the war. Both Union and Confederate

---

1 Ross's biographer, Gary E. Bolton, in *John Ross, Cherokee Chief* (Athens, GA, 1978), 1-14, provides details of Ross's ancestry of Scottish traders, mixed and full blood wives, and their offspring, but he rightly does not attempt an exact ratio. One-sixteenth is commonly used. According to Moulton, he was not a fluent Cherokee speaker. The complexity of "full blood" and "mixed blood" relationships before Removal is reflected in Theda Perdue, "Mixed Blood" Indians: Racial Construction in the Early South (Athens, GA, passim) 85-103.

authorities organized efforts to feed and shelter the refugees. Senator James H. Lane of Kansas, Union Gen. James G. Blunt, and their associates defrauded the federal government through kickbacks and fixed civilian contracts to supply troops and subsist the full blood Indian refugees.

Following the battle of Honey Springs, Confederate forces reorganized under a new commander, Gen. Samuel Bell Maxey, who reported directly to Lt. Gen. Edmund Kirby Smith, commander of the Trans-Mississippi Department. There were successful campaigns, coordinated with other Confederate forces in the department, including the defense against the Camden Expedition in Arkansas; a demonstration against Fort Smith; and, the disruption of traffic on the Arkansas River and overland supply trains to Fort Gibson. These campaigns were especially notable because Confederates refused to take prisoners from the 1st Kansas Colored Infantry and other black units in the theater.

High-level political activity on both sides attended these developments. President Abraham Lincoln needed Senator Lane's political support, despite the corruption of Lane and Blunt. There was also communication between Kirby Smith, Maxey, the Indian leadership, and the office of Confederate President Jefferson Davis and members of his cabinet about a dispute regarding the chain of command and the supply of ordnance. The story ended with the collapse of the Confederate military organization of the Trans-Mississippi and the onset of Reconstruction, also rife with division between the full bloods and mixed bloods. As a result, the Indian participants, Union as well as Confederate, shared in the loss of lands in the West, which they technically owned but were actually controlled by Comanches, Kiowas, and other Plains Indians, and which the Interior Department needed for the planned reservation system. Unfortunately, the land the Five Tribes had settled and retained lay in ruins.

Acknowledgments

I would like to thank Dr. Daniel Sutherland for his support, encouragement, and guidance in preparing this dissertation.

I would also like to thank Dr. Patrick Williams and Dr. Elliott West at the University of Arkansas for reading the manuscript and making useful suggestions. In addition, I would like to thank Dr. Brad Agnew, who directed my master's thesis, and Delores Sumner, special collections librarian, Northeastern State University, who gave me access to the collection and a place to work, and the late Sarah Erwin, librarian, and Renee Harvey, librarian, Gilcrease Museum, who provided access to the archives.

I also owe a debt my publisher Savas Beatie. Managing Director Theodore P. Savas helped develop and edit the manuscript for publication, and Joel Manuel read and corrected the final galley. Cartographer Hal Jespersen drafted the fine maps, and Lee Merideth produced the index. I am grateful.

Lastly, I want to thank my father, Harry M. Crowe, Jr. for repeatedly proofreading each chapter.

"Family on the Move." *Andy Thomas. All rights reserved.*

The Division Over Removal

The cotton culture expanded rapidly across the South during the 1820s and 1830s, an expansion that dramatically increased demand for Indian lands. There had long been pressure on the Indians to voluntarily move west of the Mississippi River. In 1803, President Thomas Jefferson wrote to William Henry Harrison, governor of Indiana Territory, about the issue. "Our system is to live in perpetual peace with the Indians, to cultivate an affectionate attachment from them, by everything just and liberal which we can do for them within the bounds of reason," explained the president. "The decrease of game rendering their subsistence by hunting insufficient," he continued, "we wish to draw them to agriculture, to spinning and weaving, [and to purchase their excess lands]. . . . They will in time either incorporate with us as citizens of the United States, or remove beyond the Mississippi."[1]

Over time, the Indians populating the southeast part of the United States made a number of land cessions, but with the election of Andrew Jackson and the passage of the Indian Removal Act, state and federal authorities increased the pressure upon the Indians to emigrate west beyond the Mississippi River. Some

---

1 Merrill D. Peterson, ed., *Thomas Jefferson: Writings* (New York, NY, 1984), 1,118.

southern Indians were resigned to the removal, but many others were absolutely against it and determined to resist rather than pick up and move.[2]

Before removal, Cherokees, Creeks, Seminoles, Choctaws, and Chickasaws occupied much of the southeastern United States. The Cherokee language was Iroquoian. The other four dialects belonged to the Muskogean language group. The Cherokees occupied northern Georgia and portions of Alabama, Tennessee, and North Carolina. The Creeks were farther south of the Cherokees in Alabama and Georgia. The Chickasaws were in northern Mississippi, while the Choctaws occupied central Mississippi and the Seminoles lived in Florida. Through years of trade and intermarriage, each of these tribes had been influenced in varying degrees by white southern culture, particularly the more wealthy mixed-bloods who adopted the institution of black slavery and the English language.[3]

Nearer the Gulf Coast, the Lower Creeks were more affected by white culture than any of the others, and many of their leaders were resigned to removal. Farther inland, the less integrated Upper Creeks opposed removal. After several land cessions, the Creek chiefs in 1824 voted that any chief who sold Creek land to the whites would be killed. When William McIntosh, a mixed-blood lower Creek chief, made an additional cession in exchange for a personal payment of $25,000 and land in the Indian Territory, about 200 Upper Creek warriors raided McIntosh's house. After allowing most of his guests to leave, they burned the dwelling and killed McIntosh and another chief. Witnesses reported that the Creeks shot McIntosh 50

2 Dorothy B. Goebel, *William Henry Harrison: A Political Biography* (Philadelphia, PA, 1974), 51-53, 93-94; Robert V. Remini, *The Jacksonian Era* (Arlington Heights, IL, 1989), 42-43; Ray A. Billington, *Westward Expansion: A History of the American Frontier* (New York, NY, 1960), 310-316; Francis P. Prucha, "Andrew Jackson's Indian Policy: A Reassessment," in *Journal of American History* (December 1969), Issue 56, 536-539; Francis P. Prucha, *The Great Father: The United States Government and the American Indians* (Lincoln, NE, 1984), 183-184; Grace S. Woodward, *The Cherokees* (Norman, OK, 1963), 1, 188-192; Ronald N. Satz, *American Indian Policy in the Jacksonian Period* (Lincoln, NE, 1975), 99-100, 296-298; Gary E. Moulton, *John Ross: Cherokee Chief* (Athens, GA, 1978), 72-95.

3 John W. Morris, Charles R. Goins, and Edwin C. McReynolds, *Historical Atlas of Oklahoma*, 3d ed. (Norman, OK, 1986), 20; Angie Debo, *The Rise and Fall of the Choctaw Republic* (Norman, OK, 1982), 1, 59-60; Arrell M. Gibson, *The Chickasaws* (Norman, OK, 1971), 159-166; Angie Debo, *The Road to Disappearance: A History of the Creek Indians* (Norman, OK, 1941), 3-5; Angie Debo, *A History of the Indians of the United States* (Norman, OK, 1979), 9-10; Daniel F. Littlefield, Jr., *Africans and Creeks: From the Colonial Period to the Civil War* (Westport, CT, 1979), 114-115; Theda Perdue, *Slavery and the Evolution of Cherokee Society* (Knoxville, TN, 1979), 58-60; Richard Halliburton, Jr., *Red Over Black: Black Slavery among the Cherokee Indians* (Westport, CT, 1977), 57-59; R. S. Cotterill, *The Southern Indians: The Story of the Civilized Tribes before Removal* (Norman, OK, 1954), 223-230; Edwin C. McReynolds, *The Seminoles* (Norman, OK, 1972), 95-96.

times. By 1827, the Lower Creeks began to migrate to the Trans-Mississippi. The Upper Creeks remained behind.[4]

In an effort to strengthen their rights to the remaining lands, in 1827 Cherokees under the leadership of John Ross created a bicameral government consisting of a National Committee and a National Council. In 1828, the two houses elected Ross as their principal chief. He had little Cherokee ancestry, but he had lived among the Cherokees all his life and was married to a Cherokee woman. The Cherokees considered Ross's native English and knowledge of American politics an advantage to resisting removal. That year, the *Cherokee Phoenix* began publication as a national newspaper to represent Cherokee interests.[5] The editors published the *Phoenix* in both English and in Sequoyah's Cherokee syllabary, which many native Cherokee speakers learned to read with relative ease.[6] The English text was intended for mixed-blood Cherokees who could not read or speak Cherokee.

By 1835, the cultural division in the Cherokee Nation—of which linguistics was a critical element—was well developed. Theda Perdue, an authority on slavery in the Cherokee nation, examined the Cherokee census of 1835 and concluded that while only some 17 percent of the people living in the Cherokee Nation in 1835 had "any white ancestors," up to 78 percent of "the members of families owning slaves claimed some proportion of white blood. . . . Among the people (including infants and small children) living in slaveholding families, 39 percent could read English, while only 13 percent were proficient at reading Cherokee. In the case of non-slaveholding Cherokees, less than four percent were capable of reading English, but 18 percent could read Cherokee." Literacy among the Cherokees in one language or the other may well have exceeded the literacy of the white Southerners moving onto Cherokee land.[7]

---

4 Debo, *The Road to Disappearance*, 85-90; Benjamin W. Griffith, Jr., *McIntosh and Weatherford: Creek Indian Leaders* (Tuscaloosa, AL, 1988), 248-252; Charles J. Kappler, ed., *Indian Affairs: Laws and Treaties*, 7 vols. (Washington D.C., 1904), vol. 2, 214-217.

5 Moulton, *John Ross*, 36-37; Woodward, *The Cherokees*, 144-145; Prucha, *The Great Father*, 189; Thurman Wilkins, *Cherokee Tragedy: The Ridge Family and the Decimation of a People* (Norman, OK, 1986), 205-206.

6 Sequoyah was three-quarters Cherokee. Raised by his Cherokee mother, he spoke no English. Convinced that the whites' method of writing could be duplicated in Cherokee he spent 12 years developing the Cherokee syllabary. Eighty-six written characters represent the various sounds of the Cherokee language. The system is remarkably effective, and native Cherokee speakers can learn the system fairly easily.

7 Theda Perdue, "Cherokee Planters: The Development of Plantation Slavery before Removal," in Duane H. King, ed., *The Cherokee Indian Nation: A Troubled History* (Knoxville, TN,

Andrew Jackson took office as president of the United States in 1829. At or near the top of his legislative agenda was the Indian Removal Bill. The legislation was hotly contested in Congress by the National Republicans (also known as the anti-Jacksonian party), including prominent leaders Daniel Webster and Henry Clay. The Democrats won a close vote, and Jackson signed the bill into law on May 28, 1830.[8]

Mississippi extended state law over the Choctaws and declared tribal government to be illegal in 1829. The Choctaws were divided over removal, and a violent civil war within the tribe nearly erupted. In June of 1830, however, they agreed to remove west of the Mississippi River. The emigration took place in three movements in 1831, 1832, and 1833. On March 24, 1832, Opothleyahola and other Upper Creek leaders signed a removal treaty and encouraged the Upper Creeks to prepare for the move west.[9]

When Georgia politicians extended state jurisdiction over Cherokee lands, the Cherokees took them to court. Under Chief Justice John J. Marshall the court ruled that the Cherokee Nation was not a sovereign state and, therefore, did not have standing in the Supreme Court.[10] The same month, to control the missionaries who opposed removal, Georgia passed a law that whites could not enter Cherokee land without a license from the state. Samuel A. Worcester, an American Board missionary who defied the law, was convicted and sentenced to four years hard labor.[11] Worcester appealed to the Supreme Court. In the case *Worcester v. Georgia*,

---

1979), 117; Perdue, *Slavery and the Evolution of Cherokee Society*, 61; Grady McWhiney, *Cracker Culture: Celtic Ways in the Old South* (Tuscaloosa, AL, 1990), 193-216.

8 Robert V. Remini, *Henry Clay: Statesman for the Union* (New York, NY, 1991), 362-363; Merrill D. Peterson, *The Great Triumvirate: Webster, Clay, and Calhoun*, (Oxford, UK, 1987), 195, 214; Robert V. Remini, *Andrew Jackson and the Course of American Freedom, 1822-1832* (New York, NY, 1981), vol. 2, 259-263; Remini, *The Jacksonian Era*, 42-43; Satz, *American Indian Policy in the Jacksonian Period*, 21-31.

9 Debo, *The Rise and Fall of the Choctaw Republic*, 51-56; Prucha, *The Great Father*, 215-219; Kappler, *Indian Affairs*, vol. 2, 310-318, 341; Debo, *The Road to Disappearance*, 97-101; Leitch J. Wright, Jr., *Creeks and Seminoles: Destruction and Regeneration of the Muscogulge People* (Lincoln, NE, 1986), 251; Michael D. Green, *The Politics of Indian Removal: Creek Government and Society in Crisis* (Lincoln, NE, 1982), 174-184.

10 Richard Peters, *Reports of Cases Argued and Adjudged in the Supreme Court of the United States* (Philadelphia, PA, 1831), vol. 5, 15-17, 20; Kermit L. Hall, ed., *Oxford Companion to the Supreme Court of the United States* (Oxford, UK, 1992), 139; Prucha, *The Great Father*, 207-210; Horace H. Hagan, *Eight Great Lawyers* (Oklahoma City, OK, 1923), 57, 71, 77-79.

11 The American Board of Commissioners for Foreign Missions was the most active of the missions among the Indians. It represented New England Congregationalists, Dutch

heard in February 1832, Marshall's ruling favored the Cherokees. In his opinion, the chief justice stated that the Constitution "[c]onfers on congress the powers of war and peace; of making treaties, and of regulating commerce with foreign nations, and among the several states, and with the Indian tribes. . . . The acts of Georgia are repugnant to the constitution, laws, and treaties of the United States."[12]

The Supreme Court adjourned shortly after handing down its important decision. Georgia's compliance with the ruling could not be determined until the next session of the Supreme Court—which would not take place for a year. Worcester had been in jail for eight months when he dropped the lawsuit, convinced "[t]hat there was no longer any hope, by our perseverance of securing the rights of the Cherokees. . . . The Supreme Court had given a decision in our favor, which recognized the rights of the Cherokees; but . . . it had become certain that the executive would not protect them." He recognized that only force could put the ruling into effect, and that force from Jackson would not be forthcoming.[13]

Among the Cherokees, the Treaty Party, also known as the Ridge Faction, favored removal. They were led by a man named Major Ridge, considered at that time to be the greatest orator in the Cherokee Nation, his son John Ridge, John's cousin Elias Boudinot, and Boudinot's younger brother Stand Watie. Major Ridge, a traditional chief, could not speak English. John Ridge and Elias Boudinot had college training, and Watie had a well-rounded education. With their land overrun by Georgia allotees and their government rendered powerless, these men believed they should take the best terms they could get and move west. On December 29, 1835, Major Ridge, Elias Boudinot, and 18 others signed the Treaty of New Echota, approved by a minority council. The treaty surrendered all lands in the East

---

Reformed, and the Presbyterian Church. William G. McLoughlin, *Champions of the Cherokees: Evan and John B. Jones* (Princeton, NJ, 1990), 18-19.

12 Peters, *Reports of Cases Argued and Adjudged in the Supreme Court of the United States*, 559, 561; Edwin A. Miles, "After John Marshall's Decision: *Worcester v. Georgia* and the Nullification Crisis," in *Journal of Southern History* (November 1973), Issue 39, 524-527, 533-543; Wilkins, *Cherokee Tragedy*, 195-198; Althea Bass, *Cherokee Messenger* (Norman, OK, 1968), 80-81.

13 *Missionary Herald* (Boston, MA, 1833), vol. 4, 184-185. In a prelude to the Civil War, South Carolina, which objected to high tariffs, asserted its right to nullify federal law it believed unconstitutional. President Jackson was willing to pressure the state to submit to federal authority, but not to force Georgia to submit to Worcester's Supreme Court victory. Concern that further resistance might cause Georgia to align with South Carolina and increase the danger of civil war contributed to Worcester's decision to drop the fight he had come to believe the Cherokees could not win. Bass, *Cherokee Messenger*, 175-176; Prucha, *The Great Father*, 211-213; Clement Eaton, *A History of the Old South* (New York, NY, 1975; reprint, Prospect Heights, IL, 1987), 334-335; Miles, "After John Marshall's Decision," 533- 543.

for $5,000,000 and new lands west of the Mississippi. They knew that the act violated Cherokee law and could cost them their lives, but they believed it was in the best interest of the Cherokee Nation. On May 18, 1836, the U.S. Senate ratified the treaty by just one vote. From that time forward, the United States insisted the treaty was valid.[14]

The Treaty Party removed west, but John Ross continued to resist the effort and traveled to Washington in 1837 to renegotiate the treaty. In part because of this, few of his followers prepared for removal, which should have been completed by May 23, 1838, at least according to the Treaty of New Echota. When the deadline came, Gen. Winfield Scott, soon to become commander of the U.S. Army, arrived to arrest the Cherokees and place them in stockades for removal. Scott ordered his men to be humane, but he was prepared to execute his orders. Ross capitulated and arranged to be put in charge of the removal. He returned from Washington in July after obtaining $1,047,067 in funds. This infuriated the members of the Treaty Party still in Georgia, who charged Ross with corruption and then left on their own. Ross organized the remaining Cherokees into 13 groups of about 1,000 each, and they departed in October and November 1838.[15]

The Chickasaws entered into a removal treaty in 1832, but it was not until the Treaty of Doaksville in 1837, which provided for land within the Choctaw Nation, that the Chickasaws began to remove. In Florida, the Seminoles fought a war against their removal until 1842, when hostilities finally ceased and most of the Seminoles had relocated to the western portion of the Creek Nation.[16]

Estimates of the loss of life among the 16,000 Cherokees on what is now known as the Trail of Tears range from as low as 2,000 to as high as 4,000 or more. The Creeks, Seminoles, Choctaws, and Chickasaws also suffered heavy losses.

---

14 Theda Purdue and Michael D. Green, *The Cherokee Nation and the Trail of Tears* (New York, NY, 2007), 91-115; Theda Perdue, "The Conflict Within: Cherokees and Removal" in William L. Anderson, ed., *Cherokee Removal: Before and After* (Athens, GA, 1991), 67-72; Wilkins, *Cherokee Tragedy*, 119-125, 142, 247, 256, 285-290; Kenny A. Franks, *Stand Watie and the Agony of the Cherokee Nation* (Memphis, TN, 1979), 1979; Prucha, *The Great Father*, 237; Kappler, *Indian Affairs*, 439-449.

15 Kappler, *Indian Affairs*, 209-213, 240, 241 footnote; *Missionary Herald*, vol. 29, 182-187; Miles, "After John Marshall's Decision," 543-544; Moulton, *John Ross*, 86-99; Mark M. Boatner, III, *Civil War Dictionary* rev. ed. (New York, NY, 1991), 728; Kappler, *Indian Affairs*, 446; Woodward, *The Cherokees*, 193.

16 Ibid., 153-162; Prucha, *The Great Father*, vol. 1, 223-226, 229-233, 268-269; Kappler, *Indian Affairs*, 209-13, 240, 241.

Removal greatly widened the division between the mixed-bloods and full-bloods, especially in the Creek and Cherokee Nations.[17]

The land that the Five Tribes settled was not in the arid West, but along the western-most edge of the geographic South. Average rainfall of 38-52 inches a year fed numerous streams and rivers. The treaties stipulated that Choctaw, Creek, and Cherokee lands (which included a hunting outlet) stretched to the western boundary of U.S. territory at that latitude (the 100th meridian). But the Five Tribes did not venture onto the Southern Plains, where the Comanches and other tribes dominated, and instead chose to stay east of the Cross Timbers, a belt of thick stunted forest with heavy undergrowth, miles wide and stretching from the southern border of eastern Kansas southwest into central Texas. The timber served as a physical barrier between the eastern woodlands and the southern plains. The area they settled varied from the wooded Ozark Uplift in the northeast, the Ouachita Mountains to the southeast, rolling savanna in the southwest, to a tall grass prairie providing excellent grazing in the northwest. The army had built Fort Smith on the Arkansas River in 1817, and Fort Gibson upstream near the confluence of the Verdigris, Grand, and Arkansas rivers, an area known as Three Forks, in 1824.[18]

The Choctaws and Chickasaws settled in the southern portion of the Indian Nations and established their tribal and mission schools, newspapers, and plantations. The military built Fort Towson above the Red River on the southern edge of Indian territory in 1824 to help oversee the area and to guard against any trouble from Mexico. The Chickasaws initially lived within the bounds of the Choctaw Nation and government, but in 1855 they attained near- autonomy in their own nation west of the Choctaws by treaty.[19]

The Lower Creeks settled above Three Forks along the valleys of the Verdigris and Arkansas rivers. The Upper Creeks settled around the confluence of the North Canadian and Canadian rivers and their northern tributaries. The two districts each

---

17 Prucha, *The Great Father*, 241, n. #58; Russell Thornton, *The Cherokees: A Population History* (Lincoln, NE, 1990), 73-76; Debo, *The Rise and Fall of the Choctaw Republic*, 56-57; Debo, *The Road to Disappearance*, 103-107; Debo, *A History of the Indians of the United States*, 125-126; Gibson, *The Chickasaws*, 167-176.

18 Morris, Goins, and McReynolds, *Historical Atlas of Oklahoma*, 5, 7, 9; Brad Agnew, *Fort Gibson: Terminal on the Trail of Tears* (Norman, OK, 1981), 3, 29-31; Robert W. Frazer, *Forts of the West: Military Forts and Presidios and Posts Commonly Called Forts West of the Mississippi River to 1898* (Norman, OK, 1965), 125-126.

19 Debo, *The Rise and Fall of the Choctaw Republic*, 58-65, 71-73; Gibson, *The Chickasaws*, 195-204, 208-222.

elected chiefs, with the Lower Creek chief ranking first. Opothleyahola, though not always chief, dominated politics among the Upper Creeks. Roley McIntosh, half-brother of the slain William McIntosh, was chief of the Lower Creeks.[20]

The division among Cherokees worsened following the Trail of Tears. A group of Cherokees known as the Old Settlers had migrated to Arkansas, beginning in the 1790s. When the Treaty Party arrived, its leaders agreed to live under the government of the Old Settlers. Later, when Ross arrived in Arkansas, he wanted to merge the Old Settlers and the Treaty Party under his control within the bicameral government established in the East. They held a council, and, encouraged by the Ridge Faction, the Old Settlers refused to cooperate with Ross. The full bloods blamed the Treaty Party for the removal from their traditional lands. On June 22, 1839, the day after the council ended, members of the Ross Party assassinated Major Ridge, John Ridge, and Elias Boudinot. Friends warned Stand Watie of the danger and the future Confederate general managed to escape. John Ross maintained that he did not take part in the killings.[21]

Chaos prevailed in the Cherokee Nation for seven years. Violence was common, and many members of the Treaty Party fled to Arkansas seeking safety. The parties held council, after council but without result. Only after President James K. Polk threatened to divide the Nation did the parties agree to end the violence and sign the Cherokee Treaty of 1846. The terms of the treaty pardoned all crimes between the parties and invited those who had left the Cherokee Nation to return in safety. Financial claims were settled, and both factions agreed to hold the land in common. The treaty stated that, "whereas serious difficulties have . . . existed between the the Cherokee Nation of Indians . . . it is desirable [they] should be speedily settled, so that peace and harmony may be restored among them. . . . All difficulties and differences heretofore between the several parties of the Cherokee Nation are hereby settled and adjusted, and shall, as far as possible, be forgotten and forever buried in oblivion." The differences remained buried until the secession crisis and the Civil War provoked total war in the Creek and Cherokee

---

20 Debo, *The Road to Disappearance*, 90, 101, 109-110, 123-124; Griffith, *McIntosh and Weatherford*, 3.

21 The author most sympathetic to the Ridge Faction believed Chief Ross did not take part in the planning of these killings. His son, who did take part, testified years later that the plotters had sent him to keep his father occupied while the killings were carried out. Wilkins, *Cherokee Tragedy*, 329-339; Morris L. Wardell, *A Political History of the Cherokee Nation* (Norman, OK, 1938), 11-19; Woodward, *The Cherokees*, 222-227.

country. In the meantime, a relative prosperity prevailed throughout the Indian Nations.[22]

Wealthy mixed-bloods used slaves to work plantations and raise livestock. Trade was conducted by seasonal steam traffic on the Arkansas and Red rivers and by a system of roads maintained by the military and tribal governments. Trading posts accommodated members of both the Ross and Ridge parties, as many immigrated south to Texas and west to the gold fields. The conservative full-bloods built cabins, raised livestock, and planted corn on small plots. Stock raising was successful in the tall grass prairie of the western Cherokee and eastern Creek Nations, where cattle numbered between 250,000 and 300,000 at the outbreak of the Civil War.[23]

Both missionaries and tribal governments established school systems. The Cherokee government built and maintained two state-of-the-art normal schools (high schools). Completed in 1851, the Male and Female Seminaries were substantial three-story brick buildings near Tahlequah, the Cherokee capital. They were boarding schools with entrance examinations and a carefully planned four-year curriculum. The Cherokee school system was superior to that of the adjoining state of Arkansas, which had no "system" to speak of.[24]

With the approach of the Civil War, division once again split the two nations. The full-blood Creeks and Cherokees favored siding with the Union, while the mixed-bloods advocated joining the Confederate cause. In the Cherokee Nation, the two opposing groups joined secret societies to organize and resist one another. A civil war within the Civil War was about to begin.

---

22 Kappler, *Indian Affairs*, 561-565; Gerard Reed, "Postremoval Factionalism in the Cherokee Nation," in Duane H. King, ed., *The Cherokee Nation: A Troubled History* (Knoxville, TN, 1979), 150-160; Woodward, *The Cherokees* 227-237.

23 Debo, *The Road to Disappearance*, 110-114, 141; *Annual Report to the Commissioner of Indian Affairs, 1859*, 178-182; Muriel H. Wright, "Early Navigation and Commerce along the Arkansas and Red Rivers in Oklahoma," in *Chronicles of Oklahoma* (March 1930), Issue 8, 65-88; William Paul Corbett, "Oklahoma's Highways: Indian Trails to Urban Expressways," (PhD diss., Oklahoma State University, 1982), 99, 101-102, 113-114, 122, 124, 126-127, 135, 138, 140-141; Clarissa W. Confer, *The Cherokee Nation in the Civil War* (Norman, OK, 2007), 35-41.

24 Woodward, *The Cherokees*, 240-243; Devon A. Mihesuah, *Cultivating the Rosebuds: The Education of Women at the Cherokee Female Seminary, 1851-1909* (Urbana, IL, 1993), 30-31; Carolyn Thomas Foreman, *Park Hill* (Muskogee, OK, 1948), 78-79; James Mooney, *Myths of the Cherokee and Sacred Formulas of the Cherokees* (1900, 1891; reprint, Nashville, TN, 1972), 147-150; Brad Agnew, "Indian Territory on the Eve of the Civil War," in *Proceedings: War and Reconstruction in Indian Territory: A History Conference in Observation of the 130th Anniversary of the Fort Smith Council* (Fort Smith, 1995), 35-39.

The Knights of the Golden Circle
and the Keetoowah Society

the Civil War approached, the opposing factions within the Cherokee and Creek Nations became further entrenched. The Cherokees formed secret societies that would have significant influence on upcoming events.[1]

Although the Cherokees had attained a degree of peace with the 1846 agreement, study of Cherokee politics and religion reveals that in the years leading to the war, "the full bloods and mixed bloods . . . participated in two separate subcultures." The coming conflict "brought into sharp focus full blood/mixed blood differences." Mixed-bloods dominated the Cherokee government, but "traditional elders . . . created the Cherokee national government . . . [and] power was still in the hands of the full bloods . . . who outnumbered the mixed bloods by about two to one." The two secret societies assumed a significant position in Cherokee politics. One proposed unity with the Confederacy, while the other favored the Union.[2]

---

1 The Creek Nation and its relationship with the Keetoowah Society is examined in Chapter 4.

2 Janet Etheridge Jordon, "Politics and Religion in a Western Cherokee Community: A Century of Struggle in a White Man's World," (PhD diss., University of Connecticut, 1975), 41-43; Christie Smith et al., "Memorial of the Delegates of the Cherokee Nation to the President of the United States, and the Senate and House of Representatives in Congress," (Washington D.C.: Washington Chronicle Print, 1866), in *Pamphlets in American History* (New Haven: Research Publications Inc.), microfilm, #190.

On May 22, 1854, the United States Congress passed the Kansas-Nebraska Act in an unsuccessful attempt to compromise sectional differences. Southerners believed their slave-based economy had to expand into the territories if it was to survive. The growing strength of the Knights of the Golden Circle was one manifestation of this belief. George W. Bickley, a Northern novelist, historian, and physician, founded the KGC at Lexington, Kentucky, on July 4, 1854. The quasi-military organization sought to extend and control the production of cotton, tobacco, sugar, rice, and coffee. Members planned to establish a commercial empire based on a slave economy that would encompass "a radius of 16 geographical degrees or about 1,200 miles, a great circle . . . that would include Maryland, Kentucky, southern Missouri, all of the states south of them, a portion of Kansas, most of Texas and Old Mexico, all of Central America, the northern part of South America, and all the West Indies."[3]

Individual chapters, or lodges, of the KGC were called "castles." There were three progressive levels of membership. First was the fighting unit known as the Knights of the Iron Fist. Second was the financial arm, or Knights of the True Faith. Third was the political inner circle called the Knights of the Columbian Star. KGC castles would form the basis for many early Confederate military units.[4]

The KGC leadership dreamed of taking advantage of political instability in Mexico by seizing the country and dividing it into territories to be admitted to the Union as slave states. An observer reported on the military nature of the society at a KGC convention in Sulphur Springs, Virginia, in July 1859: "From the presence of a large number of military men and . . . a secret southern military organization, it appears that this movement is more advanced than has heretofore been understood," he declared. "The Legion is 13,000 strong, mostly armed, and ready to march at short notice."[5]

Among the notable military men attending the convention were Ben McCulloch, Mexican War veteran and noted Texas Ranger, and Secretary of War John B. Floyd. Sam Houston, governor of Texas, also had designs on Mexican territory and considered joining forces with Bickley. Houston's friend McCulloch encouraged him in this dangerous venture. Houston consulted with Col. Robert E.

3 C. A. Bridges, "The Knights of the Golden Circle: A Filibustering Fantasy," in *Southwestern Historical Quarterly* (January 1941), Issue 44, 288.

4 Roy Sylvan Dunn, "The KGC in Texas, 1860-1861," in *Southwestern Historical Quarterly* (April 1967), Issue 70, 544-545; Bridges, "The Knights of the Golden Circle," 289.

5 Little Rock *Arkansas True Democrat*, September 7, 1859.

Lee, who was then stationed in Texas leading 2nd U.S. Cavalry. Lee refused to even consider participating in an unauthorized invasion of Mexico. When Houston realized the idea was unfeasible, and when members of the KGC began to concentrate in southern Texas in March of 1860, he ordered them to disband.[6]

In order to regroup, Bickley organized a convention in Raleigh, North Carolina, from May 7-11, 1860. There, he symbolically resigned and the members of the convention re-elected him. The convention published an "Address to the Citizens of the Southern States," which expressed the objective of the organization: "[M]ake the South strong in the Union or powerful outside the Union." The result was an "upsurge of virility," as the members realized "that the growing KGC . . . castles . . . were actually the nucleus of a Southern army."[7] The military nature of the Knights was most apparent in Texas, where there were 32 known castles. The election of Abraham Lincoln interrupted the second KGC plan to invade Mexico, but KGC activity influenced the secession movement across the South. In Texas, Unionists expressed growing alarm about the organization, apparently with good reason. In February 1861, McCulloch led a group of 125 KGC members and others and took possession of the federal arsenal at San Antonio.[8]

There was substantial KGC activity in the Indian Nations. In 1866, D. J. MacGowan, a scholar contributing to *Historical Magazine*, revealed the presence in the Cherokee Nation of the KGC and pro-South Masonic Blue Lodges "during the excitement preceding the rebellion."[9] Masonic lodges were located in most of the major settlements in the Indian Nations. E. H. Carruth, a loyalist working with the Seminoles, complained of Confederate action and federal inaction in the region. He reported that "the half breeds belong to the K.G.C.[,] a society whose sole object is to increase and defend slavery."[10]

---

6 Floyd resigned his office in the fall of 1860 in support of the South. In the winter of 1861 he was accused of transporting weapons to Southern arsenals while he was still in office, and posting military commands to remote areas to render them ineffective. Floyd returned to Washington, demanded a trial, and was found innocent on all counts. He later raised a Confederate brigade and took part in the battle of Fort Donelson, where he demonstrated poor abilities as a soldier. Thomas W. Cutrer, *Ben McCulloch and the Frontier Military Tradition* (Chapel Hill, 1993), 170-172; Dunn, "KGC in Texas," 545-551.

7 Dunn, "KGC in Texas," 553.

8 Ibid., 548 n. #13, 554-560; Llerena Friend, *Sam Houston: The Great Designer* (Austin, TX, 1954), 337.

9 D. J. MacGowan, "Indian Secret Societies," in *Historical Magazine* (1866), Issue 10, 140.

10 Annie Heloise Abel, *The American Indian as Slaveholder and Secessionist: An Omitted Chapter in the Diplomatic History of the Southern Confederacy* (1915), reprinted as *The American Indian as Slaveholder*

In the Indian Nations, as elsewhere, the KGC was pro-slavery and anti-abolitionist. For example, the constitution of the Cherokee KGC included the following articles: "No person shall be a member of the Knights of the Golden Circle in the Cherokee Nation who is not a pro-slavery man. . . . The Captain or in case of his refusal, then the Lieutenant has the power to compel each and every member of their encampment to turn out and assist in capturing and punishing any and all abolitionists in their minds who are interfering with slavery."[11]

Led by Stand Watie, a surviving leader of the Treaty Party, mixed-blood members of the KGC had failed to convince Chief Ross to negotiate a treaty with the Confederacy during the summer of 1861.[12]

The Watie faction maintained a political relationship with important Southern politicians in Arkansas. Among their contacts was Richard H. Johnson, nephew of Senator Robert Ward Johnson, who ran the political network known as the "Family," which had controlled Arkansas politics since statehood. Richard Johnson edited the most important Democratic newspaper in Arkansas, the *Arkansas True Democrat*, which promoted "the Family's" interests. The *True Democrat* reported on Bickley's connections with Mexican politicians on August 3, 1859; on the KGC convention at White Sulphur Springs, Virginia, on September 5, 1859; on a castle organizing in Little Rock in September 1859; and on a castle operating in San Antonio on May 5, 1860.[13]

---

and Secessionist (Lincoln, NE, 1992), 86 n. #122; "Necrology," obituary of Robert B. Ross. No author given, in *Chronicles of Oklahoma* (September 1930), Issue 7, 356; Carolyn Thomas Foreman, "North Fork Town," in *Chronicles of Oklahoma* (Spring 1951), Issue 29, 97.

11 Halliburton, Jr., *Red over Black*, 119-120; The complete English text of the constitution of the Cherokee KGC dated August 28, 1860, is in Appendix I of Eula E. Fullerton, "Some Social Institutions of the Cherokees" (MA thesis, University of Oklahoma, 1931).

12 Franks, *Stand Watie and the Agony of the Cherokee Nation*, 114; Wardell, *A Political History of the Cherokee Nation*, 122, 130, 134; Edward Everett Dale, "The Cherokees in the Confederacy," in *Journal of Southern History* (May 1947), Issue 13, 161; *Reply to the Demands of the Commissioner of Indian Affairs* (Washington D.C., 1866), 10-11, 13, in *Western Americana: Frontier History of the Trans-Mississippi West* (Woodbridge, CT, 1976), microfilm, reel 105; MacGowan, "Indian Secret Societies," 140; Halliburton, *Red Over Black*, 119-120; Emmet Starr, *History of the Cherokee Indians and Their Legends and Folk Lore* (Oklahoma City, OK, 1921), 143; Rachel Caroline Eaton, *John Ross and the Cherokee Indians* (Chicago, IL, 1921), 127-129.

13 Bridges, "The Knights of the Golden Circle," 291-292 (text and footnote); Lenette Sengle Taylor, "Polemics and Partisanship: The Arkansas Press in the 1860 Election," in *Arkansas Historical Quarterly* (Spring 1985), Issue 44, 315; Elsie M. Lewis, "Robert Ward Johnson: Militant Spokesman of the Old-South-West," in *Arkansas Historical Quarterly* (1954), vol. 13, Issue 13, 30.

Brig. Gen. Stand Watie, the only Native American to reach the rank of
general in the Confederate States Army.

Oklahoma Historical Society

Bickley moved the headquarters of the KGC to Knoxville, Tennessee, in 1860. The goal of the organization had shifted from acquiring territory in Mexico to supporting secession. One study reported that Bickley claimed, "doubtless with exaggeration, that the 'brains' of the South, all slave state governors save three, several members of the Buchanan cabinet, and 65,000 other Southerners were members of the Knights." Regardless of the numbers, it is likely that the "Family" was represented in the Little Rock castle. Johnson resigned as editor in 1860 to run for governor of Arkansas. He was replaced as editor by Stand Watie's nephew Elias C. Boudinot (Watie was Boudinot's surrogate father), son of Elias Boudinot, the assassinated leader of the Ridge faction.[14]

The new editor, who had been educated in the East, had co-established the successful *Fayetteville Arkansan* on March 6, 1859. The purpose of the paper, explained one historian, was "to advocate the principles of the Democratic party, and to stay the onrushing tide of abolitionism, which threatens to overwhelm the South; to advocate the building of a railroad from the Atlantic to the Pacific, and to secure the location of it on or near the 35th parallel; and to promote the causes of education."[15]

Johnson's political enemy, an Arkansas congressman and future Confederate general named Thomas Carmichael Hindman, had been writing letters to area newspapers under a pseudonym to praise his own speeches. Boudinot, however, exposed the ruse. Under the Cherokee editor, the *True Democrat* supported John Cabell Breckinridge, the Southern Democrats' candidate for president in 1860.[16]

In addition to editing newspapers, Boudinot practiced law in the state and served as secretary of the Arkansas secession convention, where he was well regarded. The convention convened on March 4, 1861, and was nothing if not contentious. A motion for secession subject to a vote of the people failed 35–39. Following the attack on Fort Sumter, the convention reconvened on May 6, 1861,

---

14 Ollinger Crenshaw, "The Knights of the Golden Circle," in *American Historical Review* (October 1941), Issue 47, 39-40; Horace Greeley, *The American Conflict: A History of the Great Rebellion in the United States of America, 1860-'65* (Hartford, CT, 1885), vol. 1, 350; Michael Dougan, "A Look at the 'Family' in Arkansas Politics, 1858-1865" in *Arkansas Historical Quarterly* (Spring-Winter 1970), Issue 29, 102; Taylor, "Polemics and Partisanship," 315.

15 Fred W. Allsopp, *History of the Arkansas Press for a Hundred Years and More* (Little Rock, AR, 1922), 462.

16 James M. Woods, *Rebellion and Realignment: Arkansas's Road to Secession* (Fayetteville, AR, 1987), 76, 83-84; Michael B. Dougan, *Confederate Arkansas: The People and Policies of a Frontier State in Wartime* (Tuscaloosa, AL, 1976), 17-22; Taylor, "Polemics and Partisanship," 317, 321-322; James W. Parins, *Elias Cornelius Boudinot: A Life on the Cherokee Border* (Lincoln, NE, 2006), 29-30.

and on May 7 voted 63-8 for secession.[17] Boudinot's close contact with the "Family" illustrated the relationship between the secessionist politicians in Arkansas and the pro-slavery faction in the Cherokee Nation.

Following the secession of Arkansas, the Confederacy created a military district that encompassed the Indian Nations. The new secretary of war, Leroy Pope Walker, ordered Texan and newly commissioned Brigadier General Ben McCulloch to take "command of the district embracing the Indian Territory lying west of Arkansas and south of Kansas. "Your field of operations will be to guard that territory against invasion from Kansas or elsewhere. For this purpose," continued Secretary Walker, "there will be placed at your disposal three regiments of volunteers, viz: one regiment of mounted men from Texas . . . one of mounted men from Arkansas, and one regiment of foot from Louisiana.[18]

Confederate Commissioner Albert Pike negotiated treaties with the four Muskogean-speaking nations, but the Cherokees under Chief John Ross resisted stubbornly. Ross professed neutrality and refused McCulloch permission to bring his brigade into the Cherokee Nation. McCulloch complied, but surrounded the Cherokee Nation with Confederate military units to convince Ross that his future lay with the South. Confederate Arkansas was east of the Cherokee Nation. The Creek and Choctaw Nations to the west and south had allied with the Confederacy and were in the process of organizing regiments. McCulloch considered positioning elements of his brigade in Kansas north of the Cherokee Nation to complete the encirclement, but he chose a less dramatic alternative.[19]

The Cherokees owned a tract known as the Neutral Lands, a rectangle of 25 by 50 miles in the southeast corner of Kansas encompassing some 800,000 acres.[20] This property afforded McCulloch an alternative to invading Kansas with his own

17 A later vote produced only one dissenter. Alfred Holt Carrigan and Jesse N. Cypert, "Reminiscences of the Secession Convention," in *Publications of the Arkansas Historical Association* (1906), Issue 1, 306, 316; Jack B. Scroggs, "Arkansas in the Secession Crisis," in *Arkansas Historical Quarterly* (Autumn 1953), Issue 12, 209-211, 222-223. Ralph Wooster, *The Secession Conventions of the South* (Westport, CT, 1962), 161-166; Parins, *Elias Cornelius Boudinot*, 30-39.

18 *The War of the Rebellion: A Compilation of the Official Records of the Union and Confederate Armies*, 128 vols. (Washington D.C., 1880-1901), Series 1, vol. 3, 575-576. Hereafter cited as *OR*. All references are to Series 1 unless otherwise noted.

19 Cutrer, *Ben McCulloch and the Frontier Military Tradition*, 205; Abel, *The American Indian as Slaveholder and Secessionist*, 149-150, 151 n. #244; Franks, *Stand Watie and the Agony of the Cherokee Nation*, 117-118; *OR* 3, 591-592, 594-596, 692.

20 The Cherokees had been seeking to sell the Neutral Lands to the United States to alleviate their financial difficulties.

John Ross, principal chief of the Cherokee Nation, 1828-1866.

brigade. Early in 1861, before the Cherokee Nation had officially sided with the Confederacy and before his regiment of Mounted Cherokee Rifles mustered at Old Fort Wayne, Stand Watie formed three companies, totaling about 300 men. McCulloch posted Watie and his men to the Neutral Lands in Kansas. As Cherokees on Cherokee land, they were less likely to provoke federal retaliation than McCulloch would have done had he invaded Kansas with his non-Indian forces. Watie, leader of the quasi-military Cherokee KGC, formed his men outside the organization of the Cherokee national government. His three companies were probably his castle of the Knights of the Golden Circle.[21]

McCulloch, writing after Ross had relented and allied with the Confederacy, stated that he considered Stand Watie to belong "to the true Southern Party, composed mostly of mixed-bloods, and opposed to John Ross, and by whose course and influence, Ross was induced to join the South." The KGC served to organize the mixed-bloods, who constituted a southern sub-culture within the Cherokee Nation in particular and the Five Nations in general. However, the KGC did not control the region, for the full-blood majority had a secret society of its own.[22]

From the mixed-bloods' point of view, the Keetoowah Society was a political organization of full-bloods created by white abolitionist Baptist missionaries to combat the slave-owning Indians. From the full-blood point of view, the Society was the continuation of a pre-Columbian institution dedicated to the preservation of Cherokee culture and religion.

On April 15, 1858, members of Pea Vine Baptist Church gathered to consider how to deal with the mixed-bloods. Bud Gritts, a native Baptist preacher and leader of the Keetoowahs, reported that "a small number of leading members of Keetoowahs got together and discussed the affairs of the Cherokees, the purpose and objectives for which they had always stood."[23]

---

21 OR 3, 691-692; Franks, *Stand Watie and the Agony of the Cherokee Nation*, 114-118, Wardell, *A Political History of the Cherokee Nation*, 122, 130, 134; Dale, "The Cherokees in the Confederacy," 161; *Reply to the Demands of the Commissioner of Indian Affairs* (Washington D.C., 1866), 10-11, 13, in *Western Americana: Frontier History of the Trans-Mississippi West* (Woodbridge, CT, 1976); MacGowan, "Indian Secret Societies," 140; Halliburton, *Red Over Black*, 119-120; Starr, *History of the Cherokee Indians and Their Legends and Folk Lore*, 143; Eaton, *John Ross and the Cherokee Indians*, 127-129; Fullerton, "Some Social Institutions of the Cherokees," Appendix I.

22 OR 3, 692.

23 Howard Tyner, "The Keetoowah Society in Cherokee History" (MA thesis, University of Tulsa, 1949), 102.

Gritts' report was written a year before the convention at which these men drafted and ratified their plan of action and code of laws. The Keetoowah organization predated the Civil War and may have existed in pre-Columbian times. As Nighthawk Keetoowah Chief Sam Smith testified in 1937, "the Keetoowahs originated thousands of years ago beyond the records and memories of men." Keetoowah was a ceremonial name for the Cherokees, representing the traditional culture and values of the Cherokee Nation of full-bloods. The word was first recorded by the British in 1730. "Kituhwu" was the town that guarded the northern boundary of the nation. Anthropologist James Mooney recorded that "its inhabitants were called Ani-Kituhwagi (people of Kituhwa), and seem to have exercised a controlling influence over those of all the towns on the waters of Tuckasegee and the upper part of the little Tennessee." The word was synonymous with Cherokee among the Delaware Indians and other Algonquian speakers.[24]

The mixed-bloods claimed that abolitionist Baptist missionaries Evan Jones and his son John B. Jones were responsible for creating the Keetoowah Society. Early Cherokee authorities, including Emmet Starr and James Mooney, stated that one or both of the Joneses organized the society.[25] Indeed, while the Keetoowah Society emphasized the preservation of traditional Cherokee culture, the Joneses were influential with most of the membership.

The tendency of subsequent writers to refer to the Keetoowah documents written in the period just before the war as the "Keetoowah Constitution" contributed to the mistaken idea that the society was created at that time. The "Deliberation" was a formal statement of the positions reached by Keetoowah leaders at the meeting at Pea Vine Church in 1858. The society enacted the Deliberation and several laws from April 1859 through July 1861.[26]

---

24 Kenneth Ernst Fink, "A Cherokee Nation of Development," (PhD diss., Union Graduate School, 1978), 82; James Mooney, *Myths of the Cherokee* in *Nineteenth Annual Report of the U. S. Bureau of American Ethnology to the Secretary of the Smithsonian Institution, 1897-98* (Washington D.C., 1900), 182.

25 Starr states that both father and son were involved, Mooney, only the son, who was fluent in Cherokee; Starr, *History of the Cherokee Indians and Their Legends and Folk Lore*, 143; Mooney, *Myths of the Cherokee*, 225.

26 An English translation of the text of the Keetoowah Convention is contained in Tyner, "The Keetoowah Society in Cherokee History," Appendix A; Benny Smith, "The Keetoowah Society of the Cherokee Indians," (MA thesis, Northwestern State University, Alva, Oklahoma, 1967), 9; Sequoyah's syllabary was in widespread use by 1830, Wardell, *A Political History of the Cherokee Nation*, 4.

There are several indications that the Joneses and Ross influenced the drafting of this document. Evan Jones established Pea Vine Church, where the "Deliberation" occurred. Bud Gritts, the author of the "Deliberation," was a member and a preacher. The Joneses were in danger of expulsion from the Cherokee Nation for abolitionist activity, and the "Deliberation" reflects their concern over that threat. In addition, the society's four stated intentions were in strict agreement with Ross's position at that time. Most important among them was neutrality, a change from the Keetoowah statement in the "Deliberation" that called for an alliance with the North. The Keetoowah expression of loyalty to the Cherokee government and constitution implies loyalty to Ross. Finally, the "Constitution" established a communications network between Ross and his full-blood political base.[27]

The Keetoowah Society was not an abolitionist society created by the Joneses, but rather a faction on one side of the cultural rift in the Cherokee Nation. Nevertheless, the Joneses had great influence with the full-bloods. During Evan Jones's early evangelical work in the East, he formed a close political relationship with John Ross by resisting removal. While Ross was in Washington attempting to negotiate new terms for the Cherokees, Jones kept him informed of the morale of the full-bloods and the depredations being inflicted on them. When Elias Boudinot authored a pamphlet defending the New Echota Treaty that was circulated in the United States Congress, Ross chose Jones to write the rebuttal. The degree to which Ross and Jones cooperated to resist removal is illustrated in the postscript of a letter from Jones to Ross: "Will another protest from the people be of any avail? If so, let me know the principal points to be dwelt on, and in the kind of style or tone rather whether confident or submissive or both mixed."[28]

As slavery became the dominant issue in the South, the southern Protestant churches endorsed the institution and gradually silenced southern moderates opposed to slavery. Jones was unique as an anti-slavery Baptist, sponsored by the

---

27 Howard Tyner, "The Keetoowah Society in Cherokee History (MA thesis, University of Tulsa, 1949), Keetoowah Convention, Laws, 1, 7, 30.

28 Evan Jones to John Ross, December 29, 1837; Evan Jones to John Ross, November 20, 1837; Evan Jones to John Ross, February 26, 1838; Evan Jones to John Ross, March 20, 1838; Gary E. Moulton, *The Papers of John Ross: 1840-1866* (Norman, OK, 1985), vol. 1, 549-551, 571-572, 599-600, 614-615; McLoughlin, *Champions of the Cherokees*, 159-166.

Baptist Home Mission Board, who came west with the Cherokees and their slaves and continued to work among them until the beginning of the Civil War.[29]

The Joneses' biographer wrote that they did not participate directly in the Keetoowah Society, but instead preferred to let the native preachers they had trained, including Bud Gritts, run a "parallel organization . . . [offering] advice only when asked, . . . [because the author believed the society was a] genuinely syncretic, grassroots political and social organization."[30] Still, one cannot be certain of the degree of the Joneses' involvement in the society.

Evan Jones gained his reputation as an abolitionist following his board's inquiry, in 1848, into the extent of slavery in his mission among the Cherokees. Only 4 of the 1,200 members of his circuit owned slaves. Aware that any suggestion of abolitionist activity could lead to his expulsion from the nation, Jones stalled until 1852, when he finally asked the four slaveowners to leave his circuit. In 1854, the expelled members complained to the Cherokee agent, George Butler, a South Carolina slave owner. Butler reported to the commissioner of Indian affairs that certain missionaries had overstepped their legitimate responsibilities by interfering with slavery. Their actions, he concluded, "if persisted in, must lead to mischievous and pernicious consequences."[31] In 1855, Butler reported to the new commissioner that he had "called the attention of your predecessor to the slavery question, I again refer to it, as it is producing much excitement in the nation. . . . I am sorry to say, the cause can be traced to the anti-slavery missionaries in the nation." Butler continued: "It is a subject of daily conversation among the intelligent portion of the community, who denounce in strong terms the movements of the abolitionists."[32]

As a result of the controversy, the Cherokee Council considered a bill to expel missionaries connected with abolitionism. For the time being, the Joneses survived the criticism and continued to operate their mission. Already active in the Creek

29 Ibid.,159-166; Southern Baptists, Southern Methodists, and others found Biblical justification for slavery in the condemnation of Ham, and Peter's failure to condemn slavery, Eaton, *A History of the Old South*, 384-388; John Ehle, *Trail of Tears: The Rise and Fall of the Cherokee Nation* (New York, NY, 1988), 299-301.

30 McLoughlin, *Champions of the Cherokees*, 348.

31 *Report of the Commissioner of Indian Affairs for the Year 1854* (Washington D.C., 1855), 114-115.

32 *Report of the Commissioner of Indian Affairs for the Year 1855* (Washington D.C.), 124-125.

Nation, the Southern Baptists came into the Cherokee Nation in 1856, but, because of their pro-slavery position, they made few full-blood converts.[33]

Jones' actions angered Reverend Samuel A. Worcester, who operated the American Board Mission at Park Hill, a few miles south of Tahlequah. He did not believe that the slave owners in his congregation were in violation of Christian doctrine, and he was angry with Jones for stirring up trouble. Worcester and Evan Jones had been at odds since Worcester dropped his legal battle against the State of Georgia and argued for removal.[34]

Worcester's assistant in translating the Bible, Stephen Foreman, a bilingual half-Cherokee Princeton seminary graduate, was a Watie loyalist. Early in the war, he recorded his southern point of view concerning northern missionaries, writing: "When I think the Jones's are the cause of all our present sufferings and losses, and will be the cause of the final overthrow of the Cherokee Nation, I am astonished, I know not what to say. Old Mr. Jones has been among us upwards of 40 years, laboring as a missionary. His son John was born and raised among us and speaks the Cherokee language perfectly."[35]

Many of the pro-southern Cherokees believed that John Jones created the Keetoowah Society in opposition to the mixed-blood secret societies. For some time, the Joneses had been aware of the mixed-blood secret organizations, which were specifically referred to in the Keetoowah "constitution." In 1855, Ross sent Evan Jones a copy of an oath, which read as follows:

> Are you in favor of supporting slavery in Kansas, in the Cherokee Nation and in other countries? You do solemnly swear that you will for the support of slavery, support any person that you may be instructed to, by the Mother Lodge, for any office in the Cherokee

---

33 McLoughlin, *Champions of the Cherokees*, 277-290, 339-343, 355-360; Robert G. Gardner, "Ebenezer Lee Compere and Problems of Civil War" in *The Quarterly Review: A Survey of Southern Baptist Progress* 37 (January-February-March 1977), Issue 37, 26-29; Robert G. Gardner, "Landmark Banner and Cherokee Baptist" in *The Quarterly Review: A Survey of Southern Baptist Progress* (January-February-March 1975), Issue 35, 63.

34 *Worcester v. Georgia*, U.S. *Supreme Court Reports* 515 (1832); McLoughlin, *Champions of the Cherokees*, 276-277, 279, 289, 292, 294, 296-297.

35 Stephen Foreman, "Journal and Letters of Stephen Foreman, Cherokee Minister," 51, typescript, Western History Collection, University of Oklahoma; McLoughlin, *Champions of the Cherokees*, 405.

Nation or anywhere else, and to assist any member that may get into a difficulty on account of being a Brother of the Secret Society.[36]

In an accompanying letter, the Cherokee chief remarked that the secret lodges were subject to a mother lodge outside the Cherokee nation. These pre-KGC, pro-slavery lodges were probably Masonic Blue Lodges.[37]

Evan Jones was involved (with aid from translators) in translating parts of the Bible. His son John had been raised in the Cherokee Nation and was truly bilingual. After taking a degree in the East, John returned to instruct the native preachers in the scriptures and establish close contact with the widely scattered full-bloods. From May 17 to September 18, 1856, he conducted 33 camp meetings, some lasting up to four days, and rode "about a thousand miles on horse-back."[38] He complained that "certain influences . . . are . . . used against us growing principally out of our position on the slavery question. . . . Our mission has become the object of detestation by many of the more wealthy."[39]

John wrote a letter published in the *Baptist Missionary Magazine* in May 1860, which was reprinted the following summer in several Arkansas newspapers: "On account of our position on the slavery question," it read in part, "we also have to contend with opposition from many of the politicians both in the Cherokee Nation & the State of Arkansas. The border papers vilify us."[40]

Slavery proponents presented a petition to federal Indian agent Robert Cowert that accused Jones of interference in Cherokee affairs. Cowert gave Jones until September 27 to leave the Cherokee Nation. Preparing to depart, Jones returned to Baptist Mission where John Ross, back from a summer in Washington D.C., had

36 John Ross to Evan Jones with enclosure, May 5, 1855; Evan and John Jones Papers, American Baptist Archives Center (microfilm), Valley Forge, Pennsylvania; Mooney, *Myths of the Cherokee*, 225.

37 McLoughlin, *Champions of the Cherokees*, 343-344; MacGowan, "Indian Secret Societies," 140; "Necrology," obituary of Robert B. Ross, no author given, in *Chronicles of Oklahoma* (September 1930) 356; Foreman, "North Fork Town," 97.

38 J. Buttrick Jones to Rev. P. Peck, September 18, 1856, Evan and John Jones Papers. A microfilm copy of the Evan and John Jones Papers is in Special Collections in the library of Northeastern State University, Tahlequah, Oklahoma.

39 Ibid.; McLoughlin, *Champions of the Cherokees*, 5-6, 40-45, 225-229; Daniel Rogers, "The Beginning and Development of Baptist History Among the Cherokee Indians" in *Miscellaneous Letters and Manuscripts relating to Cherokee History* (Tahlequah: Northeastern State Teachers College, 1933), 33; Evan Jones, journal, August 12, 1827; Evan Jones Papers, American Baptist Historical Society, Rochester, New York, microfilm.

40 J. Buttrick Jones to Rev. G. Warren D. D., November, 17, 1859, John Jones Papers.

stopped overnight. As Jones recalled, "[Ross] gave me assurance of his sympathy and appeared to be very indignant at the treatment I had received. He told me he could do nothing for me now, but he hoped the time would soon come when he could."[41]

Ross, the Joneses, and the Keetoowahs each opposed the mixed-blood faction for different reasons. The Joneses opposed the mixed-bloods over slavery, while the Keetoowahs' opposition was an effort to preserve Cherokee culture. Ross, who was no abolitionist and owned many slaves, was not involved in traditional Cherokee culture. His political strength came from the full-bloods, and he opposed the mixed-bloods in order to maintain his position as chief of the Cherokees.

The Civil War drove a wedge into this highly complex division within the Cherokee Nation. The Knights of the Golden Circle, representing the Watie faction, helped organize the pro-Confederate mixed-blood Cherokees against Ross and his full-blood political base. The Keetoowah Society sought to preserve the old Cherokee traditions and social structure while incorporating northern Baptist Christian theology. The Society helped to organize its members against the mixed-bloods who had drifted away from traditional Cherokee society and aligned with the Confederacy. The full-bloods were pro-Union and anti-Confederate from the beginning of the conflict, but the convoluted policies of Chief Ross made it difficult initially for them to express their loyalties openly.

Ross stubbornly sought neutrality to avoid involvement in the war. Pressure from the pro-South Cherokees, the strategic location of the Five Nations, the absence of federal authority, aggressive Southern diplomacy, and the Confederate early-war victory on August 10, 1861, at Wilson's Creek in southwestern Missouri, however, forced him to make a choice.

---

41 J. Buttrick Jones to Rev. G. Warren, October 25, 1860, Evan and John Jones Papers.

Alliance with the Confederacy

The secession of the Southern states occurred in two phases. The first phase followed soon after the election of Abraham Lincoln, when the states of the lower South seceded. South Carolina led they way out of the Union on December 20, 1860. Mississippi, Florida, Alabama, Georgia, and Louisiana followed. Texas joined them on February 1, 1861. That April, President Lincoln informed the governor of South Carolina that he intended to provision the Federal garrison at Fort Sumter in Charleston harbor. Jefferson Davis, the new Confederate president, was under pressure to bring the upper Southern states into the Confederacy. He ordered Gen. Pierre G. T. Beauregard to take the fort. On April 12, Beauregard began a bombardment that continued for 33 hours until the Union garrison surrendered. The event polarized the North and South and ended attempts at finding a diplomatic solution. The second phase of secession followed when Virginia left the Union on April 17, Arkansas on May 6, North Carolina on May 20, and Tennessee on June 8.[1]

Confederate officials in Texas and Arkansas urged the Indian Nations to sever relations with the Federal government, and both states sent delegations into the region. The Choctaw, Chickasaw, and Seminole leadership, although not unanimously pro-Confederate or anti-Union, saw no alternative but to align with the Confederacy. Federal military evacuation and diplomatic neglect helped

---

1 David Potter, *The Impending Crisis, 1848-1861* (New York, NY, 1976), 494-498; Wooster, *The Secession Conventions of the South* (1962; reprint, Westport, CN, 1976), 148-149, 164-165, 182, 188, 195-201.

Confederate commissioner Albert Pike to negotiate treaties with all of the Five Nations. Nevertheless, dissent remained strong among the full-blood Creeks and Cherokees.

Texas Governor Sam Houston, who had worked to bring the Lone Star Republic into the Union, refused to call a convention to consider secession. Nonetheless, delegates met in Austin on January 28, 1861. After three days of discussion, the delegates voted 166-8 to adopt an ordinance of secession, subject to a vote of the people. Texans approved the ordinance by a three-to-one margin on February 23. Four days later, a three-man delegation departed for the Indian Nations to encourage the Five Tribes to align with the Confederacy.[2]

Aside from Ross and his allies, the mixed-blood leaders in the Indian Nations generally favored the South. Many full-bloods and some mixed-bloods in the Choctaw and Chickasaw Nations wished to stay out of the war, but not with the conviction that the full-blood Creeks and Cherokees displayed because the Choctaws and Chickasaws had not been as divided over removal. On February 6, the Choctaw General Council authorized the transfer of deposits in the North to Southern banks, if necessary. Communications with the Federal government were to be kept open, but the Council resolved that the "natural affections, institutions, and interests of our people, which indissolubly bind us . . . to . . . our neighbors and brethren of the Southern States [and] that we desire to assure our immediate neighbors, the people of Arkansas and Texas, of our determination to observe . . . amicable relations."[3]

The Choctaw Council elected 12 delegates to attend a convention with the Chickasaw Nation at Boggy Depot "to consult for the common safety of these two tribes in the event of the dissolution of the American Union." The convention convened on March 11, with the Texas delegation attending. James E. Harrison, leader of the Texans, addressed the convention on March 12 to give an overview of his state's differences with the Federal government and to explain why Texas had left the Union. He reported to Texas officials that "the Choctaws and Chickasaws are entirely Southern and are determined to adhere to the fortunes of the South." He also thought the meeting was conducted "with such admirable decorum and promptness as is rarely met with in similar deliberative bodies within the States."

---

2 Stephen B. Oates, "Texas Under the Secessionists," in *Southwestern Historical Quarterly* (October 1963), Issue 68, 168-171; Abel, *The American Indian as Slaveholder and Secessionist*, 88-91; *OR*, Series 4, 1, 322.

3 *OR* 1, 682; Gipson, *The Chickasaws*, 229-241; Debo, *The Rise and Fall of the Choctaw Republic*, 2d ed., 80-83.

The Texas delegation moved on, traveling through the Creek Nation to meet with important mixed-blood families. Lower Creek Chief Motey Canard helped Harrison arrange a meeting of all the Five Nations at North Fork Town on April 8, 1861. In the meantime, the Texans left for the Cherokee Nation. John Ross "received [them] with courtesy, but not with cordiality." Ross made it clear that he remained with the Union, although he said that if Virginia and the other border states seceded, he would side with the South. Harrison believed Ross might share the fate of Sam Houston, who had forfeited his office as governor of Texas for declining to swear a loyalty oath to the new Confederacy.[4]

High water in the Canadian and Arkansas rivers prevented the attendance of the Choctaws and Chickasaws, but the Seminoles, Creeks, and Cherokees were represented. Those present named Motey Canard chairman of the North Fork Town convention, which opened on April 8, 1861. Harrison delivered a well received two-hour speech in favor of the Confederacy. The convention adjourned, and Harrison submitted his report to Texas officials on April 23.[5]

On May 15, Governor William Clark, Sam Houston's successor, informed President Davis that "the active friendship of these nations is of vital importance to the South," and forwarded a copy of Harrison's report. The Texas commissioner was confident the Indian Nations would eventually conclude alliances with the Confederacy, and praised the Five Nations for their advancements in education, agriculture, livestock production, and the quality of their homes and land. He found the mixed-bloods to be Southern "by geographical position, by a common interest, by their social system, and by blood," and declared that "they [were] . . . rapidly becoming a nation of whites." Harrison thought that the Indians could raise 20,000 soldiers if they were not restrained by Federal troops and suggested that Fort Washita, just 24 miles north of the Red River, could be captured with little effort.[6]

The U.S. Army would have none of that and attempted to reinforce the isolated post. Lt. Col. William H. Emory, 1st U.S. Cavalry, was ordered to take command of Federal forces in Indian Territory, with his headquarters at Fort Cobb

---

4 Debo, *The Rise and Fall of the Choctaw Republic*, 80-82, 143; Gibson, *The Chickasaws*, 227-232; W. David Baird, *Peter Pitchlynn: Chief of the Choctaws* (Norman, OK, 1972), 126-128; Abel, *The American Indian as Slaveholder and Secessionist*, 92-94, 155-156; H. B. Cushman, *History of the Choctaw, Chickasaw and Natchez Indians* (Stillwater, OK, 1972), 272-273, 412-413

5 Cushman, *History of the Choctaw, Chickasaw and Natchez Indians*, 413.

6 OR Series 4, 1, 322; Abel, *The American Indian as Slaveholder and Secessionist*, 94-95; T. R. Fehrenbach, *Lone Star: A History of Texas and the Texans* (New York, NY, 1991), 347.

in the Leased District, west of the Choctaws and Chickasaws. However, before he left Washington, the government changed his orders to concentrate instead all forces from Fort Cobb and Fort Arbuckle at Fort Washita. Because the region was remote, Emory's orders were discretionary. He traveled by rail to Memphis, where he boarded a boat for the journey down the Mississippi and then up the Arkansas River. When low water stranded him in Arkansas, he sent orders ahead to the commander at Fort Arbuckle to begin moving troops and supplies to Fort Washita and, if Washita was seriously threatened, move there with his entire force.[7]

In March, Gen. William S. Harney, department commander, had ordered the commander at Fort Cobb to be ready to move his troops on short notice. Arriving at Fort Smith, Lt. Col. Emory ordered him to march two companies to Fort Washita while leaving two companies behind at Fort Cobb. When he arrived on the scene, Emory decided that Fort Washita had not been sufficiently reinforced and abandoned the post to the Texans. The following day, Virginia passed an ordinance of secession and the Army changed Emory's orders once again. This time he was to move all his troops in the Indian Nations to Fort Leavenworth, Kansas.[8]

The Army entrusted Emory's orders to Lt. William W. Averell, who had just reported for duty from sick leave. Leaving Washington on April 17, he traveled by rail under an assumed name and in civilian clothing to Rolla, Missouri. After an additional 300 miles by stagecoach he arrived at Fort Smith to find the post in a state of pandemonium. Troops loyal to the Union had abandoned the fort to join Emory. The Rebels had imprisoned the quartermaster, who was to have provided Averell with transportation. For his watch and cash, the Union lieutenant obtained a saddle and an unbroken horse, which Averell mastered as he rode the remaining 260 miles. Although pursued by bushwhackers, Averell, with the help of an Indian guide, found Colonel Emory on May 2, 1861. The lieutenant joined the Union command as it moved northwest from Fort Washita to Fort Arbuckle.[9]

---

7   This area was leased from the Choctaw and Chickasaw Nations to provide a future reservation for Southern Plains Indians. The army abandoned Fort Gibson in 1857. *OR* 1, 656, 659, 660-661.

8   Ibid., 662, 663, 665, 667, 648.

9   Edwin C. Bearss and Arrell M. Gibson, *Fort Smith: Little Gibraltar on the Arkansas* (Norman, OK, 1969), 241-242; Emory, whose overall command included Fort Smith, had been instructed to move the troops there across the western border if Arkansas seceded. He left the same instructions with Captain Sturgis, who in the face of overwhelming force abandoned the fort on April 23. Arkansas seceded on May 6, 1861. *OR* 1, 659, 665. Muriel H. Wright, "Lieutenant Averell's Ride," in *Chronicles of Oklahoma* (Spring 1961), Issue 39, 2, 6-11; *OR* 1, 648.

With the troops from Forts Smith, Washita, and Arbuckle, Emory proceeded to Fort Cobb, stopping only to deal with a pursuing advance guard of Texans. Captain Samuel D. Sturgis, former Federal commander at Fort Smith, and Averell took one company and bloodlessly captured 50 Texans, whom they paroled the following day. After collecting the garrison at Fort Cobb, Emory's command traveled north toward Fort Leavenworth with the aid of a Delaware guide. On May 19, Emory reported, "I am now in Kansas, on the north side of the Arkansas River with the whole command—eleven companies, 750 fighting men, 150 women, children, teamsters, and other non-combatants. Nothing has been left behind but would have been left in time of peace." The withdrawal of the Federal troops removed the last vestige of Union authority in the Indian Nations. All remaining Indian agents were Southern secessionists. The Indians opposed to severing ties with the Federal government were placed at a disadvantage, while those in favor of allying with the secession movement gained momentum amid the spreading Southern fervor for disunion.[10]

In 1860, the voters of Arkansas had elected a secessionist governor named Henry M. Rector. In his inaugural speech, Rector announced his intention to join "a Confederacy of Southern States," and, with them, make military preparations for their defense.[11] David Hubbard, a visiting secession commissioner from Alabama, declared to Governor Andrew B. Moore prior to Arkansas's leaving the Union, "The counties bordering on the Indian nations . . . would hesitate greatly to vote for secession and leave those tribes still under the influence of the Government at Washington. . . . These Indians are at a spot very important . . . and must be assured that the South must do as well as the North [concerning treaty obligations]." Indeed, a Cherokee alliance with the South was an important element in Governor Rector's plan to take Arkansas out of the Union.[12]

Rector wrote to John Ross on January 29, 1861, to introduce his agent, Lt. Col. J. J. Gains. The governor reminded Ross, "[Y]our people, in their institutions, latitude, and natural sympathies, are allied to the common brotherhood of the slaveholding states." He also made reference to Secretary of State William H. Seward who, while campaigning for the Republican presidential nomination, had

10 Bearss and Gibson, *Fort Smith*, 241; OR 1, 648. The Regular Army numbered only about 13,000 in 1861.

11 Abel, *The American Indian as Slaveholder and Secessionist*, 112-113.

12 Ibid., 108-109. The governor of Alabama appointed one commissioner to each of the Southern states to "consult and advise" on secession and confederation. Walter L. Fleming, *Civil War and Reconstruction in Alabama* (New York, NY, 1949), 46.

proposed that the Indian Nations be "vacated" in favor of white settlement. With Seward now a prominent member of Lincoln's cabinet, Rector could portray the Republicans as a threat to Indian sovereignty while expressing hopes that Ross would find friendship and protection with the South.[13]

Ross adamantly opposed abrogating any element of the Cherokee treaties with the United States and counseled the leaders of the other tribes to follow his example. When the Southern-leaning Chickasaws asked the Creeks to hold a council of the Five Nations, Ross cautioned his delegates to the meeting, held February 17, 1861, at the Creek Council Ground. "[I]t will ever be our wisdom and our interest," he warned, "to adhere strictly to those obligations, and carefully to guard against being drawn into any complications which may prove prejudicial to the interest of our people, or imperil the security we now enjoy under the protection of the Government of the United States as guaranteed by our Treaties."[14] The Chickasaws and Choctaws, aware of Ross's opposition, did not bother to attend the meeting. The Cherokees, Seminoles, and Creeks, already present, agreed to do nothing.[15]

J. J. Gains traveled to Fort Smith to meet with the commissioner of the southern superintendency of Indian affairs, Elias Rector, a cousin of the governor of Arkansas. An Arkansas planter and secessionist, Elias Rector was in charge of the agents to the Five Nations. He wrote a short letter to Ross to introduce Gains and encourage Ross to give the governor's plans "favorable consideration." Ross was not receptive, but continued to equivocate. On the one hand, Ross complained to one of his political allies that the Federally appointed Cherokee agent, R. J. Cowert, was currently "officiously advocating the Secessionist policy of the Southern States . . . [and encouraging] the Cherokees to act in concert" with the

---

13 Able, *The American Indian as Slaveholder and Secessionist*, 58, 75, 112-113.

14 John Ross to Cyrus Harris, February 9, 1861; Jacob Derrysaw to John Ross, February 4, 1861; John Ross to Jacob Derrysaw, February 9, 1861; John Ross to George Hudson, February 11, 1861; John Ross to William P. Ross, Thomas Pegg, John Spears, and Lewis Downing, February 12, 1861; William P. Ross, Thomas Pegg, Lewis Downing, and John Spears to John Ross, March 15, 1861; Moulton, ed., *The Papers of John Ross* vol. 2, 459-460, 459, 461, 462.

15 John Ross to Cyrus Harris, February 9, 1861; Jacob Derrysaw to John Ross, February 4, 1861; John Ross to Jacob Derrysaw, February 9, 1861; John Ross to George Hudson February 11, 1861; John Ross to William P. Ross, Thomas Pegg, John Spears, and Lewis Downing, February 12, 1861; William P. Ross, Thomas Pegg, Lewis Downing, and John Spears to John Ross, March 15, 1861; Moulton, ed., *The Papers of John Ross* vol. 2, 459-460, 459, 461, 462.

South.[16] Ross warned Governor Rector that "the Cherokee people . . . [were] enviably allied with . . . the United States." On the other hand, Ross received Gains cordially and reassured Governor Rector that the Cherokees were by "their institutions, locality, & natural sympathies . . . unequivocally with the slave holding states."[17]

Following the Confederate attack on Fort Sumter, Governor Rector refused president Lincoln's request to raise an army. The Arkansas secession convention reconvened on May 6, and voted 69-1 for secession. On May 9, several Arkansas citizens politely asked Chief Ross where he stood on the crisis. Their frustration was as evident in the closing sentence of their inquiry as was their threat: "We earnestly hope to find in . . . your people true allies and active friends; but if, unfortunately, you prefer to retain your connection with the Northern Government . . . we want to know that, as we prefer an open enemy to a doubtful friend."[18]

On the same day, the Arkansas secessionist convention resolved to protect the wealth of the Indian Nations by promising "a faithful application of all money and property . . . for the several tribes west of Arkansas." Signed by convention President David Walker and attested by secretary E. C. Boudinot, Stand Watie's nephew, the document reflected the convention's desire to maintain good relations with the Indian Nations and to leave the door open for future alliances and the extraordinary man who would negotiate them.[19]

At this time, Albert Pike was the most important representative of the Confederacy in the Indian Nations. He was born in Boston in 1809, studied at Harvard, and passed the examination to be admitted as a junior, but problems with tuition led Pike to continue his education informally. As a young man he wrote and published poetry in the romantic style and may have influenced Edgar Allan Poe's verse structure in "The Raven." In 1831, the Bostonian traveled west to the Staked Plains before moving to Arkansas, where he taught school and edited a newspaper. Thereafter, he practiced law and became a successful attorney. By 1859, Pike was Sovereign Grand Commander of the Supreme Council for the Southern

---

16 OR 1, 683; John Ross to Henry M. Rector, February 22, 1861; John Ross to John B. Ogdon, February 28, 1861; Moulton, ed., *The Papers of John Ross*, vol. 2, 464-465, 466.

17 Ibid., 465.

18 Abel, *The American Indian as Slaveholder and Secessionist*, 111-112, n. #175; Parins, *Elias Cornelius Boudinot*, 38-39.

19 *OR* Series 4, 1, 307.

Jurisdiction of the Masonic Order. A man of many accomplishments, it was as an Arkansas lawyer that he had gained influence with the Five Nations.[20]

Pike had traveled on yearly hunting trips to the Creek and Choctaw Nations, where he had made many friends. In 1852, he petitioned Arkansas "Family" leader, Robert W. Johnson, head of the committee on Indian affairs, to compensate the Creek Nation for nine million acres of land ceded to the United States as punishment for siding with the British during the War of 1812. The committee recommended compensation, but the opposition managed to kill the bill. Afterward, the Choctaws and Chickasaws also sought Pike's aid for compensation for ten million acres ceded in 1830. In time, Pike and his clients succeeded. In 1856, the Choctaws and Chickasaws received $800,000 in compensation. The following year the Creeks gained a similar award, and additional settlements followed. Pike was generously compensated.[21]

A former Whig and native Northerner, Pike had not always been an enthusiastic secessionist. When Lincoln was elected, however, he wrote *State or Province? Bond or Free?*, a pamphlet advocating secession. After Arkansas left the Union, Pike wrote to Johnson, by that time a delegate to the Confederate Congress, and to Robert A. Toombs, Confederate secretary of state, about the importance of organizing Indian regiments to prevent the reoccupation of the Indian Nations by Union forces. He thought they should be led by a known professional soldier and be supplemented with white troops. These measures were designed to gain the Indians' confidence as well as to augment the defense of the region.[22]

Echoing Pike's concern was N. Bart Pearce, a West Point graduate and brigadier general of Arkansas state troops commanding in the western part of the state. In a letter introducing himself to Jefferson Davis, Pearce requested that "some steps be taken at once to secure the cooperation of the Indians in the West, and especially to prevent any emissaries of the Republicans from poisoning the

---

20 By 1880 Pike was considered the "foremost Scottish Rite Mason in the world." He rewrote the upper divisions of the Scottish Rite (4-33 degrees) and studied Eastern philosophy. His memorial is in the Masonic Temple in Washington D.C. Jay B. Hubbell, *The South in American Literature: 1609-1900* (Durham, NC, 1954), 640-644, 647; Fletcher, *Arkansas*, 94, Albert Pike, "Albert Pike's Autobiography" in *New Age Magazine* (1929-1930), Issue 38, 537.

21 Robert Lipscomb Duncan, *Reluctant General: The Life and Times of Albert Pike* (New York, NY, 1961) 151-153, 156-159.

22 Walter Lee Brown, *A Life of Albert Pike* (Fayetteville, AR, 1997), 350-351; Woods, *Rebellion and Realignment*, 162; *OR*, 3, 572-574. Pike served in the Mexican War as major and had commanded militia artillery in Little Rock, Arkansas.

Confederate Brig. Gen. Albert Pike commanded in Indian territory and
later raised, trained, and fought three Indian regiments.

Library of Congress

minds of the full bloods."[23] Davis was familiar with the region, for he had served as a young lieutenant at Fort Gibson in the early 1830s. Consideration for the alliance of the Five Nations was already a concern for the Provisional Congress of the Confederacy. It had created the Committee for Indian Affairs, which Robert Johnson later joined as senator from Arkansas. Toombs, an influential Georgian, and Pike were friends. President Davis later supported the creation of the Bureau of Indian affairs and named David Hubbard, the Alabama secession ambassador to Arkansas, as Commissioner of Indian affairs on March 16, just three weeks before Arkansas seceded.[24]

In early March Toombs drafted legislation empowering a special commissioner to treat with the Indian Nations. Following the secession of Arkansas, President Davis appointed Pike to office. Pike planned to visit the Cherokee Nation to deal with John Ross and requested supplies, including 2,000 rifles. He also warned that the Arkansas River would soon be too low for boats and would force the use of ground transportation.[25]

Events on the ground were now moving quickly. On May 13, Confederate Secretary of War Walker appointed Ben McCulloch to command the Indian district. Pike and McCulloch planned to approach Ross together at Park Hill. While in Fort Smith, they consulted with members of the Stand Watie faction. Pike planned to treat with them at the Creek agency if his negotiations with Ross failed. Anticipating no problems with the Creeks, Seminoles, Choctaws, and Chickasaws, Pike left for Park Hill on May 29 in the company of a mounted escort provided by the state of Arkansas. In closing a long letter to Secretary of State Toombs, Pike expressed his concern that Ross would eventually oppose him. "He is very shrewd," observed Pike. "If I fail with him it will not be my fault."[26]

As anticipated, the presence of McCulloch and Pike at his home did not sway Ross, who had issued a proclamation of neutrality on May 17. Like most people, Ross believed the conflict between the Union and the Confederacy would likely be short-lived, and he did not want to risk abrogating the treaties. McCulloch agreed to keep his forces out of the Cherokee Nation unless it was invaded by the Federals.

23 *OR* 3, 576.

24 Abel, *The American Indian as Slaveholder and Secessionist*, 127-132; In December 1834, Jefferson Davis's superior court-martialed Davis for insubordination when he questioned taking roll call in the rain. Davis was acquitted on February 19, 1835, and he submitted his resignation, accepted June 30; William J. Cooper, Jr., *Jefferson Davis, American* (New York, NY, 2000), 56-64.

25 Agnew, *Fort Gibson*, 116; Brown, *A Life of Albert Pike*, 353, 355-356; *OR* 3, 572-574, 580-581.

26 *OR* Series 4, 1, 359-361; Brown, *A Life of Albert Pike*, 354-357.

Confederate Brig. Gen.
Ben McCulloch

University of Arkansas Libraries

Pike published a letter promising to respect the Cherokees' neutral position, but threatened he would not treat with them again. Pike turned to the other Indian nations. He was offering good terms, and word soon spread to more receptive tribal leadership. McCulloch, meanwhile, returned to Fort Smith.[27]

The members of the Watie faction feared for their lives and, despite guarantees for their safety, failed to meet with Pike at the Creek agency. Pike sent word for the Creek, Choctaw, and Chickasaw chiefs to meet him at North Fork Town. In a counter move, Ross contacted Opothleyahola and encouraged him to form a neutral alliance among the tribes by sending delegates to a conference in the Leased District[28]

The Creeks were still divided over removal. Many, if not most, of the Upper Creeks were opposed to joining the Confederates, but the leaders in favor of neutrality were in the Leased District. The principal chief of the Upper Creeks, Icho Harjo, owned slaves and favored the South. The Lower Creeks, mixed-bloods led by Motey Canard and the McIntoshes, were overwhelmingly for the South.[29]

27 Brown, *A Life of Albert Pike*, 357; Albert Pike to the Commissioner of Indian Affairs, February 17, 1866, cited in Abel, *The American Indian as Slaveholder and Secessionist*, 135-136 n. #225; Proclamation, May 17, 1861, Moulton, ed., *The Papers of John Ross*, 469-470.

28 Brown, *A Life of Albert Pike*, 358-359; Abel, *The American Indian as Slaveholder and Secessionist*, 136, n. #228. In 1855, the Choctaws leased their land west of the 98th meridian to the U.S. as a reservation for Plains Indians. Morris, Goins, and McReynolds, *Historical Atlas of Oklahoma*, 26.

29 Brown, *A Life of Albert Pike*, 358-359; Abel, *Slaveholder and Secessionist*, 136; Gary Zellar, *African Creeks: Estelvste and the Creek Nation* (Norman, OK, 2007), 42-44; Littlefield, Jr., *Africans and Creeks*, 233-236.

The pro-southern faction of the Creeks signed a treaty with the Confederacy on July 10, 1861. The agreement promised them military protection, assumption of annuity payments, additional judicial rights, and a non-voting delegate to the Confederate Congress. Slavery was recognized as legal, and the Creek Nation was to remain free from territorial status. In return, the Creeks agreed to raise troops (to include the Seminoles) who would be armed by the Confederacy. By the terms of the treaty, these men could not be made to serve outside Indian Territory without their consent.[30]

Although dissent existed, the Choctaw and Chickasaw leadership overwhelmingly favored siding with the Confederacy, and Pike had no trouble negotiating treaties with his old friends. The treaties, signed July 12, were similar to the Creek treaty with some additional aspects. They established a Confederate district court at Boggy Depot, stated that the two nations would alternately be represented in the Confederate Congress, and outlined the procedure for becoming a state in the Confederacy. In return, the two nations would raise a regiment for Confederate service under the command of Col. Douglas H. Cooper, a former Federal agent to the Choctaws.[31]

Pike moved on to treat with the Seminoles at their agency on the Canadian River. Many of their leaders had attended the neutrality conference and were against joining the Rebels, but the Creeks had traditional influence over the Seminoles. Creek leaders Motey Canard and Chilly McIntosh, together with Pike, Superintendent Rector, and Seminole agent Charles Johnson, finally persuaded Principal Chief John Jumper and a dozen town chiefs to sign a treaty. This document, signed August 1, 1861, was similar to the Creek treaty. Approximately half of the town chiefs declined to sign and would join Opothleyahola's full-blood Creek revolt against the alliances with the Confederacy.[32]

From the Seminole agency, Pike and his companions proceeded to the Wichita Agency to treat with the Wichitas, Comanches, and other tribes in the Leased District. Pike had requested that the agent gather as many leaders as possible. Not

30 Brown, *A Life of Albert Pike*, 361. Abel, *The American Indian as Slaveholder and Secessionist*, 159; *OR* Series 4, 1, 426-443.

31 *OR* 3, 574-575, 585-587, 593-594, ser. 4, vol. 1, 445-466; Brown, *A Life of Albert Pike*, 362-363; Abel, *The American Indian as Slaveholder and Secessionist*, 75-79, 159-160.

32 Brown, *A Life of Albert Pike*, 363-364; Zellar, *African Creeks*, 45; Daniel F Littlefield, Jr., *Africans and Seminoles: From Removal to Emancipation* (Westport, CT, 1977), 180-184. The full-blood Seminoles were generally against the Confederate alliances. Since removal, mixed-blood Creeks encouraged by whites had been stealing Seminole slaves, and their number was dwindling.

only were the reservation chiefs present, but several bands of free Comanches attended, one led by the war chief Buffalo Hump. While Pike was on the Plains, the outcome of the battle of Wilson's Creek (August 10, 1861) in southwest Missouri made it more difficult for Ross to maintain his neutrality.[33]

The border state of Missouri was deeply divided over secession. Although he had run as a Douglas Democrat, newly elected Governor Claiborne F. Jackson left no doubt about his Southern rights philosophy in his inaugural speech. The Missouri assembly called for a secession convention at Jefferson City.[34] Sterling Price, a conditional Unionist originally from Virginia, presided over the convention. As a Missourian, he had served as a congressman, successful planter, colonel (brevet brigadier) during the Mexican War, and pro-slavery governor of Missouri. Francis P. Blair, Jr., a wealthy St. Louis merchant who supported Lincoln, led the Unionist delegates. Governor Jackson led the secessionists. In March, the convention, which was meeting at St. Louis, adopted a report against severing ties with the Union.[35]

Extremists on both sides, led by Jackson and Blair, refused to let the issue rest. Captain Nathaniel Lyon, a Blair supporter, drilled a pro-Union militia of "Wide Awakes" while St. Louis secessionists organized a force of "Minute Men." The shelling of Fort Sumter on April 12 provoked a confrontation at St Louis, where Lyon seized the state militia's Camp Jackson. This move convinced Price to throw his lot in with the Confederacy and spun the state into open armed conflict. Jackson put Price in command of the Missouri State Guard.[36]

Price sent word for his volunteers to gather at Boonville and Lexington, and Governor Jackson returned to Jefferson City. With Lyon now a Union general and in pursuit with Federal forces, Price and Jackson boarded a steamer and headed up the Missouri River. The governor remained at Boonville with about 400 volunteers while Price went on to Lexington. After a skirmish on June 14, Jackson and his motley force retreated south toward Ben McCulloch's command. Gathering

---

33 Ibid., 365.

34 Arthur Roy Kirkpatrick, "Missouri on the Eve of the Civil War," in *Missouri Historical Review* (March 1959), Issue 55, 99-104.

35 Ibid., 104-106; Albert Castel, *General Sterling Price and the Civil War in the West* (Baton Rouge, LA, 1968), 1-6.

36 Kirkpatrick, "Missouri on the Eve of the Civil War," 106-108; Kirkpatrick, "Missouri in the Early Months," 235-237, 240-242; Castel, *General Sterling Price and the Civil War in the West*, 24-25; Christopher Phillips, *Damned Yankee: The Life of General Nathaniel Lyons* (Columbia, MO, 1990) 156-169, 175-193, 211-214.

volunteers as he went, Price rode ahead to confer with McCulloch. The Texan's orders were to use caution regarding Missouri, but he did not hesitate to take his cavalry north to rescue Jackson's party. Eventually, the forces combined and moved north to meet Lyon near Springfield. McCulloch was in overall command of the Rebels when they fought Lyon's command at Wilson's Creek. The Southern army included Price's 5,500 troops (plus other militia who were not armed), Brig. Gen. N. Bart Pearce's 2,000-man Arkansas militia, and McCulloch's own brigade numbering about 2,500.[37]

As the opposing armies converged, neither Lyon nor McCulloch wanted to engage—but neither man was willing to retreat. With Price demanding that McCulloch attack, the Texan ordered the army to move on Springfield. The Rebels carried their ammunition in cotton socks, and when rain threatened their powder, McCulloch and Price agreed they had no choice but to halt. On the evening of August 9, the men were ordered to sleep with weapons loaded and their powder guarded against the moisture.[38]

McCulloch did not have to attack because Lyon beat him to it. His second-in-command, Col. Franz Sigel, assaulted from the south with about 1,000 men while Lyon struck from the north with another 4,500 men through the thick woods of Oak Hill. The Federals achieved complete surprise, but the alert state of the Confederate force prevented what might have been a rout. Instead, McCulloch met, counter-attacked, and routed Sigel. Price rallied his retreating line while constantly exposing himself to enemy fire. The disadvantage of the inferior weapons carried by Price's force, mostly shotguns, squirrel guns, and smoothbore muskets, was negated by the close range at which the battle was waged.[39]

After McCulloch defeated Sigel, he reinforced Price and pressed the attack home against Lyon's wing. The Union commander was leading a charge to turn the tide of battle when Rebel fire struck him down. Major Samuel D. Sturgis directed an orderly retreat, but Lyon's body was left on the field. The seven-hour battle was the bloodiest of the war to date. Total casualties (killed, wounded, and missing)

37 Phillips, *Damned Yankee*, 10-35; Boatner, *Civil War Dictionary*, 497-498; Castel, *General Stirling Price and the Civil War in the West*, 26; Cutrer, *Ben McCulloch and the Frontier Military Tradition*, 210-214, 216-222.

38 Castel, *General Stirling Price and the Civil War in the West*, 34-41; Cutrer, *Ben McCulloch and the Frontier Military Tradition*, 219-228; Phillips, *Damned Yankee*, 240-252; Edwin C. Bearss, *The Battle of Wilson's Creek*, 4th ed. (Cassville, MO, 1992), 41-50.

39 Castel, *General Stirling Price and the Civil War in the West*, 40-42; Cutrer, *Ben McCulloch and the Frontier Military Tradition*, 231-236; Phillips, *Damned Yankee*, 252-254; Bearss, *The Battle of Wilson's Creek*, 58-68.

were high, with the Confederates losing 12 percent and the Union double that at 24.5 percent. The Confederate victory at Wilson's Creek, together with the earlier success at Bull Run on July 21, boosted Confederate spirits and their confidence in the ultimate success of the rebellion.[40]

In the Cherokee Nation, faced with a widespread Federal withdrawal and the growing strength and high morale of the Southern faction, John Ross had little choice but to treat with the Confederacy. Ross's executive council (himself, Joseph Vann, James Brown, John Drew, and William Ross) had supported neutrality in late June and early July and had met on August 1 with the intention of remaining neutral. Dissension, however, was growing. Amid the volatile atmosphere, the council held a mass meeting at Tahlequah, Cherokee Nation on August 21.[41]

The orderly meeting was attended by some 4,000 men. The Cherokee agent urged the Cherokees to unite with the South. Ross, warning that only as a unified body could the Cherokee Nation retain its strength, agreed the time had come to ally with the Confederacy. "The people are here: Say, whether you are arrayed in classes one against the other—the full-blood against the white and mixed-blood citizens—say whether you are faithful to the constitution of laws of your country?" argued a frustrated Ross. He continued: "Union is strength, dissension is weakness, misery ruin! . . . When your nationality ceases here, it will live nowhere else. When these homes are lost, you will find no others like them. . . . The time has now arrived . . . for an alliance with the Confederate States upon terms honorable and advantageous to the Cherokee Nation."[42]

Following the decision to ally with the Confederacy, Ross and the executive council authorized the organization of a Confederate regiment. Members of the council were well represented and appointed John Drew, executive councilman and one of Ross' allies, colonel of the regiment. Secretary William P. Ross, the

40 Cutrer, *Ben McCulloch and the Frontier Military Tradition*, 236-237; Castel, *General Stirling Price and the Civil War in the West*, 43-46; Phillips, *Damned Yankee*, 254-256; William Garrett Piston and Richard W. Hatcher III, *Wilson's Creek: The Second Battle of the Civil War and the Men Who Fought It* (Chapel Hill, NC: University of North Carolina Press, 2000), 287; Phillips, *Damned Yankee*, 254-256; Bearss, *The Battle of Wilson's Creek*, 73-124.

41 OR 3, 673-676; Wardell, *A Political History of the Cherokee Nation*, 130-131.

42 Address to the Cherokees, August 21, 1861; Moulton, *Ross Papers*, 481; Wardell, *A Political History of the Cherokee Nation*, 131; Palmer H. Boeger, "The Indians' Decision to Go With the South in the Civil War," 41-48 in *Proceedings: War and Reconstruction in Indian Territory: A History Conference in Observance of the 130th Anniversary of the Fort Smith Council* (Fort Smith, 1995), 41-48.

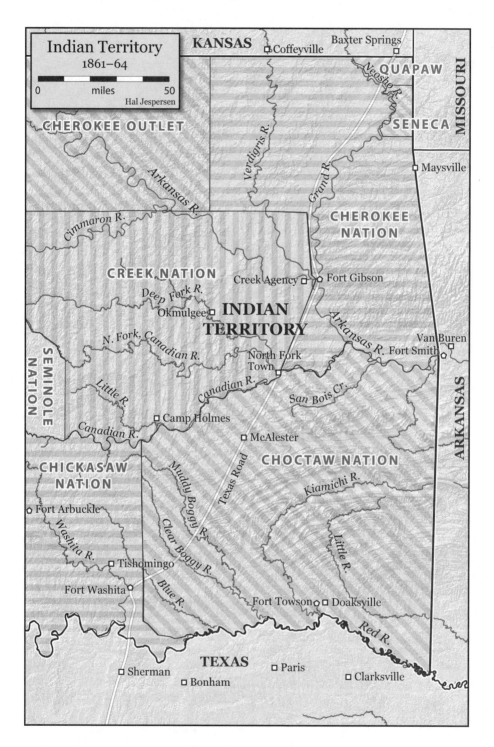

Indian Territory
1861–64

0   miles   50
Hal Jespersen

KANSAS
Coffeyville
Baxter Springs
QUAPAW
Neosho R.
SENECA
MISSOURI
Maysville
CHEROKEE OUTLET
Verdigris R.
Grand R.
CHEROKEE NATION
Arkansas R.
Cimmaron R.
CREEK NATION
Creek Agency
Fort Gibson
Deep Fork R.
Okmulgee
INDIAN TERRITORY
Arkansas R.
Fort Smith
Van Buren
N. Fork, Canadian R.
North Fork Town
SEMINOLE NATION
Little R.
Canadian R.
San Bois Cr.
Camp Holmes
ARKANSAS
Canadian R.
McAlester
CHOCTAW NATION
CHICKASAW NATION
Kiamichi R.
Fort Arbuckle
Muddy Boggy R.
Texas Road
Little R.
Washita R.
Clear Boggy R.
Tishomingo
Fort Washita
Blue R.
Fort Towson
Doaksville
Red R.
TEXAS
Sherman
Paris
Clarksville
Bonham

chief's nephew, was made its lieutenant colonel. Full-blood members of the Keetoowah Society dominated the regiment in all but one company.[43]

On September 1, Ben McCulloch wrote to congratulate Ross on his decision. That same day, he expressed his pleasure to John Drew about the decision of the Cherokee leaders, but cautioned that he could not accept the new regiment until the treaty was signed. He also informed Drew that he had authorized Stand Watie to organize and operate north of the Cherokee border against Kansas Jayhawkers. McCulloch was not concerned about legalities when it came to Watie, whom he trusted. McCulloch had officially given Watie the rank of colonel in the Confederate army on July 12.[44]

He felt differently about Drew and his men. On September 2, McCulloch wrote Secretary of War Walker concerning the situation. "Colonel Stand Watie belongs to the true Southern party," began McCulloch. "I hope our government will continue this gallant man and true friend of our country in our service, and attach him and his men (some 300) to my command. It might be well to give him a battalion separate from the Cherokee regiment under Colonel Drew. Colonel Drew's regiment," he continued, "will be mostly composed of full-bloods, whilst those with Colonel Stand Watie will be half-breeds, who are educated men, and good soldiers anywhere, in or out of the Nation."[45]

In fact, Watie soon expanded his command from a battalion to a regiment: the 2nd Mounted Cherokee Rifles. The rosters of Drew's and Watie's regiments suggests the cultural differences between their members. Most of the enlisted men in Drew's regiment gave Cherokee names or the English equivalent of a Cherokee name. Most of the enlisted men in Watie's regiment gave English names. Watie's men were loyal to him and the alliance with the Confederacy. Drew's men, most of whom were members of the Keetoowah Society, were not loyal to their colonel or the Confederacy. Instead, they were loyal to each other—and they were biding their time.[46]

---

43 Tyner, "The Keetoowah Society in Cherokee History," 27, 39-40; *OR* 8, 16-18.

44 *OR* 3, 690-691; Wilfred Knight, *Red Fox: Stand Watie and the Confederate Indian Nations during the Civil War Years in Indian Territory* (Glendale, CA, 1988), 63, 65; Abel, *The American Indian as Slaveholder and Secessionist*, 217, 226-227.

45 *OR* 3, 692. The reference to "in or out of the Nation" refers to the stipulation included in the Confederate treaties, that Indian soldiers could not be required to serve outside of the Indian Nations without their consent.

46 "Special Confederate Documents, Oklahoma Civil War Commission, 1961-1965, Oklahoma City Civil War Round Table Organized 1961," microfilm; W. Graig Gaines, *The*

Ross and the council now wanted Albert Pike to return and negotiate a Confederate treaty. They sent one of Ross's nephews to find him, and the two men met as Pike was returning to Fort Arbuckle from a meeting with some Comanches. Pike sent word ahead with Ross's nephew to expect him. He returned from Arbuckle with four men to Fort Gibson, and from there was escorted by "eight or nine companies of Colonel Drew's regiment of Cherokees, chiefly full-bloods and Pins," to Park Hill. Pike camped nearby Rose Cottage. Above the encampment flew a Confederate flag.[47]

Through Ross's influence, on October 4 Pike was able to sign a treaty with the Osages, relatively small numbers of the mixed band of Seneca and Shawnee, and the Quapaw, who had occupied two parcels of land between the Grand River and the Missouri border in what is now the far northeastern corner of Oklahoma since the 1830s. Another band of Quapaws had rejected these lands and resided in Texas until they were forced out and accepted the Creek's permission to settle on the Canadian River in 1842. The two Quapaw bands would soon be reunited.[48]

On October 7, the Cherokees signed a treaty that provided payment for the Neutral Lands in Kansas if they were lost to the North, non-voting representation in the Confederate House of Representatives, a Confederate district court at Tahlequah, and freedom to regulate trade and citizenship. All previous financial obligations of the United States would be met by the Confederacy. The Cherokees were not interested in statehood, and no method of attaining it was included. In return, the Cherokees agreed to raise a mounted regiment, two reserve companies, and additional forces as requested by the Confederate president. These units could

---

Confederate Cherokees: John Drew's Regiment of Mounted Rifles (Baton Rouge, LA, 1989), 11-16; Knight, *Red Fox*, 64-70; E. C. Boudinot to Stand Watie, October 5, 1861, in Cherokee Nation Papers; Edward Everett Dale and Gaston Litton, eds., *Cherokee Cavaliers: Forty Years of Cherokee History as Told in the Correspondence of the Ridge-Watie-Boudinot Family* (Norman 1995), 110-111, shows Boudinot lobbying for the position of Lieutenant Colonel in Watie's regiment then forming, as Ross had given his nephew the same rank in Drew's regiment.

47 Albert Pike to the Commissioner of Indian Affairs, February 17, 1866, appended to D. N. Cooley, *The Cherokee Question* (Washington D.C., 1866) in Joseph B. Thoburn, ed., "The Cherokee Question," in *Chronicles of Oklahoma* (March 1924), Issue 2, 175-176; Brown, *A Life of Albert Pike*, 369.

48 W. David Baird, *The Quapaw Indians: A History of the Downstream People* (Norman, OK, 1980), 82-85, 96-97; Abel, *The American Indian as Slaveholder and Secessionist*, n. #464; OR 4, 647-666; Muriel H. Wright, *A Guide to the Indian Tribes of Oklahoma* (Norman, OK, 1951), 220, 238-239, 242; Kappler, *Indian Affairs*, vol. 2, 383-385, 395-397; James H. Howard, *Shawnee! The Ceremonialism of a Native Indian Tribe and Its Cultural Background* (Athens, OH, 1981), 19; Grant Foreman, *The Last Trek of the Indians* (New York, NY, 1946), 71-72.

Rose Cottage

Oklahoma Historical Society

"not be moved beyond the limits of Indian country west of Arkansas without their consent."[49]

The strength of the unified Cherokee Nation was derived from the political and property rights granted in its treaty with the United States. Ross had worked for decades to cultivate influence in Washington. To maintain the legitimacy of the treaty, Ross had stalled as long as possible. However, in the face of the political convulsions around him, he gambled that his full-blood political base would remain loyal to him and that he could keep the Cherokee Nation, and his position as its leader, unified as a Confederate protectorate. The full-bloods did remain loyal to Ross, but they would not fight for the South. For this reason, Ross's plan would fail, and the ruin he predicted soon followed.

49 OR Series 4, 1, 679; Brown, *A Life of Albert Pike*, 368, 371; Abel, *The American Indian as Slaveholder and Secessionist*, 166-167.

Chapter 4

Opothleyahola's Revolt

When the war was approaching, Southern leaders became increasingly intransigent in their defense of slavery. This tendency was also evident in the Creek Nation in the continual tightening of the slave codes and the increased punishment for those who violated them. The Lower Creeks under D. N. McIntosh enthusiastically supported the South. Many Upper Creeks followed Chief Motey Canard in his support of the South, but a majority of the full-bloods refused to support Canard's policy and followed another leader in their resistance to the Confederate alliance.[1]

On August 5, 1861, the loyal Creeks declared the treaty with the Confederacy to be invalid and elected Oktarharsars Harjo (Sands) chief in place of Motey Canard. Opothleyahola, a full-blood who had been influential in Creek affairs since the 1820s, gave his support to the loyalist Indians and became the true leader in the coming movement against the Confederate alliance. Attempting to gain federal support and protection, they sent a delegation to Kansas. White Chief (Mikko Hutkee), Bob Deer, and Joseph Ellis carried a letter that described the activities of Confederate commissioner Albert Pike. They pleaded that their "Great Father" not abandon them and asked to hold a council. The delegation also carried a letter from Opothleyahola and Sands to President Abraham Lincoln asking for protection against intruders as promised in their 1832 treaty with the United States. They reminded Northern leaders that Opothleyahola, who had signed the treaty, believed in the integrity of the old agreement: "I was at Washington when you

---

1 Debo, *Road to Disappearance*, 142-147.

Opothleyahola

Oklahoma Historical Society

treated with us, and now White People are trying to take our people away to fight against us and you. I am alive," he continued. "I well remember the treaty. My ears are open & my memory is good. This is the letter of Your Children."[2]

The delegation met with E. H. Carruth, a personal representative of Republican Senator James Lane of Kansas. Carruth brought the delegation to Fort Scott to meet with Lane, who was actively lobbying for an expedition south into the Indian Territory. He hoped to lead "Lane's Brigade" with the rank of general while retaining his Senate seat. The Kansas senator encouraged the loyal Indians in their resistance. They also received support from Rev. Evan Jones, in Lawrence, but Mikko Hutkee, apparently miffed at Ross's decision, turned down Jones's offer of $25 to deliver a message to Ross. Carruth sent a letter with the returning delegation to tell Opothleyahola, "I am authorized to inform you that the president will not forget you. Our army will soon go South, and those who are true and loyal to the government will be treated as friends."[3]

Opothleyahola and Sands were aided by Seminole chiefs Billy Bowlegs, John Chuppco, and Halleck Tustenuggee. They made plans to travel with their families to the northern part of the Cherokee Nation, where good timber and water provided a suitable place for the loyal Creeks and their allies to await help from Kansas. In the beginning there were "4,400 Creeks, 1,100 Seminoles, 300 Yuchis, 250 Cherokees, 150 Chickasaws, and over 300 free Negroes and slaves."[4] At a council held on the Plains near Jessie Chisholm's trading post, south of modern Oklahoma City, many smaller tribes from the western Creek Nation, including the Quapaw band allowed by the Creeks to settle on the Canadian River, joined the movement. This increased Opothleyahola's numbers to about 7,600. To gather this

2 Opthleyahola and Ouktahnaserharjo to the President Our Great Father, August 15, 1861, cited in Able, *The American Indian as Slaveholder and Secessionist*, 244-245, 245-246, n. #491; Kappler, *Indian Affairs*, 341-343; John Bartlett Meserve, "Chief Opothleyahola," in *Chronicles of Oklahoma* (December 1931), Issue 9, 441; Debo, *Road to Disappearance*, 147.

3 Dean Tricket, "The Civil War in the Indian Territory: 1861" (continued) in *Chronicles of Oklahoma* (June 1940), Issue 18, 151-152. *Annual Report of the Commissioner of Indian Affairs for the Year 1861* (Washington, D.C., 1862), 41-43; Annie Heloise Abel, *The American Indian as Participant in the Civil War* (1919), reprinted as *The American Indian in the Civil War, 1862-1865* (Lincoln, NE, 1992), 62-64, n. #141, 71-77. Jim Lane was Lincoln's confidant concerning matters in the region. His plan to lead the invasion proved politically unworkable, and Lane's brigade accomplished little more than some Jayhawking early in the war. L. W. Spring, "Career of a Kansas Politician," in *American Historical Review*, 4 (October 1898 to July 1899), Issue 4, (New York, NY, 1963), 98-99; Castel, *General Sterling Price and the Civil War in the West*, 60l;. OR 8, 25.

4 Baird, *The Quapaw Indians*, 97-98; Jerry Leon Gill, "Federal Refugees from Indian Territory, 1861-1867," Master's Thesis (Oklahoma State University, 1967), 40.

widespread support required the careful organization of his followers, and the deception of his enemies. The group included a growing number of free blacks and slaves who were fleeing the newly stringent slave codes passed by mixed-blood Creeks during months leading up to the war. The full-bloods treated blacks, who offered valuable services as translators and cultural interpreters, more favorably than did the mixed-bloods. The flight of the mixed-bloods slaves helped to motivate Rebel pursuit.[5]

The migration followed three routes. The Seminoles and smaller tribes used the Delaware-Shawnee trail from Chisholm's Store to Black Bear Creek (in Noble and Pawnee Counties), which ran east to the Arkansas River. The western Creeks followed the Dawson Road, which linked Opothleyahola's towns of Thlopthlocco, Greenleaf's Town, Arbeka, Big Pond, and Sell's Store. Loyal eastern Creeks traveled from North Fork Town northwest along the Deep Fork River and Little Deep Fork until they met the western Creeks and Seminoles.[6]

To deceive his opponents, Opothleyahola announced that he would travel west to the Plains. Daniel N. McIntosh, William P. Adair, and other pro-Confederate mixed-blood leaders testified in 1868, "The 'talk,' put out among the people was, that the Country would soon be over-run by a great Army from the North, which would sweep over it . . . [and] that the 'Old Chief' [Opothleyahola] would lead his people, with their flocks and herds, into the wilderness westward, out of the track of the army." This diversion allowed the old chief and the other leaders to move their people, property, and livestock not west but east, across the Arkansas River into the Cherokee Nation, while diverting Cooper's Confederate force to the west.[7]

Following the signing of the Cherokee treaty, Albert Pike left for Richmond to oversee ratification of the agreements and to obtain the funding promised in the treaties. Hoping that a show of force would cause Opothleyahola's followers to disperse, Pike had placed Douglas Cooper, a former Indian agent and commander of the Choctaw-Chickasaw Regiment, in charge of the combined Confederate Indian forces. Cooper arrived with his enlarged command at the Creek council

---

5 Jerry Leon Gill, "Federal Refugees from Indian Territory, 1861-1867," Master's Thesis (Oklahoma State University, 1967), 41-42; Zellar, *African Creeks*, 41-48.

6 Gill, "Federal Refugees from Indian Territory," 47-49.

7 D. N. McIntosh et al., March 17, 1868, "Statement relative to the Exodus of Ho-poth-la-yo-hola and his followers from the Creek and Cherokee Country in the fall and winter of 1861 and '62," Letters Received by the Office of Indian Affairs, Choctaw Agency, 1867-1868, National Archives, microfilm.

ground, where he joined forces with the full-blood Cherokees under Colonel John Drew and Creek troops under D. N. McIntosh. Opothleyahola sent a delegation asking for a "friendly council at Thlobthlocco [Opothleyahola's home "town"] about 45 miles a little South of West."[8] Since the full-blood Cherokees were not eager to fight the full-blood Creeks, Cooper let Drew's regiment return to the Cherokee Nation. Cooper and McIntosh headed north and found that Opothleyahola had moved to the headwaters of the Deep Fork. An unnamed secondary Creek chief approached Cooper and assured him that Opothleyahola was friendly. He suggested Cooper camp and await communication from the old chief, and Cooper agreed. The officer camped and waited, but no message arrived. After further delays, Cooper finally moved again. As McIntosh and others later testified, "After waiting several days, the Confederate forces moved up Deep Fork to the supposed camp of Ho-poith-lo-ya-hola, but found it deserted and a large trail leading in a Northwestward direction toward the Red Fork of Arkansas, [Cimarron River] apparently a week or more old."[9]

Opothleyahola led Cooper northwest to the edge of the Plains while moving his own people east across the Arkansas River just below its confluence with the Cimarron River. These skillfully planned delaying tactics were executed while Cooper, as he later reported, was "exhaust[ing] every means in my power to procure an interview with Opothleyahola." Unencumbered by his followers, Opothleyahola gathered his warriors and prepared to fight Cooper. The skirmish about to unfold became known as the battle of Round Mountain.[10]

---

8 Throughout Pike's term of influence as commissioner and general, he continually stressed the importance to the Confederate administration of the need to match the number of Indian regiments with white troops. McIntosh et al., "Statement relative to the Exodus of Ho-poth-la-ya-holat;"; Brown, *Albert Pike*, 372-373; *OR* 8, 519-520.

9 McIntosh, et al., "Statement relative to the Exodus of Ho-poth-la-ya-holat."

10 *OR* 8, 5. The location of the Battle of Round Mountain has long been disputed. During the Civil War Centennial, two prominent Oklahoma historians, Drs. Angie Debo and Muriel Wright, reached different conclusions. Each was partly correct, which may have led to the intransigence that followed. Both placed the main body of the Loyalists' movement and the battle in proximity, when in fact hey were separate and distant events. It is about 30 miles from the battlefield to the ford across the Arkansas leading to the Cherokee Nation. Debo followed the battlefield evidence to the site in Payne County at the western edge of the Cross Timbers where the battle probably occurred. Her error, based on sparse evidence, was placing the 5,600 civilians nearby. Wright followed the migration to the crossing of the Arkansas River below the Cimarron. Her error was in placing the battle in this vicinity, where the geography—rugged, wooded hill country—does not match descriptions in the official reports and contemporary accounts. For more evidence and a description of the battlefield, see Angie Debo, "The Location of the Battle of Round Mountains," in *Chronicles of Oklahoma* (Spring 1963), Issue 41,

On November 15, Cooper advanced up the Deep Fork with 500 men of the 9th Texas Cavalry and 900 from the Choctaw, Chickasaw, Creek, and Seminole regiments. When they found Opothleyahola's camp abandoned, the Rebels followed the trail north. In his diary, Adjutant George L. Griscom of the 9h Texas Cavalry reported that they began "over pretty rough country" of the Cross Timbers. On November 16 and 17, they "pursue[d] them striking the trail that the old fellow made destroying the country as he goes—we get no feed for our horses scarcely but a little corn & not much grass." On the 18th, the pursuers took "the trail at light & follow until night when we camp without a thing for our horses, the prairies burned & no habitations near . . . now in broad Prairie of the Creek Nation," along the eastern edge of the Southern Plains.[11]

The Confederates crossed the Cimarron River on November 19. Texas scouts reported smoke five miles ahead. The Texas cavalry investigated but found only an abandoned camp. Near sundown, a man on horseback enticed about 150 Texans to follow him. The riders soon came under fire from warriors hidden in the timber along Salt Creek a few miles west of modern Yale, Oklahoma. The Texans formed a rough battle line and fired three volleys, but the loyalists had set the prairie on fire and soon outflanked them. The Rebels retreated 300 yards, attempted a stand, failed, and continued retreating another two miles as night fell.[12]

When Cooper learned of their plight he advanced with his troops. Arriving on the scene, he ordered his men to dismount and moved ahead of them in the darkness. Calling out to see if there were any Texans ahead, Cooper received a volley from the loyal Indians in response. The skirmishing soon ended, and in the morning Cooper's men found only 12 discarded wagons, scattered ponies, and some cattle. Opothleyahola's warriors had gone north to the Arkansas River,

---

70-104; McIntosh et al, "Statement relative to the Exodus of Ho-poth-la-ya-holat;" *OR* 8, 5-11, 14-15; George L. Griscom, *Fighting with Ross' Texas Cavalry C. S. A.: The Diary of George L. Griscom, Adjutant, 9th Texas Cavalry Regiment*, Homer L. Kerr, ed. (Hillsboro, TX, 1976), 4-5; Charles Bahos, "On Opothleyahola's Trail: Locating the Battle of Round Mountains," in *Chronicles of Oklahoma* (Spring 1985), Issue 63, 58-89. Gill, "Federal Refugees," 49-56, offers evidence of the migration and placed Opothleyahola across the Arkansas River with the migration substantially completed by November 15, 1861. Muriel H. Wright, "Colonel Cooper's Civil War Report on the Battle of Round Mountain," in *Chronicles of Oklahoma* (Winter 1961-1962), Issue 39, 352-397.

11 Griscom, *Fighting with Ross' Texas Cavalry C. S. A.*, 4-5; The Payne County battle site skirts the western edge of the Cross Timbers. Its geographical configuration conforms with the official reports. *OR* 8, 5-7.

12 *OR* 8, 5-6, 14-15; McIntosh et al., "Statement relative to the Exodus of Ho-poth-la-ya-holat"; Kerr, ed., *Fighting with Ross*, 5-6.

crossed, and returned to their families. Concurrently, Brig. Gen. Ben McCulloch ordered Cooper to move close to the Arkansas border. McCulloch was concerned about a possible Union campaign out of Springfield under Gen. John C. Frémont. McCulloch intended to meet it, but thought he might be forced to move south into the Boston Mountains.[13]

Opothleyahola was in communication with sympathetic Cherokee Keetoowahs in Col. John Drew's Confederate Cherokee Regiment. They put no faith in the alliance with the Rebels, and planned to unite with Opothleyahola and await the invasion of the federal army. Abolitionist missionary Evan Jones was incredulous when he heard that Ross had sided with the Confederacy and refused to believe it was voluntary. Writing to Commissioner of Indian Affairs William Dole just 19 days before the Battle of Round Mountain, Jones expressed his frustration at being unable to get a message from Kansas to Ross. He had spoken to the delegation from Opothleyahola and told the commissioner that one among them had said the full-blood Creeks, Seminoles, and Cherokees were loyal. Jones thought Ross's actions must have been forced and would only be temporary. "I was perfectly astounded at the announcement of the defection of John Ross and the Cherokees. . . . I have no doubt the unfortunate affair was brought about under stress," explained Jones, "and that it only needs a sufficient force to afford them protection to secure a speedy and cordial return to their former alliance."[14]

Many of these Cherokees apparently felt that Opothleyahola's rebellion provided adequate protection. They did not wait for Ross to act. Rather, under the guidance and organization of the Keetoowah Society, they aligned with Opothleyahola's movement.

Nineteenth century anthropologist James Mooney believed that the Keetoowah Society was active in both the Creek and Cherokee Nations. If Opothleyahola's traditional full-bloods were not members of the society, they shared the same reservations about allying with the Confederacy and were in communication with the Keetoowah organization. On the day before the fighting at Round Mountain, Confederate-allied Creek chiefs Moty Canard and Echo Harjo went into Opothleyahola's camp, where the loyal Creeks told them they were expecting help from the Cherokees. After the battle Canard and Harjo passed this

---

13 Griscom, *Fighting with Ross' Texas Cavalry C. S. A.*, 5-6; *OR* 8, 5-6, 15; McIntosh, et. al., 1868 "Statement relative to the Exodus of Ho-poth-la-ya-holat"; Debo, "Location of the Battle of Round Mountains," 89; Zellar, *African Creeks*, 50-51. Cooper lost six killed, four wounded, and one missing, while Opothleyahola suffered about 110 killed, wounded, and missing.

14 *Annual Report of the Commissioner Indian Affairs for the Year 1861*, 41.

information on to Ross. Opothleyahola and the Creek and Seminole chiefs had demonstrated great facility in controlling events and manipulating Cooper, and their plan was still unfolding.[15]

The threat from Frémont, which caused McCulloch to hold Cooper in reserve, never materialized. The Confederates soon learned that instead of going off to Kansas, "Ho-poith-lo-yo-hola had crossed the Arkansas and moved down the Arkansas . . . near Skiatooka's settlement." Opothleyahola had taken his people from the tributaries of the Arkansas River to a camp in the hills bordering the north bank of Hominy Creek, in the vicinity of modern Skiatook Lake. Cooper responded by moving to Tulsey Town with 780 men of the Choctaw-Chickasaw and Creek regiments. He planned to join with 500 of Colonel Drew's regiment and 260 of Colonel William B. Sims' 9th Texas Cavalry.[16]

Arriving at Tulsey Town, Cooper learned that Opothleyahola had moved to Chusto-Talasah (Bird Creek, north of modern Tulsa) near Captain James McDaniel's home. The non-combatants probably remained camped on Hominy Creek, which flows into Bird Creek. McDaniel, formerly a senator of the Cherokee National Committee, was captain of the First Reserve Company of Drew's regiment. His officers' names demonstrate the ethnicity of the regiment. His first lieutenant was Watt Stop, and his second lieutenants were Noah Drowning Bear and Big Sky yak too kahn. McDaniel was one of the officers who would later defect with his full-blood companies to Opothleyahola.[17]

John Drew was stationed at Coody's Bluff on the Verdigris River. Cooper reported that Drew was to meet with him "somewhere on the road to James McDaniel's. . . . From some misunderstanding Colonel Drew marched direct to Melton's, 6 miles from Hopoeithleyola. . . . Thus he arrived in the immediate vicinity of the enemy twenty-four hours or more in advance of the main body." Drew's movements may have been influenced by the actions of his disloyal

15 Motey Kennard and Echo Harjo to John Ross, November 25, 1861; Moulton, ed., *The Papers of John Ross*, vol. 2, 505; Mooney, *Myths of the Cherokee*, 225-226. Debo, "Location of the Battle of Round Mountains," 80, n. #26; *OR* 8, 7.

16 McIntosh et al., "Statement relative to the Exodus of Ho-poth-la-ya-holat"; *OR* 8, 7; Douglas Hale, "Rehearsal for Civil War: The Texas Cavalry in the Indian Territory, 1861," in *Chronicles of Oklahoma* (Fall 1990), Issue 58, 241; Stephen B. Oats, *Confederate Cavalry West of the River* (Austin, TX, 1961), 174.

17 Perhaps the Joneses contributed the Christian name of Noah to Drowning Bear.

officers, for a mass defection occurred during the early evening of December 8, 1861, the day before the battle of Chusto-Talasah.[18]

On the afternoon of December 8, Cooper gave Drew permission to send a peace delegation to treat with Opothleyahola, who had made a peace overture to gain time and perhaps facilitate the defection. Most of Drew's men who left did not return to the Confederate ranks. By late evening, Drew realized that only 60 of 480 men remained in his camp. Major Pegg, a Ross loyalist and member of the peace delegation, returned from Opothleyahola's camp and reported that Drew's position would be attacked. The remnants of Drew's regiment left their equipment behind and moved with speed to Cooper's camp two miles below on Bird Creek. Expecting action, the men remained alert all night, but no attack occurred. Early the next morning the remaining Cherokees, with help from some Choctaws and Texans, retrieved their valuable equipment that had been left untouched by the enemy. Drew reported in detail the names of the officers who joined Opothleyahola.[19]

These officers and their men did not desert because of a lack of courage. They merely abandoned a Confederacy that had never commanded their loyalty. Given the apparent organization of the defection and the irregular movement of Drew's regiment the day before, it seems probable that the action had been planned. The conspiracy may have begun weeks before if the communication between Opothleyahola and the Keetoowahs included the Creek chief's plans to move east of the Arkansas River.[20]

During the morning of December 9, Cooper sent two Creek companies under Captain Foster to scout Opothleyahola's position. At 11:00 a.m., Cooper crossed to the east side of Bird Creek and moved south across the adjacent prairie. After he covered about five miles, Captain Foster's runners arrived to report to Cooper that the advance scouting party was under fire and retreating. Simultaneously, Cooper's force also came under attack. The loyal Indians retreated to a large horseshoe bend in the creek where the men prepared to give battle. Heavy timber sheltered the creek bottom. Opothleyahola's men also occupied a hidden ravine extending from

---

18 OR 8, 7-8; McIntosh et al., 1868 "Statement relative to the Exodus of Ho-poth-la-ya-holat"; Dean Trickett, "The Civil War in the Indian Territory," *Chronicles of Oklahoma* (June, 1940) Issue 18, 272; Starr, *History of the Cherokee Indians and Their Legends and Folk Lore*, 272.

19 OR 8, 7-8, 17.

20 James G. Blunt, "General Blunt's Account of his Civil War Experiences," *Kansas Historical Quarterly* (May 1932), Issue 1, 224.

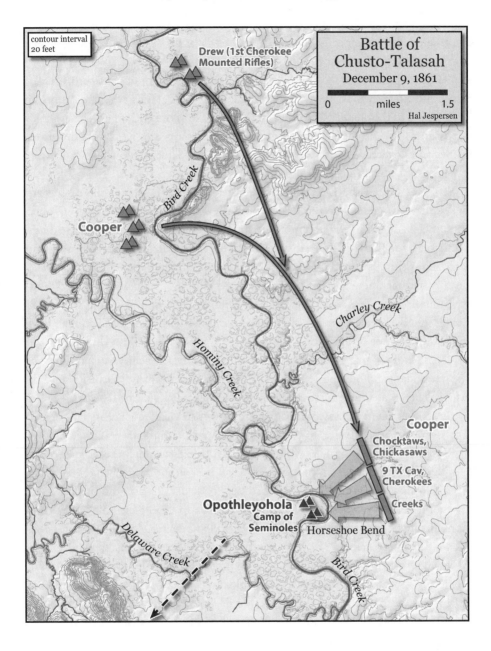

contour interval
20 feet

Drew (1st Cherokee
Mounted Rifles)

Battle of
Chusto-Talasah
December 9, 1861

0   miles   1.5

Hal Jespersen

Bird Creek

Cooper

Charley Creek

Hominy Creek

Cooper

Chocktaws,
Chickasaws

9 TX Cav,
Cherokees

Creeks

Opothleyohola
Camp of
Seminoles

Horseshoe Bend

Delaware Creek

Bird Creek

the creek into the prairie. The battle of Chusto-Talasah, the second fight in what is also known as the Trail of Blood on Ice Campaign, was about to begin.[21]

Chusto-Talasah, or "Caving Banks," was an apt description of Bird Creek, a strong-flowing stream with steep banks that dropped 20 feet to the current below. To the west of the creek was picturesque, forested hill country and Opothleyahola's base camp. Only his men knew where the fording points they would use during the battle were located. As the attacking Confederates later acknowledged, it was a well-chosen defensive position.[22]

Cooper placed the Cherokee train under a strong guard on the prairie and positioned his forces with the Creeks on his left flank. The remaining Cherokees and the Texans occupied his center, and the Choctaws and Chickasaws were on the north or right flank. When all was ready, the Confederate forces attacked the fortified position from the east. Colonel William B. Sims divided his 9th Texas Cavalry early in the action in order to serve with the Choctaws and Chickasaws when he became aware of the heavily defended ravine farther to the north. The Rebel Creeks attacked along the bend where a house with a corn crib and rail fence marked the center of the battle.

Most of the fighting took place dismounted. Both sides alternately gained and lost the advantage, but the Confederate force, in occasionally sharp fighting that lasted as much as four hours, failed to achieve a decisive victory. The battle ended with nightfall when the loyal Indians were driven or withdrew across Bird Creek. The Confederates returned to their camp. Cooper's command held the field, but had lost 15-30 killed, some 37 wounded, and suffered several hundred desertions. Opothleyahola's command, perhaps 500 in all, lost about nine killed.[23]

Following the battle, Cooper, whose men were low on ammunition, learned of another defection of Cherokees from Fort Gibson to Opothleyahola's camp. The Confederate commander decided to request help. General McCulloch had left for Richmond on December 10 to explain the situation in the distant and chaotic Trans-Mississippi theater. His cavalry commander, Col. James McIntosh—no relation to the Creek McIntoshes—remained in charge. McIntosh, who was born at Fort Brooke in what is today Tampa, Florida, knew the region well. He graduated from West Point in 1849, though at the bottom of his class, and had served as a

21 OR 8, 8-9, 16; Trickett, "The Civil War in the Indian Territory" (September 1940), 273-274.

22 Ibid., 273-275; OR 8, 14-22.

23 OR 8, 8-10, 14, 16-17, 20-21; Douglas Hale, "Rehearsal for Civil War,", Issue 68, 241-246.

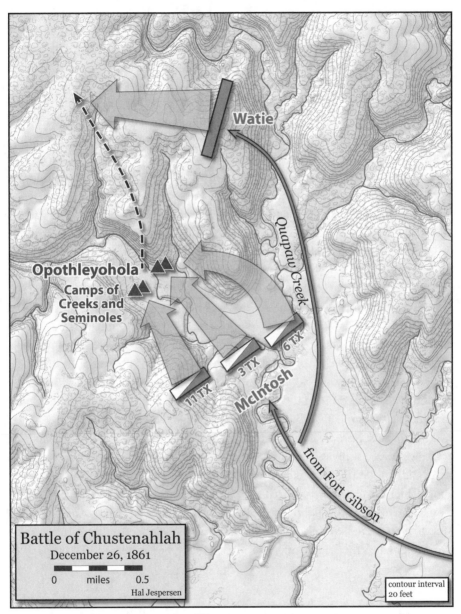

Battle of Chustenahlah
December 26, 1861

0   miles   0.5

Hal Jespersen

contour interval
20 feet

captain of the 1st Cavalry, spending time at Forts Arbuckle, Cobb, and Smith, before resigning his commission to throw his fortune in with the Confederacy.

Cooper sent a rider to Van Buren, Arkansas, to report the fluid and difficult situation he faced and to request resupply and reinforcements. He believed that more white troops would serve to curtail defections. Leaving the bulk of his troops at Choska, about 20 miles west of Fort Gibson on the Arkansas River, Cooper and a pair of companies camped across the Grand River from the fort.[24]

McIntosh's reply reached Cooper on December 14. The message assured him that the supplies, ammunition, and reinforcements he had requested would be forthcoming—though in a form Cooper surely was not expecting. When Cooper crossed the river six days later on December 20, he was surprised to find Colonel McIntosh at the head of 1,600 men of his Texas and Arkansas cavalry at Gibson. After he reinforced Cooper, McIntosh's command totaled 1,380 men. The Confederate leaders developed a plan of attack. McIntosh would move up the Verdigris toward Opothleyahola's camp while Cooper, with his force of 1,500, moved up the Arkansas River to get behind and block Opothleyahola's escape. Stand Watie, stationed to the north on the Grand River, would converge from the east with his 300 men. McIntosh left Fort Gibson on December 22 without waiting for Cooper, who was still transporting his supplies and was thus delayed.[25]

The weather turned cold as McIntosh and his cavalry rode along the Verdigris. It was snowing on Christmas night when a group of the loyal Indians tried to lure the Texans aside, but McIntosh would not be turned. On December 26, he ordered four days' cooked rations prepared and rode for the heights above Hominy Creek, a tributary of Bird Creek, to confront the loyal Indians. Opothleyahola had realized that no help from Kansas would be forthcoming, and had begun evacuating in the direction of Kansas. He had traveled north two days before Chustenahlah, the third and final battle in the Trail Blood on Ice Campaign, got underway.[26]

A rear guard protected the retreating loyal Indians. McIntosh estimated the defensive force numbered about 1,700 in "a very strong position" at the crest of a steep and wooded hill not far from Opothleyahola's main camp. The Seminoles under Chief Tustenuggee prepared to fight on foot, using the trees for cover, while mounted Creeks were held in reserve. The loyal Indians exhibited confidence, but McIntosh reported that the defenders had underestimated "the gallant resolve which animated the hearts of those in the valley below them." A company of

---

24 McCulloch wanted authorities to place an officer in command over McCulloch and Price; *OR* 8, 11-12; Cutrer, *Ben McCulloch and the Frontier Military Tradition*, 268-271; Trickett, "The Civil War in the Indian Territory" (September 1940), 278.

25 *OR* 8, 11-12, 22.

26 Chustenahlah translates to "a shoal in the stream." Douglas Hale, *Third Texas Cavalry* (Norman, OK, 1993), 80-81; Hale, "Rehearsal for Civil War," 248-249; Muriel H. Wright and LeRoy H. Fischer, "Civil War Sites in Oklahoma," in *Chronicles of Oklahoma* (Summer 1966), Issue 44, 202; *OR* 8, 12-14, 22; Gill, "Federal Refugees from Indian Territory," 65-66.

McIntosh's command crossed the creek and came under heavy fire. Others followed, forming battle lines as they moved. Another force was sent up the creek to attack on foot where the terrain was too steep for horses to safely or easily operate. When the bugler sounded the charge, the Confederates quickly overran the position in combat that included hand-to-hand fighting.[27]

The defenders fell back and offered a second stand at their camp but were soon routed, leaving McIntosh in possession of their supplies. The West Pointer reported capturing "160 women and children, 20 negroes, several hundred head of cattle, 100 sheep, and a great quantity of property of much value to the enemy . . . [leaving them] destitute of the simplest elements of subsistence." He listed the enemy's loss at 250 killed and his own as nine killed and 40 wounded. Men, women, and children fled into a storm of sleet and snow through rugged, thickly wooded country. Their misery was about to get much worse.

Stand Watie arrived just as the battle was ending. The following day he and McIntosh pursued the defeated loyalists. Watie divided his force between himself and his nephew, Maj. E. C. Boudinot, and overtook them retreating through the hill country. In a two-hour running skirmish that followed Watie reported killing "8 or 9" of the enemy and did not lose a single man in return. According to Boudinot, "[T]he enemy were seen upon every hill and in every valley . . . [and] must have numbered from 500 to 600 warriors. They made no determined stand, but were driven by our soldiers from point to point . . . [through] the roughest country I ever saw." Boudinot reported 11 enemy dead and the capture of 75 women and children; Watie later ordered them released.[28]

On December 29, Cooper arrived and began a seven-day reconnaissance to the north almost to the Kansas border. He reported killing six combatants and capturing 150, primarily women and children. One of his own men froze to death in the frigid conditions. The trails of the retreating refugees led to the Walnut River and other tributaries of the Arkansas north of the Kansas border. Opothleyahola's skillful maneuvering had ended in disaster. The promised Union army on which he had so deeply depended did not arrive. Colonel McIntosh found the letters promising aid to Opothleyahola and enclosed them in his official report.[29]

---

27 OR 8, 22-24; Trickett, "The Civil War in the Indian Territory," 278-279; Hale, *Third Texas Cavalry*, 81-82.

28 Ibid., 13, 23-25, 32-33.

29 Ibid., 12-13, 25-26; Mary Jane Ward, *When the Wolf Came: The Civil War in the Indian Territory* (Fayetteville: University of Arkansas Press, 2013), 82-87.

The refugees suffered terribly that winter. The Indians collected on the Walnut River before moving east to the upper Verdigris, where their condition was described as wretched. They had little food and no utensils with which to prepare it. Frostbite affected every man, woman, and child, and Army surgeons performed more than 100 amputations. Among the Creeks, who numbered around 4,000, 240 died during just the first two months in Kansas. The number of those who died en route will never be known. The Indian agents and the army did what they could to help and Congress directed annuity payments to the loyal Indians. Help, however—especially blankets and shelter—was slow in coming. When 2,000 ponies died of exposure and starvation, fouling the Verdigris River, the survivors had no choice but to move east to the Grand River, where conditions slowly improved and the refugees finally obtained tents. By the end of that summer about one tenth of the Creeks had perished. The death rate was comparable among the other tribes.[30]

Opothleyahola's revolt was a costly defeat, but it did not mark the end of the full-bloods' opposition to the Confederate alliances. On May 22, 1862, loyal Creeks, including a small number of African Creeks and Seminoles, became the nucleus of the 1st Regiment of the Indian Home Guard. The 2nd Regiment included Cherokees augmented by Osages, Seneca, Shawnee, Quapaw, and Delewares. These mounted regiments were initially well-supplied and well-led. Following the defeat of the Confederate forces assigned to safeguard the Cherokee Nation, Drew's reconstructed Keetoowah regiment defected and provided the brigade with a 3rd Regiment, which became commonly known as the Union Indian Brigade.

By that time the bitter war in the Indian Nations had already begun shifting inexorably toward the Union.[31]

---

30 OR Series 2, 4, 5-10; *Annual Report of the Commissioner of Indian Affairs for the Year 1862* (Washington, D.C., 1863), 138-140, 143-145; Confer, *The Cherokee Nation in the Civil War*, 118-122; Zellar, *African Creeks*, 52-53; Baird, *The Quapaw Indians*, 98; Edmund J. Danziger, Jr., "The Office of Indian Affairs and the Problem of Civil War Refugees in Kansas" in *Kansas Historical Quarterly* (Autumn 1969), vol 35, Issue 35, 261-264.

31 OR 8, 482, 576; Abel, *The American Indian as Slaveholder and Secessionist*, 270-271, n. #548-549, *The American Indian as Participant in the Civil War*, 133-116 text and n. #272; Annual Report of the Commission of Indian Affairs, 1862, 144; Wiley Britton, *The Union Indian Brigade in the Civil War* (Kansas City, MO, 1922), 61-62; Zellar, *African Creeks*, 55-56; Sharon Dixon Wyant, "Colonel William A. Phillips and the Civil War in the Indian Territory" (MA thesis, Oklahoma State University, 1964), 10.

Pea Ridge

Pike left Col. Douglas Cooper in charge of the Opothleyahola affair and started out for Richmond in late October 1861 with the goal of arranging for the ratification of the treaties. Dealing with the Confederate Congress was a time-consuming affair, but with the help of Arkansas "Family" patriarch Robert W. Johnson, head of the Senate Committee on Indian Affairs, the treaties were ratified by the first of the year.[1]

While Pike was in the Southern capital, the Senate confirmed Jefferson Davis's nomination of Pike as a brigadier general assigned to command the "Indian Country west of Arkansas and north of Texas." Pike arranged for construction of his headquarters, Fort Davis, a few miles from Fort Gibson but south of the Arkansas River. Because of Opothleyahola's revolt and the defection of Drew's regiment, Pike wanted more white troops in the region. He was given permission to raise "two regiments of infantry and two companies of artillery [from Arkansas, but only] as soon as . . . [he could] arm them."[2]

The shortage of weapons complicated Pike's recruiting efforts, but Confederate authorities guaranteed 2,000 rifled muskets for his Indian regiments. After the treaties were ratified, Pike sent word for his regiments to meet with him at Fort Davis on January 25. To obtain the treaty monies, the newly minted general

---

1 OR 8, 596-598, 605, 611, 690, 721; Dougan, *Confederate Arkansas*, 83.

2 OR 8, 690, 721; Walter Lee Brown, *A Life of Albert Pike*, 372-373; Brown, *A Life of Albert Pike*, 375-376.

returned via Columbia, South Carolina, where he received $95,000 in gold. He continued to New Orleans, where he picked up more specie plus treasury notes totaling more than $700,000. Although Pike appeared to have succeeded in his strategy of establishing a secure relationship between the Confederacy and the Indian Nations, events turned sour the moment he returned.[3]

While Pike was still in the East, Sterling Price insisted that General McCulloch join him for a raid to Lexington on the Missouri River. McCulloch had little faith in the effort and was convinced an attack even with their combined forces would fail, and that he could not operate that far from his base of supplies. The reason for his doubt was simple: He did not trust Price's undisciplined army. As a result, he refused to risk his force 300 miles north of his own base. Unfazed by the lack of support, Price set out on his own and fought the Battle of Lexington, ("Battle of the Hemp Bales") skirmishing from September 12-17 and engaging in more heavy fighting September 18-20. The raid was a tactical success, but Price and his men ended up falling back to Springfield in southwest Missouri.

McCulloch also refused to join Price in pursuit of Jim Lane's Jayhawkers. When asked by Secretary of War Judah P. Benjamin, the recipient of Price's complaints, why he did not cooperate more fully with Price or pursue Gen. Franz Sigel's retreating army of some 12,500 men, McCulloch bluntly replied, "I was assigned to the Indian Territory, with instructions to defend it from invasion from any quarter." McCulloch also explained that he was low on ammunition and that "the Arkansas State troops [had] marched for home, leaving me with about 2,500 men fit for duty, 2,000 of whom were required to defend the northwest part of Arkansas and the Indian Territory." McCulloch suggested that Price fortify Springfield and use his cavalry against Kansas Jayhawkers. The end result was a controversy that erupted in newspaper editorials and in a series of bitter letters between the supporters of McCulloch and Price.[4]

McCulloch advised Secretary Benjamin, tucked far away in a Richmond office, that an officer who was not from Missouri should command both armies. While Price lobbied for the command, McCulloch ruled himself out and suggested instead Maj. Gen. Braxton Bragg, a West Pointer who was offered command in

3 *OR* 3, 581-582, 607-608; *OR* 8, 53, 698-699, 719-721, 764; *OR* 13, 841-844; 53, 795-796; Brown, *A Life of Albert Pike*, 375-376, 378-380; Cutrer, *Ben McCulloch and the Frontier Military Tradition*, 256-257.

4 *OR* 3, 743-749; William L. Shea and Earl J. Hess, *Pea Ridge: Civil War Campaign in the West* (Chapel Hill, NC, 1996), 15-26; Castel, *General Stirling Price and the Civil War in the West*, 246-250; Cutrer, *Ben McCulloch and the Frontier Military Tradition*, 246-251.

Maj. Gen. Earl Van Dorn

Library of Congress

Arkansas in January 1862. Bragg declined. In his place stepped Maj. Gen. Earl Van Dorn, a former U.S. cavalry officer from Mississippi and the man favored by Jefferson Davis. His appointment proved to be a mistake, for he was prone to act rashly.[5]

Van Dorn had made a name for himself campaigning against Buffalo Hump's Comanche band. He was widely liked by his comrades as well as by his superiors, but he was also ambitious and arrogant. Van Dorn cared little that the band he successfully attacked was (unbeknownst to him) under the protection of an officer at Fort Arbuckle. The new appointee had big plans. His first was a fanciful scheme to defeat the Union army in northwest Arkansas, take St. Louis, and attack General U.S. Grant from the north in order to "make a reputation and serve my country." Unfortunately for the Confederacy, all it would accomplish was heavy losses in men and supplies, the death of a capable Southern general, and the abandonment of a wide swath of territory.

Van Dorn decided to move his command to Pocahontas, 12 miles south of Bentonville in northeast Arkansas, to be in a position to take St. Louis. His decision alarmed the more careful McCulloch. "This will leave the whole country open to the attack of Lane of Kansas with his Indian allies," he complained to Texas Governor Francis R. Lubbock on February 6. "General Pike's command being composed of mostly of Indians will not be able to resist without aid the force sent against them . . . . [This, together with Indian defections,] may enable [the enemy] to carry the [war] as far south as the frontiers of Texas. To prevent this," urged

---

5 On June 27, 1862, Bragg assumed command of what would become known as the Army of Tennessee. His difficult personality, coupled with trying subordinates, hampered his efforts.

McCulloch, "I would respectfully suggest that Texas should make the Indian Country or Kansas this battle ground rather than have it on her own soil. To do this she must send her own men to General Pike who will be stationed in the Indian Territory." Should Van Dorn change his mind and attack Kansas—McCulloch's preferred course—McCulloch would be there to lead them. But since there was no guarantee of that, McCulloch recommended "some experienced men from our state [be] put in command of these regiments. The President ought & will listen to the Gov of the State when he recommends a man for such a position."[6]

The Union army out west was also in the midst of change. After General Fremont's unauthorized freeing of slaves in Missouri, President Lincoln on November 19, 1861, appointed Maj. Gen. Henry W. Halleck, a West Point graduate and author of *Elements of Military Arts and Science* (1846), as commander of the Department of Missouri. Halleck, or "Old Brains" as he was also known, ordered Brig. Gen. Samuel R. Curtis, another West Point graduate and former Iowa congressman, to confront Price. By mid-February, Price had abandoned Springfield to Curtis and retreated in a running skirmish toward McCulloch's small army in northwest Arkansas. McCulloch led a force to bring in Price's command safely. His 3rd Louisiana turned away an assault against Price's rear, and Curtis let the Rebels retire toward Fayetteville. There, McCulloch had supplies issued to his men from the city's warehouses and torched what remained, burning half the town in the process.

With the city in flames, McCulloch and Price, whose combined force numbered about 16,000 men and 65 artillery pieces, moved south to a strong position near Crawford, Arkansas, in the Boston Mountains. McCulloch hoped Curtis would come straight at them in a frontal assault. The Union general seemed about to do just that when he advanced south of Fayetteville to within 15 miles of the Rebel army. After an encounter with McCulloch's cavalry, however, he disappointed the Texan by fortifying above Little Sugar Creek, near Elkhorn Tavern. General Sigel, meanwhile, occupied Bentonville to the southwest. The

---

6 Ben McCulloch to His Excellency Governor Lubboch, February 6, 1862, Governor's Papers, Texas State Library, Austin; Cutrer, *Ben McCulloch and the Frontier Military Tradition*, 280; Brad Agnew, "War against the Comanches," in *The Chronicles of Oklahoma* (Summer 1971), Issue 49, 225-229; Arthur B. Carter, *The Tarnished Cavalier: Major General Earl Van Dorn, C.S.A.* (Knoxville, TN, 1999), 40-45; Robert G. Hartje, *Van Dorn: The Life and Times of a Confederate General* (Nashville, TN, 1967), 12-13, 60, 74, 92; Shea and Hess, *Pea Ridge*, 19-26; Castel, *General Sterling Price and the Civil War in the West*, 67-68; Cutrer, *Ben McCulloch and the Frontier Military Tradition*, 277-280; OR 3, 733-734; T. Harry Williams, *P. G. T. Beauregard: Napoleon in Gray* (Baton Rouge, LA, 1955), 47, 158-159.

aggressive Van Dorn saw only opportunity and decided to attack immediately. Orders went out from Fort Smith to prepare to march. The resulting fight at Pea Ridge affected the outcome of the war in the Indian Nations and in the Trans-Mississippi West more than any other single battle.[7]

The movement of Confederate troops began on March 4 in the midst of a snowstorm. The men spent the night of March 5-6 a dozen miles from Bentonville. Brigadier General James McIntosh's cavalry left before dawn to engage Sigel, with the rest of the Rebel command to follow and complete the victory. Sigel, however, slipped out of Bentonville, repulsed McIntosh, and marched to join Curtis, whose total force now numbered about 10,500. Van Dorn had conceived a plan he believed would destroy Curtis's army. Using McCulloch's knowledge of the geography, he planned to march his army around the heavily defended Federal position by leaving the Telegraph Road for the Bentonville Detour so he could attack Curtis from the rear. Van Dorn failed to foresee that a blocked road would slow his flanking movement, and that the Federals would detect his advance.[8]

As these events unfolded, Albert Pike's return to the Indian Nations was delayed by heavy rains that flooded roads but did not raise the water level in the Arkansas River enough to permit boat traffic. When he finally arrived at Fort Davis on February 25, orders were waiting for him to join General Van Dorn. First, however, he had to distribute money to the Indian regiments, a process that consumed another three days.[9]

General Curtis, meanwhile, was entrenched in a strong position above Little Sugar Creek. In preparation for his daring flanking maneuver, Van Dorn made it appear to the Federals that his men had camped for the night. "But soon after dark," he continued, "I marched again, moving with Price's division in advance, and taking the road by which I hoped before daylight to reach the rear of the enemy."[10] Ben McCulloch objected, arguing his men needed rest. He and Price instead suggested a different flanking movement to force Curtis to withdraw. Van

---

7 OR 8, 462-463, 468, 471, 473-475, 487-489, 494, 499, 506, 516, 524-525, 528, 543-545, 556, 559-569; Shea and Hess, *Pea Ridge*, 5-7, 9-15, 22-26, 27-44, 59; Cutrer, *Ben McCulloch and the Frontier Military Tradition*, 262, 281-88; Castel, *General Sterling Price and the Civil War in the West*, 64-65; Carter, *The Tarnished Cavalier*, 47-50; Robert Selph Henry, *The Story of the Confederacy* (Garden City, NY, 1931), 46-7; Boatner, *Civil War Dictionary*, 367.

8 Cutrer, *Ben McCulloch and the Frontier Military Tradition*, 294; OR 8, 286-287; Carter, *The Tarnished Cavalier*, 52-56; Shea and Hess, *Pea Ridge*, 52-90.

9 Brown, *A Life of Albert Pike*, 385-386; OR 8, 287, 283, 755, 763.

10 OR 8, 283.

Brig. Gen. Samuel R. Curtis

Library of Congress

Dorn rejected the advice and led his proposed encirclement with Price's division. When General Pike and his Cherokee regiments arrived from Fort Davis, Van Dorn ordered them into line behind McCulloch. This placed the Cherokees on the extreme right flank of the Confederate line when they were suddenly attacked by Union troops led by Col. Peter J. Osterhaus at about 10:00 a.m.— before they had united with Van Dorn at Elkhorn Tavern.[11]

Union pickets reported a clash with a Rebel force on the Bentonville Detour. Cavalry and infantry sent to protect Curtis's train confirmed the report, and Curtis dispatched Colonel Osterhaus to investigate. His relatively small force consisted of mainly cavalry (battalions of 3rd Iowa Cavalry, 1st and 5th Missouri Cavalry), and three pieces of the flying battery, all under the immediate command of Col. Cyrus Bussey, 3rd Iowa Cavalry; and further, the 12th Missouri, 36th Illinois and 22nd Indiana Regiments, three pieces, 12 pounder howitzers, of Captain Welfley's battery, and Captain Hoffmann's battery." Osterhaus passed through Leetown and approached the Ford Road a mile to the north, which left the Bentonville Detour at 12 Corner Church to converge on Elkhorn Tavern from the west. During the march Van Dorn ordered McCulloch to take that route, while Van Dorn and Price continued on the Bentonville Detour to Telegraph Road, which led to Elkhorn Tavern from the north. The astonished Osterhaus had stumbled into McCulloch's entire army. Though heavily outnumbered, Osterhaus unlimbered his artillery and

11 Shea and Hess, *Pea Ridge*, 80-81, 85-96; Carter, *The Tarnished Cavalier*, 55-57; OR 8, 283-284, 287-288, 292; Brown, *A Life of Albert Pike*, 386; William L. Shea, *War in the West: Pea Ridge and Prairie Grove* (Fort Worth and Boulder, 1996), 45-46. Cooper and Creek Col. D. N. McIntosh's regiments were delayed and did not participate in the battle.

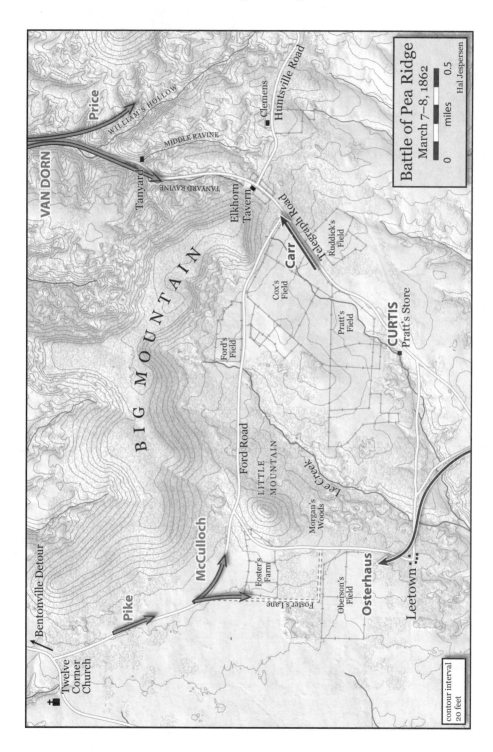

Battle of Pea Ridge
March 7–8, 1862

Hal Jespersen

0   miles   0.5

contour interval
20 feet

prepared to fight, opening fire with good effect. The result was two separate battles fought a couple of miles apart.[12]

McCulloch, who was also surprised, ordered McIntosh to reply with his cavalry, and the Texas and Arkansas regiments charged the battery. Pike's Cherokees joined in the assault. The result, Osterhaus reported, was that "a wild, numerous, and irregular throng of cavalry, a great many Indians among them, rushed towards us, breaking through our lines. A general discharge of fire-arms on both sides created a scene of wild confusion, from which our cavalry, abandoning the three pieces of artillery, retreated towards their old camping ground, while that of the enemy made their way across the fields towards the Bentonville road."[13]

"My whole command consisted of about 1,000 men, all Indians, except one squadron," reported Pike after the battle. "The enemy opened fire into the woods where we were, the fence in front of us was thrown down, and the Indians (Watie's regiment on foot and Drew's on horseback), with part of Sims' regiment, gallantly led by Lieutenant-Colonel Quayle, charged full in front through the woods and into the open ground with loud yells, routed the cavalry, took the battery, fired on and pursued the enemy, retreating through the fenced field on our right, and held the battery."[14]

Most of the teams managed to gallop away with their caissons, which deprived Pike of the ability to move the captured guns to the rear as trophies. When Watie saw another Union battery in his front, "beyond the skirt of underbrush, protected by a heavy force of infantry," Pike ordered Captain Lee to turn the captured guns to face the new threat, but "around the taken battery was a mass of Indians"—mounted troops from Drew's regiment—and "he could not induce a single man to assist in doing so."[15]

Once the Union guns began shelling them, the Indians retreated into the woods. Pike did not believe his Indian regiments would stand in the open and

---

12 *OR* 8, 199, 217, 232-233, 270-271; Shea and Hess, *Pea Ridge*, 89-96, 101-104.

13 *OR* 8, 217, 232-234, 270-271; Cutrer, *Ben McCulloch and the Frontier Military Tradition*, 298-299.

14 This was a detachment from Col. William B. Sims' 9th Texas Cavalry, present at the Battle of Chustanala. No report by William Quayle has been found. *OR* 8, 288.

15 Ibid. Shea and Hess, *Pea Ridge*, 101 and Shea, *War in the West*, 46-48, argue the Cherokee capture of the Union battery is an inaccurate "legend," and cite the St. Louis *Daily Missouri Democrat*, March 22, 1862, which gave an account of the 3rd Louisiana without Indians among the "cavalry," and James Boyal's journal (State Historical Society of Iowa, March 7, 1862), which did the same. This is wholly insufficient to reject Albert Pike's detailed after-action report backed up by General Osterhaus's own observations.

maintain discipline in the face of an artillery barrage. The new general dismounted Drew's regiment and ordered both Drew and Watie's men to take cover in the trees and await the enemies' advance. Instead, the Union guns continued with an ineffective shelling for two and a half hours. About 1:30 p.m., Pike dispatched Drew's regiment to form in the rear of two other cavalry regiments and had Watie's men move the captured battery into the woods.[16]

The Battle of Pea Ridge stamped the Cherokees with an undeserved reputation for cowardice. This impression contrasts sharply with the performance of Stand Watie's regiment during the war, as well as that of the Union 3rd Indian at Newtonia and the Union Indian Brigade at Honey Springs and elsewhere (discussed below). At Pea Ridge, Drew's Keetoowahs were not motivated to fight for the Confederacy. The notion that the Cherokees would not hold formation under heavy fire comes from Pike's official report of the battle and his later writings. Dr. Annie Abel, who wrote three volumes on the Civil War in the Indian Nations early in the last century, contributed to this error. "The Indian's most effective work was done, throughout, under cover of the woods," she concluded. "Indians, as Pike well knew, could never be induced to face shells in the open."[17] Historians have accepted this misinterpretation of the Cherokees' performance at Pea Ridge for too long. It is time to replace the nineteenth century analysis with a new interpretation based on a better understanding of the complexity of the situation they faced at Pea Ridge.[18]

The charge of McIntosh's Texas and Arkansas cavalry regiments routed the Union troops, but ended in a state of excited confusion. Only Maj. Lawrence Ross's 6th Texas Cavalry continued in pursuit of the broken enemy, during which he discovered a large Union force that he reported to McCulloch. The news prompted him to ordered Col. Louis Hebert to move the infantry onto the field. Osterhaus had reformed most of his cavalry in a field beyond a belt of timber where his own infantry, numbering around 1,600, had assembled. McCulloch's newly deployed 4,000 Rebel infantry under Hebert were in a position to threaten Osterhaus's right flank. McCulloch, a former scout against the Comanches and Gen. Zachary Taylor's chief of scouts during the war with Mexico, reverted to his former role and made a fateful decision: He would ride into the timber to get a

---

16 OR 8, 217, 288-289; 13, 954-955; Shea and Hess, *Pea Ridge*, 99-100.

17 Abel, *The American Indian in the Civil War*, 30.

18 OR 8, 288; 13, 819-820; Cutrer, *Ben McCulloch and the Frontier Military Tradition*, 286, 299; Shea and Hess, *Pea Ridge*, 144, 224, 321.

better sense of the situation so he could attack with both infantry and his reforming cavalry as soon as possible. Riflemen from the 36th Illinois spotted the mounted officer, leveled their weapons, and killed him. McIntosh compounded the fatal mistake. When he learned McCulloch was dead, he rode to the head of the 2nd Arkansas Rifles (dismounted) and advanced into the timber, where Union fire also ended his life.[19]

The leaderless regimental officers decided to call off the attack, which left Rebel hopes for the Battle of Leetown in the hands of Colonel Hebert on the Confederate left, in Morgan's Woods east of the Leetown Road. A confused and extended engagement unfolded in which Hebert gained the upper hand, though his limited success proved temporary: two-thirds of McCulloch's troops awaited orders and failed to support Hebert. Osterhaus, hard-pressed and facing potential defeat, asked Curtis for reinforcements and eventually was able to overrun the Rebels. Hebert was captured in the midst of the confused fighting in the woods.[20]

At 3.00 p.m., Major Whitfield informed Pike that McCulloch and McIntosh were dead and that 7,000 Federals threatened their left flank—3,000 of whom Whitfield had seen personally. Pike gathered troops behind fences and sent Maj. E. C. Boudinot to inform Van Dorn that he would attempt to maintain the position. However, when Pike rode "along the ridge to the rear I found the position was not tenable. . . . At this time the firing on the field had ceased. It was evident enough that the field was left to the enemy. . . . I determined to withdraw the troops and lead them to General Van Dorn." Pike went on to note, "the officers assured me that the men were in such condition that it would be worse than useless to bring them into action again that day. I accordingly sent orders to the artillery and cavalry to join me."[21]

In relatively good order Pike withdrew with the "16th and 17th Arkansas, the 1st Arkansas Mounted Rifles, the 4th Texas Cavalry Battalion . . . and Good's Texas Battery," while Watie's cavalry protected his right flank. Other units didn't receive his orders to move or ignored them. Some outfits marched to protect the train at Camp Stephens, including B. Warren Stone's and Drew's regiments; others remained on the field. After Pike and his men departed, Colonel Greer of the 3rd

19 OR 8, 218, 289, 295, 298-299; Shea and Hess, *Pea Ridge*, 99-112; Cutrer, *Ben McCulloch and the Frontier Military Tradition*, 298-304.

20 OR 8, 199, 217-219, 231-232, 237-238, 246, 249-250, 289, 295; Shea and Hess, *Pea Ridge*, 115-133, 134-149; Shea, *War in the West*, 43-54; Brown, *A Life of Albert Pike*, 391.

21 OR 8, 289.

Texas Cavalry learned of the death of McCulloch and McIntosh. Greer rounded up several regiments "that could not have exceeded 3,000 men" and at 10:00 p.m. sent a message to Van Dorn that he intended to march to him at 1:00 a.m. unless otherwise ordered. He received permission and moved out a half-hour later, reaching the Telegraph Road before first light.[22]

While McCulloch and McIntosh had been fighting what would be known as the Battle of Leetown on March 7, Van Dorn and Price were moving behind them in an effort to flank Curtis, whose men had moved down the Telegraph Road and deployed around 10:00 a.m. before reaching the high ground of Pea Ridge. Curtis had hastily repositioned some of his men from Little Sugar Creek to face the threat from Van Dorn's maneuver, and would continue moving up reinforcements as the battle progressed. The opposing sides exchanged artillery fire before the infantry engaged in a long seesaw affair with the Rebel fighters, eventually capturing Elkhorn Tavern late in the day after driving Brig. Gen. Eugene A. Carr's division back nearly a mile. Darkness ended the March 7 fighting and a freezing cold night followed. Curtis and Van Dorn consolidated their forces. Van Dorn placed elements of McCulloch's former division in the center of his line and extended his right flank to Big Mountain, where part of Watie's command also was located. Pike joined Watie to watch for a flanking movement.[23]

Van Dorn, however, had badly mishandled his wagon train, which was several hours away. During a savage artillery duel the next morning (March 8), his artillerists began to run out of ammunition. Fresh Union troops under Sigel were entering the fighting. Van Dorn had no choice but to order his army to pull out under covering fire as Curtis's men began advancing. The evacuation was easier than it should have been because Curtis did not pursue. Union losses were reported as 203 killed, 980 wounded, and 201 missing, or 1,384. Van Dorn later reported his losses as about 800 killed and wounded and 200-300 captured, but a total of about 2,000 is now deemed more accurate.

The Confederates moved to the east of the White River, up the valley, and over the Boston Mountains into the Arkansas River valley. Van Dorn made his new headquarters in Van Buren without informing Pike or Watie of his withdrawal. Pike tried to rally a few retreating stragglers before withdrawing. Watie and his men were among the last Rebels to leave the battlefield. Pike initially believed that Union

---

22 *Shea and Hess, Pea Ridge*, 143-144; OR 8, 289, 293-294, 301, 303-304; Brown, *A Life of Albert Pike*, 391-392.

23 OR vol. 8, 290; Shea and Hess, *Pea Ridge*, 224.

forces had captured his supply train, but Brig. Gen. Martin E. Green of the Second Division, Missouri State Guard, used Col. B. Warren Stone and his men to protect the train and guide it to safety. With the wagons safe, Green sent 100 men to bring up ammunition to Van Dorn. When the men eventually got through, they discovered the Confederate commander had left the field. Albert Pike, apparently believing the Southern army destroyed and dispersed, made his way through Elm Springs, Cincinnati, Evansville, and into the Cherokee Nation to Dwight Mission, where he wrote his report of the battle. Van Dorn's official report praised Stone's actions but made no mention of Pike, Watie, or the Indian regiments.[24]

On March 15, when Pike heard that one of the Confederate dead had been scalped, he issued an order forbidding the practice. It would only be allowed if Union Indians employed it—but not against white troops. Pike sent a copy of his order to Curtis with a note promising the gruesome practice would not be repeated. Scalping, he assured the Union general, was "regarded with horror by the Confederate commander." Curtis replied, "I avail myself, general, of this occasion to assure you I reciprocate the personal regard expressed by you. I would prefer that we were friends rather than foes." Curtis went on to imply that it was wrong for the Confederacy to employ Indian troops, who as far as Curtis was concerned could never be controlled. Union authorities had aided Opthleyahola and were preparing Indian troops to participate in an invasion of the Indian Nations, retorted Pike, who gathered the order and all the correspondence and had them published in a Little Rock newspaper.[25]

When the news filtered east, the papers made sure to comment. The *Boston Evening Transcript* castigated Albert Pike. "There is no pit of infamy too deep for him to fill," it editorialized. The *New York Daily Tribune* accused him of leading what it called "the Aboriginal Corps of Tomahawkers and Scalpers at the Battle of Pea Ridge." A third paper, the *Chicago Tribune*, condemned "Colonel Albert Pike . . . who deserves and will doubtless receive eternal infamy for his efforts to induce a horde of savages to butcher brave men who had taken up arms to prevent the subversion of the Republic."[26]

---

24 OR 8, 284, 290-292, 317-318; Shea and Hess, *Pea Ridge*, 240-252; Carter, *The Tarnished Cavalier*, 63-64; Brown, *A Life of Albert Pike*, 392-393.

25 Brown, *A Life of Albert Pike*, 395-396.

26 Boston *Evening Transcript*, March 15, 1862; *New York Daily Tribune*, March 27, 1862; Brown, *A Life of Albert Pike*, 397.

On April 1, Senator Charles Sumner asked the Joint Committee on the Conduct of the War to investigate what had taken place at Pea Ridge. The committee contacted Curtis, whose report arrived on June 20. The members appended the report to their already-completed business and published it. John W. Noble, adjutant of the 3rd Iowa Cavalry, inflamed passions when he reported: "I discovered that 8 of the men of the regiment had been scalped. I also saw bodies of the same men which had been wounded in parts not vital by bullets, and also pierced through the heart and neck with knives, fully satisfying me that the men had first fallen from the gunshot wounds received and afterwards [were] brutally murdered." Col. Cyrus Bussey, also of the 3rd Iowa, offered a similar account: "Of 25 men killed on the field of my regiment, 8 were scalped, and the bodies of others were horribly mutilated. . . . These atrocities I believe to have been committed by Indians belonging to the rebel army." Pike had many occasions during his long life to attempt to explain these events, but never fully did so. The participants were a small minority in one or the other regiments, each of several hundred men.[27]

Van Dorn's stunning defeat and subsequent actions tipped the balance of power west of the Mississippi River and marked the end of his time in the Trans-Mississippi. Ben McCulloch, the dependable protector of the Confederate Indian Nations, was dead. Two other generals, James McIntosh and William Slack, had also been killed or mortally wounded, and Sterling Price wounded. The tired and hungry Confederate survivors lived off the land for about a week, and thousands of Price's men deserted. The Confederacy would never again seriously threaten the state of Missouri.

General Pierre G. T. Beauregard, meanwhile, lobbied Van Dorn to move east of the Mississippi River and join forces there with Gen. Albert Sidney Johnston's army gathering in northern Mississippi, but Van Dorn (who refused to admit he had been defeated at Pea Ridge) still had hopes of capturing St. Louis. He assured Johnston on March 18 that he could support Beauregard (now Johnston's second in command) by a movement on New Madrid and perhaps St. Louis. On March 23, Johnston ordered Van Dorn to move to Memphis, but bad weather delayed Van Dorn in the delta of southeastern Arkansas. By the time he crossed the river he was too late: Johnston's Army of Mississippi had been defeated at Shiloh (April 6-7) and its commander killed.[28]

27 Duncan, *Reluctant General*, 227-228.

28 The rail from Memphis led to Beauregard's headquarters at Corinth, the important rail junction in northern Mississippi. It was from his headquarters there that General Johnston led a

Henry Rector, Arkansas's governor, was worried the Confederate army had abandoned his state. A surprised Jefferson Davis requested an explanation from Van Dorn, who reassured Davis that there were sufficient troops in the state to meet the enemy. Van Dorn explained that he had sent a capable replacement with "all the ammunition &c., that could be spared." The replacement, Maj. Gen. Thomas Hindman, a former Arkansas congressman and ardent secessionist, agreed the manpower was adequate but complained to the adjutant general that "nearly everything of value has been taken away by General Van Dorn." He urgently requested supplies and credit.[29]

Van Dorn ordered Pike to maintain himself independently, though he could request aid from Texas and Arkansas if the Federals attempted to move south. Pike's Indian troops had returned to their respective nations, so Van Dorn assigned Pike a battery and a pair of Texas regiments that were then forming and explained he did not expect him "to give battle to a large force, but by felling trees, burning bridges, removing supplies of forage and subsistence, attacking his trains, stampeding his animals, cutting of his detachments, and other similar means you will be able materially to harass his army and protect this region of the country. . . . In case only of absolute necessity you may move southward."[30]

Pike was more than disgruntled with Van Dorn, who had somehow failed to mention the Indian units in his official report on Pea Ridge. Van Dorn's leading biographer concluded that his subject "must be especially censured for his treatment of Pike throughout the campaign." Pike vowed that his Indian troops would never again leave the region on any "Quixotic expeditions into Missouri, undertaken without probability of success, or . . . any other result than utter and

---

surprise attack against U. S. Grant's Union forces at Pittsburg Landing (Shiloh) on the Tennessee River on April 6, 1862. Johnston was killed the first day of the fighting and Beauregard assumed command. Grant had narrowly held on, but received reinforcements during the night and attacked the next morning on April 7, driving Beauregard's men off the field. On October 3-4, Van Dorn and Price joined forces once more, this time east of the Mississippi River, and suffered another costly defeat at Corinth. In December, Van Dorn, now commanding cavalry, led a very successful raid and destroyed Grant's supply depot at Holly Springs, Mississippi, turning back Grant's first attempt against Vicksburg. In April 1863, a jealous husband killed Van Dorn in Tennessee. Carter, *The Tarnished Cavalier*, 127-146; 181-199; Williams, *P. G. T. Beauregard* (reprint, Baton Rouge: Louisiana State University Press, 1991), 121,147; Hartje, *Van Dorn*, 166-168; Jack Hurst, *Nathan Bedford Forrest: A Biography* (New York: Knopf, 1993), 117; Castel, *General Sterling Price and the Civil War in the West*, 110-119; OR 8, 789-790, and ibid., 10, pt. 2, 354, 371.

29 OR 13, 832-833.

30 Ibid., 795-796; Brown, *A Life of Albert Pike*, 403.

ignominious failure." Van Dorn further inflamed matters when, without Pike's knowledge, he confiscated for his own use Pike's carefully arranged shipment of 2,000 rifles and other valuable equipment.[31]

From the beginning, Pike viewed the Indian Nations as a separate entity outside the Confederate states with its own unique problems. He also believed in the obligations contained in the Confederate treaties designed to address those problems. When Van Dorn and others (who cared nothing about the integrity of the treaties) confiscated Pike's equipment and disregarded his command, he tried to defend the Indian Nations with the meager assets left to him. Like McCulloch, Pike believed the best defense of the Indian Nations was from the "formidable ramparts of the Boston Mountains." Because that option was no longer feasible after the defeat at Pea Ridge, Pike disobeyed Van Dorn's orders and retreated south down the Texas Road to the Blue River. Just 30 miles north of the Texas border he began building Fort McCulloch, which he believed would be impregnable against attack. Dissatisfied with his treatment by the Arkansas commissary system, Pike turned to Texas to procure supplies directly, bypassing the profiteers.[32]

Forts Gibson and Davis, Pike explained to Stand Watie, could not be defended, but Fort McCulloch was in a defensible position and could be supplied from Texas. Watie and Drew would remain farther north in the Cherokee Nation to harass the enemy he was certain would advance against them, especially since (as Pike believed) Van Dorn had abandoned the region. Pike instructed Watie to "give information of the approach of the enemy, harass his flanks and rear, stampede his animals, destroy his small foraging parties, and at last if he still advances, gaining his front join me within my lines and aid in utterly defeating him there."[33]

It didn't take long for a conflict to develop between Pike and General Hindman, the new Confederate commander in Arkansas. Hindman wanted Pike's funds placed in the care of Maj. N. B. Pearce, Hindman's Arkansas ordnance officer. Pike adamantly refused and flatly stated he would purchase his supplies directly in Texas. Pearce and Hindman also wanted Pike's artillery and Texas regiments transferred north to Arkansas. The frustrated Pike explained in several long letters to Hindman that this equipment and his few men were essential to the

---

31 Hartje, *Van Dorn*, 165; *OR* 13, 952; ibid., 53, 795-796, and ibid, *OR* 13, 815, 846, 952, 954.

32 Cutrer, *Ben McCulloch and the Frontier Military Tradition*, 261; Albert Pike to Stand Watie, April 1, 1862, in Cherokee Nation Papers, Western History Collection, University of Oklahoma, typescript, microfilm; Dale and Litton, eds., *Cherokee Cavaliers* (Norman, 1940), 115-117.

33 Ibid., 115-117.

plan approved by the Confederate government to maintain the Indian Nations as allies of the Confederacy. On July 11, 1862, Hindman ordered Pike to report to Fort Smith and take command of northwest Arkansas and Indian Territory. Pike instead offered his resignation. Hindman accepted it and ordered him to report to Little Rock. Ignoring the order, Pike explained to Jefferson Davis that he believed a great injustice had been done to the Indian Nations. He also published a statement to the chiefs of the Nations blaming Van Dorn and other Confederate officers for the dismal state of affairs. Colonel Cooper worked to suppress every copy of the letter he could find and ordered Pike's arrest. For a few months Pike eluded capture and continued his war of words with his commanding officers, but when he attempted to resume command that fall he was arrested. When President Davis accepted his resignation, Pike was released.

Federal forces, meanwhile, moved south of the Kansas border into the Cherokee Nation, just as Pike feared they might.[34]

---

34 OR 13, 40-41, 819-823, 827, 841-844, 846-852, 866, 869-871, 921-922, 935-943, 947-950, 954-962, 970, 973-974, 977; Brown, *A Life of Albert Pike*, 408-416. Pike continued to pursue his prosecution of Van Dorn, Hindman, and Theophilus Holmes by taking his case publicly to Richmond. He finally let the matter drop the following April.

John Ross Throws in with the Union

Historian Albert Castel long considered Kansas Republican Senator James H. Lane as nothing more than an unscrupulous and corrupt demagogue. He may well have been, but Lane had influence with President Abraham Lincoln from the opening days of his administration, when Lane organized and led a bodyguard for the Illinois politician.[1]

As a general, Lane commanded some 1,500 Jayhawkers known as "Lane's Brigade." The force engaged in a series of raids in Missouri, burning houses, looting property, and liberating slaves during September, October, and early November of 1861. He was chased back to Kansas by Maj. Gen. Sterling Price during the Lexington Campaign, though Price retreated south in the face of Maj. Gen. John C. Frémont's superior force. Lane next sacked Osceola and marched to Springfield before returning to Fort Scott with 600 freed slaves and wagons of plunder. As early as August 1861, Lane had proposed using loyal Creeks and Cherokees to defend Kansas. After the Battle of Pea Ridge, Commissioner of Indian Affairs William P. Dole requested that the secretary of the interior send two Kansas regiments and 2,000 armed Indians to occupy Indian country. Dole's goal was to clear the area of Rebel activity so the refugee Indians in Kansas could return to their homes. On March 19, 1862, the War Department ordered department commander Maj. Gen. Henry W. Halleck to send two regiments to the "Indian

1 Albert Castel, *A Frontier State at War*, 20-23, 83-85.

Senator James Lane

Kansas State Historical Society

country" and informed him that 5,000 loyal Indians would also be armed for their defense.[2]

Disapproving generals delayed the mustering of the Indian regiments until Senator Lane intervened. When he determined that it was not politically possible to be both senator and general, Lane decided to keep his Senate seat. However, he retained effective military control in Kansas by arranging for the state to be a separate department from Henry Halleck's Department of the Mississippi. He even managed to have his cavalry commander, Brig. Gen. James G. Blunt—an abolitionist Republican who had been a physician before the war—command the new Department of Kansas. As will be seen, both Lane and Blunt participated in illegal schemes throughout the war to profit from army supply contracts, but Blunt would prove more than once to be an effective field general. On the day he took command, May 5, 1862, he ordered that the mustering of the Indian regiments be continued.[3]

2 OR 3, 162, 163-164, 505-506, 516-517, 748; 8, 624-625; 53, 435-436; Gary N. Heath, "The First Federal Invasion of the Indian Territory," in *Chronicles of Oklahoma* (Winter 1966-1967), Issue 44, 409-410; Castel, *A Frontier State at War*, 34-36, 50-62, 84; Castel, *General Sterling Price and the Civil War in the West*, 48-65; Able, *The American Indian as Slaveholder and Secessionist*, 231 n. #447; Leverett W. Spring, *Kansas: The Prelude to the War for the Union* (Boston, MA, 1885), 303-305; Spring, "The Career of a Kansas Politician," 81-104; Blunt, "Account of His Civil War Experiences," 215-216.

3 Heath, "The First Federal Invasion of the Indian Territory," 409-411, Albert Castel studied graft in Kansas during the war: "Army supply contracts . . . were let out by officers in the quartermaster and commissary bureaus under the supervision of the commanding generals. A person who had contacts or understandings with these officers or who could dictate their acts was able to make great sums of money. This is exactly what Lane . . . did following Blunt's assumption of command. . . . 'Army contractors' . . . cut Lane in on their profits. . . Blunt also

The advance party of the Indian expedition got underway on June 6, 1862. When it returned five weeks later, it included John Ross and his entourage after Ross's failed attempt to keep the Cherokee Nation united under a Confederate alliance. Colonel Charles D. Doubleday, who commanded a force of infantry, cavalry, and artillery totaling about 1,000 men, moved south to confront Col. Stand Watie, who was known to be based at Cowskin Prairie east of the Grand River. Col. Doubleday sent elements of his cavalry riding down the west side of the river in an effort to cross it below Watie's position and block his route of escape. At 9:00 p.m., the Union commander opened fire with his artillery on Watie's 300-man force camped in a grove of trees. Abandoning 600 head of horses and cattle to the enemy, Watie and his men escaped east into the woods avoiding the trap waiting south of them.[4]

The commander of the expedition, Col. William Weer, ordered Doubleday to rein in his aggressive tendencies until the rest of the force arrived. Encouraged by recent intelligence, Weer reported, "[T]hey have a secret society of Union Indians called Ke-too-wah. . . . It numbers 2,000 warriors. . . . The messenger represents a sad state of oppression of Union men, and that we will be hailed as deliverers. . . . John Ross," concluded Weer, "is undoubtably with us and will come out openly when we reach there."[5]

In late June, two army columns marched south from Kansas. Colonel Weer led the 1st and 2nd Indian regiments, the 10th Kansas, a battery of artillery, and elements of the 9th Kansas. Colonel Frederick S. Salomon led the second column comprised of an Indiana battery and elements of the 2nd Ohio Cavalry and 9th Wisconsin Infantry. Weer ordered the 1st and 2nd Indian regiments to scout south one day apart along the Missouri line while his main body moved down the east side of the Grand River. Salomon, meanwhile, led his command down the west side of the river to a ford three miles above Cowskin Prairie, where the Rebels were believed to be located.[6]

The Federals intended to force an engagement with the Confederates, whose strength they estimated at 1,000 to 3,000 under a Missouri brigadier general named James S. Rains, a veteran of both Wilson's Creek and Pea Ridge. Rains' command

---

shared in this graft, as did many of the quartermaster and commissary officers." Castel, *Frontier State at War*, 84, 82-85; OR 8, 369, 370, 647-648, 829-833; 53, 517, 519.

4 OR 13, 102, 90, 63.

5 Ibid., 418-419, 431.

6 Ibid., 444, 458-460.

included Cols. Stand Watie and John T. Coffee of Dade County, Missouri. The outnumbered Rebels had no intention of fighting on Union terms. After a brief skirmish, Rains withdrew with about 600 men to Fayetteville, Arkansas. Watie's men, 10 miles south on Honey Creek, maneuvered east into the hill country above Spavinaw Creek. The Union Indians off scouting the hill country to the east had problems negotiating the rocky terrain on their unshod horses, so Colonel Weer replaced them with Kansas cavalry. These troopers made contact with Watie's men, who wisely withdrew without giving battle.[7]

Salomon sent his force down the west bank of the Grand River to Cabin Creek and on to Flat Rock Creek while he remained with Weer on the east bank of the river. Confederate Colonel J. J. Clarkson, formerly of Price's Missouri State Guard, blocked their path. Van Dorn had authorized him to raise a battalion and raid federal supply trains traveling to the New Mexico and Colorado territories. Clarkson was camped with about 300 men near the settlement of Locust Grove in the rough hill country four miles east of the Grand River.[8] At dawn on July 3, 300 men from the 1st Indian, 2nd Indian, and 9th Kansas surprised Clarkson. The small battle lasted several hours, during which the Rebels suffered heavy casualties. The Union force captured Clarkson and about 100 of his men and 60 wagons with supplies. Those who managed to escape fled south through Tahlequah to spread the alarm, and the town was soon vacated.[9]

Evan Jones, the abolitionist missionary associated with the Keetoowah Society, accompanied the expedition. He carried a message to Ross from W. G. Coffin, a federal Indian agent in charge of the Southern Superintendency: "[I] embrace the opportunity as an Agent of the Government to assure you that the United States Government has no disposition to shrink from or evade any of its obligations to the Indian tribes that remain loyal to it. . . . Mr. Jones has, during his exile, been the most unceasing advocate of your people and their rights."[10]

---

7 OR 3, 127-128; 8, 327-328; 13, 458-460, 466-467, 510; A. Franks, *Stand Watie and the Agony of the Cherokee Nation*, 129.

8 Although Grant Foreman reported that the earliest post office at Locust Grove was established on March 17, 1873, he noted that mistakes in his data would be found. Post offices were frequently discontinued and re-established. Weer reported there was a post office at Locust Grove when he was there in 1862. Grant Foreman, "Early Post Offices of Oklahoma," in *Chronicles of Oklahoma* (March 1928), Issue 6, 4, 18; OR 13, 137-138.

9 OR 13, 137-138, 161-162, 456; Series 2, 5, 21-22. Britton, *The Union Indian Brigade in the Civil War*, 65-66.

10 McLoughlin, *Champions of the Cherokees*, 402.

Two subagents, E. H. Carruth and H. W. Martin, also accompanied the expedition. Their tasks were to survey the situation and provide assistance for the loyal Indians in the Cherokee Nation in anticipation of returning the refugees in Kansas to the Indian Nations. Prominent Cherokees, such as James McDaniel, a leader of the Cherokee defectors at the battle of Bird Creek (Chusto-Talasah), returned as officers in the Indian regiments. John Ross remained at Park Hill, but William A. Phillips, future commander of the Union Indian Brigade, later testified that Ross used messengers to keep them "fully posted as to the condition of affairs." James McDaniel sent a member of the Keetoowah Society with a message urging the Cherokees still in Drew's regiment to join the Union.[11]

Weer was confident that Ross was ready to align with the North. Riding with the expedition was Ross's physician, Dr. Rufus Gillpatrick, who had served with Jim Lane in Kansas. On July 7, Gillpatrick delivered a letter from Weer to Ross (and may have delivered the message Evan Jones carried). "[I am] here to injure no one who is disposed to do what [the original federal] treaties by his nation bind him to do," Weer explained, "but am here to protect all faithful members of the tribe."[12]

Weer requested a meeting with Ross, but the Cherokee chief refused to commit, choosing instead to send copies of Weer's letter and his reply to Albert Pike. Even as the men of Drew's regiment were defecting in great numbers, Ross informed Weer that the Cherokee Nation was allied with the Confederacy. He implied that Weer understood the circumstances that had created the alliance, and that Ross could not "under existing circumstances entertain the proposition for an official interview" at Weer's location.[13]

---

11 US Congress, Senate, Committee on Claims, Report #113, 41st Congress, 2d sess., 1870; Christie et al, "Memorial of the Delegates of the Cherokee Nation to the President of the United States, and the Senate and House of Representatives in Congress," 3, 6-7; Moulton, ed., *The Papers of John Ross*, vol. 2, 515; Abel, *The American Indian in the Civil War*, 121, 122 n. #308.

12 William McLoughlin placed Jones at Park Hill with Dr. Gillpatrick and later at Park Hill with Colonel Cloud (described below), but he provided no footnotes to document the events. *Champions of the Cherokees*, 403-405; *OR* 13, 464; Charles Le Bahos, "John Ross: Unionist or Secessionist in 1861," (M. A. thesis, University of Tulsa, 1968), 118; *Washington Telegraph*, Arkansas, August 13, 1862.

13 *Washington Telegraph*, Arkansas, August 13, 1862; John Ross to William Weer, July 8, 1862, Moulton, ed., *The Papers of John Ross*, 515-516; Bahos, "John Ross," 118-119. McLoughlin, *Champions of the Cherokees*, 403. On July 17, Pike sent copies to the *Washington Telegraph* to be published beneath Pike's remarks: "To the people of Red River country in Texas. I print the following correspondence, that you may know what a true man, the Chief of the Cherokees, says to the Northern invaders of his country, at the moment when 250 Texans are leaving this camp to go home, because the law allows it, they being over 35 years of age. The enemy is in the

In response, Weer proclaimed that federal forces intended to occupy and hold the Cherokee Nation. On July 11, most of the enlisted men of Drew's regiment were sworn into Union service as the 3rd Indian Home Guard at Flat Rock Creek, (near present day Wagoner), where Weer's forces were based. The new commander was Maj. William A. Phillips, a Republican journalist who before the war had reported on "Bleeding Kansas" for the *New York Tribune*. Ross retained two companies from the old regiment at Park Hill as a bodyguard. General Blunt later explained it this way: "'Drew's Regiment' . . . offered their services to the government. I accepted their offer and had them organized and mustered as the 3rd Indian Regiment. . . . They served three years, . . . and did excellent service for the Union cause."[14]

Tensions were running high among pro-Confederate Cherokees. Tahlequah was all but abandoned, and independent bands of Keetoowahs became more aggressive as the federal expedition approached. A Moravian mission 25 miles north of Tahlequah at Oaks suffered as a result. The Moravians were pacifists, but one member, James Ward, had been a Southern Methodist. In 1854, Ward married Esther Hoyt, a mixed-blood Cherokee who had taught school at Samuel A. Worcester's Park Hill Mission. The Female Seminary was there and the Male Seminary "two miles to the Southwest." In 1858, the Wards joined the Moravian church and were living at the mission with their five children in September 1862. Although Ward maintained a neutral position, he was believed to be a Southern sympathizer. Friends warned him that his life was in danger, but he refused to leave. In early September, angry Keetoowahs shot and killed him while he was out riding his horse. Indians with painted faces searched Ward's house and took mission leader Gilbert Bishop and Mrs. Ward to a Union officer several miles distant. The officer detained Bishop, but Mrs. Ward was left with infant twins to make her own way home. She and the other missionaries promptly abandoned the mission and fled to Arkansas.[15]

At Park Hill, the Reverend Stephen Foreman, a mixed-blood, Princeton-educated assistant to the late Samuel Worcester, feared for his life. He had

---

Indian country. It is worth a 100 millions, and there are 1,300 mounted white men in it to defend it. Albert Pike."

14 Blunt, "Account of His Civil War Experiences," 224; Bahos, "John Ross," 119-121; 41st Congress, 2d session, report 113, 7; Wyant, "Colonel William A. Phillips and the Civil War in Indian Territory," 2-9; *OR* 13, 473.

15 Mihesuah, *Cultivating the Rosebuds*, 23; Muriel H. Wright, *Springplace: Moravian Mission and the Ward Family* (Guthrie, OK, 1940), 64, 67-74; *OR* 13, 273-74.

performed a funeral service on July 11 and took note of the sparse attendance. He recorded in his journal that "everybody seemed afraid to go out. . . . Women were afraid of the negroes, and men were afraid of each other, not knowing who was a friend or an enemy." After some Keetoowahs began milling around his house and stole his horse, Foreman realized he was in grave danger and slept in his cornfield. "[T]o be a Watie man or an anti-pin is to be under sentence of death," he wrote. Believing that Jones and the Pin Indians (Keetoowahs) wanted him dead, he took temporary refuge in the house of a friend.[16]

Weer sent out two patrols on July 14. Major William T. Campbell with 200 men of the 6th Kansas scouted Rebel positions south of the Arkansas River opposite Fort Gibson, and Capt. Harris S. Greeno, with one white company and 50 Cherokees, rode to Tahlequah. Campbell's thrust encountered fewer than 100 Rebels, who retreated before him and withdrew below the Arkansas River as he approached Fort Gibson about 5.00 p.m. After Colonel Weer learned the Confederates planned to move north in force that night, he personally led 600 men to reinforce Fort Gibson, arriving there at 2.00 a.m. Captain Greeno, meanwhile, found Tahlequah abandoned and moved south a few miles before camping near Park Hill. There, a black man (probably a slave sent by Ross) informed Greeno the Cherokees guarding Ross's home were friendly.[17]

Confederate forces gathered south of the Arkansas at Fort Davis in response to the federal invasion. Colonel Douglas Cooper arrived there on July 6. He anticipated that Albert Pike also would arrive soon. Cooper reported to General Hindman's commissary officer that he was "greatly in need of ammunition, especially percussion caps," for the 5,000 Indian troops he expected to assemble. The coalescing of Rebels did not pass unnoticed. On July 14 at Fort Gibson, prisoners informed Major Campbell that between 6,000 and 7,000 Rebels under

---

16 Foreman, "Journal," 33-35, 38, 41-42 (Norman: University of Oklahoma, Western History Collection), 33-35, 38, 41-42, typescript; OR 13, 161-162. The whites and the mixed-bloods derisively referred to the Keetoowah membership as Pin Indians for the crossed pins they wore to identify their membership in the society. There is an argument that not all Keetoowahs were members of the Pin society. Janey B. Hindrix, "Redbird Smith and the Nighthawk Keetoowahs," in *Journal of Cherokee Studies* (Fall 1983), Issue 8, 24; William McLoughlin, *After the Trail of Tears: The Cherokees Struggle for Sovereignty, 1839-1880* (Chapel Hill, NC, 1993), 158, 158 n. #10. Some bands of Keetoowahs operated independently from the military. Wardell, *A Political History of the Cherokee Nation*, 121; Dale and Litton, eds., *Cherokee Cavaliers*, xix; Britton, *The Union Indian Brigade in the Civil War*, 202.

17 OR 13, 160-162, 1016; Abel, *The American Indian in the Civil War*, 136-137.

Cooper were "in the vicinity" of Fort Davis, and that Pike was expected but overdue. He was to attack the federal position upon his arrival.[18]

About one month earlier, on June 17, Hindman had ordered Pike to proceed to Fort Gibson, but part of his command was furloughed and ongoing conflicts with his commanding officers hampered the movement. By July 15 Pike had only made it as far as Boggy Depot. The reported number of Indians was grossly exaggerated. In fact, Cooper's Choctaws, Chickasaws, and Creeks probably numbered fewer than 2,000. They were supplemented by another 500 Arkansas troops who had just arrived. In an attempt to strengthen his force during the night of July 14, Cooper ordered Drew's regiment to report to Fort Davis and Ross "in the name of President Davis . . . to issue a proclamation calling on all Cherokee Indians over 18 and under 35 to come forward and assist in protecting the country from invasion."[19]

Captain Greeno arrived at Park Hill the next morning. Accompanying Chief Ross were Col. William P. Ross, Maj. Thomas Pegg, and nine lieutenants of Drew's regiment. These officers disregarded Colonel Cooper's orders and cooperated with the Union officer, who formally arrested and paroled them. Ross stalled Cooper by maintaining that the treaty stipulated that Jefferson Davis himself must request additional troops. The notion of Cherokee unity within the Confederacy had broken down completely. Ross and his officers reported that members of the Watie faction had murdered several Ross supporters during the past week. The following day, Captain Greeno left Park Hill for the Grand River with 200 new Cherokee recruits riding with him.[20]

During the initial phase of the Indian expedition, Weer was optimistic about its outcome. On July 2, he reported that he had information "from the south sufficient to satisfy me that the whole tribe can be induced to surrender. . . . My only drawback is the want of supplies from my rear. If properly supplied, and not

---

18 OR 13, 161, 473, 965. The main federal force was collected west of the Grand River at that time.

19 Abel, *The American Indian in the Civil War*, 137, 161-162; OR 13, 161-162, 473, 859-868, 947-950, 963-964; Brown, "*A Life of Albert Pike*," 685, 691; William P. Corbett, "Confederate Strongholds in Indian Territory: Forts Davis and McCulloch," in Odie P. Faulk et al , eds., *Early Military Forts and Posts in Oklahoma* (Oklahoma City, OK, 1978), 71.

20 OR 13, 473, ser. 4, 1, 679. In 1869, Phillips testified on behalf of Ross's heirs: "I brought back with me twelve hundred armed and mounted Cherokees for our service, two companies of these being John Ross's body-guard, which I swore into the service in his presence. . . . In addition, he personally informed me where the enemy had ammunition stored, which I blew up, as I could not take it away." 41st Congress, 2d session, report 113, 7.

delayed with negotiations with the Indians," he added, "I can be in Fort Smith in a week."[21]

The needed supplies did not arrive. Periodically, Weer sent scouts north to locate the supply train and report back, but none of them returned. Union supply and communication lines remained closed. In the extreme heat and with inadequate sources of good water on the west side of the Grand River, the men suffered—especially those from northern states. Weer ignored reports of any disabilities amongst the men. His officers were concerned that without a secure line of communication with Fort Scott, the enemy could easily get behind them and defeat the isolated Union force in battle.[22]

On July 17, Colonel Weer and his officers met to determine their future course. Weer agreed the best move would be to return north to occupy a more strategically favorable position with better lines of supply and communication. The following day, however, Weer reversed his decision. A frustrated Colonel Salomon placed Weer under arrest and assumed command of the expedition. The white troops began withdrawing that evening, leaving the Indian regiments behind.[23]

While 200 men of the 3rd Indian Home Guard remained briefly at Fort Gibson, Col. Robert W. Furnas, commander of the 1st Indian, convened a council of the three Indian regiments at the Verdigris River in the Creek Nation. When soldiers of the 1st and 2nd Indian (many of whom were Creeks) left the ranks, Furnas moved his command to Pryor Creek near the Grand River in the Cherokee Nation. Despite his difficulties, Furnas was confident he could hold the area north of the Arkansas River. At Horse Creek, Salomon agreed to leave part of his artillery with the Indian troops.[24]

Alarmed at this turn of events, John Ross asked for protection. Major Phillips led elements of the 3rd Indian to Park Hill and camped at Rose Cottage. The Union officer later testified that his orders were "to take Mr. Ross and all the archives or other effects of the nation . . . and bring them out to prevent the enemy from getting them." Ross's concern proved to be valid, for Phillips soon learned that a contingent of Stand Watie's regiment was advancing in their direction up the Fort Gibson-Tahlequah road. Phillips divided his command and placed them on three roads that converged on the Confederate advance. With perfect timing, the Union

21 OR 13, 460.

22 Ibid., 475-476, 484-485, 511-512; Blunt, "Account of His Civil War Experiences," 223.

23 Blunt, "Account of His Civil War Experiences," 223.

24 OR 13, 481, 511-512; Blunt, "Account of His Civil War Experiences," 223-224.

troops met the Confederates and inflicted severe casualties, including killing the commander of the rebel detachment, Lt. Col. Thomas F. Taylor. Phillips' men captured 25 Rebels and counted 32 Confederate dead. Phillips later learned his men had killed three other officers and that the rebels estimated their own casualties at 125 killed and wounded.[25]

While Phillips patrolled west of the Grand River, future brigade commander Col. William S. Cloud entered Park Hill with his command and escorted Ross and his party of 37 out of danger. They traveled in a dozen carriages with their possessions and, reportedly, the Cherokee treasury of $70,000 in gold and $150,000 in Confederate paper.[26]

Once in Kansas, Ross explained to General Blunt that he never would have aligned with the Confederacy had the Union lived up to its obligation to protect the Cherokees against outside agitation. Blunt informed Secretary of War Edwin Stanton that he believed Ross and many of the Cherokees were loyal to the Union cause. Blunt advised Ross to go to Washington and visit with President Lincoln, and even provided him with a letter of introduction. Ross agreed and made the long journey east. He met with Lincoln on September 16, 1862. When Lincoln asked Ross to state his position in writing, Ross responded that the Cherokee Nation was a protectorate of the United States, and that when it was abandoned by federal authorities, the Cherokees had no choice but to align with the Confederacy. His people had sided with the Union as soon as the opportunity presented itself. Ross wanted federal forces to occupy the Cherokee Nation permanently.

Lincoln replied cautiously. Admitting no failure of treaty obligations by the United States, he promised to look into the matter. "[T]he Cherokee people remaining practically loyal to the federal Union will receive all the protection which can be given them consistently with the duty of the government to the whole country," assured the president. "I sincerely hope the Cherokee country may not again be over-run by the enemy; and I shall do all I consistently can to prevent it.[27]

25 41st Congress, report 113, 7; *OR* 13, 181-182.

26 Ibid., 595; 41st Congress, Senate, 2d Session, report 113, 7; Bahos, "John Ross," 124-125; Moulton, *John Ross*, 189-190.

27 John Ross to Abraham Lincoln, September, 16, 1862, Moulton, ed., *The Papers of John Ross*, 516-518; Abraham Lincoln to John Ross, September 25, 1862 in Roy P. Basler, ed., *The Collected Works of Abraham Lincoln* vol. 5 (New Brunswick, NJ, 1955), 439, 516-518; Moulton, *John Ross*, 175-176; *OR* 13, 486, 565-566; Brad Agnew, "Indian Territory," in Ralph Y. McGinnis and Calvin N. Smith, eds., *Abraham Lincoln and the Western Territories* (Chicago, IL, 1994), 196-198.

While Ross was in Washington, many Cherokee full-blood families fled north when the Indian regiments withdrew to Kansas and southwestern Missouri. Food and shelter were inadequate, and influenza and pneumonia were serious problems. Many stayed in the Cherokee Neutral Lands. Other refugees remained close to the regiments their relatives had joined or drifted into Missouri, where they were subject to Southern cavalry raids. Many eventually found sanctuary in Neosho, Missouri, and in western Arkansas. The addition of the Cherokee refugees swelled the number of loyal refugee Indians to about 10,000.[28]

John Ross spent the rest of the war in Washington and Philadelphia (his wife had property in the latter city). Commissioner of Indian Affairs William P. Dole grudgingly supported Ross and the Cherokee delegation of more than 30 persons with Cherokee funds. William G. Coffin, head of the Southern Superintendency, was critical of Ross for living extravagantly while his people suffered. Writing from Fort Gibson on June 16, 1864, Coffin described the poor conditions, lack of supplies, and high prices charged to the refugees. "Flour of rather poor quality is selling here at 25$ per sack of 98 lbs.," complained the agent. "The Ross Store in which John Ross, Lewis Ross & all the Ross family are understood to be interested are selling flour to Cherokees at 25$ per sack, and I very much fear that when we let another contract it will be at greatly increased prices."[29]

Ross vigorously defended himself against charges of extravagant living and claims that he had an interest in the Ross store at Fort Gibson. He pointed out that most of the people under his care were widows and their children. On May 10, 1866, in a sworn affidavit, Daniel Ross denied that John Ross had ever had any connection with the store "directly or indirectly." Furthermore, he stated that the price of flour from the date of Coffin's accusation varied from 16 to 10 dollars a sack.

Conditions at Fort Gibson remained tenuous as the 3rd Indian Regiment faced its first test in a tough battle in southwest Missouri at Newtonia.[30]

---

28 Agnew, "Indian Territory," 42; Gill, "Federal Refugees from Indian Territory," 126-137, 140-141; Huckleberry Downing et al to John Ross, January 8, 1863, Statement of Ross and Evan Jones, February 15, 1864; Moulton, ed., *The Papers of John Ross*, 527-529, 560-563.

29 Moulton, *John Ross*, 178-183; John Ross to William P. Dole, July 29, 1864; Moulton, ed., *The Papers of John Ross*, 600-601; Gary Moulton, "Chief John Ross during the Civil War," in *Civil War History* (December, 1973), Issue 19, 327; William Coffin to William P. Dole, June 6, 1864, Letters Received, Cherokee Agency, OIA.

30 Daniel Ross affidavit, May 10, 1866, Letters Received, in Cherokee Agency; John Ross to William P. Dole, July 29, 1864; John Ross to William P. Dole, August 26, 1864; Moulton, ed., *The Papers of John Ross*, vol. 2, 600-601, 607-608.

Facing Artillery

Confederate troops quickly filled the void left by the retreating Union forces. Whether they would prove sufficient remained to be seen.

On August 21, 1862, the Southern Cherokees convened a council at Tahlequah and elected Stand Watie as their chief. Major General Thomas C. Hindman, who had been organizing and arming men across Arkansas, decided to use his cavalry to prevent a unification of General Blunt's command with federal forces at Springfield. Brigadier General James S. Rains, based near the Pea Ridge battlefield, ordered a cavalry brigade under Col. Joe Shelby and Arkansas cavalry under Col. Joseph T. Coffee to a base camp six miles south of Newtonia, Missouri. On September 26, the Rebels were reinforced by Col. Douglas Cooper with Texas cavalry, Tandy Walker's Choctaws, and a battalion from Watie's regiment under Maj. J. M. Bryan. Cooper had seniority over Shelby and assumed command. When the Confederates moved north, they found the civilian population in chaos. Many frightened pro-Union Cherokee families retreated before them as refugees.[1]

Changes were afoot in the Union commands as well. The three Union Indian regiments were reassigned, one each to the brigades of Saloman, Cloud, and Weer,

---

1 OR 13, 29-42, 672-673. Colonel Shelby was generally regarded as the best Confederate cavalry commander in the Trans-Mississippi Theater Accounts vary as to when Shelby was given overall command of the brigade. It was either just before the battle or one month afterward. Daniel O'Flaherty, *General Joe Shelby: Undefeated Rebel* (Chapel Hill, NC, 1954), 118-119, 189-190, 225.

who received the 3rd Indian under Col. William Phillips. Drew's regiment, ineffective under Confederate leadership, proved to be highly motivated as the 3rd Indian in the Union army.[2]

On September 19, Col. M. W. Buster led two Confederate companies of Arkansas cavalry from Tahlequah 25 miles north to the recently deserted Moravian mission. He reported that "the houses were entirely abandoned. In several of them valuable articles of furniture and libraries were found scattered in utter confusion about the floors." An officer and two enlisted men "visited every house within a circuit of 4 miles, but found [them] . . . entirely deserted." An additional 20 men had ridden down Spring Creek and found more recently abandoned houses. "The women could not, or would not, talk English. . . . Some 200 yards below . . . one of the men found hanging to a sapling a new Federal overcoat, and [an] Indian hunting shirt . . . evidently belonging to the Pins that ran away from the house."[3]

Reports reached Colonel Weer that the reorganized Rebels numbered 11,000. He discounted the figure and suggested to General Salomon that they cooperate against the Rebels in case of attack.[4] General Curtis was justifiably concerned about the buildup. On September 27, he placed General Blunt temporarily under Maj. Gen. John M. Schofield. Blunt began moving reinforcements to the region from Fort Scott, but he was unable to consolidate his army until after the forthcoming Confederate victory at Newtonia.[5]

The main battle, which unfolded in two distinct phases after complex troop movements, occurred on September 30, 1862. Newtonia consisted of several brick

---

2 Wyant, "Colonel William A. Phillips and the Civil War in the Indian Territory," 17-18, 24, 26; Britton, *The Union Indian Brigade in the Civil War*, 84-85; Grace Steele Woodward, *The Cherokees* (Norman, OK., 1978), 281; Wardell, *A Political History of the Cherokee Nation*, 160; Abel, *The American Indian in the Civil War*, 193-194; OR 13, 42, 877. Later in the war, when Phillips commanded the Union Indian Brigade, he employed a daily regimen of drill for officers and enlisted men and required all orders to be given and received in English. He had worked to instill discipline from the time he took command of the 3rd Indian, a task made easier by the existing unity of the Keetoowah Society. The 3rd Indian would demonstrate its resolve—disproving the arguments of Annie Able and subsequent historians that Indians would not hold formation in the face of artillery—when the 3rd Indian maintained discipline under heavy rebel fire while playing a decisive role at the battle of Newtonia.

3 OR 13, 274, 275. A 10-mile scout down the Illinois River provided a similar experience. Ibid., 273-274, 276-277.

4 General Blunt considered invoking a court martial against Weer after Salomon's arrest of that officer during the expedition into the Cherokee Nation, but more pressing events convinced him to drop the matter. Castel, *Frontier State at War*, 98.

5 OR 13, 370, 653, 666, 672-674, 675-676.

houses, a stone barn, and a stone wall surrounding a two-acre lot that extended a quarter-mile west along the road from town. The battle was fought from the town northward through open prairie and fenced cornfields to several wooded ridges a mile and more distant. On September 29, Salomon ordered Col. E. Lynde, commander of the 9th Kansas Cavalry, to reconnoiter Newtonia. Lynde led four companies and a small battery to the ridges overlooking the town. After firing a few rounds from his artillery and capturing two pickets, he determined that 2,600 Rebels were there, a figure too high by at least 1,000. By dawn the following day, Lynde had been reinforced by Wisconsin infantry, giving him a total of 12 companies and six pieces of artillery.[6]

The troops Lynde had watched and shelled at Newtonia consisted of Col. Trezevant C. Hawpe's 31st Texas Cavalry, a battalion from Stand Watie's regiment under Major Bryan, and Capt. Joseph Bledsoe's two-gun battery. An artillery duel began early on September 30. Although the Confederates had only two guns, they proved so effective that Union officers referred to them in their reports. Alerted by the cannon fire, Colonel Cooper, who was with Col. A. M. Alexander's Texas cavalry regiment, rode to reinforce Newtonia. When the Confederate artillerymen ran out of ammunition, the Federals attacked the Rebel position behind the stone wall. The Confederates left the wall to repulse the attack, but were forced to return to the stone barrier by federal artillery fire. The Union forces were retreating in good order when Confederate reserves sent by Colonel Shelby reached the scene. Together with Tandy Walker's Choctaws, they attacked and routed Lynde's federals at 10:00 a.m., who retreated several miles north with heavy casualties, ending the first phase of the battle.[7]

Both sides were reinforced during the lull in the fighting. Colonel Beal G. Jeans' Missourians and Col. J. G. Stevens' Texans reinforced Cooper, which placed six Confederate cavalry regiments on the field. The arrival of Captain Sylvanus Howell's Texas battery of four guns strengthened Cooper's artillery. The 6th Kansas Cavalry reinforced the Federals at 10:00 that morning, and the 3rd Indian Home Guard arrived at 2:00 p.m. followed by General Salomon at 3:30 p.m. with the remainder of his infantry and artillery. The Union army now deployed nine

---

6 Some of these brick, two-story homes are still standing. The barn and wall were torn down in the 1950s for foundation stone. Britton, *The Union Indian Brigade in the Civil War*, 91-92; Edwin C. Bearss, "The Army of the Frontier's First Campaign: The Confederates Win at Newtonia," in *Missouri Historical Review* (October 1965), Issue 60, 288-296.

7 OR 13, 288, 291-293, 297-298; Bearss, "The Army of the Frontier's First Campaign," 301-308.

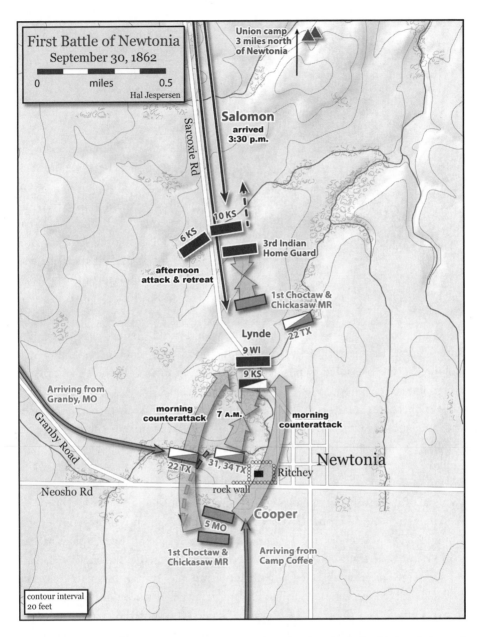

First Battle of Newtonia
September 30, 1862

0   miles   0.5

Hal Jespersen

Union camp
3 miles north
of Newtonia

Salomon
arrived
3:30 p.m.

Sarcoxie Rd

10 KS

6 KS

3rd Indian
Home Guard

afternoon
attack & retreat

1st Choctaw &
Chickasaw MR

22 TX

Lynde
9 WI

9 KS

Arriving from
Granby, MO

Granby Road

morning
counterattack   7 A.M.   morning
counterattack

Newtonia

22 TX   31, 34 TX   Ritchey

Neosho Rd   rock wall

Cooper

5 MO

1st Choctaw &
Chickasaw MR   Arriving from
Camp Coffee

contour interval
20 feet

guns. Salomon expected to be reinforced by a brigade of nearby Union Missouri militia, but these troops moved slowly and, in the end, would serve only to provide cover for Salomon's retreat. Cooper later reported that his force never exceeded 4,000 solders. Prisoners, however, reported to Salomon that Cooper's

Colonel (later brigadier general) Samuel Cooper. No genuine photo of him in uniform has come to light.

Library of Congress

Confederates numbered as many as 7,000. Union numbers are inexact, but northern commanders were certain they were outnumbered.[8]

Fresh action broke out that afternoon all along the federal front, but the hottest part of the fight was on the federal left against Phillips' 3rd Indian. At Pea Ridge, Albert Pike did not believe his Indian regiments would hold under heavy fire. As noted earlier, his viewpoint became widely known and may have strengthened Colonel Cooper's resolve to push the 3rd Indian in turning the left flank of the Union line.[9]

Colonel Sampson Folsom's 1st Choctaw joined the fight by providing Cooper with a seventh cavalry regiment. Supported by Jeans' Missouri and Stephens' Texas cavalry, Cooper sent Tandy Walker and Sampson Folsom's regiments against Phillips. "A desperate struggle between soldiers of the 3d Indian Home Guard and Folsom and Walker's regiments ensued," explained historian Edwin C. Bearss. "Several officers were cut down as they recklessly exposed themselves. Major John A. Foreman of the 3d Home Guard was killed, while Captain William Webber was wounded. The soldiers of the 1st Choctaw were saddened to see Captain Martin Folsom knocked from his horse. He was carried from the field, dying."

General Salomon directed a battalion from the 10th Kansas to reinforce Phillips, ordered three guns to roll to Phillips' left, and instructed his other artillery to concentrate their fire on the Choctaws. General Salomon directed Capt. Job B. Stockton, the commander of a battery, to support Phillips. "As soon as the rebels

8 OR 13, 287, 291, 298, 304, 1023, ser. 2, vol. 48, part 2, 963; Bearss, "The Army of the Frontier's First Campaign," 313.

9 Hartje, *Van Dorn*, 130; OR 13, 287-288, 295, 298-299, 304; Shea and Hess, *Pea Ridge*, 101, 107, 143-144; Able, *The American Indian in the Civil War*, 30.

commenced to waver the Indians commenced to advance," reported the artillerist, "and drove them until their ammunition gave out, when they retired under cover of my guns."

While this fighting was underway, Cooper erroneously believed two Union regiments of "Pin Indians and jayhawkers" were trying to turn his right flank. In response, he ordered both Capt. Sylvanus Howell and Capt. Joseph Bledsoe to concentrate their batteries on Phillips' position.[10] Phillips' men held and repulsed the Rebel flanking movement. Their stout performance prevented the outnumbered Federals from being routed and overrun by seven regiments of Confederate cavalry. Phillips' superiors commented on the 3rd Indian's performance. As General Salomon wrote in his report, "an attempt to force our left flank was nobly repulsed by Colonel Phillips, 3rd Indian Home Guards, supported by our reserve."[11]

Phillips wrote a letter to John Ross praising his regiment's performance. Ross quoted from it in a letter to Secretary of War Stanton. "The Regiment behaved very gallantly," he read. Colonel Phillips "dismounted the men and stationed them behind a fence with their rifles, and there for two hours & a half withstood seven charges of the enemy." Ross later gave Phillips' letter to Commissioner of Indian Affairs William Dole, who in turn showed it to President Lincoln.[12]

The Cherokee officers of the 2nd and 3rd Indian were flattered by the recognition, but they also asked for help. They wanted to reoccupy the Cherokee Nation, and the refugees among their people there faced horrible conditions. The officers pleaded to Chief Ross that, "[T]he few who are now at or near Ft. Scott need but be cited—No shelter—no clothing—sick barefooted and pennyless . . . . Our land and homes have been despoiled by the enemy. . . . None have escaped. . . . We need your advice and wholesome council."[13]

Retired Cherokee Supreme Court Justice Riley Keys complained to General Blunt that Colonel Weer had clearly broken his former promise to permanently

10 Bearss, "The Army of the Frontier's First Campaign," 295, 297, 299, 315.

11 Ibid., 288, 295, 297, 299. Salomon was furious with Colonel Hall, who had halted his Missouri brigade two miles in the rear of the battle rather than coming forward as ordered. OR 13, 287-288, 295-296, 299; Moulton, ed., *The Papers of John Ross*, vol. 2, 520-521.

12 John Ross to Edwin M. Stanton, November 8, 1862; Moulton, ed., *The Papers of John Ross*, vol. 2, 520-521; John Ross to William A. Phillips, January 4, 1863; Moulton, ed., *The Papers of John Ross*, vol. 2, 225-226.

13 Ibid., vol. 2, 522-23; OR 8, 288; vol. 13, 819-820; White Catcher et al. to John Ross, December 2, 1862; Moulton, ed., *The Papers of John Ross*, vol. 2, 522-523.

occupy the Cherokee Nation. "We are gratified to learn that our gallant troops have evinced a willingness to be led . . . against the common enemy wherever to be found," he asserted, but "think that we may justly pray you to allot to the Cherokees such duty . . . as will present relief and future security" to the loyal people of the Cherokee Nation.[14]

The Union Indians wanted relief, and they wanted to go home. The Confederate Indians would soon find themselves in a similar position. The sides were now clearly drawn. A civil war within the Civil War that would be severely contested in the Indian Nations had begun, with white troops participating on both sides. Eventually, the per capita loss of life and property would rival the destruction in the most war-torn areas east of the Mississippi River.

---

14 Riley Keys to General J. G. Blunt, November 24, 1862, in John Ross Papers, Gilcrease Museum, Tulsa, Oklahoma.

Chapter 8

The War for the Nations

In 1862 and 1863, the area north of the Arkansas River was heavily contested by Union and Confederate forces. Several battles involved Union forces—including the Union Indian Brigade as well as Kansas, Iowa, Wisconsin, and Colorado troops—against mixed-blood Confederate Indians, Texas, and Arkansas troops. These efforts culminated in the battle of Honey Springs on July 17, 1863. The Union victory drove Confederate military forces and thousands of refugees south of the Arkansas River, denuding the Creek and Cherokee Nations of much of its population.

The struggle began on October 22, 1862, with the battle of Old Fort Wayne. After the Southern victory at Newtonia, General Rains ordered the four Texas regiments back to his command in Arkansas. Colonel Douglas Cooper retained a battalion of Texas infantry, Howell's battery, a Creek battalion, and a Cherokee battalion under Stand Watie, who had spent the previous April and May successfully engaging Missouri militia in and around Neosho in southwest Missouri. Cooper, who was camped in the Cherokee Nation just across the Arkansas line near abandoned Old Fort Wayne was ordered by Rains to attack Fort Scott, Kansas. Cooper was awaiting the arrival of some Choctaw troops to do so when the battle of Old Fort Wayne began. His command at that time numbered only about 1,500 men.[1]

1 OR 13, 61-63, 90-95, 331-337.

The Union commander, General Blunt, was unaware that Rains had detached the Texas regiments from Cooper. He was under orders from the commander of the Army of the Frontier, Maj. Gen. John M. Schofield, to pursue the Rebels into the Cherokee Nation with two full brigades, including Phillips' mounted 3rd Indian Regiment. Blunt had a report that Cooper was at Old Fort Wayne with from 5,000 to 7,000 men. Hoping to surprise Cooper at dawn, Blunt ordered a 25-mile forced march through rugged country from Bentonville, Arkansas, west to Maysville. At two in the morning, the column inexplicably halted. When Blunt rode forward to find out why, he discovered the men in the lead had stopped to rest, and some of the exhausted soldiers had fallen asleep. An angry Blunt ordered the troops to their feet and the column began moving again as he rode ahead with his bodyguard and elements of the 2nd Kansas Cavalry, just more than 500 men. Blunt met a woman in Maysville and, posing as a Rebel, inquired about the Confederate camp. She told him that two Texas regiments had just joined Cooper. They had not. Her husband was in the camp, and she was trying to mislead Blunt. Still, Blunt believed there were 7,000 men in the Rebel camp. To hold them there until the rest of his force could be brought up, he boldly attacked with the men he had on hand.[2]

In a field 200 yards wide with timber lining both sides, Blunt's Kansas cavalry engaged a portion of Cooper's command. Because of what was later reported as "illness"—Cooper reportedly was drunk—command of the Confederate battle line fell to Col. M. W. Buster, who as recently as August had been a major in Watie's regiment. Buster had been promoted and had raised an "Indian Battalion" of mixed-blood Cherokees to fight at Newtonia. Buster did the best he could, positioning his men on the Confederate left. The main Confederate battle line probably numbered about 500 men, making the sides roughly evenly matched.[3]

Blunt sent two mountain howitzers and a dismounted company to a fence 200 yards from the Rebel line, and the engagement got underway in earnest. Dismounting the remainder of his force, Blunt reinforced his line and advanced. Colonel Buster attempted to flank Blunt's exposed right, a movement that might have succeeded had not Col. William R. Judson's 6th Kansas Cavalry and Col. William A. Phillips' 3rd Indian arrived on the field.[4] Blunt sent Judson's troopers to counter Buster's plan, and he ordered Phillips to move to the Union left to engage Stand Watie's battalion. At the same time, the 2nd Kansas charged the Confederate

---

2 Ibid., 325-328, 332-336, 754-756; Blunt, "Account of His Civil War Experiences," 1228.

3 OR 13, 183, 273, 303, 324-329, 336-337.

4 Ibid., 327, 329-330.

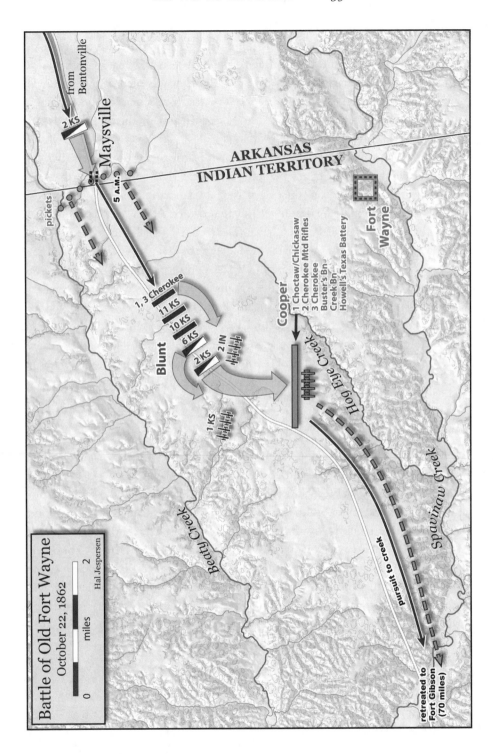

Battle of Old Fort Wayne
October 22, 1862

0   miles   2

Hal Jespersen

from Bentonville

2 KS

Maysville

ARKANSAS

INDIAN TERRITORY

5 A.M.?

pickets

Fort Wayne

1, 3 Cherokee

11 KS

10 KS

6 KS

Blunt

2 KS

2 IN

1 KS

Cooper

1 Choctaw/Chickasaw
2 Cherokee Mtd Rifles
3 Cherokee
Buster's Bn
Creek Bn
Howell's Texas Battery

Hog Eye Creek

Beaty Creek

pursuit to creek

Spavinaw Creek

retreated to
Fort Gibson
(70 miles)

line and captured Howell's battery of four cannons. The Confederate line broke. Union cavalry pursued the fleeing Rebels five miles to Spavinaw Creek before giving up and returning to Fort Wayne. Watie halted his men at the Moravian mission (modern Oaks Mission) and sent out patrols to reconnoiter and gather his scattered command. Cooper continued to Tahlequah and, on the following day, to Fort Gibson.[5]

The event proved significant, for Cooper subsequently retired below the Arkansas River into the Choctaw Nation, leaving the Indian territory north of the river firmly in Union hands. At the end of 1862, two more important battles played a key role in determining the destiny of Indian territory. At the battles of Cane Hill (November 28, 1862) and Prairie Grove (December 7, 1862), both in northwest Arkansas, General Blunt and Brig. Gen. Francis Herron defeated Thomas Hindman's Arkansans, Missourians, and Texans and forced the Rebels to retreat south of the Boston Mountains into the Arkansas River valley. At Prairie Grove, all but one company of the Creek 1st Indian Home Guards under Lt. Col. Stephen Wattles were in the line of Col. William Cloud's 3rd Brigade. Phillips and the 3rd Indian Home Guards guarded the train, while a detachment 44 men of the 3rd Indian provided effective skirmishers for the 10th Kansas. Four months later in April 1863, Union forces would once again occupy Fort Gibson, the key strategic point in the Cherokee Nation. The Confederacy had utterly failed to honor its treaties with the Cherokees and the Creeks.[6]

In an effort to salvage the disastrous situation and keep Cooper from gaining too much power in the region, Confederate authorities gave command of the Department of the Indian Territory to Brig. Gen. William Steele on January 8, 1863. Steele, a native of New York who had married into a Southern family, made his headquarters at Fort Smith and found the command in disarray. Colonel Cooper was at Perryville below the Canadian River in the Choctaw Nation with the 1st and 2nd Cherokee regiments and some Texas cavalry. General Hindman, Steele's predecessor who had been defeated at Cane Hill and Prairie Grove, had furloughed the other Indian regiments, but they were beginning to make their way back to Cooper's command. Steele's goal was to reassemble his army, reinforce it with Texans, and keep the Union forces north of the Arkansas River. He believed

5 Ibid., 327-328, 329, 330-331, 335, 337. Old Fort Wayne, also called the battle of Maysville or Beattie's Prairie, cost Blunt 14 men killed and wounded and Cooper as many as 150. Fifty Rebels were reported killed outright and buried on the field.

6 Ibid., 22, 75, 89-90, 92-93, 93-94; William L. Shea, *Fields of Blood: The Prairie Grove Campaign* (Chapel Hill, NC, 2009), 220-223; Shea, *War in the West*, 94-107, 116-117.

that if the Arkansas River valley could not be held the next line of defense for northern Texas would be the Red River. That made the Cherokee Nation the key strategic point for the defense of Texas.[7]

On March 16, Steele wrote Cooper that he wished "all of your available force be brought forward at the earliest moment to the Arkansas River. Colonel Speight's [Texas] brigade I intend to move forward as it can be supplied." Cooper was slow to move. Secretary of War James Seddon and others questioned Cooper's fitness for duty due to intemperance, but Steele protected him. Steele's superiors had instructed him to order Cooper to Fort Smith for an interview, which he did, but Cooper sent his adjutant instead of attending in person. On April 1, the secretary of war authorized Stand Watie to raise a brigade. On April 22, Steele suggested that Cooper move to Webber's Falls or farther north with his command, which included some Texas cavalry and a regiment of infantry. On May 18, Steele informed Cooper that Gen. William L. Cabell, "who is familiar with the country, says the place mentioned in your letter to fortify is as good a one as could be found." As a result, Cooper established his base camp at the stage depot of Honey Springs on the Texas Road, 25 miles south of Fort Gibson. The springs provided good water, and Elk Creek, a large wooded stream in the valley north of the depot, bisected the Texas Road, making it a good defensive position.[8]

With Confederate access to the Mississippi River corridor degrading, Steele had trouble procuring arms and ammunition. His troops were unevenly armed and his artillery inferior. As late as April 26, Steele considered bringing up troops who lacked proper ammunition. There was gunpowder in Texas, most of it manufactured in San Antonio and Mexico, if only he could get it. By May 18 he had arranged for Cooper to get powder from a depot at Bonham, Texas. The quality of Mexican gunpowder was cause for serious concern. Powder manufactured at San Antonio was "test fired" before shipping, and Steele recommended that Cooper use that powder for his cartridges. Steele also sent 1,100 pounds of lead.[9]

On June 16, Steele ordered General Cabell, commanding a brigade in northwest Arkansas, to cooperate with Colonel Cooper against the federal wagon

---

7 OR 22, pt. 2, 802, 804-805, 809, 909-910.

8 Ibid., 804, 805, 809, 810, 830, 838, 842-843; Knight, *Red Fox*, 146-147. Cooper had powerful friends in Richmond working behind the scenes to promote him despite concerns about his intemperance. They were successful and Cooper would be confirmed as brigadier general on June 23, 1863, to date from May 22, 1863. Anne Bailey, "Douglas Hancock Cooper," in William C. Davis, ed., *The Confederate General*, 6 vols. (Harrisburg, 1991), vol. 2, 27.

9 OR 22, pt. 2, 842-843, 805-806, 830-831.

trains supplying Fort Gibson from Kansas. On June 23 (the same day Cooper was being confirmed for brigadier general back in Richmond), Cooper reported that a supply train was moving south from Fort Scott and that he was sending 1,500 men to meet it at the Cabin Creek ford, about 50 miles north of Gibson (near modern Pensacola) on the Texas Road. Cabell's arrival would double the size of the Rebel army and add a battery of artillery.[10]

Both Phillips and Blunt were concerned about Rebel activity in the area, but Schofield could not grant Blunt's request for reinforcements. At General Halleck's request, Schofield in early June ordered eight regiments and three batteries to reinforce General Grant, who was besieging Vicksburg, Mississippi. Halleck assured Schofield that the troops would be returned when Vicksburg fell, and Schofield would then be free to use them in his planned offensive against General Price at Little Rock.[11]

Concerned that his supply train would be attacked, Colonel Phillips sent Major Foreman with 600 men of the 3rd Indian and a battery with a 12-pound howitzer and other lighter mountain howitzers to Baxter Springs, Kansas, to escort the train to Fort Gibson. The train stretched for miles, rumbling south from Fort Scott on June 25. Phillips reinforced Foreman with elements of the 1st Kansas Colored Infantry, commanded by Col. James M. Williams, and a battery of six pounders. The train reached Hudson's ford on the Grand River on June 26 only to find the river flooded. There was no choice but to wait for the water to fall, which meant they did not get across until June 29.[12]

Jim Lane was responsible raising the 1st Kansas Colored Infantry Regiment. He had begun recruiting "contrabands"as early as August 1862. The men hailed from Arkansas, Missouri, and the Creek and Cherokee Nations. Lane did so without permission from the Lincoln administration, which had not yet embraced the idea of black men serving in the army. Lane continued even after Secretary of War Stanton telegraphed him to stop his recruiting efforts. In the Jayhawking tradition, not all of the men were volunteers, but on January 13, 1863, they were officially mustered into service as the Kansas Colored Volunteers. The officers were all white and routinely referred to the command as the 1st Kansas Colored Infantry. Blunt would later conclude that they were his best troops. The men were

---

10 Ibid., 874, 885.

11 *OR* 22, pt. 1, 13; pt. 2, 310-311, 315; 24, pt. 3, 377, 383, 384.

12 Ibid., 378-382.

destined to play a significant role in Kansas and would take part in multiple actions in Arkansas and the Indian Nations.[13]

The confrontation over the wagon train began in the Grand River Valley on the afternoon of July 1, when the train arrived at a small stockade on Cabin Creek Ford. Watie's force of 1,500 just south of Cabin Creek consisted of elements of the Creek and Cherokee regiments, the 5th Texas Partisan Rangers, and the 29th Texas Cavalry. Watie had no artillery because the guns had been lost in the fighting at Old Fort Wayne, and Cabell's Arkansas force, including his artillery, was east of the flooded Grand River. The Union forces protecting the wagons began shelling Watie's men late in the afternoon and approached the creek under its cover. To their dismay, the water was too high to ford.[14]

The following morning, Colonel Williams of the 1st Kansas Colored Infantry decided to storm the ford and drive away the defenders. He deployed all but one company of the Cherokee 3rd Indian Regiment on his flanks, covered by artillery on either side and in the center. Leading the assault on the ford was Maj. John A. Foreman and the remaining company of Cherokees. Behind them came the 1st Kansas Colored Infantry, followed by a battalion of Colorado infantry and, after bringing up the rear, three battalions of Kansas and Wisconsin cavalry. After a 40-minute artillery barrage the 3rd Indian advanced into the chest-deep water but was forced back by heavy fire from Rebels hidden in the timber. Major Foreman was wounded twice, and his horse five times. Colonel Williams directed rifle and artillery fire against the Rebel position, and 20 minutes later the 1st Kansas infantrymen succeeded in crossing the stream. The Rebels formed a hasty battle line on the prairie opposite the creek, but the advancing Federals quickly broke it. Several of the Rebels and their horses drowned in the Grand River during the retreat and were later reported floating past Fort Gibson.

The wagon train successfully reached the fort, and General Steele's attempt to starve Fort Gibson out of Union hands had failed. In the interim, Colonel Phillips

---

13 Eugene H. Berwanger, *The Frontier Against Slavery: Western Anti-Negro Prejudice and the Slavery Extension Controversy* (Urbana, IL, 1967), 103-18; Dudley Taylor Cornish, "Kansas Negro Regiments in the Civil War," in *Kansas Historical Quarterly* (May 1953), vol. 20, Issue 20, 417-421; Dudley Taylor Cornish, *The Sable Arm:Negro Troops in the Union Army, 1861-1865* (New York, NY, 1956), 71-76; *Frontier State at War*,90-94; W. S. Burke, *Official military History of Kansas Regiments During the War for the Suppression of the Great Rebellion* (Leavenworth, KS, 1870), 407; Ira Berlin, ed., *Freedom:A Documentary History of Emancipation 1861-1867, Series II, The Black Military Experience* (Cambridge, UK, 1982), 67-73; Littlefield, Jr., *Africans and Creeks*, 239.

14 OR 22, pt. 1, 378-382. As a matter of context, July 1, 1863, was also the first day of the battle of Gettysburg more than 1,100 miles east in Pennsylvania.

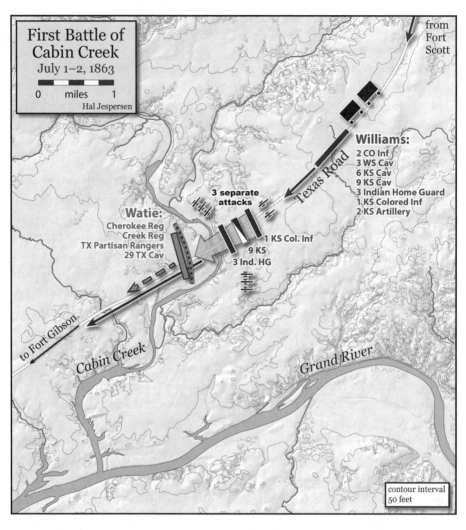

First Battle of Cabin Creek
July 1–2, 1863

0   miles   1

Hal Jespersen

from Fort Scott

Williams:
2 CO Inf
3 WS Cav
6 KS Cav
9 KS Cav
3 Indian Home Guard
1 KS Colored Inf
2 KS Artillery

Texas Road

3 separate attacks

Watie:
Cherokee Reg
Creek Reg
TX Partisan Rangers
29 TX Cav

1 KS Col. Inf
9 KS
3 Ind. HG

to Fort Gibson

Cabin Creek

Grand River

contour interval 50 feet

began building additional fortifications to better his odds of holding Gibson. The 55-year-old Watie escaped by swimming both the Grand and the Arkansas rivers on his horse and soon reported the battle loss to Cooper. "I returned yesterday [illegible] my trip up the country," Watie wrote his wife Sarah on July 12. "I had a hard trip of it, while I was gone had one of the severest fights that have been fought in this country on the banks of Cabbin Creek. . . . I am safe you must not be uneasy about me I will take care of myself I received your letter. It makes me feel good to hear you talk. I shall write to you every opportunity." The battle of Cabin Creek (fought near modern Big Cabin, Oklahoma) was not the hardest fight Watie would witness, but it was impactful despite its relatively small size. The Union would not be leaving Indian territory any time soon, and the fighting set up two later Union victories at Honey Springs and Fort Smith. It was also significant because it was the first time black soldiers (Williams' 1st Kansas Colored Infantry) had fought together with white troops.[15]

On July 5, four days after the battle, Steele wrote General Cooper that General Cabell was ordered to fall back if the interdiction of the supply train failed, so he could join a concentration of troops south of Fort Gibson. On July 7, Steele informed Lt. Gen. Edmund Kirby Smith's chief of staff, Brig. Gen. William R. Boggs, that he was reinforcing Cooper's Creeks and Cherokees with Texas units, but that Phillips' increased fortification of Gibson had rendered capture of the fort impossible without better artillery than he now possessed. Steele suggested that any troops that were not needed in northern Texas be sent south of Fort Gibson. He also rather optimistically, though with some truth, pointed out that if Fort Gibson fell, there was "little obstacle to going to the Missouri River or Kansas City."[16]

Unable to maintain himself in the field, Cabell returned to Fort Smith. Steele attempted to make good use of his presence. On July 8, Steele assured Cooper, "there will be no delay in concentrating all the troops under my command. . . . Cabell . . . informed me that he would be at Van Buren to-day. He will be moved on at once. I have written some days since to General Smith for the troops in Northern Texas." On July 10, Steele directed that Cabell "move forward, with the least possible delay . . . to some suitable camping place between Webber's Falls and Fort Gibson."[17]

Steele was aware the three rivers were falling and the effect that this could have on troop movements. On July 10, he warned Cabell that Phillips might attack and disperse Cooper's command before he could reinforce him. That same day, Steele telegraphed Maj. W. B. Blair, assistant adjutant general of the Arkansas District, to complain that requests for a resupply of ammunition in May had not been met. While Steele was directing all available forces to gather opposite Fort Gibson, Cabell's Arkansas brigade was just crossing the Arkansas River from Van Buren to Fort Smith "much broken down and weakened by his recent expedition" to Cabin Creek. Three days later on July 13, Steele lamented to Major Blair that it was taking longer than he had anticipated to ready the brigade to march. Although he was

---

15 Watie to My Dear Wife, n.d., in Cherokee Nation Papers; Dale and Litton, eds., *Cherokee Cavaliers*, 131; *OR* 22, pt. 2, 874, 909. Confederate casualties amounted to 65 men killed with the Union Army suffering between 3 and 23 dead with 30 wounded.

16 *OR* 22, pt. 2, 906, 909-910.

17 Ibid., 911-912, 916-917.

somewhat buoyed by a report from Cooper that the rivers were on the rise, the heavy artillery he expected from Texas had been "repossessed by General [John] Magruder, which leaves me with artillery less in number and caliber than is in Fort Gibson." Cooper was still waiting for General Cabell to arrive with his brigade of 1,400 men and a battery of four guns when the sun rose on July 17.[18]

On paper, however, even without Cabell's brigade it looked as though Cooper had the advantage. His ranks had increased since the battle of Old Fort Wayne. In addition to the 1st and 2nd Creek regiments, the 1st and 2nd Cherokee regiments, and Tandy Walkers' regiment of Choctaws (which had performed well at Newtonia), Cooper gained the 29th Texas Cavalry, the 5th Texas Partisan Rangers, the 20th Texas Cavalry (Dismounted), and Lee's light battery. Cooper had posted pickets stretching all the way to the south bank of the Arkansas River, and they were watching the fords as far north as the Creek Agency, south of the Arkansas River and 12 miles upriver from Gibson. Small parties occasionally crossed the river to steal cattle and harass Phillips' command, which was closely contained around the fort.[19]

General Blunt estimated Cooper's numbers, without Cabell's brigade, at 6,000 men. Phillips, guarding the refugee Indians at Fort Gibson, had under his command the 1st Kansas Colored Infantry and the 1st and 2nd Indian Home Guards, about 2,500 men all told. Cooper later lamented the absence of Stand Watie, who had been sent to Webber's Falls on an errand, but it is doubtful whether Watie's presence could have overcome the inherent problems of Cooper's command.[20]

Three elements negated whatever advantage Cooper possessed on paper. He had lost his artillery at Old Fort Wayne, and although the Texans had provided a light battery, Blunt had more and heavier artillery. The Rebel force had purchased Mexican gunpowder they had hauled north by ox-drawn wagons. It had proved, after all, to be as faulty as advertised. In anything buy dry conditions it would not

---

18 Ibid., 903, 910, 917, 921.

19 Ibid., 447, 457-462; Blunt, "Account of His Civil War Experiences," 244. Blunt's account was written in 1866. The manuscript was found in the basement of the Kansas State capitol building around 1897, but was not published until 1932. From statements contained in it, the friction between Blunt and Colonel Phillips, of which there will be more below, was well under way by the time of the battle of Honey Springs.

20 The Second Regiment of Colorado Volunteers was under Phillips' command at the battle of Honey Springs, but it is unclear whether its men were stationed at Fort Gibson, which is improbable, or arrived as reinforcements just before the engagement, which is more likely. They are not mentioned in Blunt's accounts. Dale and Litton, eds., *Cherokee Cavaliers*, 340-341.

General James G. Blunt

Gilcrease Museum Archives,
University of Tulsa

fire effectively. Last, Blunt's aggressive tactical style was too much for General Cooper to handle. Thus far in the war Blunt had prevailed in every battle, including the Prairie Grove campaign, which to that point in the war in the Trans-Mississippi Theater ranked behind only Pea Ridge in magnitude.[21]

On July 5, a report "from an unofficial source" informed Blunt that Fort Gibson was imperiled. He left Fort Scott that afternoon bound for Gibson with 350 of the 6th Kansas Cavalry, a detachment of Wisconsin cavalry, and 12 cannons. Blunt arrived at Fort Gibson early on July 11 and found the military conditions there deplorable. He blamed Phillips, but the split between the two men went beyond military matters.[22]

Having learned that Texas regiments were reinforcing Cooper, Blunt hoped to cross the Arkansas River and attack before they arrived, but he was already too late. The Texas regiments had already reached Cooper, who was also waiting for Cabell's Arkansas brigade to join him before he crossed the Arkansas and attacked Fort Gibson. Blunt decided to forestall Cooper's plans. With the Arkansas River still flooded, Blunt ordered the building of flatboats. By July 15 the river was beginning to recede. At midnight, Blunt took 250 Kansas cavalry and two

---

21 *OR* 22, pt. 1, 458; Shea, *Fields of Blood*, 261.

22 Ibid., 454, 456-457. It appears that Captain Edward A. Smith, on the right of the battlefield and Captain Henry Hopkins on the left each had four guns. Smith gave more detail. He had two six pounder iron guns and two twelve pounder brass guns; Blunt, "Account of His Civil War Experiences," 343; Willey Britton, *Memoirs of the Rebellion on the Border, 1863* (Chicago, IL, 1882), 357; Blunt, "Account of His Civil War Experiences," 243-244.

six-pound guns and crossed the Grand and Verdigris rivers and advanced 12 miles upstream to the ford adjacent to the Creek agency.[23]

About 100 Rebel cavalry on the south bank of the Arkansas fled at the sight of the six pounders. Above Three Forks, the Arkansas was shallower but still high, so Blunt had the artillery ammunition crossed by flatboat. The cavalry made its way through the current, crossed to the south bank, and rode downriver until the troopers were opposite Fort Gibson at the "mouth" of the Grand River. The Confederate pickets had fled, so Blunt commenced crossing the rest of his command. The maneuver was completed by 10:00 p.m. on July 16, and the 25-mile march to Cooper's position at Elk Creek begun.[24]

At dawn, 500 Confederate cavalry five miles in advance of Elk Creek temporarily drove back Blunt's advance guard under Lt. Col. William Campbell's 6th Kansas Cavalry. Campbell "brought up the rest of . . . [his] command at a gallop" and dispersed the Rebels at the cost of three Kansans wounded and one killed. It was about this time that Cooper noticed the dampness and intermittent rain had left him with nearly useless gunpowder. The Confederate cavalry, Choctaws, and Texans returned to their base camp at Honey Springs to replace the cartridges, but they only received more of the same filled with Mexican powder.[25]

That morning, when Blunt moved within sight of Cooper's position on the north side of Elk Creek, well hidden in the timber, he took a few men and rode ahead of the main body to try to locate the Rebel battery. Gunfire wounded one of Blunt's men and they returned to the main group without locating the battery. Blunt halted behind cover one-half mile north of Elk Creek and allowed his men to eat a meal and rest for two hours.[26]

At 10:00 a.m. Blunt assembled his men on either side of the Texas Road and advanced in two single files. When they were within a quarter-mile of Elk Creek, Blunt fanned out his lines on either side of the road, organized by company, to form a battle line opposite the Confederates. On the far right side was the 3rd Wisconsin Cavalry, dismounted. Next to it was the 2nd Cherokee Regiment, and in the center straddling the road the 1st Kansas Colored Infantry, in whom Blunt placed his highest confidence. Blair's four-gun battery supported the line. Colonel

---

23 Blunt, "Account of His Civil War Experiences," 244; *OR* 22, pt. 1, 447.

24 Britton, *Memoirs of the Rebellion on the Border*, 355-356; Blunt, "Account of His Civil War Experiences," 244; *OR* 22, pt. 1, 447.

25 Ibid., 458.

26 Ibid., 447, 452; Blunt "Account of His Civil War Experiences," 244.

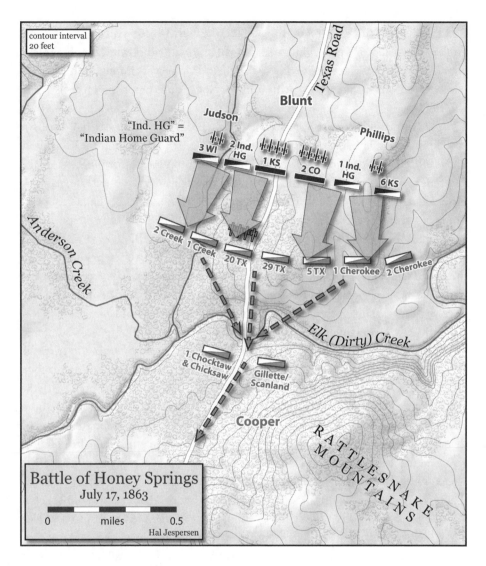

contour interval
20 feet

"Ind. HG" =
"Indian Home Guard"

Judson

Blunt

Texas Road

Phillips

3 WI   2 Ind. HG   1 KS   2 CO   1 Ind. HG   6 KS

Anderson Creek

2 Creek 1 Creek 20 TX 29 TX 5 TX 1 Cherokee 2 Cherokee

Elk (Dirty) Creek

1 Choctaw & Chickasaw   Gillette/ Scanland

Cooper

RATTLESNAKE MOUNTAINS

Battle of Honey Springs
July 17, 1863

0   miles   0.5
Hal Jespersen

William R. Judson of the 6th Kansas commanded the right flank. On the far left were elements of the 6th Kansas, followed by the 1st Cherokee Regiment and stretching toward the road the 2nd Colorado, both supported by Hopkins' battery and under the command of Col. William Phillips.[27]

General Cooper placed the 1st and 2nd Cherokee on his far right, the 1st and 2nd Creek on his far left. The Texas units held the center, bisected by the Texas

27 OR 22, pt. 1, 447-448.

Road, with the 20th Texas left of the road and the 29th Texas on the right. Cooper's artillery consisted of Lee's light battery of three mountain howitzers and another light gun. Tandy Walker's Choctaws were held in reserve, although a mistake in communication would keep them out of the battle until the Rebels were withdrawing.[28]

The battle of Honey Springs began with Blunt's batteries opening fire for several minutes. The Rebels responded and each side lost one gun in the artillery duel before Blunt ordered the Union line forward to within "forty paces" of the Confederate line. Blunt used the 6th Kansas to engage a Confederate flanking movement, which was entirely repulsed after "about an hour and a half." After two hours of fighting the Confederate line began to break. The 20th Texas, opposite the 1st Kansas Colored Infantry, was the first to give way. Blunt was particularly impressed with his black infantry. "They fought like veterans," he reported, "and preserved their line unbroken throughout the engagement. Their coolness and bravery I have never seen surpassed; they were in the hottest of the fight, and opposed to Texas troops twice their number, whom they completely routed."[29]

Other Confederate units gave way all along the line as Blunt's forces entered the timber of Elk Creek. Confederate lines reformed several times but to no avail. Cooper's forces reformed at the Honey Springs depot, where they set fire to their stores before retreating south for a mile and a half before Blunt broke off the pursuit to let his exhausted men and horses rest. The whole affair had lasted about four hours. Late in the day, Colonel Cabell's Arkansas brigade approached in the distance, but General Steele's attempt to coordinate his forces had failed and Cabell returned to Fort Smith. Blunt, meanwhile, ordered his men to camp north of Elk Creek and be ready for a counterattack the following day, but the next morning dawned quietly. The Union forces broke camp and started back to Fort Gibson.[30]

Despite the length of the fighting, Blunt reported light losses of just 13 killed and 62 wounded, "most of them slightly." He detailed the enemy's loss as follows: "Killed upon the field and buried by my men 150; wounded 400; and 77 taken prisoners." Cooper's report on his losses varied considerably from Blunt's tabulation. According to Cooper, he lost 134 killed and wounded and 47

---

28 Ibid., 461-462.

29 Ibid., 448.

30 Ibid., 447-462.

prisoners.[31] Discrepancies of this type are common for Civil War battles, but Blunt's report of only 13 killed is rather remarkable given that he reported the battle "was unremitting and terrific for two hours" before the Texans' lines began to break. Several sources attest to the problem with the Confederate gunpowder, including Cooper's official report, historian Joseph Thoburn's interview with a veteran of the Texas unit who delivered the powder, General Steele's official report, and the recollections of the participants interviewed for the *Indian Pioneer History* series. The Mexican powder, though probably not the only source of powder among such a diversity of units, almost certainly accounts for Blunt's low casualties against a numerically superior force in a defensive position. Houston Rich, born in 1879 in the Sequoyah district, testified about the experience of his two grandfathers in Watie's brigade. "As the battle continued it began raining, and about noon, the ammunitions got wet and powder in many instances would not explode," he recalled, "a cannon would be prepared with powder and cannon balls, a fuse would be lighted, and if it fired at all, it had no force." Blunt was aggressive, but on that day he was also lucky.[32]

Cooper regrouped his defeated command 25 miles south of Honey Springs, and General Steele promised to bring reinforcements and take command. By July 25 Cooper had returned to the vicinity of Honey Springs and had sent cavalry patrols to within five miles of the Arkansas River. Blunt, suffering at this time from a prolonged illness, reported to General Schofield that he believed Steele was assembling an army of 9,000 men and intended to attack Fort Gibson. Steele was a professional soldier (West Point Class of 1840) who had held the rank of captain in the U.S. Army. His actual strategy was to maintain sufficient strength near Fort Gibson to prevent it from being supplied until the garrison evacuated.

As usual, Blunt was determined to move against his opponent first, regardless of his strength, but he was hoping for reinforcement by Col. William F. Cloud's Kansas cavalry regiment of 1,500 men and an artillery battery. Cloud was not then assigned to Blunt's district, but he responded to Blunt's repeated requests and arrived from Fayetteville on August 21. Blunt began crossing the Arkansas River with some 4,000 men on August 22, 1863.[33]

31 Ibid., 460.

32 OR 7, 75-76; ibid, 43, 388, 401; OR 22, pt. 1, 33, 458; Joseph B. Thoburn and Muriel H. Wright, *Oklahoma: A History of a State and Its People* (New York, NY, 1929), 345, 346 n. #18.

33 OR 22, pt. 1, 32-33, 411.

By then, General Steele was losing his enthusiasm for engaging Blunt. Large numbers of Cable's brigade were deserting, and Steele had confirmed the degraded condition of his Mexican gunpowder. "The powder which had been received from Texas was found to be worthless when exposed to the slightest moisture," he complained, "a night's heavy dew converting it into a paste." He decided to give up the operation. Colonel D. N. McIntosh took his Creeks west along the Canadian River, Cabell followed his brigade back to Fort Smith, and Steele, Cooper, and Watie withdrew into the Choctaw Nation along the Texas Road toward the Red River.[34]

Blunt caught up with Steele's rear guard at 10:00 a.m. on August 25. There was a running skirmish between some Choctaws, who had two howitzers, and Cloud's 2nd Kansas Cavalry. At Perryville, Blunt decided to end the chase. Steele's main force and his baggage were miles ahead with rested horses, while Blunt's own horses were spent. The Union general satisfied himself with the more easily attainable goal of burning the town of Perryville and moving toward Fort Smith.[35]

Blunt expected Colonel Cabell to defend Fort Smith, but to his surprise he did not do so. Steele had ordered Cabell to continue south to rendezvous with a stronger force thought to be in the area and then return to contest Fort Smith. Blunt sent Cloud in pursuit and there was a fight 16 miles south of Fort Smith on an ominously named hill called the Devil's Backbone. Cloud prevailed and Cabell, his ranks reduced by desertion to fewer than 1,000 men, retreated south along the border between Arkansas and the Choctaw Nation, hoping eventually to link up with Steele in Texas. Union Maj. Gen. Frederick Steele began an expedition out of Helena on August 11, 1863, which by September 10 had forced Maj. Gen. Sterling Price to abandon Little Rock without fighting a major battle, and had left the Union army in uneasy possession of the Arkansas River valley.

The war for the Indian Nations was effectively over, but not its attendant misery.[36]

---

34 Ibid., 33, 597, 465-466.

35 Ibid., 33, 597-600; Blunt, "Account of His Civil War Experiences," 246-247.

36 *OR* 22, pt. 1, 606; Castel, *General Stirling Price and the Civil War in the West,* 153-160.

Southern Refugees

After the Battle of Honey Springs, the Cherokee and Creek Nations were abandoned as the Confederate mixed-blood refugees fled south to settle on tributaries of the Red River. They were supported by the resources of the southern Cherokee Nation and Confederate military authorities. Southern Baptist missionaries associated with the Cherokees also collected clothing and supplies from across the South for the refugee camps along the Blue River. The Cherokee delegate to the Confederate Congress obtained a credit line from the Confederacy to help people in the camps. Once well-off slave owners fared a little better by renting houses or staying with friends and relatives in North Texas.[1]

The oppressed condition of the mixed-blood refugees in the Cherokee Nation began with the Union expedition from Kansas in June 1862, which ended with John Ross realigning with the Union. During that time, members of the Keetoowah Society—called "Pins" or "Pin Indians" for the pin they wore in their

---

1 Mary Jane Warde, *George Washington Grayson and the Creek Nation, 1843-1920* (Norman, OK, 1999), 74-76; Christine Shultz White and Benton R. White, "Now the Wolf Has Come: The Civilian Civil War in the Indian Territory," in *Chronicles of Oklahoma* (Spring 1993), Issue 71, 74-76; "'Holding Our Family Together': The Civil War Experiences of the Creek Graysons" in *Proceedings: War and Reconstruction in Indian Territory: A History Conference in Observance of the 130th Anniversary of the Fort Smith Council* (Fort Smith, 1995), 122-123; Confer, *The Cherokee Nation in the Civil War*, 124-140.

collar or lapel to identify themselves—harassed Cherokee families loyal to the Confederacy.[2]

The descriptions of conditions by the refugees who left written and oral records illuminate the experiences, however imperfectly, of the thousands of refugees who left no records. The story of several refugees, as told in the pages that follow, is enlightening.

*   *   *

Stephen Foreman, a Princeton-educated, bilingual Presbyterian minister who had worked with Samuel Worcester to translate the Bible into Cherokee, kept a journal. Widowed one year, Foreman lived at Park Hill with his six children. Full-blood Cherokees stole his two slaves, his riding horse, four other horses, oats, and two saddles and bridles. Fearing for his life, he slept in his cornfields and with neighbors while trying to get word from the Ross camp as to whether he was targeted to be killed. Ross replied that he had no control over the Pins and suggested that Foreman would be safe at Ross's home, Rose Cottage. A friend of Foreman's had sought refuge in Texas, but Foreman was reluctant to leave his children for long, and he was not prepared to take them with him. He was not the only victim. Anyone aligned with Watie and the Rebels was fair game. As Foreman put it, "No one who has a good horse or any good property is safe." He did not see how the Cherokee Nation, thus divided, could survive. Like many other Cherokees aligned with the South, he blamed the Reverends Evan and John Jones for the division.[3]

To escape being murdered in their homes, some hid in basements with trap doors covered by carpets and seated women holding infants. When the men fled south, the women and children often stayed behind, at least initially, because the outcome of the war was uncertain and their own lives were not threatened. Still,

---

2 The terms Pin or Pin Indian were used to refer to the Union Indian Brigade commanded by Colonel Phillips. Watie and others often used the term in this way. Others, particularly civilians who were their victims, referred to their non-military, full-blood tormentors as "Pins." They were closely associated with the Keetoowah Society. Dale and Litton, eds., *Cherokee Cavaliers*, 57; Indian Pioneer History Collection, vol. 4, 124; vol. 76, 179; vol. 92, 376, microfilm; Clarissa W. Confer, "Indian Territory Homefront: The Cherokee Nation in 1862," in *Proceedings: War and Reconstruction in Indian Territory: A History Conference in Observance of the 130th Anniversary of the Fort Smith Council* (Fort Smith, 1995), 111-116.

3 Foreman, "Journal," 27, 51, 22, 27-28, 34-35, 42, 44, 46, typescript, Western History Collection, University of Oklahoma, Norman.

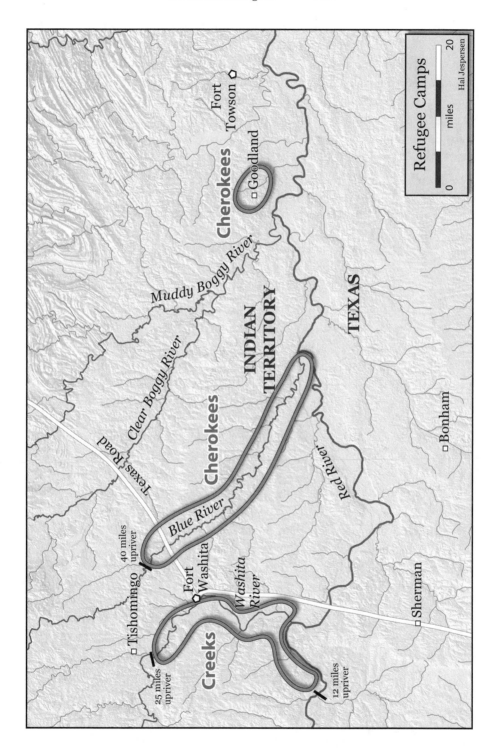

people continued to be tormented. There were repeated instances of "Pin Indians" ripping apart feather bedding and stealing food. They emptied or burned smokehouses, turned livestock out into growing crops to trample them, and simply stole the stock they wanted. "Pin" women participated by "ransack[ing] house[s]." Many people hid their bedclothes and other items of value in basements or under sub-flooring until late in the evening when they were more likely to be left alone.[4]

There is a break in Foreman's journal from August 6, 1862, until December 25, 1862. "This morning one year ago my best earthly friend left me and my children for a better and happier world than this," he recorded in the last entry before the break. "She is now where I trust there is no pain, nor sorrow nor trouble. Little did I think one year ago that in that same house in which she died, we should have so much trouble, and that I in particular should be hiding myself from some of my own people, probably some of my own neighbors who wish to kill me."[5]

By the time Foreman resumed his journal, he and his children had abandoned their house and many of their belongings to take refuge at the Creek agency south of the Arkansas River near present-day Muskogee. There was some "excitement" because the Federals were not that far away at Fort Gibson. The day after Christmas, a Union patrol crossed the river under a white flag and left a letter from Colonel Phillips to Col. Daniel N. McIntosh in an attempt to make peace among the Creeks. The riders said they would be back the next day without the white flag. They kept their word.[6]

McIntosh, who had fewer than 100 men, watched from a hilltop a mile distant on December 27 as the Federals moved onto agency land. Foreman and others observed from somewhat farther away. The mounted enemy force, which consisted of white officers and about 250 Creeks and Cherokees, burned Fort Davis and rode into the small community at the Creek agency. Except for ransacking the town store they left private property alone. Foreman rode south with McIntosh and his men to Elk Creek, where he stayed at the home of Lewis McIntosh. A Union officer asked Foreman's eldest daughter Suzie, who was always left in charge when her father was forced to flee, whether there were any men

---

4 Indian Pioneer History Collection, vol. 4, 102, 124-125; vol. 67, 451-452; vol. 31, 388; vol. 76, 179; vol. 92, 376; W. D. Polson to Sarah C. Watie, April 16, 1863, in Cherokee Nation Papers; Dale and Litton, eds., *Cherokee Cavaliers*, 121, gives the date as April 10, 1861.

5 Foreman, "Journal," 54.

6 Ibid., 55-58.

present. She replied that there were none. Three or four shots were fired and the soldiers stole some stock and left.[7]

When Foreman received word the next day that the town had been left undisturbed, he returned with the mail express and found his children unharmed. The Federal column had left Fort Gibson, but the patrol was enough for Foreman to make plans to move to North Fork Town on the Canadian River, which, together with the Arkansas River into which it flowed, marked the southern border of the Cherokee Nation. He attempted without success to arrange for two wagons for his family and some of their belongings.[8]

It was important for Foreman to learn what Watie's plans were so he could act accordingly. For three days he traveled alone east along the Canadian River to do so, encountering many friends and acquaintances along the way who had sought refuge along the southern boundary of the Cherokee Nation. Watie had left his military camp on the Canadian River to meet with General Cooper, so Foreman and several others remained there to await his return. Watie, thought Foreman, could properly advise the widespread refugees "exposed to the mercy of the Pins." Debate erupted over whether they should move farther south below the river and out of the Cherokee Nation. With Watie still gone, Foreman spent a Sunday preaching at the Cherokee officer's camp. The congregation sang hymns in their native tongue. Foreman preached in English while another preacher, Reverend Cory, translated into Cherokee.[9]

The following day, Foreman received a request from Lt. Col. R. C. Parks to become chaplain of the 1st Cherokee Regiment. He gave it serious consideration for two days before declining. His responsibility to his family made the request impossible. He continued waiting on Watie, despite the unsettling news of two cases of smallpox that had broken out in a nearby camp. The weather was cold and getting worse, the rain turning to sleet and then snow. With the military camp on the south bank of the Canadian River, Foreman worried he would be stranded

---

7 Ibid., 58-59.

8 Ibid., 59-60, 62.

9 Watie's preferred campsite on the Canadian was at Briartown near the home of his friend, Tom Starr, patriarch of the Starr family; Foreman, "Journal," 67. It is a mistake to assume there were no Cherokee speakers in Watie's brigade, but most were not fullbloods. English speakers were not allowed in the Keetoowah Society.

there because of rising water. On January 15, 1863, he crossed to the north bank and found shelter at the nearby home of Reverend Cory.[10]

Anxious for Watie's return, on January 23 Foreman rode with two other men to the bank opposite the camps. To their keen disappointment, Rebel soldiers told them that Watie still had not returned. The next day, a Saturday, Reverend Cory announced that Foreman would preach on the morrow. "We had a pretty good full house of individuals from Tahlequah, Flint, Going Snake, and Saline," Foreman recorded in his journal, "who have been forced to abandon their homes by their own people, the Pins." Foreman preached in Cherokee. Apparently, many Cherokee speakers were not members of the Keetoowah society.[11]

By January 31 Foreman was back at the Creek agency without having had a meeting with Watie. He spent the next few months struggling against the weather, traveling widely to obtain enough flour and meal so that his family would not have to rely entirely on meat for their diet, dodging Federal patrols south of the Arkansas River, and preaching an occasional sermon. To his dismay, he learned that cattle had been allowed into his house at Park Hill and his fences had been torn down, opening his fields to the remaining livestock. Somehow he remained hopeful that the war would end soon and he could farm his own land once more. Meanwhile, he planted a spring garden at his place at the Creek agency.[12]

The relationship of Stand and Sarah Watie provides further evidence of refugee conditions. Sarah, who was living at that time in Rusk, Texas, hated being separated from her husband. "I cant stay away so long from you it grieves me to think that we are so far from each other," she wrote on May 20, 1863. "[I]f anything should happen we are to far of[f] for to help each other be a good man as you always have been, and have at the end a clear conscious before God and men is the advice of your wife." Between letters and all else she managed, Sarah worked at her loom to provide homespun clothing for the family.[13]

---

10 Foreman, "Journal," 67-70. Apparently Watie's men were camped just south of the Canadian River in the Choctaw Nation.

11 These are four of the nine political districts in the Cherokee Nation. Foreman, "Journal," 74, 75.

12 Ibid., 75-98. There is a gap in Foreman's journal after April 22 until July 18, 1863. The Cherokee Nation, like the southern states, was open range. If a farmer wanted to protect his crop it was his responsibility to fence it to protect it from the livestock of others.

13 S. Watie to My dear husband, May 20, 1863, Cherokee Nation Papers, microfilm. Sarah Watie used little punctuation and regularly capitalized only "I" and "God." Dale and Litton, eds., *Cherokee Cavaliers*, 126, n. #55.

Many of Sarah's subsequent letters reflect her concern that the family's condition as refugees had deprived their younger children Solon ("Watica"), Josephine ("Ninnie"), and Charlotte ("Jessie") of an education. Of their older sons, 12-year-old Eugene Cumiskey had died recently, and the eldest, Saladin Ridge (born circa 1845), was off serving as a captain in Watie's brigade.[14]

The morals of her oldest son especially concerned Sarah Watie. She penned a letter to "My Dear Half" on June 8 about a disturbing report that had reached her. "Saladin [has] killed a prisoner," she informed Stand, "write and tell me who it was and how it was tell my boys to always show mercy as they expect to find God merciful to them," she implored of her husband. "I am afraid that Saladin never will value human life as he ought. If you should ever catch William Ross don't have him killed. . . . I know they all deserve death but I do feel for his old mother" . . . She continued, "I want them to no that you do not want to kill them just to get them out of your way I want them to know you are not afraid of their influence always do as near right as you can."[15]

Sarah's letters contain everyday details of practical survival. She would have someone tend the corn if she had to spend the summer in Rusk, Texas, where she was nursing her seriously ill sister. She sent Stand a horse, kept another not strong enough to travel, and informed him of their value in Texas.[16]

Many Rebel sympathizers hoped they would be able stay in the Nation and return to their homes, but after their defeat at Honey Springs, any chance of maintaining themselves within the Cherokee Nation was lost. The loss of the battle 12 miles south of the southern boundary of the Cherokee Nation and the attending Pin harassment overwhelmed those families aligned with the Confederacy. Hope

14 W. D. Polson to Dear Aunt Sarah, April 16, 1863; Mrs. Sarah C. Watie to Stand Watie, May 20, 1863; S. C. Watie to My Dear half, June 8, 1863, in Cherokee Nation Papers; S.C. Watie to My Dear Husband, August 21, 1863; S. C. Watie to My Dear Stand, December 12, 1863; S. C. Watie to My Dear Husband, September 4, 1864, in Cherokee Nation Papers; Dale and Litton, eds. *Cherokee Cavaliers*, 121-122, 124-126, 128; n. 60, 128-129, 135, 146, 187; Franks, *Stand Watie and the Agony of the Cherokee Nation*, 137; David Keith Hampton, *Mixed Bloods: Additions and Corrections to Family Genealogies of Dr. Emmet Starr, vol. 1., Cordery, Ghigau, Ridge-Watie, Sanders and Ward* (Lincoln, AR, 2005), 251-252.

15 S. C. Watie to My Dear Half, June 8, 1863; Dale and Litton, eds., *Cherokee Cavaliers*, 128-129. William Ross, whose mother was John Ross's sister and his father of Scottish heritage, attended English-speaking schools and then graduated first in his class from Princeton University in 1844.

16 Ibid.

for reestablishing family life in the Nation was gone, and entire families prepared to depart. Indeed, the abandonment of the Cherokee Nation became wholesale.[17]

Some people managed fairly well. A well-prepared family might have two wagons loaded with provisions, with family members riding horseback and driving cattle, sheep, and dogs. Many slipped away peacefully. Others, in proximity to the Union army or Pins, barely got away with the clothes on their backs. Once they were on their way most people migrated toward the Texas Road, which was the main avenue south. Images of women riding with a feather bed for a saddle abound in the oral record. Many participants commented how odd the scene looked with houses full of furniture, one including a piano, left abandoned in their wake. Crops ripening in the fields were left to rot or feed others, and a half-starved horse tethered in a barn.[18]

The experiences of the refugees varied in other ways. Some women and their extended families of women and children tried to stay behind. They banded together, three and four families at one location, but continued to suffer harassment and other offenses. Many people eventually gave up and went south to the camps along the Red River. Only a few stayed until the end of the war.[19] People who had families in Arkansas traveled there. Some moved only as far as Van Buren or Fort Smith before turning back into the Choctaw Nation toward the refugee camps. Those who had the means rented housing in North Texas. This was generally true of slaveholders had who managed to keep at least some of their wealth. Robert M. Jones, for example, the richest man in the Choctaw Nation, maintained several plantations along the Red River worked by more than 500 slaves.[20]

17 James M. Bell to Caroline Bell, May 29, 1863, in Cherokee Nation Papers, Western History Collection, University of Oklahoma, microfilm; Dale and Litton, eds., *Cherokee Cavaliers*, 126-127; *OR* 22, pt. 2, 1104-1105; 41, pt. 2, 1046.

18 Indian Pioneer History Collection, vol. 10, 9, 486-487; vol. 11, 68, 135; vol. 12, 526; vol. 14, 83-84, 484-485; vol. 15, 83-84; vol. 20, 18-19; vol. 23, 256-257; vol. 34, 286; vol. 43, 333; vol. 52, 32; vol. 53, 355-356; vol. 84, 253; vol. 85, 465; vol. 88, 339; Confer, *The Cherokee Nation in the Civil War*, 126-129.

19 Indian Pioneer History Collection, vol. 4, 122-127; vol. 11, 290; vol. 14, 83-85; vol. 31, 388-389; vol. 42, 5170; vol. 78, 191-192.

20 Ibid., vol., 43, 288; James M. Bell to Stand Watie, n.d., folder, 3955; to Sarah Watie, December 17, 1863; Ann to J. M. Bell, September 18, 1863; Caroline Bell to J. M. Bell, April 12, 1864; W. J. Deupree to James M. Bell, October 27, 1864, in Cherokee Nation Papers; Arrell M. Gibson, *Oklahoma: A History of Five Centuries* (Norman, OK, 1981), 100.

"I have been here with sister Nancy nearly all summer," Sarah Watie wrote her husband Stand from Rusk County on July 28, 1863, "but I have no hope that she will get better for her life seems to hang on a thread. I am in a thousand troubles," she continued, "for I have just heard that you are falling back that is bad I do not no where you will find a place to hide here." Sarah shared rumors of bad news. "You have heard before this time that Vix burg has fallen that seems to distress the people more than any thing else . . . it is thought there is something wrong about it by it, being given up on the fourth of July. . . . I hope they will make peace I see in the papers that the people of New York are tired of this war and are crying for peace I wish it was over with."[21]

Sarah wrote Stand again on August 21. She had moved back to her home in northern Texas, leaving their son Watica with Nancy so he could attend school. "I have a great many things to tell you that will make you laugh and some that would not," she admitted. "I never knew so much of this world as I do since I come to this country. I used to think that every one had some sort of soul." Now she was not so sure.[22]

The Civil War punished everyone in this part of the country, including the wealthy. Ella F. Coody was a young Cherokee aristocrat who turned 16 at the time of Honey Springs. Her father was William Shorey Coody, who had left for the new country as an Old Settler, the faction that removed before the rift over the Treaty of New Echota. William's first wife died and his 17-year-old daughter, who had just graduated from a school in Philadelphia, succumbed to typhus. On a subsequent trip to Washington City he met Elizabeth Fields, the daughter of a friend, and returned with her to the Cherokee Nation, where Stephen Foreman married them at Park Hill in 1843. Ella and her brother Will were born of this marriage. William Coody decided it was time to move from the family home on Bayou Manard, a few miles southwest of Fort Gibson, and find a new home.[23]

21 S. B. Watie to My Dear S., July 28, 1863, in Cherokee Nation Papers, microfilm; Dale and Litton, eds., *Cherokee Cavaliers*, 132-33.

22 S. B. Watie to My Dear Husband, August 21, 1863, in Cherokee Nation Papers, microfilm; Dale and Litton, eds., *Cherokee Cavaliers*, 135-136.

23 Ibid., vol. 107, 451-453. This account is from Ella Coody Robinson's testimony in 1938 when she was a lucid ninety-one year old living in Muskogee. Indian Pioneer History Collection, vol. 107, 451-484. As she put it, outside of her refugee experience to Texas, she had lived her entire life in the Cherokee Nation. Technically, Muskogee, on the south bank of the Arkansas River is in the old Creek Nation. Bayou Manard is one of the French place names around Three Forks including the Verdigris, Grand, and Illinois rivers that date to French trappers in the region long before Removal.

An ice-encrusted cliff on the south bank of the Arkansas River below the mouth of the Grand River caught his eye, and he decided to build a new home at its summit. He named his new estate Frozen Rock. His slaves cleared the land for agriculture and constructed a 10-room, two-story house with materials shipped by steamer from Little Rock and Fort Smith. The Frozen Rock Landing became the last steamboat stop before Fort Gibson during the navigable season. Ella recalled that "comfortable quarters were built for the Negro servants; a good log cabin with space for a yard, a chicken yard and a garden was given each family." While the estate was being constructed, the newlyweds traveled by steamer to New York to purchase furnishings, which they shipped to New Orleans and from there to Frozen Rock. Life was good for the Coody family during these pre-Civil War years. Mrs. Coody had six indoor slaves to help her, plus a coachman and a laundress. An active social interaction thrived between the Coodys and the officers at Fort Gibson.[24]

William Coody died in Washington in 1849 and was buried in the Congressional Cemetery. Four years later in 1853, Ella Coody's mother Elizabeth married John Vann, whose father was Joseph "Rich Joe" Vann of Webber's Falls.[25] The Vanns sold Frozen Rock and built a 14-room home near Webber's Falls, adjacent to two neighboring plantations on a bluff overlooking the Arkansas River valley. The plantation was self-sufficient, with slaves acting as carpenters, blacksmiths, and shoemakers. Homespun wool provided some of their clothing, and wheat was ground for flour. Vann sold surplus pecans in Fort Smith, and twice a year took a flatboat to the fort, which slaves polled back upstream loaded with sugar, coffee, and other supplies. House guests were frequent.[26]

When the Civil War started, Vann enlisted in Watie's regiment as a captain. Ella Coody's brother, Will, also enlisted. Because of the uncertainty of the time, Ella's parents sent her with two other privileged girls to be enrolled in a Catholic boarding school at Fort Smith. The school was already overcrowded, and only John Drew's daughter was accepted. Ella attended school in Van Buren for one year before returning home. While there, she watched on one occasion as Confederate troops

---

24 Indian Pioneer History Collection, vol. 107, 452-454, 457-458.

25 The richest man in the Cherokee Nation before and after removal, Vann was a notorious alcoholic. He was killed when he took his private steamer down the Arkansas, and up the Mississippi and Ohio Rivers to attend the Kentucky Derby. He got into a race with another steamboat and supposedly held a pistol at the slave crew forcing them to throw sides of bacon into the boiler for more steam until it exploded.

26 Indian Pioneer History Collection, vol. 107, 456, 458-461.

marched through town for four hours "in perfect order." She also saw them return after their defeat at Pea Ridge in disorder, and witnessed their wounded being treated in the schoolhouse and in other buildings.

Ella returned to Webber's Falls, where the family heard the artillery duel at Honey Springs. When no news arrived as to its meaning or result, John Vann's sister, Mrs. Perry V. Brewer, became concerned. "When she became panic stricken, she always came to my mother, who at all times tried to keep her balance," Ella recalled. When news finally filtered in that Will had been taken prisoner, Elizabeth traveled to the Union camp to discover his whereabouts. The Vanns' overseer, a Kentuckian who managed operations when Vann was away, was also absent at this time. Black Union troops came through and ransacked the house. Elizabeth returned and became uncharacteristically distraught over the incident. Later that same day Colonel Phillips' men arrived. Elizabeth begged the officer to let her remove the furniture from the home he was about to torch, but he refused and set fire to the residence. All the family could salvage were "two or three mattresses, a few quilts, and one or two pieces of furniture." What little they had left was moved into a pair of abandoned slave cabins. The cabins were empty because the slaves had liberated themselves, taking Vann's racehorses and other riding stock with them. The next day, a neighbor reported their predicament to authorities and returned that evening to make them a meal.[27]

When he heard about his family's plight Captain Vann returned as fast as he could and found a small vacant house for them to occupy. Ella Coody described the deteriorating conditions: "Some of our neighbors who had not been burned out gave us a few things but in a few days Union troops set fire to the little village and burned the whole place out." Several of the mothers and their daughters became alarmed at rumors that they were not safe and took shelter at a Confederate camp nearby where the officers were known to them. Colonel Brewer provided an escort to a camp on the Canadian River where his wife was staying. By August, they were moving south again. "We traveled slowly as it was hot and Mother was not

---

27 Indian Pioneer History Collection, vol. 107, 472. Thoburn and Wright, *Oklahoma*, 344-345 and n. #15; Indian Pioneer History Collection, vol. 43, 402-403, vol. 84, 255. Robinson reports accurately that troops under Phillips entered the Cherokee Nation in April 1863. Phillips moved to Webber's Falls and on April 25 defeated a detachment of Watie's men, who retreated across the river. Robinson refers to the burning of her house as occurring at the same time, but she discussed the Battle of Honey Springs earlier, implying her house was burned after the battle. She also recalled hearing artillery during the battle and a panicked relative coming to their "house" to seek advice from her mother. The two separate events occurred in April and July, 1863, but it is uncertain which event preceded the burning of the family house.

well," recalled Ella. Most of the Choctaws and Chickasaws had fled south. "We could find vacant cabins to camp in and would stop and rest and cook. We found plenty of late vegetables. . . . What we missed so much was sugar, coffee, white flour, milk and butter. . . . There was no regular company traveling together. Some would stop to rest and some would hurry on, but we were never alone."[28]

Captain Vann was with them when they traveled southeast along San Bois Creek from below Briartown, where they probably forded the Canadian River. It was a difficult journey, and Ella found she preferred riding her pony instead of sitting in a wagon. When Ella's "little half- brother Charles" fell sick with fever the party stopped so they could nurse him back to health. Within ten days he was dead. They buried him in the wilderness and continued on their journey. More bad news awaited. Ella's full brother Will had not been captured in the fighting at Honey Springs, but killed. The family camped on the San Bois for six weeks to rest and recover from the horrific double loss.

John Vann grew more concerned with each passing day because the weather was turning colder. It was imperative that they find winter quarters. John rode ahead and secured a military ambulance to go back and pick up his family. They arrived at Carriage Point (near present Durant) and stayed a night at a boarding house. The following morning the family moved on and stayed with Major Vore's family while Captain Vann located and rented a two-room house at Bloomfield Academy, near Colbert's Ferry on the Red River in the Chickasaw Nation. The family finally had a place to live and would remain there more than a year. At the end of their stay, Elizabeth Vann gave birth to a son.

Many families from Webber's Falls settled in the area. Crops were abundant. They made shoes by sewing canvas onto leather salvaged from boot tops and made use of looms to make dresses. One young woman dyed lace curtains and made a dress. The young people socialized by attending dances where fiddlers accompanied them in the "polka, schottische, waltz and Virginia Reel." When Ella and her family finally left Bloomfield Academy they moved to Preston, Texas, on the south bank of the Red River. There, Ella met Lt. Joe Robinson, and the couple wed in 1866.[29]

*   *   *

---

28 Indian Pioneer History Collection, vol. 107, 472-475; OR 22, pt. 1, 315-316, 602; Ibid., pt. 2, 266.

29 Ibid., 473, 474-475477-479.

Stephen Foreman's journal picks up again on July 18, 1863, the day following the fighting at Honey Springs. He was heading south with a single borrowed wagon, and was jealous of a traveling companion who had two full wagons and extra riding stock. Foreman had been forced to leave his children behind with Suzie, his eldest daughter, in charge. After they arrived at North Fork Town near the confluence of the Canadian River and North Fork of the Canadian River, Foreman returned for his children.[30]

When he finally crossed paths with Colonel Watie, Foreman asked the Confederate colonel, who had a much better grasp of the true military situation, whether the families should remove farther south to Boggy Depot in the Choctaw Nation. Watie agreed they should go and suggested it might make a good winter camp. When Foreman disclosed that he was holding some public school funds, Watie sent Joseph Martin to get them. Foreman, however, refused to turn over the money. It was not lawful for him to release the funds, and as a Cherokee, he wanted to maintain legality even in chaotic times.[31]

The Foreman family remained at North Fork Town until August 24, when there was sufficient alarm—though false alarms were common—to induce him to move once more. Forman loaded the wagon in the night, all the while regretting that it was necessary to leave behind "some books that had been used in the family, and half-worn garments of those who had died, and other small articles such as augers, gimblet, awls, candle sticks, etc, all were necessary in a family." Once packed they traveled to the home of a "Mr. Scales" south of the Canadian River in the Choctaw Nation.

The following day, while attempting to find a team of oxen that could pull more than his small horses, could Foreman met "Major Vann," who returned with him to the Scales home. News arrived that North Fork Town had been burned to the ground by the Federals, but Vann did not think the Union army would come much farther. He was wrong. Just after dark on August 26, Federal forces arrived without warning and searched Scales' house. Fortunately they did not harm anyone, but they did steal Foreman's rifle, saddle, and three valuable horses.[32]

---

30 Foreman "Journal," 98-105.

31 Ibid., 101-103.

32 Ibid., 106-109. This is almost certainly the same Captain John Vann, the man Ella Coody's mother married. It was likely when he had gone ahead to find transportation for his family left behind on San Bois Creek.

Foreman left and spent the balance of the night in an empty home a few miles away. When he returned to his family and their friends, the Wades, who had joined them while moving south, they decided the Texas Road was too unsafe to travel. Foreman scouted for a safer route and became separated from his family when the Wades continued south along the Texas Road with Foreman's children. Foreman thought they were heading for the home of Governor Winchester Colbert, leader of the Chickasaw Nation and one of Mrs. Wade's relatives. When he found no sign of his family there, he ate a quick meal and was about to leave when word arrived that his family had been seen at Perryville on the Texas Road between North Fork Town and Boggy Depot.[33]

"Many of them are in a very destitute condition," Foreman wrote regarding the condition of the Creek and Cherokee refugees he observed as he traveled. "All they are with now is a pony, one or two pot vessels, and a few old dirty bed clothes and wearing apparel. . . . But many who passed I was acquainted with, and knew them to be in good circumstances, having an abundance of everything." Now, he lamented, "their all is put into one or two small wagons."

The Texas Road reached its namesake at Colbert's Ferry on the Red River, which was operated by slave labor. Elizabeth Kemp Mead's father had married a Colbert, and they lived nearby. "The refugees from the Cherokee Nation came in bunches and settled near us during the war," she recalled. "They were without food, and I have often seen them gathering the tender leaves from Mulberry trees and cooking them for greens. Father would kill beef and hogs and divide out among them; also, let them have corn to make bread."[34]

Foreman fell ill while at Governor Colbert's, and when he was finally well enough to travel, he moved about 12 miles south of Boggy Depot to rest at "Mr. Ballentine's place." By September 11 his health was improving and he reported on his condition in a letter to his daughter. He had received two reports that she and the other children were well, but he remained anxious for them. Foreman was not well enough to travel farther, however, and wanted the children to come to him.

By September 13, the family was together again three miles from Boggy Depot. "[We] were in a very retired place where we have a plenty of good water and timber, and being able to draw rations, we are well off all things considered," expressed Foreman with no little relief. "After passing through the troubles and excitements in consequence of the late stampede, I thought it was really pleasant to be with my

33 Foreman, "Journal," 110-114.

34 Indian Pioneer History Collection, vol. 7, 162-163; Foreman "Journal," 116-117.

children again although it was in the woods and to read the Bible and reflect on the goodness of God towards us." Foreman and his family, aside from son John, who was in Watie's Confederate brigade, spent the rest of the war in Texas.[35]

While the Foremans made their home in Texas, Sarah Watie remained saddened about the continuation of the war and its effect on her marriage. On December 12, 1863, the Cherokee general's wife wrote Stand that she was dispirited after his visit to her and his return to winter's quarters. "We [get] along [illegible] as we can under the circumstances we always [illegible] about under more disadvantages than any one else we all ways feed more folks than any body else and get less thanks," she complained. "Send us all that you can in the way of work tools ploughs and other things we have no such things send me a loom if you can without too much trouble," she requested. "I have spun every day since you left and still all are bare for clothing except Jack and Ninny. . . . I am sorry you are not so well as you were at the beginning [of the] war so [many of] our friends have died." She concluded by instructing her husband to "bring Saladin [with you] for I don't like for him to be there when you are not there."[36]

The experiences of Sarah Watie, Ella Coody, Stephen Foreman, and others reflect the sufferings of the thousands of less fortunate refugees whose experiences have passed into history unrecorded. They traveled into camps along the tributaries of the Red River. Many of the Creeks were gathered around Fort Washita in the Chickasaw Nation. Some didn't leave their nations. In addition to harassment from the Pins, they fell prey to "bushwhackers," criminals who stayed behind or came in from Missouri and Arkansas to terrorize the defenseless. Generally speaking, the lives of women and children were spared, but their property was not. The bushwhackers preyed on vacant as well as occupied homes, and often left nothing but ashes in their wake.[37]

35 Foreman, "Journal," 116-118.

36 S. C. Watie to Stand, December 12, 1863, in Cherokee Nation Papers, microfilm; Dale and Litton, eds., *Cherokee Cavaliers*, 146.

37 Indian Pioneer History Collection, vol. 7, 244; vol. 21, 68; vol. 65, 407-408, vol. 68, 12; vol. 76, 320-321; Confer, "Indian Territory Homefront," 110-116.

Intervention

Cooperation between Cherokee leaders and Con-federate authorities, both military and civilian, brought some degree of order to the chaos. The Cherokee Nation passed an ordinance to furnish aid, including schools, to the refugees on May 30, 1863, and elected J. L. Martin commissioner in charge. Brig. Gen. William Steele appointed the same officer as issuing agent to supply the indigent camps along the Red River from Confederate military supplies.[1]

On August 8, 1863, Stand Watie complained to Sutton S. Scott, Commissioner of Indian Affairs, of the South's military failures. Watie complained that at least 6,000 Cherokee refugees had lost everything and were dispersed across the Creek and Choctaw Nations and south into Texas. Watie planned to have a census taken, and advised the commissioner that the Confederacy needed to provide food, clothing, and shelter for the refugees. The relief ordinance passed by the Cherokee convention provided an organization, but it needed money to function and the Cherokee leadership asked that the annual payments due them by treaty be advanced for that purpose. Concerned about the fate of his people, Watie asked, "Shall I continue to encourage them, or shall I at once unveil to them the dread truth that our country is to be hopelessly abandoned, and that they are to receive

---

1 OR 41, pt. 2, 1047; James M. Bell to Caroline Bell, May 29, 1863; Dale and Litton, eds., *Cherokee Cavaliers*, 126-128.

the reward of poverty and ruin for their unswerving fidelity to the Southern cause?"[2]

Boggy Depot, on the Clear Boggy River at the junction of the Texas Road and the Butterfield Stage Route below the Canadian River, evolved into a major staging point. "I have just returned to this place," Martin wrote Watie from the depot on September 22:

I have been looking out a place to take our people. I have found an excellent place for them down on the Blue Creek . . . about ten miles about the mouth of Said Creek [into the Red River]. There are plenty of water with good timber and summer & winter range forage Boddies of good cane and to all appearances a healthy location. I shall commence moving our people about Thursday. Genl Steele promised me he would furlough all the soldiers who had families and friends to take care of to build houses.[3]

By August of 1864, the Blue River was home to the Cherokees from 40 miles upstream at Tishomingo to its mouth at the Red River, with others "at Goodland 20 miles West of Fort Towson." The number of Cherokees receiving aid from the government was 2,906, although Watie estimated the actual number of refugees to be higher.[4]

The refugee Creeks were camped from the confluence of the Washita and the Red Rivers, 25 miles up the Washita and 12 miles up the Red River. They had built crude shelters and were "reasonably comfortable and healthy." That June, there were 1,364 children and 3,307 adults, for a total of 4,671. By July, the number had increased to 4,823. The chiefs had allowed a few people who were not technically destitute to be enrolled, but Col. R. W. Lee, Assistant Superintendent of Indian Affairs, thought it would be unwise to make an issue of it.[5]

The Chickasaws had enrolled 785 refugees, but the issuing agent, Reverend J. C. Robinson, had fed only 584 from a depot at Robinson's Academy. The Choctaw refugees were scattered along streams around Boggy Depot and in the mountainous terrain along the Kiamichi River that extended northeast to the

---

2 *OR* 22, pt. 2, 1104-1105.

3 J. L. Martin to Col. [Watie], September 22, 1863, in Cherokee Nation Papers; Dale and Litton, eds., *Cherokee Cavaliers*, 138-139; Indian Pioneer History, 78, 138-139.

4 R. W. Lee to S. B. Maxey, October 1, 1864 in Allen C. Ashcraft, "Confederate Indian Department Conditions in August, 1864," in *Chronicles of Oklahoma* (Autumn 1963), Issue 41, 277-278; *OR* 22, pt. 2, 1,004-1,005.

5 Ashcroft, "Confederate Indian Department Conditions," 275.

Arkansas border. Around Fort Towson were 800 adults and 600 children. Most of the young men were away in the Southern army. The rolls were yet to be completed, but Lee expected the total Choctaws enrolled would be 4,480. Work was underway to establish depots on the Kiamichi River at Johnson's Station and Boggy Depot.[6]

The Seminole refugees were living west of Fort Washita with some Creek families with which they retained close ties. The enrolled Seminoles numbered 574 and the Creeks 441. "Reserve" Indians west of Fort Washita (Plains Indians remaining on the reserve) numbered 532 and Osages 241. The grand total on government relief was 14,790. This did not include those in the army and those maintaining their independence or being maintained by their own governments.[7]

The relief effort combined not only the assets held in trust by the Confederacy and the Cherokee Nation, but also the Confederate military, which had the capacity to supply the refugees. Brigadier General Samuel Bell Maxey replaced General Steele as commander of the District of the Indian Territory on December 11, 1863. Maxey and his wife Marilda were residents of Paris, Texas, 15 miles south of the Red River and the Choctaw Nation. He graduated 48th out of 49 from West Point in 1846 and served in the Mexican War. Maxey later resigned from the Army, took up the practice of law, and moved to Texas. He was elected to the state legislature, but the war intervened before he took office. Maxey raised the 9th Texas Infantry and was elected its colonel. He served in and around Tennessee, where he was promoted to brigadier general on March 7, 1862.[8]

On December 29, 1863, Maxey wrote his wife from Doaksville, just north of his headquarters at Fort Towson. "I not only have control of the troops, but am ex officio Superintendent of Indian Affairs," he explained, "and these latter duties are not well defined. Amongst other things I have to feed hundreds of indigent Indians."[9] He would later revise that figure up to 14,000. Choctaw leader Peter P. Pitchlynn warned Maxey that the refugees were taxing the resources of the plantations along the Red River, and urged him to organize some relief. Maxey forwarded Pitchlynn's letter to the Trans-Mississippi Department commander, Lt.

6 Ibid., 278-279.

7 Ibid., 279-280, 282.

8 Boatner, *Civil War Dictionary*, 520. Maxey would eventually be promoted to major general by Gen. E. Kirby Smith, but the higher rank was never confirmed. He served two terms in the U.S. Senate after the war. His home in Paris, Texas is now a popular tourist attraction.

9 Maxey to his wife, Doaksville, December 29, 1863, in Samuel Bell Maxey Collection, Gilcrease Museum, Tulsa.

Gen. E. Kirby Smith, and promised Pitchlynn that something could be done if they worked together.[10]

The plight of refugees in his district, as well as in western Arkansas and northern Texas, appalled Maxey. He found "many [families] in a state of destitution, others nearly so. Whilst a few had the means of subsistence left, they were themselves homeless wanderers." He felt compelled to do all he could for them, not only because of treaty obligations but also for humanitarian reasons. Maxey allowed 1,500 bales of cotton to be sold in Mexico to finance the purchase of clothing and supplies for the refugees, and recommended close scrutiny of these transactions to avoid the corruption that ran rampant in the region.[11]

Assistant Superintendent R. W. Lee also was concerned. He blamed the inefficiency of the relief operation on a shortage of labor and wagons to deliver stores over long distances. Lee argued that Indian troops and refugees should, at least in part, be supplied by civilian contracts rather than by the army commissary. He also thought a permanently assigned train of wagons should be detailed to Warren, Texas. A depot there could supply, through sub-depots, the Cherokees, Creeks, Seminoles, and most of the Choctaws, with the balance of refugees being fed and supplied from Fort Towson.[12]

Lee appointed an inspector of camps to oversee the construction "of a manufactory for making looms and spinning wheels, a wagon shop and blacksmith shop" to aid the Creek refugees. Once it was finally begun, he considered it very successful and suggested that at a cost of only $850.00, the production might even be tripled. He considered the cost charged to customers to be fair, and not an abuse of government subsidies, and recommended that the employees be compensated beyond the small amounts allowed by regulations. Lee also urged that adequate quantities of cotton and wool be maintained.[13]

To maintain this system, each depot had an issuing agent who appointed an inspector of refugee camps. These inspectors visited each camp at least once a month and reported issues to the Superintendent of Issues, who was in overall charge of the acquisition and distribution of food, clothing, and other supplies, as well as the overall efficiency of the operation. Lee recommended that two

10 OR 53, 1,034-1,036. Smith was promoted to full general, to date from February 19, 1864.

11 Maxey to Scott, August 23, 1864, in Maxey Collection.

12 R. W. Lee to S. B. Maxey, August 20, 1864, in Ashcraft, "Confederate Indian Department Conditions," 274.

13 Ibid., 275-276.

additional officials be appointed. One, a Supervisor of Rolls, would constantly update and confirm that the rolls were accurate—a responsibility currently charged to the Superintendent of Issues. The other post was a transportation master to hire reliable teamsters. Because the military physicians were occupied with the Confederate army, Lee decided to employ civilian doctors. To support this system, he recommended that the pay for the employees be adequate to prevent turnover.[14]

General Maxey wrote to the Commissioner of Indian Affairs concerning Lee's recommendations. Maxey concurred with most of them and explained, "the system adopted was an experiment and as faults presented themselves I have endeavored to correct them." On one point Maxey disagreed: Lee's recommendation to supply the refugees through commercial civilian contracts rather than through the army commissary. "Under ordinary circumstances I would recommend the contract system," explained Maxey. "I cannot do so now as owing to the depreciation of the currency and the size of contract but for competition would enter the [illegible] and they most likely from designing speculators a class for which I have no sort of use." The contrast between Maxey's integrity and the corruption of Kansas officials cannot be overstated.[15]

Maxey's system impressed Commissioner Scott, and the two men became good friends. Scott was satisfied that conditions in the Indian Nations were much improved, and gave the credit to Maxey. On September 23, 1864, Scott asked Maxey to use his printing press to publish a circular from a text enclosed by Scott and to distribute it in order to encourage those in the Indian Nations who had supported the Confederacy.[16] Maxey published the circular on September 29. It acknowledged setbacks in the war, complimented the manner in which the people had borne them, and acknowledged that they were all part of a greater struggle. If they continued to act as they had during the last two years, it extolled, victory would be theirs. The circular also encouraged the Choctaws and Chickasaws to fill the vacancy of their delegate to the Confederate Congress because Robert M. Jones had resigned. On October 10, Scott, who was returning to Richmond, informed Maxey that he had given Robert C. Miller, the new dispersing agent requested by

---

14 R. W. Lee to S. B. Maxey, August 20, 1964 in Ashcraft, "Confederate Indian Department Conditions," 280-282.

15 Maxey to Scott, August 23, 1864.

16 S. S. Scott to E. Kirby Smith, August 27, 1864; S. S. Scott to Maxey, September 23, 1864, Maxey Collection.

Maxey, an additional $75,000.00 for the superintendency. Miller was to report to Maxey.[17]

The Choctaw government was late to bring effective relief to their own refugees from the northern Moshulatubbee District south of the Arkansas and Canadian river system. Change came with the election of Principal Chief Peter P. Pitchlynn on October 6, 1864. Pitchlynn used his inaugural address to both houses of the legislature at Armstrong Academy to appeal for continued unity and resistance to the enemy in defending "the last home of the Choctaws." He called for "appointing some suitable agent to visit the Choctaw refugees and report their condition at the earliest day practicable that the executive may submit the same to General Maxey and have their wants and necessities relieved if possible." Pitchlynn "also recommend[ed] that prompt and energetic efforts should be made by all the civil officers of this government and all good and law abiding citizens to suppress the thieving and robbing that prevails to such a fearful extent." A proclamation to the Choctaw people called on military and civilian officers to enforce the law, and to sustain the "great many among us [who] are helpless and dependent upon us for protection."

In response to a complaint by one of Maxey's dispersal agents that there were only eight wagons to transfer supplies from Texas to the refugees, the council passed measures in October requiring the district chiefs to supply more wagons and to employ enrolling agents to identify and locate Choctaw refugees so they could be fed and supplied. Later that year the council approved spending $25,000 for cotton and wool cards to manufacture cloth. In April 1865, during the final weeks of the war, Brig. Gen. Douglas Cooper reserved 2,500 bushels of corn for the exclusive use of "poor and indigent" Choctaws.[18]

Maxey and Scott were gratified by their achievements, as was Gen. Kirby Smith. They had accomplished a great deal given the immensity of the problem

---

17 S. S. Scott to Maxey, September 23, 1864; Circular, September 29, 1864, SB 58; S. S. Scott to Maxey, October 10, 1864, in Maxey Collection.

18 The Inaugural Address of Gov. Pitchlynn, n. d., photocopy, Peter P. Pitchlynn Papers, Gilcrease Museum; Proclamation by the Principal Chief of the Choctaw Nation, n.d., Pitchlynn Papers; L. C. Dixson Superintendent of Issues, Doaksville, To the Hon Council of the Choctaw Nation, Armstrong, October 8, 1864; An act for the relief of certain persons herein named, approved October 11, 1864; An act requiring the District Chiefs of this Nation to employ or make arrangements with Citizens to hire wagons to haul supplies for the indigent and Choctaw Refugees, approved October 13, 1864; S. B. Maxey to Saml. S. Mosely, December 9, 1864; D. H. Cooper to P. P. Pitchlynn, April 14, 1865, in Pitchlynn Papers.

they faced. But the Indian refugees were still the victims of war, and it would be a mistake to minimize their ongoing suffering.

Help for the displaced also came from the religious community, particularly from Southern Baptists, and from as far away as Atlanta, Georgia. One of Watie's chaplains, Ebenezer Lee Compere, played a key role in relief efforts. Compere was born February 6, 1833, in the vicinity of Montgomery, Alabama. His father, a minister in a Creek Baptist church in Mississippi, baptized Ebenezer when he was 16. The son studied at Mercer University and graduated from Mississippi College. He became an ordained minister in 1858, earned a master's degree in 1860, and moved to Fort Smith.[19]

In November 1854, the Cherokee Baptist Convention was established in Georgia. Its leaders planned to send missionaries around the world and specifically among the removed Cherokees whose original land they now occupied. One scholar who has studied the convention concluded, concerning its membership, that, "At its height, about 1860, it was comprised of more than 250 churches in eight associations, with a total membership of 15,540, led by about 190 ordained or licensed ministers." It was associated with the *Landmark Banner and Cherokee Baptist* newspaper and operated a male and a female seminary. On August 21, 1861, the convention and Compere reached a formal agreement for Compere to become a missionary to the Cherokees. He had been warned of the missionary work by abolitionists in the northern part of the Cherokee Nation, so he began preaching at nearby Webber's Falls to both civilians and the Cherokee regiments. Compere also maintained a small congregation at Fort Smith.[20]

In 1863, probably in April, Compere joined the army as chaplain to the 2nd Cherokee Regiment. During the initial refugee period before the battle of Honey Springs, Compere worked east of the Mississippi River to obtain religious literature for the troops and cloth, clothing, quilts, and blankets for the refugees. On June 29, 1863, the *Macon* (GA) *Christian Index* published a graphic report of the suffering of the refugee women and children written by Compere. It concluded, "My dear brethren and sisters. . . . I can not press you to help them, but if it will be a pleasure

---

19 Gardner, "Ebenezer Lee Compere and Problems of Civil War," 23-24. Professor Gardner published two other articles on this subject: "Ebenezer Lee Compere, Cherokee Georgia Baptist Missionary," *Viewpoints: Georgia Baptist History* (1976), Issue 5, 91-102, is nearly identical to the one cited above; "Missionary-Chaplain to the Cherokees: Ebenezer Lee Compere," *Oklahoma Baptist Chronicle*, 18 (Spring 1975), Issue 18, 5-32, is a longer treatment with appendixes. The predominant sources for all three are several Southern Baptist newspapers that supported Compere's efforts among the southern Cherokees.

20 Gardner, "Ebenezer Compere and Problems of Civil War," 25-28.

to you to divide with these suffering ones . . . then let any church . . . put up in a box such articles as may be useful, . . . and I will take pleasure in trying to get these goods to the Cherokee people."[21]

Compere remained east of the Mississippi River for several months, with several Southern Baptist newspapers following his progress. The Atlanta *Baptist Banner* encouraged donors to send him blankets and quilts as well as clothing. At Cartersville, Georgia, one church donated enough funds for a bale of osnaburg, a heavy cotton cloth used for work clothes and sacks. A group of women in Rome, Georgia, organized to collect money and clothing. Compere promised that all donations sent to him at the *Baptist Banner* by the end of July would be included in the shipment. The executive committee of the Baptist Convention also encouraged contributions.[22]

On July 4, 1863, Lt. Gen. John C. Pemberton surrendered Vicksburg, Mississippi, to Maj. Gen. Ulysses S. Grant. That Southern disaster, together with the fall of Port Hudson to the south five day later placed the length of the Mississippi River in Union hands, further isolating the Trans-Mississippi theater. Friends doubted that Compere could get his stores across the river without being captured. Compere assured the faithful that with God's help he would get through. The executive committee repeated its appeals, and Compere advertised a system whereby donors could deposit their contributions at one of several towns. He planned to start west by the end of August.[23]

On September 12, the *Baptist Banner* published a letter of thanks received from Compere, who was at that time in Enterprise, Mississippi (Clarke County) near the border with Alabama. He hoped his friends would not worry about him and reminded them that he placed his trust in God: "It would not be prudent to say how I will get over the river. But be sure God will provide a way. And may He ever bless and preserve you is my prayer." By October 8, he had reached Clinton, Mississippi, just west of Jackson and about 30 miles east of Vicksburg. There, he wrote long letter to General Grant explaining that he was on "a mission of mercy for suffering

21 *Macon Christian Index*, Georgia, June 29, 1863. This newspaper, along with the *Atlanta Baptist Banner*, are on microfilm at the Southern Baptist Archives at the Southern Baptist Convention building in Nashville, Tennessee.

22 *Christian Index*, June 27, 1863, June 29, 1863, July 23, 1863, July 4, 1863, July 11, 1863, July 18, 1863; E. L. Compere to U. S. Grant, October 8, 1863, Compere Papers, Southern Baptist Archives; Gardner, "Missionary-Chaplain to the Cherokees," 17-19. For a discussion of the importance of southern Protestant churches to the unity of the South, see Samuel S. Hill, Jr., *The South and the North in American Religion* (Athens, GA, 1980), 47-89.

23 *Christian Index*, July 23, 1863.

women and children, Cherokees," and it was urgent that he return to the Indian Nations. "I have been furnished by voluntary contributions . . . and I respectfully ask, in the name of suffering humanity," he pleaded, "that you will give me protection through your department for the above named goods—religious reading—and the requisite number of wagons and teams for the transportation." He assured Grant that nothing would go to the Confederate army.[24]

Whether the letter resulted in Grant's blessing remains unknown, but we do know that Compere crossed the Mississippi in December 1863 to deliver his goods. On July 1, 1864, Watie ordered Lt. S. G. McLendon to arrange transportation for another shipment, but he could find only one of the four wagon teams needed. Teamsters were reluctant to risk stock and equipment, even when offered barter in place of nearly valueless Confederate currency. It would be several months before the supplies crossed the river, and not until sometime in November or early December would they leave Shreveport for distribution among the Cherokee refugees along the Blue River.[25]

Compere was back in Atlanta by December 17, 1864. The *Baptist Banner* celebrated the success of his earlier mission and proclaimed that such true devotion to the Southern cause deserved further aid. The paper asked for donations of "clothing, osnaburgs, cotton cards, money, cotton etc. . . . Let everyone give promptly and liberally, remembering that all articles of clothing are scarce beyond the Mississippi River." Whether they succeeded in delivering a third shipment is not known.[26]

Additional aid came through the Confederate Congress and the Cherokee representative in Richmond, E. C. Boudinot. Boudinot had taken his seat on

---

24 Christian Index, September 12, 1863; E. L. Compere to U. S. Grant, October 8, 1863, E. L. Compere Papers, Gardner, "Missionary-Chaplain to the Cherokees," 20-21. Gardner concluded that because the letter was in Compere's possession, it must have been returned to him and therefore got through to the Union command. He acknowledged General Grant was not in Vicksburg at the time, but Compere asked that, in case of Grant's absence, it be given to the next in command. Gardner believes Union authorities cooperated. The letter Compere possessed could just as easily have been a copy. There is no way to know whether the letter got through, or if it did, its result.

25 Ibid., 206; Gardner, "Missionary-Chaplain to the Cherokees," 23-24.

26 Baptist Banner, December 17, 1864; *Macon Christian Index*, December 22, 1864; Gardner, "Missionary-Chaplin to the Cherokees," 25-26. Both Gardner, and Dale and Litton, *Cherokee Cavaliers*, 206-207, mistakenly link Watie's adjutant, Captain Thomas F. Anderson, and Sergeant John Walker who were taking a wagon east across the Mississippi, with Compere. They were on an important military mission unrelated to Compere's mission. Without Professor Robert G. Gardner's research concerning Compere, we would be left only with the fragments in Dale and Litton, and this entire episode would be lost to history.

October 7, 1862, and being well-received by the Congress, was in a position of influence to aid the refugees.[27] On August 9, 1863, Watie, writing as principal chief rather than as an army officer, gave Boudinot instructions. With the Confederate Congress not then in session, Boudinot was to proceed to Shreveport and have discussions with Kirby Smith and Commissioner Scott about how to raise relief funds and implement the relief ordinance passed by the Cherokee Convention. If no funds were forthcoming, Watie urged Boudinot, as agent of the Cherokee Convention, to proceed to Richmond and arrange funding through the Confederate Congress. Boudinot responded on November 4, 1863, that neither Smith nor Scott was willing to extend funds unless the other would take personal responsibility, and neither man would do so. Boudinot obtained $10,000 under his personal signature and told Watie that he would have $40,000 from Congress by early January. On January 24, 1864, Boudinot informed Watie that he had obtained a $100,000 credit from the Confederate Congress—but it would have to be repaid and was tied to the equivalent value in gold. The Confederate Congress had protected itself against the inflation that was devaluing its currency. The bill passed with only one negative vote and President Davis signed it. Boudinot blamed the delay—it was only a few weeks, but they were desperate ones—on Commissioner Scott, who had not performed in Richmond as he said he would.[28]

Boudinot complained to Watie on April 7 that Scott had left Richmond for the Indian Nations with the $100,000, but had managed to get only as far as Mississippi before circumstances forced him to return to Richmond—though not before he had sent a check for $44,500 to Watie. He even sent a duplicate check on March 8, in case the first was lost.[29] The Cherokee Nation's treasurer was to take proper

---

27 *Journal of the Congress of the Confederate States of America 1861-1865*, 7 vols. (Washington: Government Printing Office, 1904-1905) vol. 3, 420, 521; vol. 5, 502, 513-514; vol. 6, 276, 520, microfilm. Robert Jones, a Choctaw planter, took his seat representing the Choctaws and Chickasaws (a seat that alternated between the two nations) on January 17, 1863. T. Paul Wilson, "Confederate Delegates of the Five Civilized Tribes," in *Chronicles of Oklahoma* (Fall 1975), Issue 53, 353-366.

28 Stand Watie to Elias C. Boudinot, August 9, 1863, in Cherokee Nation Papers; Dale and Litton, eds., *Cherokee Cavaliers*, 143-144, 150; *Journal of the Confederate Congress*, vol. 3, 620; Parins, *Elias Cornelius Boudinot*, 55.

29 S. S. Scott to Stand Watie, March 18, 1864. It is the copy sent from Richmond, S. S. Scott to Stand Watie, March 18, 1864, that survives in the Cherokee Nation Papers. Elias Cornelius Boudinot to Stand Watie, April 20, 1864; Elias Cornelius Boudinot to Stand Watie, May 7, 1864; Elias Cornelius Boudinot to Stand Watie, July 13, 1864; Elias Cornelius Boudinot to Stand Watie, July 25, 1864; S. S. Scott to Stand Watie, July 27, 1864, in Cherokee Nation Papers; Dale and Litton eds., *Cherokee Cavaliers*, 153, 157-159, 181, 182.

identification to the government "depository" at Shreveport, where he was expected, and cash the check for small bills. Scott personally delivered the balance to the Cherokee treasurer at Fort Washita in August.[30]

The Cherokees were operating more independently than the Creeks because of their credit line from the Confederate Congress. "The Cherokees have a wheel and loom manufacturing, wheelwright and blacksmith shops on quite an extended scale, which turn out a considerable amount of work for the benefit of the indigent families," explained Commissioner Lee. "These are conducted under the charge of the authorities of the Nation, without expense to the [military] government. They are well supplied with hands [slaves], and have furnished most of the families the Articles needed for household and other purposes, at moderate rates." They also procured their own cotton and wool. Small pox for a time had ravaged the Cherokees, but it had subsided.[31]

By the spring 1864, the Cherokees were relatively comfortable and healthy. Major General James G. Blunt's situation, however, was about to change for the worse.

---

30 Elias Cornelius Boudinot to Stand Watie, April 20, 1864; Elias Cornelius Boudinot to Stand Watie, May 7, 1864; Elias Cornelius Boudinot to Stand Watie, May 7, 1864; Elias Cornelius Boudinot, July 13, 1864; Elias Cornelius Boudinot to Stand Watie, July 25, 1864; S. S. Scott to Stand Watie, July 27, 1864; Dale and Litton, eds., *Cherokee Cavaliers*, 153, 157-159, 181, 181-182, 182. These letters from Boudinot to Watie are not in the Cherokee Nation Papers. Inflation was evident in Richmond where Boudinot's pay was $250.00 per month, but his room and board was $350.00.

31 R. W. Lee to S. B. Maxey, October 1, 1864; *OR* 22, pt. 2, 1,104-1,105. Wilson, "Delegates of the Five Civilized Tribes to the Confederate Congress," 360.

The Travails of General Blunt

After the Union victory at Old Fort Wayne on October 22, 1862, Maj. Gen. James G. Blunt wanted to occupy Fort Gibson with the Indian Brigade and return the refugees to the Cherokee Nation. Blunt and Brig. Gen. (and U.S. Senator) Jim Lane had made plans to defraud the Federal government through a kickback scheme from suppliers to both the army and the refugees. Their plot would eventually be exposed and foiled, but not before both men made tidy sums. Unfortunately, neither man suffered the severe consequences each deserved until after the war. Here is how this unlikely tale unfolded.

The Indian agents called the Cherokee refugee camp in the Cherokee Neutral Lands "Camp Dry Wood." The Creeks were near the Sac and Fox Reservation, and William G. Coffin, Superintendent for Indian Affairs, Southern Superintendency, with offices in Leavenworth, tried to get the Cherokees to move there also. Blunt, however, intervened and informed the Cherokees that the U.S. Army would take them back to their homes, which is what the Cherokees desired. Blunt had them moved to Neosho, Missouri, much to the chagrin of the Indian agents who were responsible for caring for the refugees. The general had not consulted with the agents, and they complained of the exorbitant cost of shipping food and clothing 80 miles from their depot in Kansas. Coffin hired an additional special agent, A. G. Proctor, to assist Justin Harlan, the agent to the Cherokees.[1]

---

1 L. N. Hilderbrand, James Water, Liki Ki, Joseph Dubal to W. G. Coffin, October 31, 1862; Wm. G. Coffin to the Cherokee Refugee Indians, October 31, 1862; William Coffin to W. G

At the highest levels, the thoroughly honest intention was to return the refugees to their homes. On October 24, 1862, two days after the Battle of Old Fort Wayne, Maj. Gen. Samuel R. Curtis, commander of the Department of Missouri (which encompassed Missouri, Kansas, Arkansas, and the Indian Territory), reported on the military situation to Maj. Gen. Henry Halleck. "The enemy . . . under Cooper and Stand Watie [were] some 5,000 to 7,000 strong," explained Curtis, and "The engagement . . . resulted in the total rout of the enemy. . . . The enemy in precipitation fled beyond the Boston Mountains. All the organized rebel forces of the West have thus been driven back to the valley of the Arkansas River, and the Army of the Frontier has gallantly and successfully accomplished its mission. We will now enter the Indian Territory," he concluded, "and restore the refugee Indians to their homes."[2]

On January 13, 1863, General Curtis gave Col. William Phillips command of the 8th and 9th Districts of the Department of Missouri, which consisted of the Indian Territory and some counties in northwest Arkansas. The loyal Cherokee Council was planning a legislative meeting at Cowskin Prairie in the northwest corner of the Cherokee Nation. Phillips moved part of his command there to protect them. He also sent wagon trains filled with corn and flour south to Park Hill, Fort Gibson, and a nearby mill.[3]

On February 11, Phillips wrote A. G. Proctor that he planned to relieve the "suffering condition of the Cherokee helpless women and children" whose husbands and fathers were in his brigade. He would do so by returning them to their homes by March 1, which would give them time to put in a crop. Phillips urged Proctor and his superiors to provide "seeds of all kinds" and "agricultural implements."[4] Superintendent Coffin advised Commissioner Dole back in Washington that, on the advice of Phillips, Harlan, and Procter, "I have directed the removal of all the Cherokee Indians at Fort Scott and at Neosho to their homes in the Cherokee Nation, but not, I must confess, without some misgivings as to the

---

Coffin to William Dole [Commissioner of Indian Affairs] November 10, 1862; William Coffin to W. G. Coffin to William Dole, November 10, 1862; H. N. Martin to Col. W. G. Coffin, December 20, 1862; W. G. Coffin to A. G. Proctor, December 24, 1862; W. G. Coffin to Major B. S. Henning, December 28, 1962; W. G. Coffin to Justin Harlan, December 29, 1862; W. G. Coffin to Wm. P. Dole, January 1, 1863, Letters Received, OIA, Cherokee Agency.

2 *OR* 13, 324-325.

3 Ibid., 22; *OR* 13, pt. 2, 40, 55, 85, 96-97.

4 W. H. Phillips to A. G. Proctor, February 11. 1863, Letters Received, Cherokee Agency.

safety of the movement." The Seneca, Shawnee, and Quapaw refugees, however, spent the remainder of the war with the Ottawas in Kansas.[5]

While Phillips sent scouting parties throughout the area and south of the Arkansas River, the Cherokee Council passed resolutions to abrogate the Confederate treaty, remove disloyal Cherokees from office, and outlaw slavery in the Cherokee Nation. On February 23, General Blunt wrote Phillips that his intention was to occupy the Indian country in the summer and that Phillips should work to clear the region of guerrillas. Phillips, in a series of communiqués from February through March with Curtis and Blunt, proposed to occupy the Cherokee Nation and Fort Smith. He believed he could enlist loyal recruits from below the Arkansas River. General Curtis was certain Phillips could not hold Fort Smith until the Arkansas was in Union hands. Blunt favored moving south to the Arkansas and returning the refugee Indians to within a radius of Fort Gibson, Tahlequah, and Park Hill, but the refugees desperately wanted to return to their homes. A delegation from the Cherokee regiments twice presented Phillips with a petition to take their families home. Blunt pressured the Indian agents to cooperate, and Phillips assured Coffin and Harlan that the Cherokee Nation had been swept clear of Rebels. By April 2, Colonel Phillips occupied Park Hill and Fort Gibson, and Harlan had arrived at Tahlequah with 7,000 refugees. Others straggled in during the summer of 1864.[6]

The Cherokees dispersed, and the Union army and the agents established supply depots. Superintendent Coffin established his agency near Park Hill in the Cherokee Male Seminary building. The women, with help from the children, began planting crops while Phillips moved most of his force to Fort Gibson to erect earthworks. (He renamed the post Fort Blunt.) Phillips also moved the refugee train to Gibson and grazed his stock south of the post. At the beginning of May, Coffin informed Dole that the Indians had planted their crop but that Harlan had not sent him a census. Worse, he said, "General Blunt informs me that nearly all his

---

5 W. G. Coffin to Wm. P. Dole, February 24, 1863, Letters Received, Cherokee Agency. At the same time, Senator Lane and Senator Pomeroy were maneuvering in the Senate for the removal of all Kansas Indians to the south of Kansas border. David S. Buice, "The Civil War and the Five Civilized Tribes: A Study in Federal-Indian Relations" (PhD diss., University of Oklahoma, 1970), 150-159; Baird, *The Quapaw Indians*, 99-102; *Report of the Commissioner of Indian Affairs, 1862*, 143-144; *Report of the Commissioner of Indian Affairs, 1864*, 330; *Report of the Commissioner of Indian Affairs, 1865*, 292.

6 Abel, *The American Indian in the Civil War*, 255-60; OR 22, pt. 2, 55, 56, 60, 61, 85, 96-97, 100-101, 108-109, 111, 113-115, 121, 126, 137, 139, 147, 149, 153, 162-163, 165, 167, 168, 170, 181, 190-191; *Report to the Commissioner of Indian Affairs for the Year 1863*, 196.

forces have been drawn from him for the purpose of reinforcing Gen. Francis J. Herron in Missouri, and that he should not at all be surprised but what the force which is left with the Refugee Cherokees would have to fall back into Kansas."[7]

Eight Creek chiefs sent their "Great Father," President Lincoln, a lucid description of what they had been through: Opothleyahola's revolt, Kansas refugee camps, the failed return to their farms, and their current precarious position at Fort Gibson, with Rebel pickets on the south bank of the Arkansas River. "Now your help and protection we stand in need of very much," they wrote, "for they are not with us & we feel as if we are alone." At the highest level, the Union plan to return the refugees failed because they misunderstood the depth of the division between the full-bloods and mixed-bloods and the willingness of both parties to continue the contest.[8]

Stand Watie was not about to allow the full-bloods peaceful access to their farms when the mixed-bloods were denied access to theirs. Watie took control of the situation by disrupting the attempt to restore the full-blood refugees to their homes. On May 20, 1863, he led a raid on Fort Gibson that captured 1,500 cattle and killed 26 of Phillips' men. According to Phillips, 4,000-5,000 Rebels, including Texans from Van Buren, were massing south of him. Eight days later the Rebels crossed the river and attacked a supply train rolling out of Fort Scott, Kansas. When Phillips, who had anticipated the attack, repulsed the effort, the Rebels retreated south of the river. General Blunt ordered the 1st Kansas Colored Infantry at Baxter Springs to reinforce Phillips at Gibson, but the regiment was slow in arriving. Blunt had no other troops to send because General Schofield had sent eight regiments and three batteries east to take part in Grant's Vicksburg campaign.[9]

On or about June 3, Watie crossed his command of some 800 men over the Arkansas River 28 miles below Fort Gibson, kicking off a long raid through the Cookson Hills to Park Hill and Tahlequah until June 16. "Rebel Indians, under the command of Stand Waitie," reported the Cherokee agent at the latter place, "entered the Territory and robbed the women and children of everything they

---

7 W. G. Coffin to Wm. P. Dole, May 2, 1863, OIA; Schofield sent Herron and eight regiments to support Grant at Vicksburg. OR 24, pt. 1, 96-103; *Report of the Commissioner of Indian Affairs, 1863*, 175, 179, 195-196, 196-197, 199-200, 204; OR 22, pt. 2, 276-277; Britton, *The Union Indian Brigade in the Civil War*, 206-207.

8 Creek Chiefs to the President of the United States, May 16, 1863, Letters Received, OIA, Creek Agency.

9 OR 22, pt. 1, 337-338, 341-342; Knight, *Red Fox*, 151-154, 156-157.

could find, and took off horses, cattle, wagon, farming utensils, &c., drove off the inhabitants, and laid open their farms to be entered and eaten up by stock. . . . Robbing, sometimes murdering and burning . . . without abatement." The refugees, he continued, "were compelled to leave their crops and homes and seek protection at Fort Gibson."[10]

Watie divided his Confederates into two groups at Tahlequah. One under his personal command rode to Maysville while the other rode to Evansville (both on the Arkansas line), where they continued harassing the full-bloods. The groups reunited on Spavinaw Creek and attempted to cross to the west bank of the Grand River, but the water was too high. Riding downriver, they attempted another crossing at Salina but met the same problem. Watie then guided his men through Tahlequah on the afternoon of June 15. Major John Foreman, Phillips' most trusted officer, was trailing Watie with elements of the Third Indian. Notified of their whereabouts, Phillips put 500 men in the field. A skirmish ensued that killed seven Rebels. After Col. Douglas Cooper made a demonstration on the south bank of the Arkansas River before crossing some Texans and Choctaws to reinforce Watie, the Rebels rode south along the Arkansas and finally crossed at Webber's Falls.[11]

On July 11, 1863, the same day Blunt arrived at Fort Gibson before the Battle of Honey Springs, Superintendent Coffin was at Leavenworth preparing a supply train for Fort Gibson. To determine conditions at Gibson, Coffin had sent his clerk, Henry Smith, with the earlier train that became involved in the First Battle of Cabin Creek. Smith reported back to Coffin on July 16 that Phillips had secured an area one and one-half miles square for the Indian Brigade and about 6,000 Creek, Seminole, and Cherokee refugees, mostly women and children. Phillips planned to move Harlan and the Cherokees to Tahlequah, but deteriorating conditions led to an agreement by the agents (and even Phillips himself) that repatriation of the refugees should be halted.[12]

On August 8, Harlan recommended the refugees be taken back to Kansas. Coffin concurred, and on the last day of the month, while Commissioner Dole was away inspecting conditions in Kansas and the Cherokee Nation, Coffin notified the acting commissioner of Indian affairs, Charles Mix, that he, agents Harlan and

10 *Report of the Commissioner of Indian Affairs, 1863*, 179.

11 Ibid., 348-352; *OR* 22, pt. 2, 310-311.

12 *Report to the Commissioner of Indian Affairs, 1863*, 210-213.

Proctor, and Colonel Phillips recommended moving all willing refugees back to Kansas. He estimated only 2,000 would voluntarily return.[13]

By September, government officials were considering how to proceed. Agent Harlan wrote Superintendent Coffin that Congress should appropriate $400,000 in addition to the Cherokees' annual interest payment. Coffin reported to Dole that he was unsure how the 7,000 refugees in the Cherokee Nation and those who remained behind in Kansas could be supported. He knew it would be expensive and requested an additional $300,000 for that fiscal year. Phillips still thought the refugees should return to Kansas for the winter, but George A. Cutler, the Creek agent, believed that if the traffic on the Arkansas River could be placed under Union control and the refugees were properly defended, the quality of the country would allow them to live independently after one year.[14]

An important additional factor that would affect the fate of the refugees was the fiscal schemes dreamed up by Senator Lane, General Blunt, and those in league with them. The interests of the refugees were not their primary concern. Much more important was the money that could be made by defrauding the government through contracts to supply the refugees and the army commissary and quartermaster. The fraud was accomplished through collusion with suppliers, chiefly McDonald and Company, in which Lane and Blunt were silent partners entitled to 25 percent of the profits.[15]

Reports of "abuses and irregularities" concerning the commissary in Blunt's district cast suspicion on the general even before his victory at Honey Springs. On May 24, 1863, President Lincoln replaced General Curtis, the commander of the Department of Missouri and an ally of Senator Lane and General Blunt, with Maj. Gen. John M. Schofield. The move alarmed Lane, who had campaigned to organize a new department with Blunt as its commander. Lincoln hoped that Schofield could stop the political infighting on the western border between the conservative faction of the Republican party, led by Missouri Governor Hamilton R. Gamble, and the radical faction led by Lane. Lincoln had not removed General Curtis because of any particular malfeasance, but because he was in Lane's camp. The president wanted Schofield to govern fairly and remain above the factionalism. "If both factions, or neither, shall abuse you," he advised Schofield, "you will

---

13 Ibid., 215-218.

14 Ibid., 176, 178, 183.

15 Castel, *Frontier State at War*, 83-85.

probably be about right. Beware of being assailed by one and praised by the other."[16]

Shortly after taking command, Schofield ordered that contracts to supply the quartermaster and commissary at Fort Leavenworth have the approval of the "chief quartermaster and commissary of the department."[17] At the suggestion of Gen. Robert Allen, the department's chief quartermaster, Schofield limited Blunt's access to the Leavenworth quartermaster, Maj. L. C. Easton, by assigning Blunt to northern Kansas and Fort Scott. Blunt ignored Schofield's order and continued to arrange contracts that were profitable to him, and even tried to continue giving orders concerning contracts to Easton until that officer complained to General Allen.[18]

"I am endeavoring to correct the irregularities and abuses to which my attention has been called by the headquarters of the army," Schofield appealed to General Halleck on July 5. "The order and decision from which General Blunt appeals were made with that object." When Halleck confirmed that Major Easton was no longer subject to Blunt's orders, Schofield prepared to relieve Blunt entirely if he did not comply with the proposed directives.[19]

Blunt was fully aware of the charges Schofield was making and that the new department commander had previously criticized him in a lengthy letter to Halleck. Justifiably worried about what might be coming, Blunt began making wild accusations against his enemies, specifically Governor Carney of Kansas, Governor Gamble of Missouri, and General Schofield. On July 26, 1863, a little over a week after the Honey Springs fight, Blunt defended himself against the charges of "abuses and irregularities" to Secretary of War Edwin Stanton. His "irregularities," Blunt suggested sarcastically, were his victories at Cane Hill, Prairie Grove, and Honey Springs. He labeled Major Easton a "traitor" and called Carney and Superintendent Coffin embezzlers. "Two greater thieves do not live," he alleged. "Their wholesale robbery of those poor, unfortunate refugee Indians is so gross and outrageous that their names are a stench in the nostrils of every loyal Indian—man, woman, and child." Blunt wasn't finished. He accused his enemies in Kansas and Missouri of being pro-slavery, and demanded Carney file formal

---

16 John M. Schofield, *Forty-Six Years in the Army* (New York, NY, 1897), 68-69.

17 *OR* 22, pt. 2, 327.

18 Castel, *Frontier State at War*, 154-155; *OR* 22, pt. 2, 326-327.

19 Ibid., 319, 326-327, 392-393; Robert Steven Jones, "General James G. Blunt and the Civil War in the Trans-Mississippi West" (MA thesis, Oklahoma State University, 1990), 138-141.

charges about his treatment of civilians to President Lincoln so there could be a "court of inquiry."[20]

On July 31, Blunt sent Lincoln a similar letter that accused Schofield of "cowardice and imbecility." Blunt charged that Carney, Gamble, and others were conspiring with Schofield to withhold reinforcements to Fort Gibson in order to destroy him. The last half of the letter recounted his victory at Honey Springs.[21]

Lincoln followed his own advice not to take sides in the conflict between the conservative and the radical Republican factions. What most angered him was the usurpation of civil law at Atchison, Kansas, where civilians had been lynched. Lincoln telegraphed Blunt to report to him on this matter before he made a decision on whether to relieve him, which could account for the lapse of three weeks before the president replied to the general's unbecoming tirade. "I regret to find you denouncing so many persons as liars, scoundrels, fools, thieves, and persecutors of yourself," he informed Blunt on August 18. Concerning Blunt's military situation, Lincoln acknowledged, "Your military position looks critical, but did anybody force you into it? Have you been ordered to confront and fight 10,000 men with 3,000 men?" Lincoln reassured Blunt that he was generally satisfied with his actions, but there was "one thing [that] dissatisfied" him: Blunt's interference in a civilian court case "twenty-five miles outside your lines" and handing the defendants over to a "mob to be hanged. . . . Judge Lynch sometimes takes jurisdiction of cases . . . but this is the first case within my knowledge wherein . . . the military has come to [his] assistance."[22]

That August and September Schofield ordered three officers, Col. J. V. DuBois and Capts. S. C. Benham and R. A. Howard, to investigate the charges of "gross frauds and corruption in the administration of the staff, departments in those Districts" under Blunt's command.[23] The investigation did not take long. On October 2, Schofield telegraphed Halleck of his intention to relieve Blunt. Knowing his removal would complicate his relations with Senator Lane—whose political support Lincoln still needed—the president told Schofield to wait. Lane was a leading supporter of Lincoln for the Republican Party's nomination for a

---

20 *OR* 22, pt. 2, 398-399.

21 Ibid., 53, 565-566; Blunt, "Account of His Civil War Experiences," 239-241.

22 *OR* 53, 567.

23 J. M. Schofield to E. D. Townsend, October 3, 1863, Letters Received, Office of Adjutant General, Main Series, 1861–1870, National Archives, microcopy #619, roll 190, hereafter referred to as Schofield Report. There are 115 pages of reports, letters, circulars, and inspections in this record.

second term, while Kansas Senator Samuel Pomeroy was openly supporting Secretary of the Treasury Salmon P. Chase.[24]

Lincoln asked Schofield to forward the allegations against Blunt—but not his recommendations for action. Schofield responded that he sought permission to "dismiss from the service . . . such commissioned officers in this department as are well known to be worthless or incompetent, and, generally, such delinquents as would in my judgment be infallibly dismissed if brought before a court-martial." Halleck warned Schofield that the recommendations would only make more enemies for him, but reassured the general that they would generally be followed.[25]

In fact, the reports generated by the investigation that Schofield had received and forwarded to Lincoln contained no direct evidence against Blunt. DuBois told Schofield that he could not prove the allegations because he did not have the power to place men under oath, but that there were so many men involved in corruption, fraudulent transactions, and moral outrages that DuBois "became convinced that Sodom was a pure city compared to the Kansas Border." Two men involved in the graft at Leavenworth had told Senator Lane that unless they were promoted to colonel, they would "blow the whole concern[,] Lane, Blunt, & Babcock." Lane, who as a brigadier general controlled the promotion of officers, made sure the blackmailing officers were promptly promoted. With their demand granted, they remained silent. DuBois learned from Governor Carey that Lane and Blunt received a percentage of the profits for supplying beef to the army. There were also reports of false claims for forage paid by the quartermaster, and numerous other charges. When DuBois asked officers why they had not pressed charges, they replied, "Because they are Lane's friends & I can get no promotion in Kansas if I offend his Party." A cavalry captain at Webber's Falls detailed profiteering by officers of the 13th Kansas Infantry during their forays into Missouri, but this thievery was mostly on a small scale, amounting only to the theft of a blooded horse, a wagon and a team, and trunks of undisclosed contents.[26]

24 William Frank Zornow, *Lincoln and the Party Divided* (Norman, OK, 1954), 23-40; William Frank Zornow, "The Kansas Senators and the Re-election of Lincoln," in *Kansas Historical Quarterly* (May 1951), Issue 19, 133-144.

25 OR 22, pt. 2, 597; H. W. Halleck to Schofield, Washington, October 12, 1864, Schofield Papers, Halleck file, box 40, Library of Congress. The reply is obviously to "your letter to Col Townsend of the 3rd," dated October 3, 1863. The date on this copy is in conflict with the record cited in following note dated October 12, 1863. OR 22, pt. 2, 319, 586, 588, 595-597.

26 OR 22, pt. 2, 595-597. He did not severely criticize General Ewing, who commanded the Department of the Border, which was also under inspection together with the Department of the Frontier. There is some confusion about the terms "department" and "district." Schofield

The report filed by Captains Howard and Benham was equally suggestive and demonstrated the kind of large-scale fraud perpetrated on the government by Blunt and his cronies. The two officers found that only the 2nd Colorado Infantry and the 1st Kansas Colored Infantry could drill properly. Discipline was wanting everywhere. Their analysis of the military situation in the Indian Nations was accurate to the point of prescience. "In the country through which we passed, which had evidently been well settled, not a house was left from . . . spoilation. . . . They had been destroyed by Union troops. . . . The only portion of this country within our possession," continued the report, "are the garrisoned towns and posts. No persons can travel over it in safety without an escort. . . . The supply trains are not safe from capture."[27]

As an example of the fraud, Howard and Benham detailed the purchase by the Fort Scott quartermaster of 1,115 cavalry horses, 151 artillery horses, and 325 mules from September 10, 1862 to June 27, 1863. These purchases were from a single contractor at Leavenworth who had gained favor initially through competitive bidding. On May 29, 1863, Blunt discontinued competitive bidding by making the price for cavalry horses no higher than the current contract price of $129.45. Howard and Benham charged that subsequent purchases of horses and mules, compared with local availability at more competitive prices, could have resulted in defrauding the government of $15,000. The investigators also questioned Blunt's decision to supply 500 horses at $129.45 each from Leavenworth to a Kansas regiment in Springfield, when its proper quartermaster was in St. Louis, where cavalry horses were available for just $103.50 each.[28]

There was also a report that persons bidding for the U.S. Army's beef contract were told that they had been underbid and were paid $100 to be absent when the bids were opened. On top of all this, cattle belonging to the Indians were being stolen. Howard and Benham also charged that Fort Gibson was not being properly supplied from Fort Scott, and in a separate report Howard stated that the horses and mules at Gibson were in a deplorable condition, "all more or less unfit for service from starvation." Their condition further facilitated the cattle theft by reducing the number of patrols capable of preventing it. The remainder of the

---

also planned to replace Kansas and Missouri troops with troops from other areas who did not carry local prejudices. John V. Dubois to Schofield, October 2, 1863, Schofield Report.

27 Robert A. Howard and S. C. Benham to J. V. DuBois, October 2, 1863; H. R. Neal to Dubois, September 8, 1863, Schofield Report.

28 Thomas Moonlight to M. H. Insley, May 29, 1863, Schofield Report.

inspection concerned the generally poor condition of Blunt's command, one that could only be improved "when the crowd of dishonest speculators and contractors . . . are driven off by the exercise of a correct military discipline and a worthier example of soldierly conduct exhibited by the officers it will resume its position as an army of American soldiers."[29]

Before Schofield could take action against Blunt, however, that officer saw action of his own. On October 4, 1863, Blunt left Fort Scott to take his command to Fort Smith. He traveled with a 14-piece band and a bandwagon pulled by six mules. A 12-year-old drummer boy and a journalist from *Leslie's Weekly* rode with the band. The wife of an officer at Fort Gibson also joined the procession in a buggy driven by cavalryman Charles Davis. Among Blunt's officers was Maj. Henry Curtis, son of Gen. Samuel R. Curtis. Blunt also brought along eight wagons to carry his official papers, personal banner and sword, and supplies needed at Fort Smith. Forty-five troopers of Company I, 14th Kansas Cavalry, and 40 troopers the 3rd Wisconsin Cavalry, mostly new recruits, provided an escort.[30]

On October 6, the column approached Baxter Springs, a few miles north of the Kansas line on the Fort Scott to Fort Gibson road. Fort Baxter, commanded by Lt. James Pond, had been constructed that July. One writer described it as "consist[ing] of some log cabins with a total frontage of about 100 feet, facing east toward Spring river. Back of the fort, and of the same width, was a large space enclosed by embankments of earth thrown up against logs and about 4 feet high." Blunt's wagons were so spread out by the time the train was approaching the fort that Blunt ordered a halt so they could come together and so the bandwagon could be moved to the front of the line for his grand arrival. While the train fell into place, Blunt noticed about 100 men in blue emerge from the woods on horseback 500 yards to the east. For a few moments Blunt thought Lieutenant Pond was drilling his cavalry. In fact it was not Lieutenant Pond at all, but William Clarke Quantrill and his infamous raiders.[31]

---

29 Robert A. Howard to John V. DuBois, September 30, 1863; Robert A. Howard and S. C. Benham to J. V. DuBois, October 2, 1863, Schofield Report.

30 OR 22, pt. 1, 688, 693; Blunt, "Account of His Civil War Experiences," 247; Edward E. Leslie, *The Devil Knows How to Ride: The True Story of William Clarke Quantrill and his Confederate Raiders* (New York, NY, 1996), 272-273; Castel, *Frontier State at War*, 159-160.

31 OR 22, 688-689, 693-694, Blunt, "Account of His Civil War Experiences," 247; Castel, *Frontier State at War*, 160; Albert Castel, *William Clarke Quantrill: His Life and Times* (New York, NY, 1999), 151; Leslie, *The Devil Knows How to Ride*, 273; William Elsey Connelley, *Quantrill and the Border Wars* (New York, NY, 1956), 422, 424. Fort Baxter is also called Fort Blair.

The Rebel guerrilla chief, born in Ohio but associated with war-torn Kansas and Missouri, had decided to spend the winter in Texas. His route out of Missouri, however, carried him near Fort Baxter and what he thought was a target of opportunity. The Union garrison consisted of only 25 white cavalrymen and 65-70 men from the 2nd Kansas Colored Infantry. Quantrill divided his command into two columns. His own caught some of the garrison, mostly black troops from the 2nd Kansas Colored Infantry, out on the prairie. The Rebel riders killed some and drove the rest back into the fort's earthworks. The second column charged the fort directly. Some managed to get inside, where Lieutenant Poole rallied his men and repulsed them. Lieutenant Poole was later awarded the Medal of Honor for his defense of the small bastion. An intervening ridge prevented Blunt and his command from hearing or seeing any of this, even though they were only about 400 yards north of the fighting. Quantrill's divided command was moving back out toward the prairie when Blunt made his unexpected appearance. It was unfortunate timing for which the general and men would pay a steep price.[32]

The undisciplined manner in which the first mounted force approached convinced Blunt something was amiss. The suspicious general formed his two companies into a line of battle and ordered the train, clerks, and band to the rear. Only about 65 inexperienced Union cavalrymen held the line. Quantrill's troopers advanced to within 300 yards when Blunt rode ahead of his men. Some of the Rebels opened fire as they rode, and the entire force was joined by two companies that had been concealed in the woods. The 100 riders had suddenly swelled to as many as 300.[33]

Quantrill's men had fired only a few shots before Blunt's entire force bolted. A furious Blunt had no choice but to join them. The guerrillas were better mounted than his cavalrymen and quickly caught up with them. Once they did, the killing began. Blunt, who was well mounted, rode west with Major Curtis until a large ravine or gully blocked their way. (A number of his escort cavalrymen would later be found dead in that ravine.) With little choice in the matter, Blunt leaped his horse across. Although thrown onto the horse's neck, he somehow managed to hold on for another mile before regaining his saddle. Curtis's mount took a shot in the flank just as it prepared to make the jump. The horse fell with its rider into the

32 Castel, *William Clarke Quantrill*, 144-150; Leslie, *Devil Knows How to Ride*, 257-270; William Elsey Connelley, *Quantrill and the Border Wars* (New York: Pageant Book Co., 1909), 421-422.

33 OR 22, pt. 1, 688-689, 693-695, 700-701; Blunt "Account of His Civil War Experiences," 247-248; Castel, *Frontier State at War*, 160; Castel, *William Clarke Quantrill*, 150-151; Leslie, *The Devil Knows How to Ride*, 273-274; Connelley, *Quantrill and the Border Wars*, 425-427.

gully, throwing Curtis free before it regained its footing and ran wild about the field. Trapped, Curtis surrendered and handed his pistol to an unnamed guerrilla, who promptly shot him through the head with it and announced to anyone within earshot that he had just killed General Blunt.[34]

Blunt's band members tried to get away to the southwest in their wagon, and one of them killed a guerrilla who rode alongside demanding their surrender. After rumbling about 50 yards the wagon lost its left front wheel. The guerrillas attacked with the intent of killing the occupants, including the journalist from *Leslie's Weekly* and a 12-year-old boy. They threw their bodies onto the wagon and set it afire. The boy was later found 30 feet from the wagon with most of his clothes burned away. At the beginning of the massacre, Lydia Thomas, the wife of an officer at Fort Gibson, escaped when her driver turned their buggy west and drove the team full speed for three miles. The horses were spent, but Lydia and her driver managed to catch two riderless horses and rode away. They eventually found Blunt with the survivors of his command, which by that time numbered just 15 men.[35]

In his 1866 autobiographical sketch Blunt recalled that "in this affair eighty-seven men, including escort, clerks, teamsters, servants, and musicians were killed. All who fell wounded or were taken prisoner were inhumanely murdered."[36] Blunt and nine men left to shadow Quantrill while the rest made for Fort Scott, with one assigned to escort Lydia Thomas. After the massacre Quantrill and his men got drunk, ate a meal, and rode for the Cherokee Nation. Quantrill vetoed a second attack against Fort Baxter, but sent George Todd under a flag of truce to ask for Lieutenant Pond's surrender, which was refused. Although by that time most of the small garrison was dead, Todd promised to take care of the Union prisoners if Pool would treat guerrilla casualties. Pond agreed. Quantrill reported three of his men killed that day. One was placed in Blunt's ambulance. The raider had also captured two black men. One was known to them as having collaborated with the abolitionists and "Red Legs," or Jayhawkers. Once they arrived in the Cherokee Nation, they had the collaborator dig two graves in an abandoned garden. When he finished digging, they promptly killed and buried him and their

---

34 OR 22, pt. 1, 689, 691-692, 694-697, 701; Castel, *Frontier State at War*, 160; Castel, *William Clarke Quantrill*, 151; Leslie, *The Devil Knows How to Ride*, 274-275; Connelley, *Quantrill and the Border Wars*, 425-427.

35 Leslie, *Devil Knows How to Ride*, 274-277; OR 22, pt. 1, 689, 692, 695-696; Blunt, "Account of His Civil War Experiences," 247-248; Castel, *William Clarke Quantrill*, 151-152; Connelley, *Quantrill and the Border Wars*, 428-429.

36 Blunt, "Account of His Civil War Experiences," 248.

white casualty and moved on. The other captured black was spared because he had previously saved a member of Quantrill's band from arrest by Jayhawkers. He would become their barber once in Texas.[37]

Blunt left scouts to watch the guerrillas while he returned to the scene of the massacre. Quantrill crossed the Grand River and continued south to Cabin Creek, where he turned west to avoid Fort Gibson, crossed the Verdigris River, and turned south to cross the Arkansas River 18 miles above Gibson at Choska. There, the Rebel guerillas promptly murdered 12 Creek soldiers from Colonel Phillip's command. On October 11, the raiders camped on the North Canadian River and awoke to find themselves surrounded by Rebel Col. D. N. McIntosh and 1,500 Creek soldiers. Quantrill had been flying Blunt's flag, but when McIntosh found out the circumstances he took the raider to Cooper's camp, where they were given rations. Quantrill and his men stayed nearly a week with Cooper before proceeding to Colbert's Ferry. They spent the winter in the vicinity of Sherman, Texas.[38]

On October 19, General Schofield, with Washington's concurrence, relieved General Blunt from command at Fort Smith, ordered him to report to Leavenworth, and replaced him with Brig. Gen. John McNeil. Blunt received the news at Fort Scott, where he had gone following the massacre. He reported to Schofield that he would travel from Scott to Fort Gibson with supplies and 1,200 men before going on to Fort Smith to be relieved. Letters from Col. William Weer and Brig. Gen. Thomas Ewing imply the supplies to be carried by Blunt were provided by McDonald and Company. Weer suggested Blunt was carrying contraband, but McNeil inspected the train on December 1 and found only normal and much-needed supplies. At Fort Smith, Blunt found authorization from the secretary of war for him to organize the 11th U.S. Colored Infantry Regiment. On December 10, Blunt informed Stanton that the regiment was making progress and that he wished to be reassigned. However, he warned the war secretary that he would not report to Schofield, whom he accused of cowardice for not supporting his campaigns in 1862 and 1863. Blunt even read the letter aloud to General

---

37 Ibid.; *OR* 22, pt. 1, 699, 701; Barton, *Three Years with Quantrill*, 141-142; Castel, *Frontier State at War*, 160; Castel, *William Clarke Quantrill*, 152-154; Leslie, *The Devil Knows How to Ride*, 278-280; Connelley, *Quantrill and the Border Wars*, 434.

38 Chosky is spelled Choska on road maps, but the town no longer exists. *OR* 22, pt. 1, 689, 699, 700-701; Barton, *Three Years with Quantrill*, 142-144; Castel, *William Clarke Quantrill*, 153-154; Leslie, *The Devil Knows How to Ride*, 280-281; Connelley, *Quantrill and the Border Wars*, 435-436.

McNeil and his officers, one of whom, Captain Vaughan, he had accused of being Schofield's man.[39]

On New Year's Day 1864, Lincoln and Halleck divided the Department of Missouri into three departments, each commanded by someone acceptable to the local political power. General Curtis, with Blunt as his subordinate, received the Department of Kansas, which included Indian Territory and Fort Smith. Major General William S. Rosecrans received the Department of Missouri, and Maj. Gen. Frederick Steele the Department of Arkansas. Blunt, who had been summoned to Washington, discussed with Lincoln the prospects of a campaign into Texas. He arrived back at Fort Smith on March 12.[40]

To his dismay, Blunt reached Fort Smith only to discover that Halleck had transferred his troops to General Steele. Just over a month after his return, he replied to Commissioner of Indian Affairs William P. Dole's inquiry as to whether it was a good idea to return the remaining refugees "to their homes." Blunt explained that after two years of experience he was "clearly of the opinion that the best interests of the refugee Indians, as well as of the government, require that they should be removed to their homes at as early a day as practicable." Blunt lobbied Dole to use his influence to provide more troops to General Curtis, Blunt's immediate superior, and for the two western tiers of counties in Arkansas to be included in Curtis's new department. Blunt insisted that "Fort Smith must be the depot and base of all military operations in the Indian country, and also the depot for supplying the Indians," and where he would profit the most from their presence.[41]

In April, Col. William R. Judson complained to Brig. Gen. Nathan Kimball, commanding at Little Rock, about Blunt's interference in army supplies and his collusion with "McDowell & Co. for whose benefit this army has been run." General Kimball forwarded Judson's telegram to Halleck, who enclosed it in a confidential letter to Lt. Gen. U. S. Grant. Even without definitive proof, Halleck had heard enough about Blunt. He recommended that Indian Territory and Fort Smith be removed from Curtis's jurisdiction and attached to the Department of Arkansas, thus limiting the operations of Curtis and Blunt to the state of Kansas.

---

39 OR 22, pt. 2, 663, 666, 681-682, 689-690, 692-693, 727-728, 735-736; Blunt, "Account of His Civil War Experiences," 249-250.

40 OR 22, pt. 2, 666; OR 34, pt. 2, 7; Blunt, "Account of His Civil War Experiences," 249-250.

41 Blunt, "Account of His Civil War Experiences," 250; *Report of the Commissioner of Indian Affairs, 1864,* 322-323.

On April 16, 1864, Grant, by then the Army's commanding general, approved the change, and on April 17 General Orders No. 164 formalized Blunt's reassignment to Fort Leavenworth.[42]

The political maneuvering and deceit bothered Schofield enough to write about it in his memoirs after the war. "It was very difficult for me to comprehend the political necessity which compelled Mr. Lincoln to give his official countenance to such men as Lane and Blunt in Kansas," he mused, "but such necessity was thought to exist. I suppose a great statesman should use in the best way he can the worst materials as well as the best that are within his reach," he concluded, "and, if possible, make them all subserve the great purposes he has to accomplish."[43]

---

42 OR 34, pt. 3, 79-80, 160-161, 178, 196.

43 Schofield, *Forty-Six Years in the Army*, 11-12. Schofield was eventually rewarded for aiding Grant's Vicksburg campaign and cooperating with Lincoln and Halleck with a corps command during the Atlanta campaign under Sherman. He successfully commanded Union forces at the Battle of Franklin below Nashville on November 30, 1864, against a massive assault by Gen. John B. Hood's Army of Tennessee. Schofield followed Sherman and Sheridan as commander in chief of the U.S. Army (1888-1895). Boatner, *Civil War Dictionary*, 726-727.

Fort Gibson

By the spring of 1864, agent Justin J. Harlan had made his own assessment of the conditions in the Cherokee Nation. Not surprisingly, it differed markedly from General Blunt's official reports.

Superintendent Coffin had requested that Harlan provide a census of the Indians. "In your letter of November 10, 1863," replied the frustrated agent, "you inform me that in March next you intend to remove the Indians now in Kansas to their homes, and ask my advice as to what seeds and farming implements should be furnished them." The removal order triggered Harlan to candidly list the multiple problems that paralyzed his embattled Fort Gibson post from all sides. "[Phillips] keep[s] the whole Indian force wholly idle," he began. "Jayhawk the country for cattle for use and abuse —horses to run off to Kansas—all the corn they can use and destroy—and garden vegetables—and when they have gotten all they could find—leave Stand Watie to glean and return to Fort Gibson." The women and children work hard and suffer, he explained. They "shall have raised more corn and potatoes, recruited what horses are left them, and gathered together their for beef and milk, upon which they can make out a scanty subsistence. . . . The adored Stand Watie and his thieves and murderers," he added, "come . . . when they please, stay as long as they please, steal as much as they please." Harlan wasn't finished: "We have not been able to take [a census] and never will while the rebels hold all the country, as they do out of the reach of the guns of Fort Gibson."[1]

---

1 J. Harlan to Wm. G. Coffin, December 7, 1863, Letters Received, Cherokee Agency, OIA.

The agent did keep track of the refugees who applied for provisions, and he soon recognized that many did not apply at all, or lived too far away along the Arkansas border to reach the post. They had been robbed of all their belongings, including their horses. Men and older boys were in danger of being killed, and women and children of being robbed. Still, new applicants arrived daily. By this time the number of Cherokees registered for relief totaled 7,280. Add in Creeks and Seminoles and the number reached 8,002. More would come down in the summer of 1864, swelling the number to around 16,000—not including the men comprising the Indian Brigade.

Harlan complained of the soldiers "drinking, dancing, sleeping, getting sober and getting well of sundry diseases not brought on by any particular piety." Although Colonel Phillips had sent out three modest patrols, Harlan pointed out that there was no real opposition to the Rebel raiders, who crossed the Arkansas River easily just 15 miles from the fort. "[H]undreds of families," he added, were "without a single article of bed clothing and winter upon them."[2]

The Cherokee leadership attempted to improve the difficult conditions. On January 8, 1864, acting chief Smith Christy and others sent a plan to Colonel Phillips to establish three communities at places where there was housing and fenced farms in the districts of Tahlequah, Saline, and Sequoyah. They wanted the military, in the form of mounted Cherokees under Christy's command, to protect these communities from Rebel raiders. The federal government, they added, could deliver tools and seed for planting in spring. They proposed a general pardon for all deserters. If the government was unable or unwilling to implement this plan, they explained, "500 picked men" from the Indian Brigade under the control of the "Cherokee National Executive" could act as a militia to protect the new communities, with the remainder of the brigade mustered out of the army to farm.[3]

In February, Maj. Gen. Samuel Curtis inspected Kansas and the Cherokee Nation from Fort Scott to Fort Gibson, the Arkansas River valley to Van Buren, and then back to Fort Scott. The land was excellent, he reported to President Lincoln, and "cattle and hogs run wild[,] . . . but the Indians have entirely abandoned their widely scattered farms, and there is no other food in the country."

2 J. Harlan [to Coffin], December 7, 1863, Letters Received, OIA. This is a separate letter from note 1 of the same date; Confer, *The Cherokee Nation in the Civil War*, 123-124.

3 Smith Christy to William Phillips, January 8, 1864, in Samuel Curtis Papers, State Historical Society of Iowa, Des Moines. This letter is also in Letters Received, Cherokee Agency, OIA.

Curtis' inspection included some of the refugee camps, and the experience apparently had a strong effect on him.[4]

The *Cherokee Tomahawk* described Fort Gibson and its surroundings thusly. "If it was in Kansas, it would be called a city. . . . Together with its suburbs—Log Town—Mud Town— Skin Town, etc. . . . Although not exactly a 'City of Refuge,' it may be styled a refugee city. . . . It has a saw-mill, . . . a ferry boat and a bakery, warranted pure. . . . The hopeful look for that millennium when a railroad shall run down Grand River, and . . . Quarter Masters cease to reign on earth."[5]

"The bottom across Grand River is full of Creeks who have built a great many cabins and cut down nearly all the timber across there," observed William P. Ross. "Your Uncle George's steam mill is put up on the opposite bank of the Grand River near the ferry landing and we frequently hear its puff and whistle. A great many cabins have been put up also on this side of the river, all around us," he continued. "Fred and Juno, Dred and Caroline, and a good many others of the colored folks live around here. There are several stores here besides ours but we have much custom."[6]

General Curtis wrote to Secretary of the Interior John P. Usher that he was aware of the request to establish guarded farming communities, but neither he nor Colonel Phillips was about to make promises they could not keep. The cost of feeding refugees at Fort Gibson, explained Curtis, was much higher than feeding them in Kansas, and Kansas officials needed to understand the situation before sending more refugees south to Gibson. Equally important, the Indian Brigade, far from being disbanded, had to be reinforced if Curtis was going to secure the area. He told President Lincoln that he needed at least 15,000 troops, although he despaired about ever getting them. "Hoping Mr. President that in the great army movements which you have to consider," penned Curtis, "you will indulge me in anxious petitions in favor of your devoted but much neglected friends in this Department. I have heard much of the troubles of Kansas," he continued, "but my personal observations during the past four weeks have brought to my notice more of the havoc of war and savage cruelty and infamous barbarity on the part of rebel foes than human imagination can confess." Curtis concluded, "I have returned to

---

4 S. R. Curtis to A. Lincoln, February 28, 1864, in Curtis Papers.

5 "A Frivolous History of Fort Gibson" (1939), unpublished typescript in Special Collections, Northeastern State University, Tahlequah, OK, 276.

6 Ibid., 274.

Headquarters after 800 miles of travel a wiser but sadder soldier in your devoted service."[7]

The deteriorating conditions in the Cherokee Nation were further reflected by the ongoing attempts of the northern Cherokee leadership to establish an orphanage there. On April 12, 1864, Superintendent Coffin strongly urged approval of a proposal submitted by the Cherokee leaders to Commissioner of Indian Affairs William P. Dole. Thirteen members of the National Council had signed the letter in the Cherokee syllabary with English names alongside. Twelve were members of either the lower or upper house of the Cherokee legislature, and the last was a supreme court judge. They proposed using the Female Seminary building in Park Hill to shelter, feed, and educate 1,000 orphans, as well as 1,200 children whose fathers had been killed but whose mothers were still living. The previous fall, the National Council had created a board of trustees to receive money from the Cherokee Orphan Fund, only to be reminded by U.S. officials that Cherokee funds were now invested in Confederate securities. Having gotten nowhere on that occasion, they were trying again through their agent. The Cherokee leadership argued that the U.S. government was obligated by treaty to the Cherokees and that the funds must be found elsewhere and distributed to their treasurer, Lewis Ross. Federal authorities were unable to do much of anything to help the refugees at Fort Gibson, and local authorities were doing all they could to exploit them. Their only protectors were Colonel Phillips and the Indian agents.[8]

Adding to the Indians' woes, General Blunt found yet another way to use them for his personal gain. In addition to his fraudulent handling of supplies to the refugees, it became fairly clear to observers by the summer of 1864 that he, Senator Lane, and others were profiting from the theft of Indian cattle. On September 2, 1863, agent Harlan had reported that less than six months earlier thousands of cattle had been grazing west of the Grand River, but now few were to be seen. "From the best information, entirely reliable, I can get," he explained, "I think it safe to say that more than four-fifths have been taken by white men professing loyalty to the United States, or by those in their employ." Blunt was no longer in control at Fort Smith, but he still had influence in Kansas. His participation in the

---

7 S. R. Curtis to J. P. Usher, March 11, 1864, Letters Received, Cherokee Agency, OIA; S. R. Curtis to A. Lincoln, February 28, 1864.

8 Smith Christy, Act. Principal Chief, et al. to Justin Harlan, March 19, 1864; J. Harlan to W. G. Coffin, March 17, 1864, W. G. Coffin to William P. Dole, April 12, 1864, Letters Received, Cherokee Agency, OIA. The March 19 letter may be a later copy.

ongoing defrauding of the government is difficult to follow, but Senator Lane and McDonald & Company were still involved, and it is likely Blunt was as well.[9]

Colonel Phillips might have been able to control the cattle thefts, but by October of 1863 his brigade was no longer mounted and the land was too vast to cover on foot. The Indian Brigade was designated officially as infantry, but had operated as mounted infantry by providing their own horses. Rough use and poor forage had rendered their remaining horses all but worthless. Phillips tried unsuccessfully through the winter of 1863 and into the spring of 1864 to acquire fresh mounts. Henry Halleck sympathized with Phillips' plight, but Maj. Gen. Frederick Steele and Brig. Gen. John M. Thayer dismissed Phillips' request as too expensive.

On July 10, 1864, Colonel Phillips gave General Thayer a new reason to buy horses. He had arrested nine men, whites and Indians, with a herd of stolen cattle on the Verdigris River near the Kansas border. Phillips's men killed the two leaders trying to escape. These men had been paying the others $5.00 a day to drive cattle north into Kansas. Phillips also reported a herd of 800 head at Osage Mission, and griped that he could do little without cavalry. His complaint was demonstrably true considering the size of the tall grass prairie stretching from the Arkansas River across the Verdigris River valley to the Grand River, and from the Kansas border south to Three Forks. When Thayer denied Phillips's request to mount the Indian Brigade, the vast Indian cattle herds were left exposed. The cattle were mostly owned by mixed-blood ranchers whose loyalties were with the South.[10]

Colonel Phillips ordered Capt. H. S. Anderson to ride to Kansas and investigate the cattle thefts. On July 19, Phillips was able to report that at least 6,000–7,000 cattle with Cherokee and Creek brands had been stolen during just the last month, with many taken as far north as Fort Scott. Whites were using the Osages as scouts. On July 30 and without any explanation, General Thayer relieved Phillips of his command and ordered him to Fort Smith, where he was immersed in court martial duty. In other words, effectively rendering him unable to interfere with the cattle theft.[11]

The Indian agents also began to notice irregularities. Agent Upson wrote Commissioner Dole that no habitat in any of the United States territories was

9 *Report of the Commissioner of Indian Affairs, 1863,* 180.

10 Robert A. Howard to John V. DuBois, September 30, 1863, Letters Received, by the Adjutant General; *OR* 41, pt. 2, 107-108, 123-124.

11 Ibid., 265, 476.

better suited than the Indian lands for raising cattle, and he regretted that they were being stolen—not just by the Rebels, but by Unionists as well. On June 15, 1864, Superintendent Coffin, who had just arrived at Fort Gibson with 5,000 more refugees, reported that groups of whites and loyal Wichitas had been driving cattle north for the last two years and selling them cheaply to whites.[12]

The main culprit was McDonald & Company. The company did not purchase the stolen cattle directly, preferring instead that thieves—sometimes with the aid of Wichita and Osage guides—drive the beef north to Kansas. There, the cattle were sold for pennies on the dollar to "cattle brokers" working with McDonald & Company, who then purchased them at prices well below what the federal government was charged. In return the company made large profits selling the livestock to the U.S. Army and to the Office of Indian affairs, which then used the beef to supply the refugee Indians. By the end of the war, virtually all of the Cherokee and Creek stock, between 250,000 and 300,000 head, had been stolen. Lane and Blunt received 25 percent of the profits for not interfering with the massive theft. In one case, the senator and the general each received $20,000—their share of a single six-month contract to supply the refugees with food.[13]

The corruption was first exposed in 1864 by Colonel Phillips and then in 1865 by the Indian agents. Phillips, who believed he had been relieved of his command through the "influence of McDonald & Company," joined a campaign in Kansas newspapers against the fraud and corruption. On August 4, a contributor from Fort Smith signed only as "Refugee" wrote to the *Kansas State Journal* complaining that "the least respectable of the Red Leg organization . . . are running the machine with a vengeance. During the past week hundreds after hundreds of mules and horses have crossed the river en route to Kansas. . . . A few are growing rich," he observed. "McDonald in a year will make a million dollars. He has the beef contract at ten dollars a cwt [hundredweight]."[14]

A month later on September 8, the newspaper *White Cloud Kansas Chief* ran a reprint from the August 25 *Atchison Champion* in the form of several questions for

---

12 *Report of the Commissioner of Indian Affairs, 1864*, 32, 303-305.

13 Ibid.; *Report of the Commissioner of Indian Affairs for the Year 1865, 1866*, 252, 271, 273, 286; *New York Tribune*, May 21, 1866; *Boston* [MA] *Commonwealth*, May 26, 1866, June 2, 1866; OR 41, pt. 4, 605.

14 OR 41, pt. 2, 476, 605-606; Wyant, "Colonel William A. Phillips and the Civil War in the Indian Territory," 71-73; Annie Heloise Able, *The American Indian Under Reconstruction* (Lincoln, NE, 1994), 85-89; *Lawrence Kansas State Journal*, August 4, 1864.

Senator Lane: "What percent of the proceeds of the sale of 2000 head of cattle, stolen from the Indian Country . . . is to be given to the 'Corruption Fund' that your friends claim already amounts to $100,000, to see to your re-election to the United States Senate next winter?" Concerning cattle theft: "Fifteen thousand eight hundred dollars was recently received for a drove of cattle stolen from the Indian country. One of your particular friends received the money in Leavenworth. How much was your share?" It also reported that Lane allowed others to profit from the refugee Indian supplies in return for his political support, and that they had offered Colonel Phillips $7,000 to let the "hay contract at Fort Gibson 'run easy.'"

Five weeks later, the same paper featured a long address by Phillips in support of the reelection of President Lincoln that fall. The first paragraph concerned Lane, the upcoming Senate race, and "the greatest indignities and perversions of power that ever disgraced a State." Phillips threatened, "Knowing what I do, I cannot remain silent and see six years more of oligarchy, corruption, and overthrow of your legitimate authority."[15]

On October 28, Maj. Gen. George Sykes, commanding the District of South Kansas out of Lawrence, alerted General Curtis to the growing cattle problem. "In regard, General, to the cattle business," began Sykes, "I see but one way to control it, and that is to seize all cattle coming from the Indian Territory into the State, and hold them for the benefit of the government. Two-thirds of them are stolen," he added, "and the Government has a far better right to them than thieves."[16]

Major General Francis J. Herron, who was looking into the corruption at Forts Smith and Gibson, showed his appreciation for Phillips's bold stand by arranging for him to take command again at Fort Gibson. A visit to the latter place convinced Herron that the fort required a strong and honest hand. "[M]atters [are] controlled here by the same influence that governs at Fort Smith, and indeed the same that governs the entire District of the Frontier," Herron explained to Phillips. "The contract to furnish them supplies is let every six months, and for the first six months of 1864 was taken by A. McDonald & Co."[17]

Herron's advocacy of Phillips to command the post included the declaration that he "is the best officer they have ever had in the Indian Brigade. . . . [He] was removed by the influence of McDonald and Co." Herron strongly suggested he be

---

15 *White Cloud (Kansas) Chief,* September 8, October 13, 1864.

16 *OR* 41, pt. 3, 461-462.

17 Ibid., pt. 4, 605.

reinstated. His wish was granted, and Phillips resumed command of the Union Indian Brigade on December 29, 1864.[18]

Phillips had wanted to carry on his campaign against corruption when he received the order to take command at Gibson. "I would have preferred to meet and expose the powerful organization that I fear is not dead yet," he wrote Herron. "I was willing to stake my reputation on the struggle, but God knows best." He also did his best to restore discipline at the fort, although in responding to instructions to protect Indian rights, Phillips realized his task was not an easy one. "This I shall do," he explained, "but with the organizations above and below me to a large extent at the mercy of those who are in league with the plunderers. Captain [David S.] Vittum was named by General Blunt provost marshal of Southern Kansas," he added in abject frustration. "Only think of one of the most noted cattle thieves being the police officer on the border."[19]

As a result, Phillips's return to command at Fort Gibson presented him with a series of problems, including fraud in his commissary, the continuing cattle theft, mounting supply problems, ongoing care for the refugees, and the need for a sound military strategy to protect the region. He ordered his officers to keep accurate records of all transactions, and directed his commissary officer, Capt. George L. Gaylord, to produce his delinquent November and December reports. Suspecting irregularities, he asked General Thayer to send the district commissary officer, Capt. S. S. Peck, to inspect the commissary at Fort Gibson. Two days later, Phillips asked Peck personally, and encouraged him to root out "not only fraud, but forgery."[20]

Phillips did not trust Thayer's command at Fort Smith to provide an honest prosecution of fraud, and he tried several avenues to get around that roadblock. He asked Maj. Gen. Edward R. S. Canby, the commander of the Military Division of the West Mississippi in New Orleans, to make the Indian Territory a separate district from Fort Smith so he could conduct his own court-martial trials. "I do not deem it necessary to multiply the other numerous reasons which might be alleged

18 Ibid., 605-606, and ibid., 48, pt. 1, 542.

19 Ibid.

20 W. A. Phillips to S. S. Peck, January 14, 1865, Letters Sent, Record Group 393, vol. 92, Department of Arkansas, Letters and Orders, National Archives, hereafter referred to as Fort Gibson Letterbook. This record also includes an Abstract of Letters Received, January 3, 1864– May 29, 1865 (91 pages) and a book of Phillips' daily orders and Courts Martial, January 4, 1863–January 31, 1864 (256 pages); Circular, January 6, 1865; Colonel Commanding to George Gaylord, January 12, 1865; Colonel Commanding to John M. Thayer, January 14, 1865; W. A. Phillips to S. S. Peck, January 14, 1865.

for the request which I desire to bring to your attention," Phillips explained to Canby. He also informed Maj. Gen. J. J. Reynolds, commanding the Department of Arkansas, of his efforts to combat corruption and he continued urging Captain Peck to join his investigation at Gibson.[21]

Phillips reported to Colonel Haynes, chief commissary officer of the "West Mississippi," on January 28 that two clerks under commissary officer Gaylord had fled, one before his return to Fort Gibson and another more recently. He instructed Lt. A. W. Robb in Kansas to notify military authorities if the police failed to arrest the fugitives. Meantime, he asked for a replacement commissary officer and ordered an inventory of all the "stock, funds, and all the public property" possessed by Gaylord, to be compared against military and sutlers' monthly reports.[22] The indefatigable Phillips also discovered that Gaylord had committed fraud. In his continuing attempts to have the matter dealt with beyond the influence of Fort Smith, Phillips alerted Colonel Haynes, "I may want to refer the matter to you. The truth is, I have little inclination to send parties to Fort Smith for a trial unless there is a change there."[23]

Phillips also attempted to combat the on-going cattle theft. When he learned that stolen cattle were being herded at Coody's Bluff on the Verdigris River north of Gibson, Phillips detached scouts there and instructed the escort of a returning refugee supply train to proceed to Coody's Bluff after the train reached Kansas. He gave orders to all escorts that no one, military or civilian, should leave their trains, and that all unauthorized whites found in the Nations were to be arrested.[24]

A general order issued above Phillips's signature on January 11, 1865, that required all cattle dealers to report to Fort Gibson, where both the Indian leadership and the provost marshal would judge their legitimacy. He forbade Confederate sympathizers from buying or selling at Fort Gibson, and required sellers to obtain permission before disposing of contraband cattle. He also ordered

21 W. A. Phillips to E. R. S. Canby, January 21, 1865, Fort Gibson Letterbook; OR 48, pt. 1, 606; W. A. Phillips to J. J. Reynolds, January 27, 1865; W. A. Phillips to S. C. Peck, January 27, 1865, Fort Gibson Letterbook.

22 Proceedings of the Board of Survey Convened at Fort Gibson January 29, 1865; W. A. Phillips to Colonel Haynes, January 28, 1865, Fort Gibson Letterbook.

23 W. A. Phillips to Colonel Haynes, February 3, 1865; W. A. Phillips to A. W. Robb, January 28, 1865, Fort Gibson Letterbook.

24 W. A. Phillips to Wilson Hunter, January 1, 1865; W. A. Phillips to Capt. Falalla, January 4, 1865; W. A. Phillips to Major James A. Phillips, January 5, 1865; W. A. Phillips to Lieut. Theophilus McLain, January 6, 1865; W. A. Phillips to Major James A. Phillips, January 12, 1865, Fort Gibson Letterbook.

Union patrols to stop the wanton butchering of Indian cattle, and required handlers of the military herd to account for every head by ownership and brand.[25]

Phillips continued to remind his superiors about the deplorable situation. He warned the secretary of the interior on February 3 to be wary of the dishonesty of suppliers such as McDonald and Fuller. He warned that Fuller was lobbying to be made the Creek agent. Phillips informed General Canby on February 16, "For nearly a year past there has been a systematic and wholesale plundering and driving of stock from the Indian Nations to Kansas."[26] As an example, he pointed to the 3rd Wisconsin Cavalry's Captain Vittum, who had brought out two herds, one with 500 head, after which Vittum had been appointed provost marshal at Fort Scott. Phillips told Maj. Gen. John Pope in Missouri that both Union cavalry and civilians had made several raids on Indian cattle and afterward obtained "bogus bills of sale."[27]

None of Phillips' measures against cattle theft, however, could be enforced unless the Indian Brigade was remounted. As a result, the theft continued until there was nothing left to steal, despite a law Congress eventually passed to punish people who interfered with Indian agents, who were alone authorized to sell Indian cattle, authorizing prison sentences up to three years and fines up to $5,000.[28]

Even the corn women and children planted with hoes on one- to ten-acre plots was taken into this system of corruption. Refugees who had arrived early enough to plant a good crop in 1863 saw their harvest seized by Union suppliers and the Army. They were thus reluctant to grow another crop in 1864, but agent Harlan encouraged them to do so and warned Superintendent Coffin and Commissioner Dole that the military needed to prohibit anyone but Indians from buying Indian corn. Coffin concurred and told Dole, "[There is a] necessity to have the War Department issue an order to the military authorities at Fort Gibson, with sufficient penalties prohibiting any person but Indians from buying, or taking under any plea whatever the grain which is now being raised by defenseless

---

25 *OR* 48, pt. 1, 516-518.

26 W. A. Phillips to Maj. Genl. Canby, February 16, 1865, Fort Gibson Letterbook.

27 W. A. Phillips to Maj. Genl. John Pope, February 16, 1865, Fort Gibson Letterbook. The fact that Phillips made no complaint to General Thayer may be evidence Phillips believed Thayer was complicit.

28 *Report of the Commissioner of Indian Affairs, 1865*, 269.

Cherokee woman and children."[29] Nothing was done. The crop was stolen or bought cheaply for $1.00 to $2.00 a bushel by agents of McDonald & Company, which then resupplied the indigent Indians with their own corn and billed the federal government through contracts to supply the refugees from $5.35 to $7.00 a bushel.[30]

Phillips's concerns mounted. In January 1865, he had to supply both his troops and the refugees. His problem was eventually solved when riverboat steamers from Fort Smith replaced the overland supply route from Fort Scott. Until then, the wagon trains had been a vulnerable lifeline. On January 3, Phillips sent 300 men to escort a train down from Fort Scott. Desperate for breadstuffs, he sent additional scouts north to watch for the wagons from Kansas, and south to watch for Confederate raiders. A wagon train arrived from Fort Scott on January 14, but only 55 sacks of flour came with it, which would not sustain his people for long. A refugee train arrived from Fort Scott on January 23, and another shortly thereafter from Fort Smith. Phillips sent Lieutenant Robb to escort both trains when they traveled to Fort Scott to ensure that supplies were reloaded and sent south within eight days. On February 2, Phillips offered to trade salt to General Thayer in return for ten wagons of other badly needed supplies, and sent Capt. Thomas Pegg on February 10 to meet a train of 25 wagons approaching Hudson's Ford on the Grand River north of Gibson. The rivers were rising, and Phillips was hoping, as an alternative, that flour would be shipped from Fort Smith by boat. Despite these efforts, the condition of soldiers and refugees at Fort Gibson remained precarious until the end of the war.[31]

To the dismay of the hard-working Colonel Phillips, Confederate forces from south of the Arkansas River would soon capture a large supply train from Fort Scott on its way to Fort Gibson in a spectacular and a tragic campaign.

---

29 J. Harlan to Col. Coffin, July 30, 1864; J. Harlan to W. P. Dole, September 30, 1864; W. G. Coffin to Wm. P. Dole, August 8, 1864, Letters Received, Cherokee Agency, OIA.

30 *Report of the Commissioner, 1864*, 345-346; J. Harlan to W. P. Dole, September 30, 1864; *OR* 48, 543; *Report of the Commissioner of Indian Affairs, 1865*, 270-279; *OR* 41, pt. 3, 462.

31 W. A. Phillips to Brig. Genl. Thayer, January 3, 1865; W. A. Phillips to Brig. Gen'l. John M. Thayer, January 6, 1865; W. A. Phillips to Brig. Gen'l. John M. Thayer, January 14, 1865; W. A. Phillips to Brig. Gen'l John M. Thayer, January 23, 1865; W, A. Phillips to Brig. Gen'l. John M. Thayer, January 25, 1865; W. A. Phillips to Colonel Stephen H. Wattles, January 25, 1865; W. A. Phillips to Lt. W. A. Robb, January 26, 1865; W. A. Phillips to Capt. S. C. Peck, February 2, 1865; W. A. Phillips to Brig. Gen'l. John M. Thayer, February 2, 1865; W. A. Phillips to Capt. Thomas Pegg, February 10, 1865; W. A Phillips to Ass't Adj't Gen'l, February 12, 1865, Fort Gibson Letterbook.

Chapter 13

The Rebellion Continued

After the Confederate defeat at Honey Springs, the Rebel military was reorganized under Brig. Gen. Samuel Bell Maxey, a Texan who reported directly to Lt. Gen. E. Kirby Smith, commanding the Trans-Mississippi Department from his headquarters at Shreveport, Louisiana. Stand Watie and other Cherokee, Creek, Choctaw, and Chickasaw leaders declared continued loyalty to the Confederacy and would often conduct operations of varying size together in the coming year as they did their best to coordinate efforts in Arkansas and elsewhere.

Most of the men of the Indian brigades were furloughed at this time to help their families. Watie, who kept a detachment of his brigade in the field, told the leaders of the other nations that, if necessary, they could unite without white troops to recover their losses. In August of 1863, Colonel Watie assured the governor of the Creeks, "[If we resolve] never to be enslaved by an inferior race, and trodden under the feet of an ignorant and insolent foe, we, the Creeks, Choctaws, Seminoles, and Cherokees, never can be conquered by the Kansas Jayhawkers, renegade Indians, and runaway negroes."[1]

Watie wasn't finished. "[T]he Indians true to the South, must place small reliance upon the promises of assistance from abroad," he declared in a letter to the governor of the Choctaw and Chickasaw Nations. "We should . . . test our whole strength to defend our homes alone. . . . By a united and unyielding opposition of

---

1 OR 22, pt. 2, 1105.

our Indian forces alone, we can make our fair country an unpleasant, if not an untenable, home for our enemies." E. C. Boudinot gave copies of Watie's letters to President Jefferson Davis. Maxey provided copies to Kirby Smith.[2]

Sarah Watie's brother, James M. Bell, wrote a long letter to his wife Caroline from Boggy Depot on September 2 explaining the situation they faced. "People in Texas think we have an army," he began,

> ... in line well equipped ... two Choctaw two Creek two Cherokee of three regiments each at a thousand ... men besides two Batts [battalions] which will make ten thousand now if I was to tell you that five thousand men is the most that I have known in camps at any one time you would be surprised. ... Col Watie is still back on Arkansas River I don't believe our regiment will leave our country. We are preparing to go back Col Watie has promised as soon as we whip the Feds we can go home.[3]

Sometime in early November Watie fought back. With a force estimated by the Federals to be between 500 and 800 cavalry, Watie raided Tahlequah and Park Hill. "[I] took Dannie Hicks [illegible but not John] Ross, would not allow them killed because you said Wm Ross must not be killed on old Mrs (illegible) Ross account," he wrote in a letter to Sarah describing the action. "Killed a few Pins in Tahlaquah. They had been holding council I had the old council house set on fire and burnt down also John Ross' house. Poor Andy Nave was killed," he continued, "he refused to surrender & was [shot] by Dick Falds I felt sorry as he used to be quite friendly toward me before the war, but it could not be helpt."[4]

Kirby Smith provided some assistance on December 11 when he gave Maxey overall command of the newly created District of Indian Territory, with Douglas Cooper commanding the Indian troops. The new geographic command area was the result of an important Grand Council meeting at Armstrong in November. Several resolutions were passed and the Council sent a letter to President Davis lobbying for a separate Department of Indian Territory and the raising of three brigades, one from the Choctaws and Chickasaws, one from the Creeks and Seminoles, and one from the Cherokees. Three brigades made a division, and a division rated a major general to command it. The Council strongly recommended

---

2 Ibid., 994-996, 1106, 1103.

3 Jim to Carrie, September 2, 1863, in Cherokee Nation Papers; Dale and Litton, eds., *Cherokee Cavaliers*, 137-138.

4 Stand to My Dear Sally, November 12, 1863, Cherokee Nation Papers; Dale and Litton, eds., *Cherokee Cavaliers*, 144-145.

Brigadier General Samuel Bell Maxey

Texas State Library and Archives Commission

General Cooper fill that role and replace William Steele as commander of the district. Steele was removed through the influence of Watie and Boudinot in Congress, with the agreement of President Davis.[5] The Council sent Choctaw Capt. Campbell LeFlore to Richmond to lobby for Cooper. The adjutant general of the army, Gen. Samuel Cooper (no relation), had recommended that Douglas Cooper be placed in command of the new district. Kirby Smith disagreed, however, arguing that he did not think promoting Cooper was "wise or necessary." A few days after Maxey had taken command of the district, Richmond authorities placed Cooper in command of the Indian troops. The ambitious Cooper was not without influence of his own in Richmond, but on February 20, 1864, Kirby Smith, speaking through his adjutant, flatly stated that Cooper was under the command of Maxey. The controversy, however, did not end there.[6]

Maxey wrote often to his wife Marilda in Paris, Texas. "I am expected to defend and recover the lost territory of the Nation, and keep the Federals out of Northern Texas," he complained on December 29. "Truly this is a Herculean task. Even the troops I have are to a large extent Indian and no infantry. It is the first

---

5 *OR* 22, pt. 1, 1103; Elias Cornelius Boudinot to Stand Watie, January 24, 1864, in Cherokee Nations Papers; Dale and Litton, eds., *Cherokee Cavaliers*, 150-153; Parins, *Elias Cornelius Boudinot*, 56. William Steele was supposed to stay in command of white troops to help familiarize Maxey's transition with the command, but refused when he heard of his demotion.

6 Cooper's strongest influence and support was among the Choctaw leadership. *OR* 22, pt. 1, 1,100-1,102; ibid., 34, 1,007, and ibid., 53, 920-921, 968-969; Able, *The American Indian in the Civil War*, 317; *OR* 34, pt. 2, 824-825, 1,007-1,008.

army I ever heard of without infantry. If I do succeed, I think I ought to be entitled to some credit."[7]

Maxey's troops included a reliable Texas cavalry brigade under Richard M. Gano. A member of a prominent family of preachers in the First Christian Church (Disciples of Christ), Gano would go on to baptize more than 16,000 people in Dallas following the war. He had already served under Brig. Gen. John Hunt Morgan, first commanding two companies of Texas cavalry and then an entire Kentucky brigade. Gano gained invaluable experience in the first three of Morgan's four raids into Kentucky and Tennessee and was reassigned in 1863 to command a brigade of Texas cavalry in Arkansas. For reasons of health, he was drilling Texas cavalry on the Red River when he received the assignment that October. He was promoted to brigadier general, but would not receive official confirmation until the final weeks of the war.

"I have a Brigade of four regiments and six pieces of artillery, so somebody will be hurt before the Yanks get to Dallas," Gano boasted to his wife Mattie. "I am more uneasy about you than myself. Dear Mattie, continue to trust in God. Read the Bible oft, pray often and talk to the little boys of Heaven and of Christ. Jesus will take care of the lambs. Kiss all for me. Love, love, love from your devoted husband."[8]

Maxey's first concern was to determine Federal strength in comparison with his own. He questioned a newspaper article's estimate of the number of Union troops at Fort Smith. With two white and two black infantry regiments, two batteries of artillery, three cavalry regiments, and 600 miscellaneous men, Maxey estimated the enemy had around 4,000 in the vicinity of Fort Smith and Waldron. To match them, he had posted his own brigade at Laynesport on the Red River at the border with Arkansas. He also recalled Watie from the Creek Nation and posted his command at Carriage Point on the Texas Road about 10 miles north of Colbert's Ferry on the Red River. General Cooper was working to reassemble the other Indian regiments.[9]

---

7 Maxey to his wife, December 29, 1863; Boatner, *Civil War Dictionary*, 520.

8 R. M. Gano to Mattie Gano, October 12, 1863, in Gano Papers, Abilene Christian University; Walter Prescott Webb, ed., *The Handbook of Texas*, vol. 1 (Austin, TX, 1952), 669-670; Boatner, *Civil War Dictionary*, 322-323, 566-568, 770; OR 22, pt. 1, 34, pt. 2, 1048.

9 S. S. Andrews to S. B. Maxey, December 11, 1863, in Maxey Collection; D. H. Cooper to S. B. Maxey, December 28, 1863; S. B. Maxey to R. M. Gano, December 30, 1863; S. B. Maxey to S. S. Anderson, January 1, 1863, in Unofficial Letterbook, Maxey Collection, typescript corrected by the author from the original; OR 22, pt. 2, 1108.

Maxey reported this to Kirby Smith, who suggested the Federal spring campaign would advance by either the Line Road, which extended south from Fort Smith along the border between Arkansas and Indian Territory, or the old military road from Fort Smith to Fort Towson, Maxey's headquarters. Maxey disagreed. The old military road passed through a rough and mountainous country and had not been used for years. It would not support the passage of wagons and artillery without repair, he insisted. Nevertheless, Maxey posted five companies of Choctaws and Chickasaws under the command of Lt. Col. James Riley at Lennex Mission, on the upper reaches of the Kiamichi River, to watch the old road. On the Line Road, General Gano's brigade was at Laynesport operating in conjunction with [Brig.] Gen. William L. Cabell's brigade west of Washington, Arkansas. Maxey did not think the Federals were ready for "two brigades with cavalry."[10]

Maxey believed an attack would come from Fort Gibson down the Texas Road. Watie was his main line of defense there. Maxey planned to assemble two Indian Brigades and narrow his field of defense by moving north in the spring on Waldron, Fort Smith, and Fort Gibson. Maxey and Kirby Smith established a spy system in order to gain intelligence concerning Federal troop movements and strength, and carefully chose men and women with access to Union camps and who could be trusted to supply accurate information. Maxey instructed Cooper, his new subordinate, to do the same.[11]

Before the campaign began, Maxey asked his wife Marilda in January 1864 to travel to Fort Towson, where the food was good and conditions were as "good as could be expected in the Nations." He wrote frequently that month, asking her to give "kisses" to their daughter and thinking of the future. "[I hope] to have our own little house and garden and orchard and be out of debt. . . . If I can manage to make enough to buy you a negro woman, and buy 2 or 3 more men—I can spend a great deal more time at home when we get 'our little place.'"[12]

Maxey's plans were interrupted when the leaders of the Indian Nations organized a Grand Council to meet at the Armstrong Academy in the Choctaw Nation beginning Monday, February 1. Maxey told his wife that he had to attend, but hoped to be back in time to send for her the following week. His plans were further hindered by a raid by Col. William Phillips' Indian brigade and a

---

10 S. B. Maxey to E. Kirby Smith, January 15, 1864, Unofficial Letterbook, Maxey Collection.

11 Ibid.; S. B. Maxey to D. H, Cooper, January 15, 1864, in Unofficial Letterbook, Maxey Collection.

12 Maxey to his wife, January 13, 1864, and January 16, 1864, in Maxey Collection.

detachment of Kansas Cavalry south out of Fort Gibson. Watie could not attend the Council, but sent Capt. John Spears as a delegate in his place.[13]

On the day the Council began, Phillips started his raid, which would take him from Gibson past the Creek agency to the Creek Council ground and on to North Fork Town, where he skirmished with Confederate troops. Phillips' plan was initially more ambitious. He camped his men south of the Arkansas on January 31 with 12 days of rations. They were traveling light with only a few tents and two light howitzers. Although he had a detachment of 300 men of the 14th Kansas Cavalry with him, he expected the remainder of the 14th to join him at North Fork Town and cover his left flank down the Texas Road, to cross the Red River, and to deliver a sound defeat to the Rebels. As is so often the case when trying to coordinate far-flung movements, the expected reinforcements did not arrive. Phillips gathered corn, put up a crib, and waited three days in vain for the Kansans before finally moving on.[14]

On February 9 and 10, Phillips sent scouts along the north side of the Canadian River to the Little River. He arrived there with his whole force on the 11th. He moved onto the Middle Boggy River, where a fight broke out with some Chickasaws, Choctaws, and Texans. He sent his infantry and train back to the Little River and took 450 cavalry to the upper reaches of the Clear Boggy, in the Chickasaw Nation, on February 14. Once there he sent out two patrols but was unable to make contact with the enemy. On February 16 Phillips was back with the rest of his command on the Little River in the Seminole Nation above Fort Arbuckle. He sent forces up the Canadian and the North Fork to clear the area of Rebels before riding north to cross the Arkansas River above Gibson and return to the fort. Phillips, who returned with his train there on February 24, filed what was surely an exaggerated report that claimed he killed 250 Rebels while suffering only four wounded.[15]

One purpose of the expedition had been to induce Confederate-allied Indians to take advantage of President Abraham Lincoln's Proclamation of Amnesty and

---

13 Maxey to his wife, January 29, 1864, in Unofficial Letterbook, Maxey Collection; Stand Watie to Jno Spears, January 29, 1864, in Cherokee Nation Papers; Franks, *Stand Watie and the Agony of the Cherokee Nation*, 155.

14 *OR* 34, part 2, 467-468; pt. 1, 108-109; Wm Gallaher to Lt Col Stephen H. Wattles, January 30, 1864; Wm Gallaher to Major John Foreman, January 30, 1864; Wm Gallaher to Cap Sol Kaufman, January 30, 1864, in Fort Gibson Letterbook.

15 *OR* 34, pt. 1, 106-112; Ibid., pt. 2, 329-330, 467-468; Wm Gallaher to Maj Chas Welletts, January 31, 1864, in Fort Gibson Letterbook.

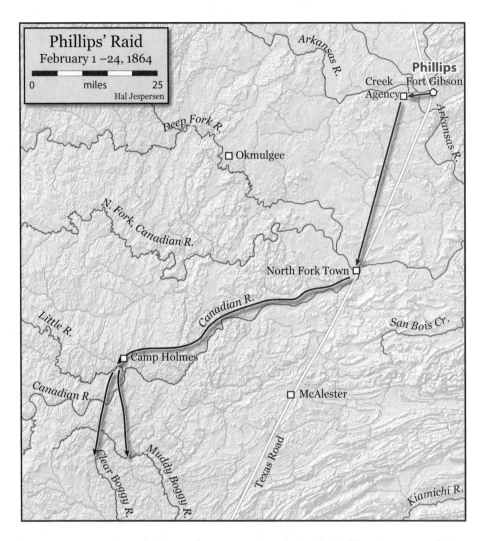

Reconstruction, issued December 8, 1863. Colonel Phillips interpreted the proclamation to apply to the Southern aligned Indian Nations even though it specifically referred to voters in the 1860 election, as well as to Southern states in rebellion.[16] It was translated and distributed, along with private letters, to the leaders of the Choctaws, Chickasaws, Creeks, and Seminoles. The proclamation

---

16 Lincoln proclaimed that if one-tenth of the number of people in a seceded state who had voted in the presidential election of 1860 swore a loyalty oath, the state would be reconstructed as a member of the Union.

Colonel William Penn Adair

Oklahoma Historical Society

had no effect. The Indian leaders forwarded the letters to Maxey as an indication of their loyalty to the Confederate cause.[17]

Maxey, meanwhile, finally arrived at the Armstrong council to address the delegates on February 5. He announced his intention to retake lost ground by pushing the Union fores out of Waldron, southeast of Fort Smith, retake Forts Smith and Gibson, and occupy the Arkansas River valley before moving farther north. General Cooper wrote to him that the speech had a good effect. Past Creek chief Moty Kanard asked for a copy.

While at Armstrong, Col. William Penn Adair, a Cherokee Nation attorney and former politician allied with Watie, approached Maxey with a letter from the Cherokee colonel. In it, Waite proposed a bold raid on Kansas as far north as Humbolt on the Neosho River. Maxey replied in his own letter that he wanted to confer with Watie about the "Spring Campaign," though he did not make any formal commitment.[18] Once back at Fort Towson, Maxey wrote Kirby Smith's adjutant, Col. S. S. Anderson, that Watie's plan might prove effective—especially if it was done a little in advance of his own plan to move north of the San Bois Mountains to the Arkansas drainage. This move would place Waldron on Maxey's

17 *OR* 34, pt. 1, 107, 109-111; pt. 2, 995, 997; Basler, ed., *The Collected Works of Abraham Lincoln*, (New Brunswick, NJ, 1953), vol. 7, 53-56; Abel, *The American Indian in the Civil War*, 322-324; Eric Foner, *Reconstruction: America's Unfinished Revolution, 1863-1877* (New York, NY, 2005), 35-37; James M. McPherson, *Battle Cry of Freedom: The Civil War Era* (New York, NY, 1988), 698-699.

18 S. B. Maxey to Stand Watie, February 5, 1864, in Cherokee Nation Papers. This letter is not in Dale and Litton, eds., *Cherokee Cavaliers*.

right, Perryville on his left, and Fort Smith to his font. Colonel Adair urged Watie to meet with Maxey, and the two men did so (probably at Fort Towson). Maxey came away impressed: "I wish I had as much energy in some of my white Commanders as he displays."[19]

Still, Maxey remained concerned about the defense of Boggy Depot. "[T]he commissary has succeeded in collecting a valuable [store] of supplies including a large amount of pork at Boggy Depot—The force there is Bass' remnant of a Regiment," he wrote adjutant Anderson. "Is all together too small [to] guard it and yet I have no force to send." He also mentioned several reports from spies about Federal troop strength. One report indicated that a force from Fort Smith would attempt to take Boggy Depot in the spring. "Unless I am greatly deceived," he added in a postscript, "the possession of this country and northern Texas would be the most serious blow the enemy has ever struck this Dept. I hope therefore he [Kirby Smith] will understand that I am thus urgent." He also referred to a battalion of Texas sharpshooters, which had yet to report to Maxey because its members lacked guns, that he intended to send to help defend Boggy Depot.[20]

By February 17th and possibly before, Maxey became aware of Phillips' wide-ranging raid. He had not received any news from Boggy Depot since February 14, and the lack of communication was troubling. Maxey was concerned enough to order the hogs there moved to Fort Towson, but he believed the men deployed at Boggy Depot could rebuff Phillips if so challenged. As it turned out, the issue was never tested because Phillips rode west around Boggy Depot.[21]

Maxey inspected Boggy Depot during the next few days and was called upon to give a speech to Texas troops, and another the following day to Creeks. Once he finished there, he rode on to Fort Washita for an inspection. Phillips believed his raid had isolated the Choctaw Nation and effectively ended the rebellion in the Creek, Chickasaw, and Seminole nations, though why he thought such a thing remains uncertain. In reality, his ride across enemy geography had no real effect.

19 S. B. Maxey to S. S. Anderson, February 7, 1864, in Unofficial Letterbook, Maxey Collection; Richard Fritz to Stand Watie, February 7, 1864, in Cherokee Nation Papers. This letter is not in Dale and Litton, eds., *Cherokee Cavaliers*; OR 34, pt. 2, 958-960; Britton, *The Union Indian Brigade in the Civil War*, 342-344.

20 S. B. Maxey to S. S. Anderson, February 7, 1864; OR 34, pt. 2, 995. Thomas C. Bass, 20th Texas Cavalry, OR 34 pt. 2, 876, 1,110.

21 Memo of information this day devised from confidential spy sent by me to Fort Smith, February 17, 1864, S. B. Maxey to Lieutenant General, February 17, 1864, in Unofficial Letterbook, Maxey Collection. Rampp and Rampp's account of Phillips' raid, *Civil War in the Indian Territory*, 62-68, concluded that Phillips reached Boggy Depot on February 9.

Maxey, meanwhile, made plans for the approaching spring campaign. Before returning to Fort Towson, he took time to describe the situation in a letter to his wife. "[T]he excitement is now over. . . . The enemy has returned to Fort Gibson. If he is not already there he [soon] will be. . . . The Old War Chief Watie is on the trail with full directions from me in a personal interview," he continued. "He fully understands my plans, and if he has the strength will carry them out. The great trouble . . . about which I have more anxiety than all others is arms—Oh for 2000 good guns and I would place Northern Texas in safety."[22]

Maxey knew the key to strengthening the poorly equipped Indian brigades was to arm them properly. On February 25 and 26, he received reports concerning the the condition of arms in the district. According to Assistant Chief Ordnance Officer J. J. Du Bose, Watie's brigade was better armed than Walker's Choctaws: "A few Enfield rifles were seen, with a few, very few, Mississippi rifles in the line; the remainder were composed of double-barrel guns, Texas rifles, sporting rifles &c." Neither unit was considered well-armed. A report by Inspector General R. W. Lee, District of Indian Territory was as disheartening as it was direct. More than one-third of the Texas troops and as many as one-half of the Indian troops were unarmed. "The Indians in this district are eminently faithful and zealous," added Lee, "and with good arms in their hands would be brave allies, able to protect themselves from all attacks not more formidable than those that have hitherto assailed them, and to extend to us valuable co-operation in our good cause." Repeated promises broken, he warned, "evidences . . . intentional faithlessness."[23]

Maxey wrote a long letter to Kirby Smith on February 26 concerning these matters. Phillips' raid, he explained, had accomplished little, and he had dispatched Watie to make sure Phillips had returned to Gibson, and, if not, "to drive him back," and if the possibility arose, "smash it up." The central issue of the communication was the arming of his men and the breaking of their treaty obligations. Maxey took pains to point out that the failure to uphold their promises to the Indians had not only affected "the honor of the Confederacy, but the future relations of the Indians toward our Government." "The arms in the hands of most of the troops are miserable apologies," penned the frustrated district commander. Military prudence, Maxey continued,

22 OR 34, pt. 2, 537; Maxey to his wife, February 25, 1864, in Unofficial Letterbook, Maxey Collection.

23 OR 22, pt. 2, 297-299, and ibid., 34, pt. 2, 997-998.

would say these men ought by all means to be armed or disbanded; but as your supply is, as I judge from your letters, inadequate for the demand, then military prudence would say distribute these guns where they are most needed and to the best troops. In that view of the case, it would likely be long before I get a supply.

While keeping his superior so informed, Maxey dispatched an officer to Shreveport to oversee the acquisition of a supply of arms. "I am now getting interested in this command," he concluded, "and I want to succeed and can do it with anything like adequate means."[24]

While General Maxey tried to arm his men, Union commanders improved on plans to supply Colonel Phillips at Fort Gibson. General Curtis inspected the fort while Phillips was away on his raid and was impressed by the improved fortifications. Shipments of supplies might be made more secure by floating them down the Grand River by keel boats, believed Curtis. After their cargoes had been secured, the boats could be disassembled and used for lumber. Curtis instructed his quartermaster, Capt. M. H. Insley, to travel to St. Louis and investigate these supply possibilities. "[A]scertain what provisions have been made for having light-draught steam-boats to run above Little Rock. You should have one or two such under your own control," he instructed. "Such boats should run to Fort Gibson when they can," he continued, "but, when they can go no farther, the supplies for points above should be stored at Van Buren. . . . Until we can certainly start the river line . . . you will run trains between Fort Scott and that post with the utmost energy and prudence."[25]

The problems, insisted Colonel Phillips, went well beyond just supplies. When the Union colonel returned to the fort in March, he unofficially complained to General Curtis that his authority was being undermined by General Blunt. Could the Indian Nations, he inquired, be made a separate department reporting directly to Curtis? Phillips also suggested that a combination of white and Indian officers would substantially improve the internal command structure. Curtis did not approve either suggestion, but he did reassure Phillips that Blunt had no ambitions beyond reorganizing the Indian Brigade. However, Curtis also tactfully reminded Phillips that, even though Blunt commanded the Indian Territory, Phillips should feel completely free to report directly to Curtis if he ever found Blunt unavailable.

24 *OR* 34, pt. 2, 994-996.

25 *OR* 34, pt. 2, 468.

Curtis also sent a copy of this reply to Blunt, ostensibly for his review, but in fact to demonstrate his support for Colonel Phillips.[26]

At the higher levels of Union command, strategic plans were being put in place to draw elements of Maxey's command more prominently into the shooting war. Halleck and Lincoln had for some time been considering a campaign to occupy Texas. It would be a complex movement requiring the coordination of troops converging from two separate directions. Frederick Steele would move south with 8,000 men men out of Arkansas, link up with another 4,000 under Brig. Gen. John Thayer, and march to Shreveport, while Maj. Gen. Nathaniel Banks moved up the Red River to Shreveport with 27,000 men and 19 gunboats. The two armies would continue upriver into northern Texas.[27]

Kirby Smith did not have enough men to defeat both enemy forces at once, so he transferred 4,000 of Maj. Gen. Sterling Price's men to reinforce Maj. Gen. Richard Taylor along the Red River. Once Banks was defeated, so the plan went, the men would be shuttled back north to reinforce Price in a confrontation with Steele. In the interim, Price would harass and slow Steele with cavalry under Brig. Gens. John S. Marmaduke and Joseph O. Shelby. Price and Kirby Smith believed Steele's immediate target was Washington, Arkansas, the home of Arkansas' exiled Confederate state government. When Price positioned himself between that point and the advancing Federals, Steele turned eastward down the Camden Road and occupied the fortified town of Camden. Steele seemed to have the advantage, but he was desperately short of rations.[28]

---

26 OR 34, pt. 2, 524-527, 537-539, 590-591, 711-712, 754-755, 789-780, 791-792; Castel, *A Frontier State at War*, 84-85.

27 Ludwell Johnson, *Red River Campaign: Politics and Cotton in the Civil War* (Baltimore, MD, 1958), 3-48; Robert L. Kerby, *Kirby Smith's Confederacy: The Trans-Mississippi South, 1863-65* (New York, NY, 1972), 290-292. When these two columns failed to rendezvous, the southern movement under Banks became known as the Red River Campaign, and the northern movement under Steele as the Camden Expedition. Neither was successful. Banks suffered a significant defeat and nearly lost his entire navy on the falling Red River, which may well have swung the balance of power back to the Confederacy in that region. Steele's campaign prevented five Confederate cavalry brigades from reinforcing Richard Taylor for use against Banks.

28 Daniel Sutherland, "1864: 'A Strange Wild Time,'" in *Rugged and Sublime: The Civil War in Arkansas*, Mark Christ, ed. (Fayetteville, AR, 1994), 110-114; Thomas A. DeBlack, *With Fire and Sword: Arkansas, 1861-1874* (Fayetteville, AR, 2003), 108-112; Kerby, *Kirby Smith's Confederacy*, 298-299, 311-313; Gary Dillard Joiner, *One Damn Blunder from Beginning to End: The Red River Campaign of 1864* (Wilmington, DE, 2003), 123-127; Castel, *General Sterling Price and the Civil War in the West*, 173-176.

On March 26, one of Maxey's spies reported that something was underway at Fort Smith, and two days later another confirmed 4,000 troops and cavalry, including the 18th Iowa Infantry and the 1st Kansas Colored Infantry, had left Fort Smith to join General Steele at Arkadelphia. Steele needed these men to round out the full complement he expected to march south to join General Banks. He also needed the supplies he expected them to bring, but the Fort Smith contingent only arrived with 10 days of rations.[29]

Maxey received orders from Price on April 2 to join Brig. Gen. William L. Cabell at Washington, Arkansas. He also received copies of Price's authorization to use troops from the District of Indian Territory and intelligence that Union troops had united at Arkadelphia. Maxey ordered General Gano to assemble his brigade and proceed to Washington, Arkansas. Gano joined General Marmaduke on April 6. With Watie unavailable, Maxey notified Kirby Smith that he would take Tandy Walker's Choctaws with him. The Indians would play a significant role in the upcoming battle of Poison Spring.[30]

On April 17, 198 wagons escorted by 500 men from Col. James Williams' 1st Kansas Colored Infantry, 195 cavalry from the 2nd, 6th, and 14th Kansas Cavalry regiments, and two guns left Camden to forage for corn. After traveling 18 miles toward Washington, Williams dispersed the command to forage as widely as possible and reassembled it at midnight. By this time most of the wagons had been filled with corn and other plunder. Without resting his men, Williams began the return trip to Camden marching east on the Washington Road. The column was reinforced by 375 infantry from the 18th Iowa, and 90 more cavalrymen from the same three Kansas regiments, and another pair of artillery pieces. The 1st Kansas Colored Infantry marched mostly in front, followed by miscellaneous cavalry, guns, and wagons, with the 18th Iowa bringing up the rear. The column was strung out and many of the men completely exhausted. According to Williams, "fully 100 [of the Kansas infantry] "were . . . unfit for duty." Shortly thereafter the head of the

29 To General, March 26, 1864; from John Forthman, March 28, 1864, in Unofficial Letterbook, Maxey Collection; Sutherland, "A Strange Wild Time," 112-113.

30 OR 34, pt. 3, 729, 824, pt. 3, 726, 728-729, 733, 745-746, 760-761; S. B. Maxey to O. J. Downs, April 8, 1864, in Sam Bell Maxey Papers, Center for American History, University of Texas, Austin. Marmaduke was a capable officer and an 1857 graduate of West Point. Boatner, *Civil War Dictionary*, 513.

column encountered Confederate pickets in front of a stand of woods in the vicinity of Poison Spring.[31]

The Rebel pickets belonged to General Marmaduke's command. The general had set out to intercept the Federal train on the same afternoon Williams had left to forage, but called off the raid when he learned the Union column had been reinforced. The following morning (April 18), Marmaduke set out again with the understanding that he would be reinforced by Maxey's 1,500 cavalry and four artillery pieces. Marmaduke moved with 2,000 men and eight guns. Once his scouts located the returning Union column, Marmaduke's escort fought a brief clash for possession of a hill, and deployed his command in the woods behind it facing west. His battle line straddled the Washington Road, with Cabell's 1,200 men and four guns on one side and his own 800 men and four guns on the other. Williams was effectively cut off.

Maxey's arrival could have caused command problems because he outranked Marmaduke, but he deployed his cavalry according to Marmaduke's plan without objection. Maxey took up a position south of and generally parallel to the road in more woods, with Walker's Choctaws on the left and Gano's brigade on the right. It took Maxey about half an hour to get his guns into good firing positions. Gano was absent because he had suffered a wound in the arm in a skirmish "near Munns Mill," so his brigade was under the command of Col. Charles DeMorse. The brigade included the 29th Texas Cavalry, which had been routed at Honey Springs by the same 1st Kansas Colored Infantry they had now isolated. Another part of Maxey's line, the left side with Tandy Walker's Choctaws, caught the eye of one observer: The Indians were "a tough looking lot. . . . There were 400 or 500 of them, mounted on ponies dressed in all sorts of clothing. . . . Some had 1 gun, some two, and there was one or two that had 3 guns."[32]

The two Confederate lines of battle formed a rough L-shaped front. Marmaduke's plan was for Maxey to attack first from the south "and turn the enemy's right flank and when this force was warmly engaged to open rapidly with the artillery in front." Once Maxey was engaged Marmaduke would follow suit and advance his line. Colonel Williams could see little of this maneuvering, but it was

31 OR, 34, pt. 1, 743-744; Sutherland, "A Strange, Wild Time," 114-15; DeBlack, *With Fire and Sword*, 111-112; Joiner, *One Damn Blunder from Beginning to End*, 128-129.

32 OR 34, pt. 1, 783; William Franklin Avera and E. H. Cathey, Jr, "Six Generations: Avera-Cathey," 3-20, unpublished manuscript, Arkansas History Commission.

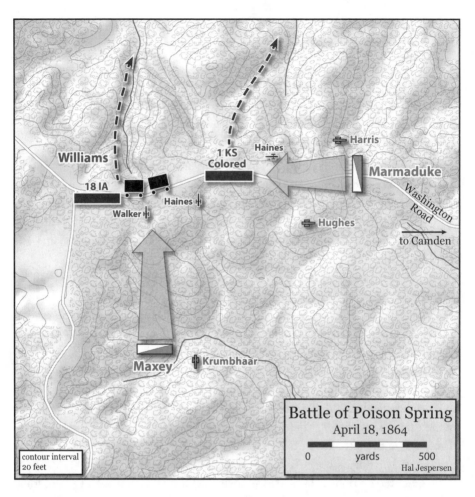

Battle of Poison Spring
April 18, 1864

contour interval
20 feet

0   yards   500

Hal Jespersen

clear the enemy was present in strength. He parked the train "as closely as the nature of the ground would permit" and deployed his men for battle.[33]

Williams called up the original escort and placed the reinforcements at the rear of the train. Up at the front, Maj. Richard G. Ward left four companies of the Kansas Colored Infantry facing east toward Marmaduke and turned four more to face south toward Maxey, where more movement seemed to be taking place. Two companies were held in reserve. Williams unlimbered his artillery and fired a round

33 OR 34, pt. 1, 744, 819, 841-844, 846-848; pt. 3, 790-791, 818-819, 826, 841-842; Sutherland, "A Strange, Wild Time," 115-116; Deblack, *With Fire and Sword*, 112-113; Joiner, *One Damn Blunder From Beginning to End*, 129; John N. Edwards, *Shelby and His Men; or ,The War in the West* (Cincinnati, OH, 1867), 273-274. For an illustration of this battlefield tactic see Richard E. Beringer, et al, *Why the South Lost the Civil War* (Athens, GA, 1986), 160.

to try and determine whether the Confederates in his front also had artillery. There was no response. The left side of Maxey's line was partially visible, and Williams sent troopers from the 2nd and 6th Kansas Cavalry regiments to investigate. The riders advanced about 400 yards before a fitful smattering of small arms fire knocked several men from their saddles and turned back the curious Union troopers. Just as the Union cavalry fell back the Rebel artillery crossfire commenced. Maxey's guns opened fire from 600 yards away, joined soon thereafter by Marmaduke's artillery 1,000 yards east of the head of the train. Once the initial shelling died away, Maxey's dismounted cavalry advanced out of the woods.[34]

Maxey's line was turned back after 15 minutes of fighting, after which he reopened with his artillery. Major Ward knew he was in serious trouble and requested reinforcements, so Colonel Williams sent him the two reserve companies (G and K) of the 1st Kansas. By this time the Rebels had found their footing and were advancing on both fronts. "Finally," Maxey would later report, "the whole line moved forward a sheet of living fire carrying death and destruction before it." Major Walker's command repulsed Maxey's line two more times, mostly with artillery, but Ward bluntly informed Williams that he could not withstand another advance. Williams ordered him to hold until the 18th Iowa could move into position behind them to support a withdrawal. When Williams' horse was shot from under him, Ward gave him his own. Rebel pressure mounted, and Ward withdrew his Kansas infantry, which was running low on ammunition, west toward the 18th Iowa, reforming twice in the process. before the men finally broke.[35]

The Union artillerists spiked their guns before joining what rapidly escalated into a rout north toward marshy ground. The long wagon train was abandoned as the Rebel cavalry continued in pursuit across nearly two miles of mostly open ground, slaughtering as they rode. "[We] were obliged to bring our wounded away the best we could," Major Ward reported, "as the Rebels were seen shooting those that fell into their hands." "[S]eeing that our train was lost, my first idea was to save the men. So I ordered them to scatter . . . with the hope of being able to form on the

---

34 OR 34, pt. 1, 744-745, 751-752, 841-844, 846-848; Sutherland, "A Strange, Wild Time," 115-116; Deblack, *With Fire and Sword*, 112; Joiner, *One Damn Blunder from Beginning to End*, 129; Edwards, *Shelby and his Men*, 274.

35 OR 34, pt. 1, 745, 752-753; Sutherland, "A Strange Wild Time," 116; DeBlack, *With Fire and Sword*, 112-113; Joiner, *One Damn Blunder from Beginning to End*, 129; Edwards, *Shelby and his Men*, 275; To Gen., Hd. Maxey's Division, in Camp, April 21, 1864, file 104, in Maxey Collection. This copy is in a four-page letterbook containing fragments of three or four letters, including a lengthy fragment of Maxey's official report.

left of the Eighteenth Iowa," explained Lt. William Gibbons of the 1st Kansas Colored Infantry. The lieutenant climbed a hill in his front, from which he "could distinctly see the rebels shooting down our brave but fatigued boys." After praising the performance of his command, he added, "I would especially mention First Sergeant Berry, Company I (supposed to be dead), whose efforts to keep his men in their place, urging them by all the endearments of freedom to keep their ground, were unceasing. He was a brave soldier and a noble man."[36]

Marmaduke wanted to continue the pursuit but Maxey—exercising his superior rank—countermanded his orders. The nearly 200 wagons were the valuable prize, and Maxey wanted to capture them. He knew it would take some time to organize and move them away, and he needed to do so before Union reinforcements were sent out from Camden and overtook them in the same manner.

Of the 438 participants from the 1st Kansas Colored Infantry, reported Colonel Williams, 117 were killed, and 65 wounded made it back to Union lines. Confederate losses, estimated Marmaduke, "will not much exceed 20 killed and 60 wounded." General Kirby Smith arrived on April 19 and visited the battlefield. Writing to his wife the next day, he mentioned that only two blacks were among the 200 Union prisoners. One of Maxey's staff officers replied to a Union request three days after the battle concerning a captured army doctor and a plea that they be allowed to bury their dead. "I have the honor to state that assist. surg. [assistant surgeon] Thos. Lindsey is temporarily detained at these Hdqs. Having been found irregularly within our lines. I am advised that it is your desire to bury the negroes of your army killed in the engagement near Poison Springs on the 18th Inst. The whites have been buried." Maxey's command refused to take prisoners from Kansas Colored Infantry units until the end of the war.[37]

"I beg leave to call special attention to the Choctaw Brigade," Maxey wrote in his report. "These people," he continued,

36 OR 34, pt. 1, 746, 748-749, 754, 756; Edwards, *Shelby and his Men*, 275.

37 OR 34, pt. 1, 746, 820, 826, 842; Sutherland, "A Strange Wild Time," 116-117; DeBlack, *With Fire and Sword*, 112-115; Joiner, *One Damn Blunder from Beginning to End*, 128-129; Edwards, *Shelby and his Men*, 275-276; Gregory J. W. Urwin, "'We Cannot Treat Negroes . . . as Prisoners of War': Racial Atrocities and Reprisals in Civil War Arkansas," in Anne J. Bailey and Daniel E. Sutherland, eds., *Civil War Arkansas: Beyond Battles and Leaders* (Fayetteville, AR, 2000), 213-223; Anne J. Bailey, "Was There a Massacre of Poison Spring?," in *Military History of the Southwest* (Fall 1990), Issue 20, 168; Charles H. Lothrop, *A History of the First Regiment Iowa Cavalry Veteran Volunteers: From Its Organization in 1861 to Its Muster Out of the United States Service in 1866* (Lyons, IA, 1890), 182.

came of their own volition. No law or treaty compelled them to do so. They were placed on the extreme left of the attacking division. Nobly, gallantly, gloriously they did their duty. They fought the very army (Thayer's from Fort Smith) that had destroyed their once happy homes, insulted their women, and driven them with their children destitute upon the world, and many an avenging blow was struck; many yet will be. The troops from Missouri, Arkansas, and Texas vied with each other in honorable emulation.[38]

Colonel De Morse, who had led Gano's brigade, was also impressed with the performance of the Indians. " [T]he Choctaws, who, from their position flanking nearly to the enemy's rear were better able to pursue them advantageously, continued keenly on their track and did splendid service, which it is not my province to detail."[39]

News of the event spread quickly. "White soldiers, no less than Indians, had become exasperated by the Negro outrages on Prairie d'Ane, & I understand that little quarter was given," wrote Southern missionary Henry Merrell. "Indeed I have heard our own people call it the 'Poison Spring Massacre.'" Other reports claimed the Choctaws took scalps.[40] "There were 10 negroes killed to one white Fed," confirmed a Confederate soldier (probably Alfred Hearn of the 10th Arkansas Cavalry). "They made the negroes go in front and if the negro was wounded, our men would shoot him dead as they passed and what negroes that were captured have, from the best information I can obtain, since been shot."[41]

The *Washington* (Arkansas) *Telegraph* ran an account by a participant that confirmed the general course of the fighting: "The enemy stood their ground and

---

38 OR 34, pt. 1, 843.

39 Ibid., 847.

40 Henry Merrell, "The Autobiography of Henry Merrell: Industrial Missionary to the South," James L. Skinner, ed. (Athens, GA, 1991), 367-368; Roman J. Zorn, ed., "Campaiging in Southern Arkansas: A Memoir by C. T. Anderson," in *Arkansas Historical Quarterly* (Autumn 1949), Issue 8, 243; Gregory J. W. Urwin, "Poison Spring and Jenkins' Ferry: Racial Atrocities during the Camden Expedition," in Mark K. Christ, ed., *All Cut to Pieces and Gone to Hell: The Civil War, Race Relations, and the Battle of Poison Spring* (Little Rock: August House, 2003), 125.

41 Dear Sallie, April 20, in Mark K. Christ, "Who Wrote the Poison Spring Letter?," in Mark K. Christ, ed., *All Cut to Pieces and Gone to Hell* (Little Rock: August House, 2003), 100; Gregory J. W. Urwin, "Poison Spring and Jenkins Ferry: Racial Atrocities during the Camden Expedition," in Christ, 107-137; Gregory J. W. Urwin, "'We Cannot Treat Negroes . . . as Prisoners of War:' Racial Atrocities and Reprisals in Civil War Arkansas," in Gregory J. W. Urwin, ed., *Black Flag Over Dixie: Racial Atrocities and Reprisals in the Civil War* (Carbondale, IL, 2004), 132-147.

fought well until we were within forty or fifty yards of them, when they broke in utter rout, leaving the ground literally covered with their dead. We pursued them two or three miles." "We captured the whole train, four pieces of artillery, many small arms and a few prisoners. Fully 500 were killed, mostly negroes," reported Col. John C. Wright of Crawford's brigade. "We fought dismounted and pursued the fleeing enemy some two and a half miles when we were ordered back." A Rebel trooper named W. C. Braly wrote home to his mother, "Our cavalry cut off a supply train near Camden capturing over five hundred wagons and killing nearly a whole regt of negroes." Fear of the Choctaws spread. Local resident Elizabeth Watts wrote her son to complain that Walker's regiment had stolen all her hogs. When she told one of her slaves to check on them, the man refused out of fear for his life.[42] Although several rumors blamed the Indians for the massacre, it is readily apparent that many Confederate units took part in the killing. Kirby Smith praised Maxey and his command and singled out the performance of Walker's Choctaw brigade. With that, he ordered Maxey to return to his district.[43]

Frederick Steele, meanwhile, had received word that Banks had been defeated at Mansfield, Louisiana, on April 8, his campaign in shambles, and that he was retreating toward Alexandria. He declined Banks' entreaty that he continue his march to join him because the Rebels were now being reinforced in his sector. Kirby Smith had decided Steele was a real threat, but exposed and potentially vulnerable to a counter-thrust. He called for the return of Sterling Price's infantry and more from Taylor's small army confronting Banks. Steele wisely abandoned Camden and withdrew northwest with Kirby Smith's motley command in pursuit. The opposing forces fought a bloody affair on the last day of April at Jenkins' Ferry, southwest of Little Rock, in what turned out to be the major battle of Steele's Camden Expedition (the northern portion of the Red River Campaign). Smith's failure to catch Steele before he could cross the Sabine River, coupled with the

---

42 *Washington* (Arkansas) *Telegraph*, May 11, 1864; John C. Wright, *Memoirs of Colonel John C. Wright* (Pine Bluff, AR, 1982), 142; OR 34, pt. 1, 784, 789, 835, 836, 137; W. C. Braly to My Dear Ma, May 7, 1864, in Amanda Braly Papers, Special Collections, University of Arkansas, Fayetteville; Elizabeth Watts to My Dear Son, May 9, 1864 in "Poison Springs Battle Recalled by 1864 Letter," in *Ouachita County Historical Quarterly* (September, 1987), Issue 19, 14.

43 James M. Dawson to Dear Father Sister and Brothers, May 5, 1864 in James Reed Eison, ed., "'Stand We in Jeopardy Every Hour:' A Confederate Letter, 1864," in *Pulaski County Historical Review* (Fall 1983), Issue 31, 52.

bungled nature of his piecemeal attacks, ended his chance to destroy the main Federal army in Arkansas. Steele returned with his army to Little Rock.[44]

Kirby Smith was very satisfied with General Maxey's handling of a difficult district, and he had never placed much faith in Brig. Gen. Douglas A. Cooper. Smith thought the matter of who ranked whom had been settled months earlier, until Maxey tendered his resignation because other officers who participated in the Camden Expedition were being promoted over him. The implication was that he had not done his duty, and "by quietly submitting," he would seem to "tacitly acquiesce in that decision."[45]

Maxey was popular among his officers, and a petition was circulated that he had the "entire confidence of the Indian Nations as a people . . . of the army . . . [and] of the people of the Northern Sub District of Texas." The petitioners requested that Smith not accept Maxey's resignation. When Cooper learned what was happening, he protested to both Maxey and Smith that Jefferson Davis had promised him command of the department. He sent them copies of President Davis's address to the General Grand Council, Steele's removal order, the order giving him command of the Indian troops, and the recommendation of the highest ranking general in the Confederate army, Samuel Cooper, dated December 11, 1863, that he "be placed in the entire command of the Indian Department."[46]

Cooper's effort outraged Maxey, who launched a protest of his own to Maj. George Williamson, assistant adjutant general under Kirby Smith. "I never intend any man or combination to drive me when I know I am on firm ground," Maxey argued. "I greatly desire to fulfill his [Kirby Smith's] expectations and it would be a matter of just pride if I can successfully administer this District through all surrounding difficulties." The reason he did not have Cooper arrested for insubordination, explained Maxey, was because he "works through others and does not show his hand" and has "considerable influence with the Indians." To arrest him would ultimately be a "detriment to the service," he concluded.[47]

44 OR 34, pt. 1, 845-846; Sutherland "A Strange Wild Time," 117-123; DeBlack, *With Fire and Sword*, 114-117; Joiner, *One Damn Blunder from Beginning to End*, 129-134; Kerby, *Kirby Smith's Confederacy*, 312-314; Castel, *General Sterling Price and the Civil War in the West*, 179-183.

45 S. B. Maxey to S. S. Anderson, May 20, 1864, in Maxey Collection.

46 Douglas H. Cooper to E. K. Smith, May 29, 1864; Douglas Cooper to W. R. Boggs, May 29, 1864, in Maxey Collection.

47 S. B. Maxey to Maj Gen Williamson, June 3, 1864, in Maxey Collection; OR 34, pt. 1, 1,184, and ibid., pt. 4, 669.

Kirby Smith decided on his own to promote Maxey and addressed him as "Maj. Gen." in a June 8 communication apologizing for the delay in his elevation in rank. The delay, explained Smith, was because of bureaucratic problems. He reassured Maxey that he had complete confidence in him, a gesture Maxey appreciated. Smith, meanwhile, ordered Cooper to report to his new superior, and considered the controversy resolved. He was wrong. Campbell LeFlore, a delegate to Richmond from the November 1863 Grand Council, explained in a long letter to Maxey why the question of rank continued to fester. LeFlore had met with Jefferson Davis twice, he explained, and was confident that Cooper had indeed been promised command of the district. All LeFlore and others who supported Cooper wanted was "justice." Unwilling to back down, Maxey replied to Laflore on June 28. "A different construction has been placed twice officially by the highest military authority in the Trans Miss Dept.," he explained. "The energy of patriots should be devoted to prompt and harmonious action, giving every aid that unity, honesty & energy can give." The tenacious problem remained unresolved.[48]

Seven weeks earlier in Virginia, President Davis had recommended that Stand Watie be promoted to brigadier general, which the Confederate Congress confirmed four days later on May 10, 1864. E. C. Boudinot shared the good news with Watie that he had "procured the appt. of Uncle Stand as Brig. Genl." and credited Arkansas senators Robert Johnson and Charles Mitchell for having pressed Davis on the matter. Because of the distance involved and problems with Confederate mail, notifications did not always reach the Trans-Mississippi, and on May 24 Watie was still referring to himself as colonel. Maxey boasted to his wife on June 13 that "Watie has been made a Brigadier on my recommendation," but as late as June 20 Maxey was still addressing Watie as colonel.[49]

The spring of 1864 brought with it another campaign season. General U. S. Grant was promoted to lead all the Union armies and was accompanying Maj. Gen. George G. Meade's Army of the Potomac in a major offensive against Gen. Robert

48 Kirby Smith promoted Maxey on his own to major general without permission from President Jefferson Davis. The Confederate Senate never affirmed the new rank, and Maxey remained a brigadier general until the end of the war. Warner, *Generals in Gray*, 216. S. B. Maxey to Campbell Leflore, June 28, 1864, in Maxey Papers; E. Kirby Smith to S. B. Maxey, June 8, 1864; S. B. Maxey to E. K. Smith, June 12, 1864; Williamson to Cooper, June 14, 1864; Campbell Leflore to S. B. Maxey, June 26, 1864, in Maxey Collection.

49 Elias C. Boudinot to W. P. Boudinot, June 2, 1864; Dale and Litton, eds., *Cherokee Cavaliers*, 166 (this letter is not in the Cherokee Nation Papers); M. to his wife, June 13, 1864, in Maxey Collection; Franks, *Stand Watie and the Agony of the Cherokee Nation*, 159; Dale and Litton, eds., *Cherokee Cavaliers*, 157-158; Stand Watie to D. H. Cooper, May 24, 1864; *OR* 34, pt. 4, 686; Parins, *Elias Cornelius Boudinot*, 58.

E. Lee's Army of Northern Virginia. Another offensive under Maj. Gen. William T. Sherman was driving south into Georgia against Gen. Joseph E. Johnston's Confederate Army of Tennessee. Other movements, smaller in nature but designed to further press the shrinking Confederacy, were also underway. In the Trans-Mississippi, Confederate leaders shifted their military interests to the Arkansas River valley and Fort Smith. Watie raided Scullyville, in the northeast corner of the Choctaw Nation near Fort Smith and destroyed some Union fortifications. On May 19, he sent Lt. Col. James M. Bell, Sarah Watie's brother, to Fort Smith, with 100 men. Bell's raid killed an officer and took three prisoners, from whom Watie learned that General Thayer had returned from the Camden Expedition with five steamboats on the Arkansas River. Three of the boats had returned to safely to Little Rock, but Watie suspected they were preparing for a run to Fort Gibson. He assigned men to watch the water level and inform him when it was navigable to Gibson.[50]

Watie thought there might be between 4,000 and 5,000 men at Fort Smith, but a spy who had been there put the number at no more than 2,700. Rumors circulated that the Federals would soon evacuate, but reports to the contrary also abounded. Cooper sent word that General Thayer had returned with 1,700 white troops and 300 Indians, and recommended to Maxey that Col. Jackson McCurtain of the 3rd Choctaw, who was operating on Winding Stair Mountain in the Ouachita Mountains, leave his wagons south of the mountains to keep them safe from Federal raids. Colonel William F. Cloud, with five regiments of Union cavalry, was campaigning against General Shelby's cavalry brigade, which controlled the Arkansas River at Dardanelle. Reports during the first two weeks of June indicated only 1,800 infantry and cavalry at Fort Smith. The confused state of affairs continued without definitive intelligence one way or the other.[51]

Rebel troops also were on the move. Watie shifted Creek troops from camps along Mill Creek, near modern Tishomingo, north of the San Bois Mountains on Brazil Creek, which flows into the Poteau River from the west. A few weeks later,

50 Stand Watie to D. H. Cooper, May 24, 1864; Stand Watie to Sarah Watie, June 1, 1864, Dale and Litton, eds., *Cherokee Cavaliers*, 164-165.

51 Stand Watie to D. H. Cooper, May 24, 1864; Endorsement from D. H. C., May 25, 1864; Robert P to General S., May 25, 1864; Robert Pierce to Gen., June 1, 1864; Sam Gunter to General, June 13, 1864; E. W. Adair to Col., Endorsed by D. H. Cooper, June 15, 1864, in Unofficial Letterbook, Maxey Collection. These reports were sent to Cooper, who forwarded them to Maxey. *OR* 34, pt. 4, 109, 121, 361-362.

they moved to San Bois Creek, which flows into the Arkansas from the south. Watie sensed an opportunity to hit the Federals and set a plan in motion.

Watie ordered George Washington Grayson to take 300 men and Lieutenant Forester's battery of three guns to Pleasant Bluff on the south bank of the Arkansas, about five miles below the confluence of the Canadian and Arkansas rivers where the channel passed close to the south bank. The Creek Nation had sent the bookish Grayson to college in Fayetteville for two semesters before he joined the Creek brigade as a private. He was eventually promoted to lieutenant and, at the age of 21, to captain. At the head of a company of the 2nd Creek Mounted Volunteers, he earned the nickname Tulwa Tustunugge (Wolf Warrior). Grayson, on his first detached command, positioned and concealed the artillery along the bluff while Watie waited south of the Canadian River across from Tom Starr's place at Briartown for the Arkansas to rise. Colonel Adair's command was watching the river from the north side, farther upriver at Webber's Falls.[52]

In Fort Smith, meanwhile, plans were underway to send a large Federal shipment of supplies by wagon—Watie later reported it consisted of "150 bals [barrels] of flour, 16,000 pounds of bacon & considerable quantity of store goods." General Thayer informed Colonel Phillips that 50 "wheel-mules" would soon arrive at Fort Gibson from Fort Scott, and he wanted them escorted to Fort Smith to assist with supply trains.[53]

Captain M. S. Adams, Thayer's commissary of subsistence, wrote his counterpart under Phillips, Capt. G. L. Gaylord, that Phillips was to "deliver to McDonald and Fuller 500 barrels of flour; also an order for 20 sacks of green coffee and 15 barrels of brown sugar" that had been lent by the sutler to feed troops at Fort Smith. Trains were on the way from Fort Scott, and Phillips was to retain no more than a 20-day supply for his command. Lt. George Huston would be in charge of the shipment and, on the return trip, was to pick up a store of lime waiting

---

52 Pleasant Bluff was also referred to by contemporaries as Pheasant Bluff; G. W. Grayson, *A Creek Warrior for the Confederacy: The Autobiography of G. W. Grayson*, W. David Baird, ed., (Norman, OK, 1988), 41-45, 47-55, 59-61, 76, 79-82, 82, n. #10; Stand Watie to Captain [T. B. Hieston], June 13, 1864, in Unofficial Letterbook, Maxey Collection; OR 34, pt. 1, 1012; Warde, *George Washington Grayson and the Creek Nation*, 77-78.

53 OR 34, pt. 1, 1,012-1,013; and ibid., pt. 4, 687. Wheel mules were trained to be harnessed closest to the wheels of a wagon; Stand Watie to Capt. [T. B. Hieston], June 13, 1864; W. P. Adair to Watie, June 14, 1864, in Unofficial Letterbook, Maxey Collection.

for him at the mouth of the Illinois River. The sternwheeler *J. R. Williams* carried a 25-man escort from the 12th Kansas under Lt. Horace Cook.[54]

The *J. R. Williams* left on the morning of June 15 and steamed about 50 miles upriver without incident until Watie's Rebels opened fire with cannons and small arms. The artillery fire was well delivered and struck the sternwheeler several times above the water line, killing two of the men aboard. The Kansas infantry fired one ineffective volley before the doomed vessel struck a sand bar along the north side of the river. Two more Kansas men died in the scramble to get ashore and out of harm's way. Lieutenant Huston and the captain had little choice and surrendered the boat while Lieutenant Cook and most of his men escaped to Fort Smith. Cook's decision to abandon the *J. R. Williams* did not sit well with General Thayer. Two sources reported the steam engine had been damaged during the bombardment, but Captain Grayson later recalled that it worked well enough to move the boat to the south bank of the river. Elated by the success, Watie's men unloaded some of the cargo on a sand bar, but had no wagons to transport the captured supplies. Most of Watie's men, including Grayson's Creeks, took what booty they could carry and left. Two women, one white and the other black, were on the boat when it surrendered. Watie kept the black woman as a cook.[55]

Colonel John Ritchie of the 2nd Indian Home Guard, who had learned about the debacle from Cook's retreating Kansans, arrived at noon on the north bank with 40 men to drive the rest of Watie's men away from the wreck. By this time the river, which was continuing to rise, began carrying away some of the cargo that had been unloaded onto the sandbar. Watie set fire to the *J. R. Williams* and shoved the flaming hulk into the current. The burning sternwheeler drifted downstream.[56]

Ritchie and Watie traded shots across the river the following day while the 2nd Kansas Colored Infantry under Col. Samuel J. Crawford marched from Fort Smith along the south bank of the Arkansas. Watie was aware of the approaching Federal infantry and left on the afternoon of June 17. Captain Grayson remained to keep watch until sundown. During his withdrawal, Watie met Major Campbell with 150 Chickasaws, who had been sent by General Cooper to reinforce him. He retired to the Iron Bridge on San Bois Creek and threw out pickets to protect his position.

---

54 *OR* 34, pt. 4, 503, 687.

55 Ibid. 503-504, vol. 34, part 1, 1,011-1,012, 1,013, Grayson, *A Creek Warrior for the Confederacy*, 82-84.

56 Ibid., 83-84; *OR* 34, pt. 1, 1,013, pt. 4, 504; Warde, *George Washington Grayson and the Creek Nation*, 78-79.

Colonel Crawford's Kansas troops drove in Watie's pickets and Crawford brought his battery forward and fired a few rounds, but decided against a major fight and retired.[57]

Maxey focused his attention on Fort Smith as he moved men into the Arkansas River valley. General Cooper, who was still in command of only the Indian troops, met with Maxey on June 24 and asked him to put his military plans for the district in writing. In an eight-page letter to Cooper, Maxey outlined his intentions within the restraints of Kirby Smith's instructions: "No move should be made endangering the command. . . . [and Smith also] "require[d] this force to cooperate with movements in Arks." Initially, Maxey and Kirby Smith had discussed moving on Fort Smith, but this plan assumed the lower Arkansas River valley, including Little Rock, would fall into Confederate possession that spring. Once Fort Smith fell, they believed Fort Gibson would follow. Smith, however, was being pressured by Richmond to move his Louisiana troops east of the Mississippi River. Without those troops, Little Rock could not be taken, and without possession of the lower Arkansas, an assault on Fort Smith was unlikely to succeed. Even if it was taken, it could not be held.[58]

Maxey, who was aware that Brig. Gen. Joseph Shelby's cavalry brigade was disrupting shipping on the lower Arkansas and White rivers and placing wagon trains to Little Rock at risk, came up with an alternate plan. Given Shelby's operations, Fort Smith was more likely to be supplied from points north, either from Fort Scott or Springfield. A letter captured by Watie on the *J. R. Williams* stated that Colonel Phillips was not to keep supplies for more than 20 days, and that Fort Gibson would be supplied by trains from Fort Scott. "[W]hilst always holding the main command ready to cooperate with movements below," he wrote Cooper,

---

57 OR 34, pt. 1, 1,013, pt. 4, 504; Grayson, *A Creek Warrior for the Confederacy*, 84-87.

58 S. B. Maxey to D. H. Cooper, June 25, 1864, in Maxey Papers, Center for American History, University of Texas; Kerby, *Kirby Smith's Confederacy*, 324-331; OR 41, pt. 4, 1,068-1,069. Maxey mentions these instructions to Cooper on June 27, 1864, in S. B. Maxey to General Boggs, July 15, 1864; Ibid., part 2, 1,007, where the editors assign it "not found," although Maxey sent Boggs a copy for Kirby Smith to read. Maxey also referred to this letter mapping out his strategy in S. B. Maxey to E. Kirby Smith, November 8, 1864, ibid., pt. 4, 1,036. A copy of the lost original, dated June 25, 1864, is in the Sam Bell Maxey Papers, Center for American History, University of Texas. This important letter places the military activity of 1864 in the Indian Nations in a strategic context, and negates the myth that conditions in the Indian Nations had descended into guerilla warfare—and especially that Watie cooperated with Quantrill, which he did not do. Under Maxey, Watie maintained communications and service with the Confederate command under Kirby Smith to the end of the war and remained in Indian territory after Kirby Smith and others had fled to Mexico.

"and never endangering the command by an initial move in force against a superior force, or a fortified place too strong to be taken without great sacrifice not compensated by advantages, we can never the less be of great service to this Territory and the Country and to movements in Arks."[59]

Maxey advocated a loose cooperation with Shelby by operating in the Cherokee Nation north of the Arkansas River. "My plan is to communicate with Shelby, see what we may depend on in that way, keep parties constantly on the alert in the direction of Fort Smith and a watch upon Gibson." He intended to "send out strong bodies well mounted and armed north of the Arkansas between Smith and Gibson on the line of communications & capture & destroy every wagon that the enemy may have out on any of the roads." With "Shelby operating in the same way with parties of his command the evacuation of Ft Smith is forced. It is needless to add that when that goes Gibson falls."[60]

The following day, Maxey pointed out to Cooper, who had suggested concentrating against Gibson, that if Fort Smith was abandoned Gibson would be theirs as well. Maintaining Gibson without control of Fort Smith would be difficult because supplies would have to be hauled all the way from Texas. Unless Confederate operations at Little Rock could prevent reinforcements from reaching Fort Smith, an attack there—where, by Cooper's own count there were 4,000 to 5,000 well-armed men in the vicinity—would be impractical. Maxey planned to keep Federal troops isolated at the forts and perhaps force their abandonment. It was with this in mind that he kept a close watch on the troop movements at Fort Smith.[61]

Regiments from Iowa, Kansas, Missouri, and Arkansas frequently moved to and from Fort Smith, which left the Rebels uncertain of the garrison's true strength. Cooper's agents sent him varying reports of Federal strength, which he forwarded to Maxey. A report dated June 15, 1864, claimed there were 1,800 men at Smith. By July 2, spies were reporting that the Union command had sent three regiments to Little Rock, including the 9th Kansas Cavalry. Colonel William F. Cloud was campaigning against Shelby. Back at Fort Smith, black troops were busy cutting down all the trees within one-quarter to one-half mile of the fort and

59 S. B. Maxey to D. H. Cooper, June 25, 1864; OR 41, pt. 1, 923-930.

60 Ibid.; OR 34, pt. 4, 687; OR 41, pt. 1, 191-192; OR 34, pt. 3, 1,027-1,028; OR 34, pt. 4, 1,068-1,069; Castel, General Stirling Price and the Civil War in the West, 197; Edwards, Shelby and his Men, 302-318.

61 OR 34, pt. 4, 697-698; OR 41, pt. 2, 998-999, 1,000, 1,007, 1,086-1,087, 1,096.

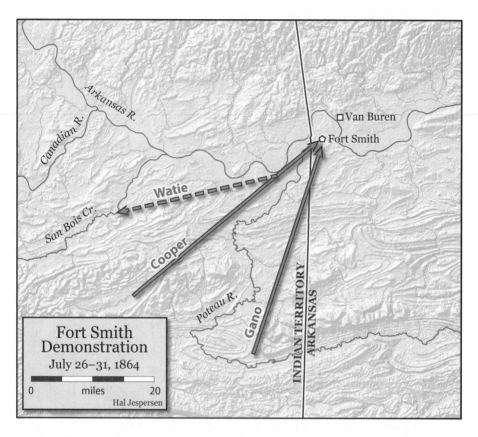

digging rifle pits. One of Cooper's agents prepared a map of the new fortifications springing up at Fort Smith.[62]

Reports from June 30 through July 5 raised the number of troops at Fort Smith to between 3,800 and 4,000. On July 7, Watie reported 3,800 including 1,200 cavalry. This was down from a high of 4,600 before three black infantry regiments departed for Little Rock. On July 12, reports arrived that work on the fortifications at Fort Smith had stopped and Union troop strength had dropped to just 1,500. One spy reported that only five regiments were present. Cooper thought it might be a trap meant to induce an attack and shared his concern with Maxey.[63]

62 OR 41, pt. 1, 24; Sam Gunter to General [Cooper], June 13, 1864; E. W. Adair to Col. n.d.; Endorsement, D. H. Cooper to [Maxey], June 15, 1864; R. D. Ford to Cooper, July 1, 1864; Stand Watie to Maxey, July 7, 1864, in Unofficial Letterbook, Maxey Collection. A Union report confirms the Ninth left on July 2.

63 John Toothman to S. B. Maxey, June 30, 1864; Stand Watie to General [Cooper], July 7, 1864; attached note from Cooper, n.d.; B. D. Ford to [Cooper], July 5, 1864; Robert Pierce to

Maxey concluded in a summary of his intelligence that between 1,500 and 2,000 troops had left Fort Smith around July 1 to deal with Shelby, that the fort was well-supplied, and that the estimates of the troops remaining were around 2,500. The number was small enough, Maxey concluded, to order a series of demonstrations against the Federals. The first was on July 26, when General Gano moved up with approximately 600 Texas and Choctaw cavalry near Fort Smith on the east side of the Poteau River. Cooper's scouts reported "a body of Federal cavalry (supposed to be Arkansans) camped near Caldwell's, and other detachments on Massard Prairie five miles from Fort Smith." The original plan, no doubt with strong input from Gano, was for him to remain with most of his men south of Devil's Backbone Mountain and send the remainder to attack what was thought to be a superior Union cavalry force. The Rebels would then purposely retreat, hoping to lead their pursuers into a trap 10 miles below.[64]

On the morning of July 27, Gano discovered the Union cavalry at Massard prairie was not as strong as Cooper expected, so he left a small detachment south of Devil's Backbone Mountain and took the rest of his force, which included the 2nd Choctaw and Col. J. W. Wells' battalion, with him. The move surprised about 200 men of the 6th Kansas Cavalry grazing stock seven miles from the fort. Gano's raid killed and wounded about 50 Federals and captured 127, together with 400 revolvers, 200 rifles, horses, and other valuable supplies. Once the fighting ended and the spoils collected, he returned south of Devil's Backbone to the James Fork of the Poteau and made camp.[65]

As part of the continuing pattern of attacking black troops without mercy, Watie planned to attack a haying party near Fort Smith north of the Arkansas River. As usual, the force consisted of Kansas Colored Infantry, supported by white cavalry. Cooper intended to use the remainder of his force in a demonstration before Fort Smith to cover Watie's operation, to determine the military strength at Smith, and perhaps to encourage an evacuation of the post. On July 29, Watie and 200 men from his brigade joined elements of the Choctaw Brigade—principal agents of the slaughter at Poison Spring—and part of Howell's Battery at Scullyville Prairie. The raid against the haying party, however, was cancelled when

D. H. Cooper, July 12, 1964; D. H. Cooper Endorsement, July 13, 1863; J. McCustin to General [Cooper], July 12, 1864. N. Hays to Col., July 12, 1864, in Unofficial Letterbook, Maxey Collection.

64 OR 41, pt. 1, 31; Summary of information Fort Smith, Hd Qrs, n.d., probably written by Maxey, Unofficial Letterbook, Maxey Collection; OR 41, pt. 1, 31.

65 OR 41, pt. 1, 25-26, 29, 31-32.

they discovered the Arkansas was too high to ford. Watie rejoined Colonels Adair and James M. Bell with the rest of the Cherokee Brigade and prepared to move concurrent with Gano and press Fort Smith.[66]

On the morning of July 31, both columns advanced simultaneously, Gano from the south and Watie from the west. The advancing Rebels pushed Federal pickets back into the rifle pits surrounding the fort and engaged in what General Maxey later described as a "picket fight," though it also involved what became a deadly artillery duel. After the garrison recovered from the shock of the appearance of the Rebels in strength, a Union battery appeared, unlimbered, and opened fire against Captain Humphreys' light battery, "with shot and shell passing harmlessly over our heads for some time," reported Cooper. Later, one of the Federal rounds blew off the leg of a Rebel gunner and killed three battery horses. Another shell, he continued, "swept off the head from the shoulders of one of Gano's men."

By this time it was getting dark, and with enemy infantry within striking distance the decision was made to withdraw. Gano's men formed the rear guard. Cattle and other supplies were rounded up, commissary stores hauled away, and another $130,000 worth burned. Of the 2,000 to 2,5000 Rebels engaged, Cooper reported one killed and five wounded (one mortally). General Thayer, who did not know the Rebels had retired, rounded up six companies of civilians and placed them in the rifle pits, where they remained all night in case of an attack. He did not believe that Forts Smith or Gibson would be taken, but he was unable to go out and fight the way he wanted to because of a lack of healthy horses able to move his artillery (14-16 pieces), or mount sufficient cavalry in the brutal July heat. The day after the demonstration, Gano's men drove a herd of cattle back to Riddle's Settlement. Watie's troops moved to San Bois Creek, and Cooper's men to Limestone Prairie. The new deployments left Watie and Gano operating in the Arkansas River watershed.[67]

*   *   *

On the political front, Maxey printed a circular of a July 11 address Watie had made to the National Committee and Council of the Cherokee Nation. The Cherokee general had reviewed the recent history of the Nation, including the assembly in Tahlequah in 1862, its alignment with the Confederacy, the "deliberate

---

66 Ibid., 31-33.

67 Ibid., 24, 29-30, 31-35.

treachery" of John Ross, and, most particularly, the wartime sacrifice of his people. "The destitute condition of the people had been represented to the authorities of the Confederate Government, and I am gratified to be able to state that measures had been taken to supply them with provisions." He recommended placing "all Cherokee male citizens between the ages of eighteen and forty-five [in service for the duration of the war]." By that course, concluded Watie, "We may securely expect a final triumph.[68]

The Confederate leadership was aware that conditions at Fort Gibson were perilous. One of Watie's officers forwarded to him a captured letter written by a Union officer to his wife in response to her request for permission to travel to the fort. "[Y]ou do not know what you ask," he admonished. The garrison had dismantled the houses for fortification materials and they were desperately short of food. "Here we are 13000 Indians & 2000 soldiers to night with no provisions," he explained. "I issued the last ounce of flour yesterday." He intended to send an escort to Fort Smith the next day to return with supplies. "I am afraid to estimate the suffering & Starvation that must occur."[69]

Hoping to exploit the deteriorating situation, Maxey on August 18 wrote Kirby Smith for permission to allow Watie to make a raid he had proposed into Kansas as far north as Humbolt, raiding enemy installations and operations and encouraging tribes in the western part of the state to join him in an attack into the eastern half. A movement against Fort Gibson only made strategic sense if there was simultaneous equivalent action against Pine Bluff and Little Rock, and no such effort was planned that fall. "Should General Watie prove successful," explained Maxey, "it will be such a diversion as will prevent movements south from Fort Smith or Fort Gibson, and if well conducted will be attended with material results." Kirby Smith approved the plan in August and advised that it be implemented by October to coincide with a major movement by General Price into Missouri. What Smith failed to share with Maxey was that he had received orders from the secretary of war dated July 21, 1864, that "the Indian Territory west of Arkansas is hereby constituted a separate district of the Trans-Mississippi" and General Cooper was to

68 OR 41, pt. 2, 1046-1048.

69 Husband Ale to Dearest Jennie, June 30, 1864, in Unofficial Letterbook, Maxey Collection. Also captured was a letter from Colonel Phillips to Fort Scott complaining about the scarcity of supplies. W. A. Phillips to C. W. Blair, July 1, 1864, in Unofficial Letterbook, Maxey Collection.

command it. Smith quietly shelved the order, intending to wait until the fall campaign season was nearly over before vigorously protesting it.[70]

Watie, meanwhile, refused to remain stationary while awaiting Smith's approval of his plan. On August 31, he crossed the Arkansas River above Fort Smith with about 300 men to take a second run at the haying operation that high river had prevented him from completing during the demonstration against Fort Smith. He attacked three days later. The Federal force was stronger than anticipated, with 70 cavalry and 350 infantry, but somewhat dispersed. The raid wounded several of Watie's men but he managed to kill "several negroes" and take "twelve prisoners [white men]." Watie had shown for a second time that no one in Maxey's command would take prisoners from the Kansas Colored Infantry.[71]

Support for Watie's plan was growing. A day earlier, Maxey had assured the Commissioner of Indian Affairs, Col. S. S. Scott, that after the setback of Honey Springs, Kirby Smith urged him to do everything possible to encourage the people of the Indian Nations. He had done his best to meet all the important leaders, he explained, and had made speeches at Armstrong, Boggy Depot, and Limestone Prairie. The Indian leaders, he continued, now believe in the alliance's ultimate success. Watie had been north of the Arkansas River the past winter, and Phillips' raid had been turned back. "The Choctaw Brigade . . . [in the] Battle of Poison Spring behaved most gallantly receiving just praise from the army and people," declared Maxey, who went on to recount Watie's capture of the *J. R. Williams*, the "demonstration" at Fort Smith, and Phillips' failed attempt to gain the loyalty of the Indian leadership. Even his printing press had been busy, working hard to spread good news to maintain morale.[72]

---

70 *OR* 41, pt. 1, 777, 781-782; pt. 2, 1,019, 1,072, 1,032; pt. 3, 971, 991.

71 J. M. Lynch to Caroline Bell, August 31, 1864; Dale and Litton, eds., *Cherokee Cavaliers*, 184 (this letter is not in the Cherokee Nation Papers); *OR* 41, pt. 2, 1095-1096. Kirby Smith had suggested to General Taylor that he show no mercy to armed ex-slaves on June 13, 1863, but this suggestion was countered by Secretary of War Seddon on August 13, 1863 when he ordered that the white officers be summarily dealt with, but the blacks be disarmed and returned to their masters. Nathaniel Banks was raising many black regiments in Louisiana under the title Corps d'Afrique. Maxey's comment to Boggs concerning Watie's raid was "It seems that Watie has had a little brush near Fort Smith with the Corps d'Afique, burning hay, & c." The Corps d'Afique consisted of 18 regiments raised in Louisiana by order of General Nathaniel Banks, John D. Winters, *The Civil War in Louisiana* (Baton Rouge, LA, 1963), 238. *OR* 15, 717; ibid., 22, pt. 2, 965; ibid., 26, pt. 1, 688-689; Kerby, *Kirby Smith's Confederacy*, 110-112.

72 S. B. Maxey to S. S. Anderson, August 23, 1864, Maxey Collection. This is the same letter in which Maxey reported on the organization of the refugees and the system to feed and shelter them. The second half of that long letter concerns political and military matters.

The importance of the Indian Nations to the Confederacy was something its leaders had been pushing since the earliest days of the war. Richmond, however, was a long way from the Trans-Mississippi Theater. "If the Indian Territory gives way the granary of the Trans Miss Department, the breadstuff and beef of this and Arkansas army are gone [and] the left flank of Holmes army is turned," Maxey had earlier expressed to Kirby Smith. "[N]ot only the meat and bread, but the salt and iron of what is left of the Trans Miss Department." Maxey lamented that the "wonderful importance of regain[ing] Fort Smith and Fort Gibson and to expel the enemy from the Territory has never been realized by those not conversant with the geography of this country."[73]

Maxey, who had a firm grasp of what was happening in the Nations and what the people were thinking, warned Kirby Smith that the argument originally used by the Confederacy to recruit the Indian Nations—that the Union had abandoned them—could become a Union tool against them. That May, he wrote again to the department commander about the importance of holding the Nations, declaring that if the Indian country was taken its inhabitants would have nowhere to go and would despair. "Should it ever be the misfortune of this people to fall under Federal rule again, no treaty will be made," warned Maxey. "It will be seen as conquered country and . . . be parceled out among freed negroes the offcomings of Europe and the descendants of Jeremiah."[74]

To Commissioner Scott Maxey stressed the importance of honoring the treaties. He endorsed President Davis's plan for a full division of Indian troops and urged the commissioner to use his influence to see that the 3,000 rifles promised be delivered. "In making this report I have frequently refereed to military matters— the superintendency and the military affairs of the territory are so intimately blended that they cannot be separated," explained the general. "Although it is not strictly in the line of your duty, I would ask that you aid all in your power the securing and delivery of these guns."[75]

While Maxey worked to keep all the puzzle pieces in place, General Gano contributed to the growing momentum for a raid north of the Arkansas, although with changing strategic goals. "I feel in rather a good humor to day and somewhat hopeful because . . . you are going to send me an order to go north of the Arkansas River, and do all of the damage to the Yanks I can," he penned Maxey. "I have been

73 Ibid.

74 Ibid.

75 Ibid.

anxious about it, but seems so much delay on our part while the Feds are moving Trains & Regiments to and fro and the finest opportunities, offered to whip them in detail. . . . If we were ordered or allowed to move forward Gen. Stand Watie would cooperate with us, but General Cooper is very cautious, and I am satisfied some good opportunities have and are being presented. What say you?"[76]

The advance north finally got underway on September 7 when General Price crossed the Arkansas River at Dardanelle in what would be known as Price's Missouri Expedition. With him were three organized divisions of cavalry totaling 10,000 to 12,000 men.[77] By September 12 Gano and Watie also were on the move, riding independently up the Texas Road above Perryville toward the Arkansas River. The two leaders had agreed on an informal joint command, each leading his own brigade even though Gano ranked Watie. Much was expected of them. "[T]he President spoke in the highest terms of you in the interview I had with him last," E. C. Boudinot informed Watie the day before he set out. "[H]e replied in answer to the remark I made that Stand Watie had penetrated far into the enemy's lines—'Yes he will go as far as anybody.'"[78]

The raid would eventually net clothing, supplies, wagons, and livestock beyond everyone's expectations, but nothing could relieve Sarah Watie's concern about the human toll being extracted by the war as the expedition was getting under way. "You must write to me what clothes you need most," she told her husband in a letter from Lamar, Texas. Many of the soldiers she knew were without proper clothing. "I am all out of sorts this war will ruin a great many good people they will not only loose all their property but a great many will loose their character," she prophesied wisely, "which is of more value than all of their property.[79]

The initial goal set by Watie and Gano was to disrupt a haying operation on Flat Rock creek, near the Grand River, and then capture a supply train thought to be making its way to Fort Gibson from Fort Scott, Kansas. Maxey stressed that this part of the expedition was just a "dash," and the real raid into Kansas would follow. Watie's command comprised elements of the 1st Cherokee under Lt. Col. C. N. Vann, the 2nd Cherokee under Maj. John Vann, Creeks under Lt. Col. Samuel

76 Gano to Maxey, August 29, 1864; Gano to Maxey, August 31, 1864, in Maxey Collection; OR 41, pt. 2, 1096; pt. 3, 930.

77 OR 41, pt. 1, 88-89, 92-93, 99-100, 107-108, 110-111; Kerby, *Kirby Smith's Confederacy*, 324-329, 334, 339-340; Castel, *General Sterling Price and the Civil War in the West*, 203-207, 209.

78 Ibid., 189.

79 S. C. Watie to My Dear Husband, September 4, 1864; Dale and Litton, eds., *Cherokee Cavaliers*, 187-188.

Chekote, and Seminoles under Col. John Jumper, a total of 800 men, all mounted. Gano led his Texas cavalry brigade and Howell's battery of six guns, numbering around 1,200 men.

On the same day Gano and Watie left on the raid, Maj. Henry Hopkins rolled out of Fort Scott for Fort Gibson as an escort for 300 Federal wagons, four ambulances, and 90 privately owned sutler's wagons. He knew it was dangerous, and "moved with as much dispatch as the conditions of the animals would permit." The initial escort consisted of 120 mounted and 140 dismounted men from the 2nd, 6th, and 14th Kansas Cavalry regiments.[80]

The two Rebel forces came together at Camp Pike on September 13 and moved to Prairie Springs the next day. With Watie's brigade leading the way, they left the Texas Road and moved northwest to avoid Fort Gibson. Major John Vann's detached command of 150 men was ordered to take the right flank and watch the Arkansas River for Federals, but none were found in that direction. Vann forded his command at the Creek Agency, scaring away a lone Federal trooper, and scouted upstream for six miles along the north bank of the river, where Watie and Gano crossed their commands. The water was high and the crossing took six hours, with ammunition for the artillery being carried across with special care.[81]

Gano and Watie camped in the river bottom four miles south of Choska. The next day they followed the road from Choska north to Sand Town, where they crossed the Verdigris River and moved east toward the Grand River. Lieutenant Colonel Clement Neeley Vann with 200 men of the 1st Cherokee rode out to guide Captain Strayhorn and a detachment of the 30th Texas Cavalry in order to get between the Union haying party on Flat Rock Creek and the Grand River, about a mile to the west. The rest of the command followed slowly behind. When the the head of the column reached Blue Mound, the two generals and their staffs climbed to the top and used a telescope to view the working haying party a few miles distant. They were not expected. Watie and Gano moved their commands to within one mile of the enemy camp. The forthcoming action would be a tough fight for the 2nd Kansas Cavalry, but for the 1st Kansas Colored Infantry, it would be nothing less than a slaughter.[82]

---

80 *OR* 41, pt. 1, 766-767, 777, 781, 785, 788; pt. 3, 930.

81 Major Vann was Ella Coody's stepfather; *OR* 41, part 1, 785, 786, 788-789.

82 Blue Mound is located about a mile and a half west-north-west of the intersection of Highways 69 and 51 at Wagoner, Oklahoma; *OR* 41, pt. 1, 771-772, 785, 788; Warde, *George Washington Grayson and the Creek Nation*, 79.

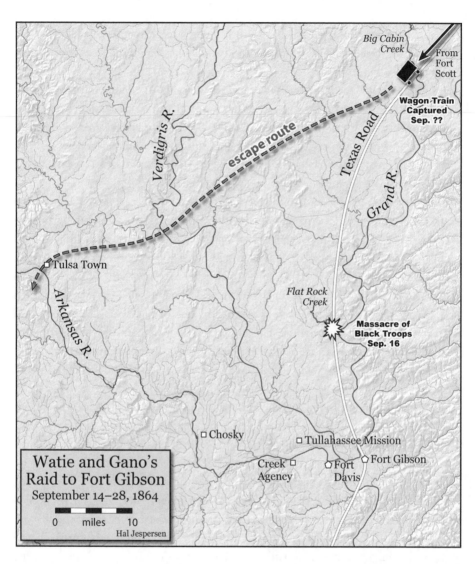

Big Cabin
Creek   From
Fort
Scott

**Wagon Train
Captured
Sep. ??**

escape route

Verdigris R.

Texas Road

Grand R.

☐ Tulsa Town

Arkansas R.

*Flat Rock
Creek*

**Massacre of
Black Troops
Sep. 16**

☐ Chosky   ☐ Tullahassee Mission

Creek ☐   ○ Fort   ○ Fort Gibson
Agency   Davis

**Watie and Gano's
Raid to Fort Gibson**
September 14–28, 1864

0   miles   10
Hal Jespersen

Gano moved two regiments to the right flank and positioned Howell's battery, "Gano's Guards," and other detachments in the center. Howell's battery was not unlimbered for action because it would not needed. The booming guns would also be heard by the Union supply train and those in Fort Gibson, giving away their position and the fact that the Rebels were traveling with artillery. Watie's men took up the left side of the front. With Vann and Strayhorn behind them, the haying party was virtually surrounded. Union Capt. Edgar A. Barker was in command of the haying operation but had only about 125 men to protect it, including 37 infantry and 88 cavalry. Not all of his troopers were mounted.[83]

When pickets brought word that Rebels were near, Captain Barker ordered his men to take up a position in a gully just west of the creek. Barker, meanwhile, together with 25 troopers, cautiously advanced toward the enemy line, discovered its strength, and withdrew under fire. Watie and Gano quickly advanced their commands to within 200 yards of the main Federal position, triggering a fitful fight that lasted about 30 minutes. Somehow the heavily outnumbered Union troops managed to repulse three advances of Confederate cavalry. Barker knew his situation was desperate and ordered his dismounted cavalry and infantry to scatter into the timber toward the Grand River. The mounted cavalry, which Watie estimated at 65 men, made a break toward the main Confederate line. A few were killed and wounded, many were captured, and 15 managed to slip through. The Federal camp belonged to Gano and Watie.[84]

For a few minutes everything was quiet. "It did not appear that there was anything for us to do more than burning the camps and the great ricks of hay that stood about the field," recalled Captain Grayson, the Creek who Watie had earlier posted to Pleasant Bluff to await the *J. R. Williams*. "Presently, however, some of our men discovered a negro hiding in the high weeds near the creek and shot and killed him. At another point one was found and shot, and it now appearing that these were to be found hid in the weeds, the men proceeded to hunt them out much as sportsmen do quails." Some of the black troops tried to surrender, but to no avail. Captain Barker reported that of the 37 black soldiers, only four escaped. Once the hunting and massacre of unarmed troops ended, the Rebels burned the mowing machines, hay, and wagons and camped nearby.[85]

Meantime, at Baxter Springs, Kansas, Major Hopkins' escort of the 200 wagons rolling to supply Fort Gibson was reinforced by 50 Cherokees under Captain Ta-la-lah. On the night of September 17, five days into the journey and still 70 miles from Fort Gibson, Hopkins received a disturbing communication from Col. Stephen H. Wattles. Fort Gibson's commander ordered Hopkins to move "with all possible haste" 15 miles to Cabin Creek station and join forces there with

83 Ibid.

84 *OR* 41, pt. 1, 772, 785. Gano reported that he sent an officer with a white flag to ask for their surrender. He was fired on. Barker makes no mention of it.

85 Grayson, *A Creek Warrior for the Confederacy*, 95-96; *OR* 41, pt. 1, 772, 785, 789. Barker reported 40 wounded, missing, and killed, and 66 taken prisoner; Warde, *George Washington Greyson and the Creek Nation*, 79-80.

Lieutenant Palmer and his 170 Union Cherokees and "await further orders." Rebels, he warned, "estimated at 1,200 to 1,500 strong, with infantry" were north of the Arkansas and moving "with the intention of attacking the train." Lieutenant B. H. Whitlow, 3rd Indian Regiment, would reinforce Hopkins with 140 Creeks and Cherokees and Major Forman would join him with mountain howitzers and six companies of the 3rd Indian.[86]

Whitlow reinforced Hopkins, but Forman did not. Hopkins crossed his train from a wooded flood plain on the north side of Cabin Creek up a cutback to the top of the bluffs that formed the south bank of the creek. The defenders drove heavy branches into the ground around a house to fortify it from small arms fire, and a stock pen to the north also offered some protection. Ten large hay ricks were placed in a line in front of and running north of the house, and the wagons and teams were moved north of the ricks along the bluffs. A forest enveloped them for about 100 yards to the south and the west, beyond which the land opened to a gently rising prairie. Major Hopkins, who now had 610 men, increased the number of his pickets. With nothing left to do, he waited for Wattles' promised "further orders" hoping they or more men arrived before the Rebels did.[87]

Federal prisoners, meanwhile, told Watie that the large wagon train was expected soon. The Cherokee general dispatched Major Vann north up the road to scout for it. Vann rode about four miles and ran into enemy pickets, prompting Watie to send reinforcements. As it turned out, the Federals belonged not to the train but to reinforcements heading for Cabin Creek to assist Hopkins. Watie camped for the night, September 17, 23 miles north of Cabin Creek on Wolf Creek. The following day Gano learned 300 enemy were posted at Cabin Creek, so he set off with 400 of his own men and two guns to inspect the depot. When he got there and realized the enemy wagon train had already arrived, he sent word back to Watie to bring up the rest of the force as soon as possible. Watie joined Gano about midnight. "We agreed to move on the enemy at once," reported Watie, "who was aware of our approach, but entirely ignorant of our numbers."[88]

With the moon high and behind them, the two Rebel generals moved ahead and formed a battle line on the elevated prairie half a mile from the Federal front. Gano's three Texas cavalry regiments formed on the right, Howell's battery in the center, and Watie's Indian brigade on the left (first the Cherokees, then the

---

86 OR 41, pt. 1, 769-770, 785.

87 Ibid., 772, 786, 790.

88 Ibid., 786, 789.

Seminoles, and finally the Creeks on the far left). The Federals, Watie believed "had decidedly the advantage in position." When all was ready, Gano and Watie advanced their commands to within 500 yards of the Federal position. A Union officer approached, reported Gano, "and when he learned that we were Rebels, he called on God to damn us, and invited us forward." When the Confederate general asked if the Federals would surrender, the officer replied that he would find out and let him know in five minutes. "I waited fifteen," continued Gano, "and hearing some wagons moving I advanced my line about 3:00 a.m." The Federals opened fire.[89]

Major Hopkins later reported the opening as "1 o'clock," when the Rebels fired on his lines "with artillery and small arms and moved upon my lines with a yell." The trapped officer would later report, "[I] was not informed they had any artillery until it opened fire on my lines." Within minutes the civilian teamsters fled, jumping on mules and riding north as fast as they could get away. The firing and darkness spooked some of the teams, which "ran over the cliff and the wagons crushed the teams to death," recorded Gano. Knowing the position was strong, the train had been stopped, and "not being able to see the fortifications," Gano prudently withdrew to wait for dawn. About an hour later sounds reached his line of the Federals attempting to move the train to the rear. The Rebels fitfully advanced through the dark a second time and opened fire with both musketry and artillery. Watie's Creeks on the far left found and turned the Federal line and captured several wagons, but Gano once more called off the fight to wait for sunrise.[90]

At first light the Rebels spotted the wagons and mules in the timber and "what appeared to us to be immense earthworks," wrote the Rebel commander, "but afterward proved to be immense hay ricks." Gano relocated his artillery forward to hit both wagons and the hay ricks and ordered Watie to dispatch "Colonel Vann with the two Cherokee regiments across to capture all the wagons that might have left before day." Vann "gained the position," reported Watie, "no wagons were crossing." The Cherokees returned for ammunition, and the Creeks again flanked the Federal right to get behind enemy lines.

"Now appeared a crisis," wrote Gano. A gully "twenty-five yards in the rear filled with armed men who had not yet participated" confronted them. "We were

89 Ibid., 773, 786-787, 789-790.

90 Ibid., 767, 770, 771, 786, 790. Gano report that he pulled back his command on two occasions, but Watie, ibid., 786-787, does not mention a pause or temporary withdrawal once the advance began.

compelled to fall back," he continued, "but not one man of the gallant Thirtieth started from that murderous fire until I ordered them to do so." A final shifting of the guns and commands assured victory. "Crash after crash of shells swept Yankees, negroes, Pins, and mules away from the land of the living," continued Gano, who had a tendency toward exaggeration, "while every regiment and company poured in volley after volley." A final push and the Union line broke, the defenders scattering into the woods. Before the collapse Major Hopkins had been making every effort to rally the teamsters and the wagon-masters, but the turning of his flank and his loss of position rendered his effort to get his train away "useless." "A general stampede ensued," was how Watie recorded the event. The survivors moved through timbered bottom lands to make their way as best they could to Fort Gibson. Hopkins sent dispatches ahead that the train had been taken, and he would report he lost most of his train and that his killed, wounded, and missing did not exceed 35. Despite the nearly six hours of fitful fighting, Gano reported his losses as just "6 killed, 48 wounded—3 mortally."[91]

The Rebel leader gave two different accounts of the size of the train, one claiming 247 wagons and the other 255. Watie counted 250. Both officers estimated the value of the wagons at $1,500,000 in greenbacks, and, after all the fighting and destruction, 130 wagons were still serviceable, as were 740 mules. The Rebels gathered all the clothing and supplies they could salvage, burned everything else, and began moving the wagons southwest toward Pryor's Creek. While Watie moved, Gano's Texans repulsed an attack from Fort Gibson and kept the Union force occupied during the night by maintaining his position and moving an empty wagon over a rocky stretch of trail to suggest the train was still nearby. Watie moved the train across Pryor's Creek and west and a little south to cross the Verdigris in the vicinity of Claremore's Mounds. The Federals had few options and returned to Gibson. Gano returned to the train and expected a fight at the Arkansas River that never materialized.[92]

On September 21, Watie informed General Cooper from Bird Creek that he was going to cross the train at Tulsa Town and would follow Cooper's route of 1861 when he had chased Opothleyahola. Watie crossed the river but changed his plans and turned south toward the Creek Council Ground and North Fork Town,

---

91 Ibid., 768, 770-771, 786-787, 790-791.

92 OR 41, pt. 1, 787, 791. According to Major Hopkins, a few wagons and an ambulance escaped, but there is still a discrepancy in the numbers reported by Gano because records show 294 wagons and four ambulances started the journey. Some of the private sutler wagons may have turned back before the train reached Cabin Creek.

where he arrived on September 28. "[F]or three days and nights our boys were without sleep, except such as they could snatch in the saddle or at watering places," Gano reported about the return trip. "They dug down banks, cut out trees, rolled wagons and artillery up hills and banks by hand, kept cheerful, and never wearied in the good cause, and came into camp rejoicing on September 28."[93]

The operation elated General Maxey, who issued a general order of praise. "Throughout the expedition I am rejoiced to say perfect harmony and good will prevailed between the white and Indian troops, all striving for the common good of our beloved country," he observed. "For gallantry, energy, enterprise, dash, and judgement, and completeness of success this raid has not been surpassed during the war."[94]

Kirby Smith was also impressed and issued a general order to mark the event. "The General commanding announces to the army the complete success of one of the most brilliant raids of the war." Smith recounted the success of the raid and concluded, "[T]he celerity of the movement, the dash of the attack, and their entire success entitle the commands engaged to the thanks of the country."[95]

When Sarah Watie learned of her husband's success, she penned a letter grounded in her domestic concerns for his well-being. "I thought I would send you some clothes but I hear you have done better than to wait on me for them," she wrote on October 9 from Lamar, Texas. "I have been looking for you to send me some brown domestic and some calico. I have not a sheet till I make it is all I can do to keep clothes on the children. I wanted to send them to school," she continued, "but the board is 200 a month apiece and 12 in provision what must I do. I want to have your advise on it."[96]

The successful raid raised flagging morale. All the men involved received new clothing and other supplies, and the wagons and mules proved invaluable. Still, it was just one raid. If the the Confederate command had permitted Maxey to operate north of the Arkansas River for the remainder of the season, as he had hoped and planned to do, he might have enjoyed further success. Such was not to be.

In October, another large wagon train left Fort Scott for Fort Gibson and arrived without incident.

---

93 Ibid., 791, 783-784.

94 Ibid., 793.

95 Ibid., 794.

96 Sarah to Stand, October 9, 1864, Cherokee Nation Papers, typescript; Dale and Litton, eds., *Cherokee Cavaliers*, 200-201.

Chapter 14

The War Ends

October 1864, friends in the Indian Nations and northern Texas informed General Maxey that Douglas Cooper was about to replace him as commander of the district. J. R. Johnson, an officer serving under Cooper at Fort Washita, passed on the rumor to Maxey, adding the news "has given me no little cause of uneasiness. I have not slept soundly since I heard it."[1]

The news also deeply concerned Maxey. "Rumor has been rife in a quiet sort of way for the last two weeks that Genl Cooper was to supersede me in command of the District," he wrote Brig. Gen. William R. Boggs, the commander of the Louisiana district in Shreveport. "This has caused no little excitement here and in Northern Texas. . . . When compelled to answer private letters from respectable gentlemen about it . . . [I] could then only say that I had no knowledge of such change." Boggs initially replied in jest that an order had been issued giving the command to Don Carlos Buell, a Union major general who had recently resigned under pressure, before assuming a more serious tone: "Gen. [Kirby] S[mith] has kept the order and written to Richmond requesting its revocation. Col. Scott [Commissioner of Indian Affairs] will also take the matter to the President."[2]

Kirby Smith held onto the order elevating Cooper to command of the district for more than two months before finally contacting Richmond on October 1, 1864,

1 J. R. Johnson to S. B. Maxey, October 16, 1864, in Maxey Collection.

2 S. B. Maxey to W. R. Boggs, October 24, 1864, Maxey Collection; W. R. Boggs to S. B. Maxey, October 28, 1864, Maxey Collection.

to protest it. "[S]erious injury would result to the service were this order enforced," he informed his distant superiors. "I have delayed its publication awaiting further instructions. General Maxey . . . has with skill, judgment, and success administered his duties. . . . His removal, besides being an injustice to him, would be a misfortune to the department." Smith concluded that he "would respectfully refer the department to Colonel Scott, the Commissioner of Indian Affairs regarding the civil administration of General Maxey's District."[3]

Maxey's command status was as uncertain as his plan to force the evacuation of Forts Smith and Gibson, which was interrupted by the new commander of the District of Arkansas. Major General John B. Magruder had served on the Virginia Peninsula earlier in the war, but wasn't up to the demands of front line combat service in the Eastern Theater. President Davis shipped him west to command Texas, New Mexico, and Arizona, where he enjoyed more, if limited, success. After Sterling Price left on his mounted Missouri expedition, Magruder was tapped to assume the Arkansas command. Maxey's plan to move against Forts Smith and Gibson didn't sit well with new new commander, who expressed concern about the vulnerability of Washington, Arkansas, where the Rebel state government still resided. Magruder convinced Kirby Smith to order Maxey to stand down, which had the effect of holding General Gano's brigade south of the Arkansas River, away from the supply trains running from Fort Scott. Cooperation with Magruder was one of Maxey's duties, but he did not believe his planned operation put Washington in any imminent danger.[4]

Magruder, however, had plans of his own. With the help of Gano's brigade, he intended to take on Brig. Gen. Frederick Steele at Little Rock. Kirby Smith reviewed the plan and concurred, believing something should be done to help support Price's large-scale mounted raid, which was now rumored to be returning south from Missouri. When it became apparent that Steele was too strong at Little Rock after being reinforced in late October, Magruder turned his attention to Fort Smith. Relations between Maxey and Magruder, however, remained strained.[5]

Maxey, meanwhile, rode to the Choctaw capital of Chahta Tamaha [modern Bryan County, Oklahoma] to attend a Grand Council meeting at the Armstrong Academy on November 4. William P. Adair and D. N. McIntosh had invited Maxey to speak to the Council the following day, where Maxey could reinforce his

3 OR 41, pt. 3, 971; Boatner, *Civil War Dictionary*, 174.

4 OR 41, pt. 4, 999, 1,032, 1,036, 1,039.

5 Ibid., 1,001, 1,019, 1,020, 1,028-1,029, 1,032-1,033.

position as commander of the district. The Confederate general delivered a three hour speech "on the administration Civil & Military and their duties to each other and the Confederacy." In later discussions he informed General Boggs he would inspect Fort Washita and Boggy Depot, and be back at Fort Towson by Saturday. Maxey also informed Kirby Smith that the Council had passed "a resolution fully endorsing my administration, civil and military."[6]

Maxey was at the Choctaw capital when an inquiry from Magruder arrived that stirred his blood. What was the best route from Washington to subsist cavalry moving on Fort Smith from Camden? Magruder also asked about the fortifications and troop strength at Fort Smith, and how many men and artillery it would take to capture it. Magruder was curious about what troops in Maxey's command besides Gano's brigade could participate in the venture, the route they should take, and when the movement could be completed. This interfered with Maxey's plans for Forts Smith and Gibson. The frustrated officer rode the next day to Fort Washita, informed General Cooper of Magruder's request, and handed him a copy with his reply. "[H]e has given but short notice and this seems to be a sudden notion," complained Maxey, "as but a short time ago he attempted to move Gano's brigade to the neighborhood of Fulton." He asked Cooper to advise him in his response, and to send his reply to Boggy Depot, which Maxey expected to reach on November 8.[7]

In his report dated the same day, Maxey complained to General Boggs, who was still at Shreveport, about Magruder's plan. "[H]ad my troops been left north of the Arkansas six weeks longer," lamented Maxey, "I believe supplies would have been so depleted and forage cut off by burning all the hay that both forts would have been forced to evacuate very shortly. I fear now," he continued, that "he is too late & without grass he cannot get forage for a larger move."[8]

Smith, however, encouraged Maxey to cooperate with Magruder. In a letter dated November 4, Smith explained that complications with supplies and an increase in General Steele's strength made a campaign around Little Rock impossible. Smith wanted to support General Price's withdrawal from Missouri in

---

6 Although E. C. Boudinot had initially supported Cooper's three brigade plan, W. P. and D. N. McIntosh, together with Watie, firmly supported Maxey over Cooper. S. B. Maxey to W. R. Boggs, November 6, 1864, and S. B. Maxey to D. N. McIntosh and W. P. Adair, November 4, 1864, in Maxey Papers, University of Texas; OR 41, pt. 4, 1,035-1,036.

7 OR 41, pt. 4, 1,024; S. B. Maxey to D. H. Cooper, November 6, 1864, in Maxey Papers, University of Texas.

8 S. B. Maxey to W. R. Boggs, November 6, 1864.

case he was unable to winter there, and believed the occupation of Fort Smith was the best way to accomplish that goal. Confederate control of the fort would make it much easier for Price to retreat safely and secure the Indian Nations and northern Texas for at least six months. Smith had already shared these ideas with Magruder and had instructed him to relay the details of the campaign to Maxey.[9]

Maxey's attitude improved with the news that Smith was behind the plan. That night, he sent Cooper a copy of Smith's communication and reiterated that Cooper's biggest problem in cooperating with Magruder would be forage for his horses. He also remained concerned that the campaign was being undertaken too late in the season. "[N]evertheless if Genl Magruder undertakes this matter and carr[ies] it out he will be of wonderful service to the Dist. And I want to give him all the help possible," explained Maxey.[10]

Cooper replied to Maxey the following day that adequate forage would be available on a route from Washington through the Ouachita Mountains using the Caddo Gap, at the headwaters of the Caddo River leading to Waldron. Cooper recommended that Gano's brigade at Laynesport join Magruder at Waldron. A captured dispatch from Col. Stephen H. Wattles commanding at Fort Gibson to General Thayer, commanding Fort Smith, included the depressing news that "General Price is retreating, hard pressed, having been defeated near Fort Scott, Cabell and Marmaduke, with 1,200 men and 13 pieces cannon, captured." Cooper would have trouble with forage, but he promised to attempt to meet Magruder's cavalry commander, Maj. Gen. John Wharton, in the vicinity of Fort Smith if there was time. Cooper estimated Union strength there at 3,000 men, with timber cut away from all approaches. Maxey forwarded copies of Cooper's reply to Magruder and Smith and began moving back to Fort Towson the same day. Both Maxey and Cooper continued to note that their operation north of the Arkansas would have been successful if left alone.[11]

On November 12, Magruder ordered John Wharton to begin moving on Fort Smith. Magruder, who still did not trust Maxey, al planned to send Gano's cavalry to Fort Smith, but on November 13 he received all of Maxey's and Cooper's reports and could see they were cooperating. In the following days, the Confederate military concentration shifted from Fort Smith to Price's retreating

---

9 Note from Maxey's Adjutant T. M. Scott, November 8, 1864, in Maxey Papers, University of Texas; OR 41, pt. 4, 1028-1029, 1034.

10 S. B. Maxey to D. H. Cooper, November 8, 1864, in Maxey Papers, University of Texas.

11 OR 41, pt. 4 1,037-1,039, 1,042-43.

army. Magruder hoped Wharton could supply Price somewhere near the Caddo Gap and recommended that Gano gather supplies on the Texas Road. That same day, Magruder advised General Boggs that Price's route would be through Fort Gibson. He called off the attack on Fort Smith but left Wharton in the Caddo Gap in case he might be helpful.[12]

Sterling Price was not only retreating, but had been routed out of Missouri. He entered the state in September with about 12,000 cavalry and 14 artillery pieces had moved slowly toward St. Louis. Major General William Rosecrans, however, had reinforced the city and Price soon determined it was too well defended to attack. He shifted his command toward Pilot Knob, southwest of St. Louis, drove Brig. Gen. Thomas Ewing's heavily outnumbered defenders into Fort Davidson, and attacked on September 27. Price's careless assaults were repelled several times at the cost of some 1,000 in killed and wounded and the fort never fell. The defenders evacuated during the night, leaving him with a hollow victory at best and his dreams of taking St. Louis in ruins.

Riding north and then west, the Rebels found the capital at Jefferson City too strongly defended to assault and continued riding and fighting toward Kansas City, with Generals Rosecrans and Alfred Pleasonton in pursuit and General Blunt at Westport, south of Kansas City, with Kansas and Colorado Regulars and militia. The opposing forces came together at Westport on October 23, where a Union command under Maj. Gen. Sam Curtis crushed Price's outnumbered army. With some 30,000 participants (22,000 Union and 8,500 Confederates) Westport was the largest battle fought in the Trans-Mississippi. Given its size, total casualties were remarkably low at some 510 Confederates and 350 Federals. Two Confederate generals, John Marmaduke and William Cabell, were captured, along with most of their men and all of their artillery. Jo Shelby covered the Rebel rear as Price retreated south toward the Indian Nations with his battered remnants. Price's defeat army, an anxious Magruder telegraphed Shreveport on November 16, was completely "demoralized" and incapable of further fighting.[13]

Price's defeat ended further operations for the season and Smith made plans for Magruder's command to go into winter quarters on the Red River downstream

---

12 Ibid., 1,037-1,039.

13 Sutherland, " A Strange Wild Time," 134-139, 142, 145-146; DeBlack, *With Fire and Sword*, 123-131; Castel, *General Sterling Price and the Civil War in the West*, 209-217, 228-237; Kerby, *Kirby Smith's Confederacy*, 340-352; David Eicher, *The Longest Night: A Military History of the Civil War* (New York, NY, 2001), 754-757. For a detailed study of Price's Raid, see Castel, *General Stirling Price and the Civil War in the West*, 189-255.

from Laynesport. Most of the Arkansas troops would do so as well, although Smith moved part of his force to Texas to preserve forage supplies along the Red River.[14]

Maxey stood ready at Doaksville to provide Price with supplies and invited the defeated general to ride to Fort Towson, if convenient. Price declined and made directly for Bonham, Texas, which he reached by November 24. Many of his men, however, fell out of the strung-out column and were more than happy to take advantage of Maxey's assistance. "Price's men have been arriving here for four or five days, singly, in squads, and every way," Maxey reported. "Their horses are miserably poor . . . and many are being abandoned on the prairies." By the time Price reached Texas only about one-third of his command was still armed, and their horses were unfit for further service. Unable to provide suitable mounts, most of the men would eventually reorganize as infantry. On November 30, Price began moving his command into winter quarters at Laynesport. The Little Missouri and the Ouachita rivers, considerably south of the Arkansas, formed the new Confederate frontier.[15]

The Indian brigades were also going into winter quarters. Sarah Watie hoped to entice her husband to spend the coming month in Texas. "I can get a house [illegible] with three rooms to it tolerable comfortable and ten acres of land," she wrote Stand in early November. "Mr. Russel offered me that house . . . if you could get a black man for him Old man Russel thinks that you are such a great man that you can get a negro," she continued. "I told him I did not have any idea you could make such a deal but he wanted the man so bad that he seemed to think that you could make a ne[gro]. Write next mail." Sarah's wish would pass unfulfilled. A few days later Watie's adjutant, Thomas F. Anderson, secured a house at Boggy Depot and Watie and his men spent the winter there.[16]

Around the same time Lt. Col. Elias C. Boudinot, Watie's nephew, grew concerned about plight of the southern Cherokee refugees. He toured their camps and despaired at the trying conditions he found there. There were critical shortages of almost everything, particularly cotton cards necessary for processing cotton into homespun. The day after Commissioner Scott's circular of encouragement was published, Boudinot expressed his frustration in a letter to Maxey, which he

14 *OR* 41, pt. 4, 1,052, 1,053-1,054, 1,061-1,062.

15 Ibid., 1,056-1,059, 1,067-1,068, 1,076-1,079, 1,084, 1,101-1,102.

16 S. C. Watie to My Dear, November 2, 1864, in Cherokee Nation Papers; Dale and Litton, eds., *Cherokee Cavaliers*, 202-204, 208-209, 212-213; Thomas F. Anderson to Stand Watie, November 5, 1864; Stand to Sallie, January 20, 1865; T. M Scott to Stand Watie, February 12, 1865, in Cherokee Nation Papers.

followed up with letters to Watie urging, as Boudinot always did, that action be taken to help them.[17]

Although the present system outlined by the relief ordinance was largely Boudinot's own creation, he urged Maxey to scrap it and let the military handle the system of providing rations to the refugees. He wanted to use funds allocated by the Confederate Congress and the Commissioner of Indian Affairs to pay for looms, cotton cards, better shelter, and other needed supplies. He had warned Watie on October 3 that the refugees holding old issue currency would soon lose one-third of its value if forced to trade it in for newly issued currency, and he vowed to prevent that from happening. Somehow, using his considerable political influence in Richmond, he succeeded. (The Confederate government apparently allowed the residents of the Indian Nations to exchange the currency at the same value.) The gesture was a sign of appreciation for the nearly indefensible military front these destitute Cherokees had fought so long to hold. Boudinot also suggested the Cherokee Council appropriate up to $15,000 to purchase cotton cards, and explained that Congress would provide another $50,000 by November or December. "Don't fail to call the council and recommend the measures I have before suggested for God's sake and the sake of the naked refugees, let some person go across the river and buy cotton cards," Boudinot urged Watie on October 31 from Washington, Arkansas. "And let them do it quickly, it will soon be too late." Despite this assistance, conditions for most refugees remained wretched to the end of the war and beyond. In many cases it was not until 1867 before they returned to their nations in substantial numbers.[18]

As always, the question of obtaining better arms deeply concerned Indian leadership and General Maxey. On November 9, the Grand Council passed resolutions requesting 3,000 rifled muskets promised by Jefferson Davis the previous February. In early December, a delegation consisting of Cols. William P. Adair and Daniel N. McIntosh, together with John Jumper and Peter P. Pitchlynn, traveled to Shreveport to present the resolution to Kirby Smith.[19]

---

17 E. C. Boudinot to Maxey, September 30, 1864, in Maxey Collection.

18 Cornelius to Uncle, October 31, 1864, Cherokee Nation Papers, microform; Parins, *Elias Cornelius Boudinot*, 60-61.; Elias Cornelius Boudinot to Stand Watie, October 1, 1864; Elias Cornelius Boudinot to Stand Watie, October 3, 1864, in Cherokee Nation Papers; Dale and Litton eds., *Cherokee Cavaliers*, 194-195, 195-196, 202; E. C. Boudinot to Maxey, September 30, 1864.

19 *OR* 41, pt. 4, 1,115, and ibid., 53, 1,030-1,032.

Maxey prepared Smith for their arrival. "I bespeak for them your most favorable notice," he began. "You will find them men of intelligence, fully acquainted with the condition and wants of the Indians, and thoroughly imbued with the spirit of patriotism. . . . General Watie, who is the principal chief of his nation, recommends . . . Capt. Thomas F. Anderson, assistant adjutant-general of his brigade, to be sent after these guns.[20]

Kirby Smith met with the delegation on December 17. The War Department had sent 25,000 rifles to Selma, Alabama, but Union control of the Mississippi River prevented their delivery into the Trans-Mississippi. Smith agreed to allow Captain Anderson and Sgt. John Walker to go to Selma "with authority to receive and bring 3,000 rifles across the Mississippi River for the sole use of the Indian Division." He gave them a letter for Lt. Gen. Simon Buckner, the commander of the District of West Louisiana, that ordered him to provide assistance if asked to do so.[21]

Anderson kept Watie informed of their progress, including the high cost of hotels. Writing from the Veranda Hotel in Shreveport on December 16 and 18, 1864, Anderson exclaimed, "At the rate of $35.00 a day pr man & horse, not including necessary bitters, it makes a mans pile grow beautifully less every day." Because the Trans-Mississippi Department was short of money, he had drawn only $1,000 to cover his and Walker's expenses, but he was confident more money could be found east of the Mississippi. He sent Watie a newspaper and commented on the latest news inside: "Persons who ought to be able to form a tolerable correct opinion seem to be hopeful and think that even should Sherman succeed in reaching the coast he will do so in a very crippled condition."[22]

Two-thirds of the way across Louisiana, Anderson and Walker stopped at a signal corps camp at Caldwell Parish to have their wagon repaired. Anderson proved he had a sense of humor when he penned Watie, "Nearly every Bridge has been swept away and since leaving Shreveport John and myself have got to be amphibious animals. Had it not been for a certain Bottle, containing a quantity of

---

20 Ibid., 1031; Thomas F. Anderson to Stand Watie, February 19, 1865, in Cherokee Nation Papers; Dale and Litton, eds., *Cherokee Cavaliers*, 240-242.

21 *OR* 41, pt. 4, 1,115, 1,116.

22 Thos J. Anderson to Stand Watie, December 16 and 17, 1864, in Cherokee Nation Papers, microfilm; Dale and Litton, eds., *Cherokee Cavaliers*, 205-206. Anderson was referencing General Sherman's March to the Sea through Georgia. Anderson also told Watie that Reverend Compere's last shipment was on its way from Shreveport, but Anderson was not, as Dale and Litton incorrectly concluded, connected with Compere's humanitarian efforts.

Texas Bois d'Arc, [illegible] would often have stuck in the mud [illegible]. The prospect for a Christmas Eggnog this evening," he added, "is very promising." The two agents planned to cross the Mississippi at Jackson's Point, south of Natchez, but the attempt to obtain the rifles failed. Anderson was back acting as Stand Watie's assistant adjutant the following May, just as the war was ending.[23]

On the first day of 1865, General Grant informed General Halleck that the temptation to abandon Forts Smith and Gibson must be resisted. The movement of wagon trains south from Fort Scott to Gibson and Smith had resumed without serious trouble from the Rebels. Colonel William Phillips, who had orders to hold Fort Gibson even if Fort Smith was abandoned, informed Secretary of War Stanton on January 8 that he had 1,463 troops in camp and 382 on escort duty. Phillips believed he could hold his post with a good regiment of white infantry if half his Indian troops were mounted.[24]

The lack of good cavalry horses continued to plague Phillips, who lobbied hard for more and better mounts. On February 9, he informed Maj. Gen. Joseph J. Reynolds, commander of the Department of Arkansas, that he planned to attack Forts Towson and Washita, as well as Boggy Depot, in April 1865. Intelligence indicated that most of Rebel Indian force was on furlough and would not return until May. If he did not attack, Phillips argued, they would eventually attack him. General Blunt was also lobbying for more troops to defend against the "forces of Stand Watie, Cooper, and Gano, together with a portion of the force [of] . . . General Price, numbering in all about 7,000." Both commanders were worried about what the Confederates had planned for the spring. Blunt asked that Phillips quickly report any movement below his position.[25]

At Gibson, meanwhile, the refugees, by this time mostly Creeks, numbered between 8,000 and 10,000. The Cherokees had moved away from the camps but were still dependent on Fort Gibson for supplies. The total dependent population was approximately 20,000. Colonel Phillips informed Stanton that he did not advise moving the Indian regiments because the Union troops offered the only real protection on which the refugees could rely.[26]

---

23 Thos F. Anderson to Stand Watie, Dece,ber 26, 1864 and February 19, 1866, in Cherokee Nation Papers, microfilm; Dale and Litton, eds., *Cherokee Cavaliers*, 226-228, 240-242.

24 *OR* 48, pt. 1, 391, 403, 456-457.

25 Ibid., 789-790, 851-852.

26 W. A. Phillips to Secretary of War, January 8, 1865, in Fort Gibson Letterbook.

The plight of the refugees weighed on Phillips. On February 2, he complained to General Thayer that he had nothing to issue the "suffering thousands" except beef and salt. The Creeks wanted to go home, but Phillips would not allow it because he could not protect them there. Alternatively, Chief Sands of the Creeks proposed moving his people west of the Verdigris around Tullahassee Mission within the Creek Nation, but north of the Arkansas River. Phillips liked the idea and used it to make another request for horses. He did not get them, but on February 20 he informed his new commander, Brig. Gen. Cyrus I. Bussey, that he planned to move most of the Creeks as Chief Sands requested. Two companies of infantry would protect them there while they planted a crop and established themselves.[27]

Phillips informed the Commissioner of Indian Affairs on February 27 that General Bussey concurred with him that seed corn, sweet potatoes, and Irish potatoes from Kansas should be supplied to the refugees. Until then, he asked that supplies be sent by boat from Fort Smith. Little was done, and the refugees continued to suffer. On March 7, Phillips pleaded with Bussey that he had had nothing to issue for six weeks and that it was vital to get a crop in as the growing season was fast approaching. Phillips furloughed eight to ten men from each company to help the women and children with the planting and suggested to Bussey that "if a boat load of seed corn and potatoes could be shipped here within the next two weeks, its advantages would be incalculable." Phillips issued an order to provide 10 days of military rations to the Indians, but Bussey countermanded it. A frustrated Phillips turned to General Reynolds for assistance and urged him to ship supplies and seed. Thankfully, back pay arrived for the soldiers and those with money bought commissaries and seed for those still short of funds. Phillips continued pressing for "seeds of all kinds" for the refugees, to little avail. "I believe enough corn has been planted to secure the loyal Indian refugees from starvation and the contractors, next year, if we have a season," he wrote with some hope to General Reynolds on April 19. "I allowed a large number of the soldiers to go and assist the women and children in fencing and putting in corn," he continued. "The seed corn was of great advantage. A large amount has been planted. The furloughed soldiers are returning promptly, at the expiration of the short time

27 W. A. Phillips to Brig Gen'l John M. Thayer, February 2, 1865; W. A. Phillips to the Secretary of the Interior, February 3, 1865; W. A. Phillips to Brig Gen'l Cyrus Bussey, February 20, 1865, in Fort Gibson Letterbook.

allowed. We have regimental gardens and are making a government farm. All is still quiet in front."[28]

The Union colonel instructed the commander of the detachment at Mackey's salt works to drill his men two hours every day and to hold a dress parade each afternoon, and expected the arrival of new horse teams for the pair of howitzers he had requested. Phillips wrote General Thayer and others in early January that he was doing all he could to prepare his men to hold the country north of the Arkansas River.[29] If his troops were not mustered out in March to help with a crop, as he had earlier suggested they should be, he hoped to mount 1,000 men and leave 800 infantry to serve at Gibson. "[I have] designed by the 20th of April to take the mounted men and the howitzers and move rapidly on Boggy, Towson, and Washita," he informed Reynolds on February 9, 1865. "I should like in addition to have one battalion of white cavalry; but, if necessary, could do without them." If the Rebels can't "maintain their military organization in the country they lose everything," he concluded. "Attack is the best defense. Their Indian troops are mostly furloughed until May; and if we do not attack them, they will attack us."[30]

Phillips' supplies, however, had all but run out. Rations were cut to eight ounces of flour per day per man. Further cuts might make the flour last until February 25. He suggested that since the Grand River had risen, a boat be sent from Fort Smith with supplies. Two days later Phillips learned his wagon train from Fort Scott had been stranded by high water at the Neosho (or Grand) River ford. On February 27, the steamers *Virginia Barton* and *Ad Hine* arrived at Fort Gibson from Fort Smith with his much-needed supplies.[31] With the wagon train still stranded, Phillips reported that he was going to halt supply from Fort Scott and

---

28 W. A. Phillips to Brig Gen'l Cyrus Bussey, March 7, 1865, April 7 and 19, 1865, in Fort Gibson Letterbook; W. A. Phillips to Commissioner of Indian Affairs, February 27, 1865; W. A. Phillips to Brig Gen'l Cyrus Bussey, February 28, 1865; W. A. Phillips to Major Gen'l J. J. Reynolds, March 10, 1865; W. A. Phillips to Brig Gen'l Cyrus Bussey, April 4, 1865, in Fort Gibson Letterbook.

29 W. A. Phillips to Brig Gen'l John M. Thayer, January 23, 1865; W. A. Phillips to Gen'l Thayer, January 4, 1865; W. A. Phillips to Lt. Col Bassett, January 4, 1865; W. A. Phillips to Lieut Theophilus McLain, January 6, 1865; W. A. Phillips to the Secretary of War, January 8, 1862; W. A. Phillips to Major Hunt, January 19, 1865; W. A. Phillips to the Secretary of the Interior, February 3, 1865, in Fort Gibson Letterbook.

30 W. A. Phillips to Major Gen'l. J. J. Reynolds, February 9, 1865, in Fort Gibson Letterbook.

31 W. A. Phillips to Commanding Officer, Escort for Gibson Train, February 20, 1865; W. A. Phillips to Brig Gen'l Cyrus Bussey, February 20, 1865; W. A. Phillips to Brig Gen'l Cyrus Bussey, February 22, 1865; W. A. Phillips to Brig Gen'l Cyrus Bussey, February 27, 1865; W. A. Phillips to Brig Gen'l Cyrus Bussey, February 27, 1865, in Fort Gibson Letterbook.

bring everything up by boat. Relieved at not having to deal with the sutlers at Fort Scott, Phillips turned back a civilian train from Kansas and ordered oxen at Fort Scott to be transferred to Fort Gibson. On April 1, the *Virginia Barton* and the *Lotus* delivered supplies, relieving Phillip's plight.[32]

Farther south, meanwhile, uncertainty and a losing war effort plagued the Rebels. "I find that I cant get along here [with] out help. I have a home here without anything," Watie wrote his wife Sarah from his winter quarters at Boggy Depot. "Send . . . my box with what clothes you may judge to be sufficient few cooking things if you have any which you can do without Don't forget my big tin cup & whatever you may be able to send me," he urged, "which you do not particularly need at home . . . if you can get it send about 400 lbs of flour I can trade it for pork 1 lb for three . . . try to come & stay with me a few days stay as long as you can as we can live in a house without sponging on any of our friends."[33]

The remaining winter months for the Confederates might have been relatively uneventful but for the negative response to Kirby Smith's efforts to deprive Cooper of command of the District of Indian Territory. To his dismay, Richmond ordered Smith to summarily carry out the order and install Cooper in command of the Indian Territory. He tried to soften the blow to Maxey by asking him to come to Shreveport to serve in some capacity there, but Maxey did not believe there was anything he could legitimately do there commensurate with his rank. Three weeks later on February 14 Smith put Watie in command of the Indian division and made Douglas Cooper Superintendent of the Bureau of Indian Affairs; Smith had often defied or delayed Richmond's directives, and he was still not ready to promote Cooper to command the district.[34]

The upshot of all this was that Maxey was able to resign his position with some grace. "[T]he duties of Superintendent and District Commander have so long been discharged by the same officer that they are now so intimately blended as to be difficult of separation," he informed Smith's adjutant. "[F]or the good of the service, and to enable the business of the District to be conducted . . . I respectfully

32 W. A. Phillips to Brig Gen'l Cyrus Bussey, February 28, 1865; W. A. Phillips to Brig Gen'l Cyrus Bussey, March 8, 1865; W. A. Phillips to Brig Gen'l Cyrus Bussey, April 1, 1865, in Fort Gibson Letterbook.

33 W. A. Phillips to Brig Gen'l Cyrus Bussey, February 28, 1865; W. A. Phillips to Brig Gen'l Cyrus Bussey, March 8, 1865; W. A. Phillips to Brig Gen'l Cyrus Bussey, April 1, 1865, in Fort Gibson Letterbook.

34 W. A. Phillips to Brig Gen'l Cyrus Bussey, February 28, 1865; W. A. Phillips to Brig Gen'l Cyrus Bussey, March 8, 1865; W. A. Phillips to Brig Gen'l Cyrus Bussey, April 1, 1865, in Fort Gibson Letterbook.

ask to be relieved of service in the District of the Indian Territory at the earliest moment which in the opinion of the General Commanding the Department my service can be spared."[35]

Maxey's resignation left Smith with no reason to continue stonewalling Cooper's promotion, and he finally put Cooper in command of the district on February 21. Three days later, Maxey published an address to the people who lived within his district. "[It is] upon every officer and soldier and upon every citizen of the district the absolute necessity of harmonious and united action," he urged. "With this success cannot be doubtful; without this disasters will certainly come. It is his [Maxey's] opinion that the prospects for ultimate success were never brighter than at this moment."[36]

As news of Maxey's removal and resignation spread, tributes and requests poured in from Gano's and Cooper's junior officers. M. L. Bell asked to be relieved so that he might continue serving under Maxey, wherever he ended up. Another officer, S. S. Anderson, expressed his knowledge of the appreciation Kirby Smith felt for Maxey. Lee Alexander testified that Maxey was the best commander under whom he had ever served. R. W. Lee expressed despair over the decision to remove Maxey. Finally, Brig. Gen. Henry E. McCulloch of Texas congratulated Maxey for bringing direction to what was otherwise confusion and discord.[37]

As spring approached, General Cooper began mapping a possible campaign for his new command. On March 15, 1865, he informed Watie that Fort Smith was being well supplied and suggested the Cherokee general collect his command, supplies, ordnance, and horses from Texas, where they had been foraging through the winter, and be ready to move on the enemy by the first of May. There would be no spring campaign in the Indian Nations, however, or anywhere else in the Trans-Mississippi in 1865.[38]

None of them yet knew the war was rapidly winding down east of the Mississippi River. Robert E. Lee had surrendered the Army of Northern Virginia on April 9, and Gen. Joseph E. Johnston was about to do the same with his forces

35 Stand to Sally, January 20, 1865; Dale and Litton, eds., *Cherokee Cavaliers*, 208-209.

36 *OR* 41, pt. 3, 971; ibid., pt. 1, 1,387-1,388; W. R. Boggs to S. B. Maxey, February 9, 1865, in Maxey Collection.

37 M. L. Bell to S. B. Maxey, February 20, 1865; S. S. Anderson to "My Dear General," February 23, 1865; Lee M. Alexander to S. B. Maxey; Henry E. McCulloch to S. B. Maxey, March 4, 1865; R. W. Lee to S. B. Maxey, March 6, 1865, in Maxey Collection.

38 T. M. Scott to Stand Watie, March 15, 1865, in Cherokee Nation Papers; Dale and Litton, eds., *Cherokee Cavaliers*, 217-218; Kerby, *Kirby Smith's Confederacy*, 408-411.

in North Carolina. The news was still slowly making its way west and south. Union authorities were better informed, but the ending of the war in the east did not mean the fighting was over in Indian Territory. By May 15, however, military authorities ordered Colonel Phillips to muster his three regiments out of service.[39] Cooper, however, had received reports that General Blunt was poised to attack with a strong force from Fort Gibson. Cooper sent out scouts from Adair's and Watie's camps, ordered Tandy Walker to assemble the Choctaw brigade, made arrangements for a daily express between Fort Washita and Boggy Depot, and informed his adjutant that he was ready to "take the field." The threat from Blunt never materialized.[40]

Conditions in the Confederate Trans-Mississippi Department deteriorated rapidly and desertions increased. Kirby Smith announced on May 18 that he was moving his headquarters from Shreveport to Houston, Texas. When Magruder informed Smith one week later that his Arkansas command was collapsing, Smith realized the end was indeed at hand and surrendered the Trans-Mississippi Department on May 26, 1865.[41]

The Indian Nations were not included in Smith's surrender, and thus retained their independence and command of their armed forces. Cooper recommended that a Grand Council be convened and advised authorities not to enter into any agreements with the United States until he heard from the government in Richmond—a rather optimistic plea by that late date. Richmond had fallen nearly two months earlier and President Davis was in Federal captivity. The leadership scheduled a council on June 10 at Armstrong Academy. On May 26, the same day Kirby Smith surrendered, E. C. Boudinot contacted General Reynolds, commanding the Department of Arkansas, and offered to help negotiate the surrender of the Cherokees. The Union general rebuffed the offer.[42]

The confused state of affairs was further confirmed by a letter from Sarah Watie to her husband. "We heard you was captured and have not heard any thing to the contrary we hear that Gen K Smith has surrendered and then we hear that he has not," wrote a worried Sarah from Lamar County, Texas, on May 21. "I hear they have set a price on several of there heads and you are included that is the

---

39 *Ibid.*, Kerby, 163-164, 243; W. A. Phillips to Bri Gen'l Cyrus Bussey, April 19, 1865; W. A. Phillips to Maj Gen'l J. J. Reynolds, May 15, 1865, in Fort Gibson Letterbook.

40 *OR* 48, pt. 2, 1301-1302, 1303-1304, 1305, 1310-1312, 636, 687.

41 Kerby, *Kirby Smith's Confederacy*, 421-424.

42 *OR* 48, pt. 2, 1317, 1319, 630-631.

rumor I do not want people to believe it for some of them would be after [illegible] I hear that Cooper will not give you anything. If he does not I believe that they are speculating." Sarah continued, "I do not want you to do anything of that kind I would live on bread and water [illegible] to have it said you had speculated of your people I believe you have always done what you thought best for your people and I would like to die [illegible] [holding that] belief."[43]

"No definite news yet great deal of confusion amongst the troops more particularly the white portion," Watie replied to his wife from Boggy Depot. "I have thought best to send off the majority of them home on furloughs, hints have been thrown out that they would help themselves to the public property.... I think I can manage the rest.... I only write to let you know I am still in the land of the living—love to all."[44]

Union Col. Asa C. Mathews, a commissioner sent by General Herron, informed Watie on June 9 that he had the authority to sign peace treaties with the "tribes" that had aligned with the Confederacy. Mathews and his adjutant, William Vance, traveled to the council at Armstrong, but it had adjourned before they arrived. They wanted Watie to meet with them at the home of past Choctaw governor Robert M. Jones near Doaksville. Peter Pitchlyn of the Choctaws was there, and they sent invitations to Winchester Colbert of the Chickasaws, John Jumper of the Seminoles, and Samuel Chekota of the Creeks.[45]

"We leave this morning in time to go as far as Jarretts have agreed upon the cessation of hostilities with the comms [commissioners] they will leave tomorrow," Watie wrote Sarah from Jones's home on June 23. "Genl Smith had surrendered the whole department on the 26th May—the grand council will convene 1st day of Sept when a comr is expected to arrive—I will return home soon as our council is over at Nails Mill. Jumper & Checota are expected in today try to have Cornelius [E. C. Boudinot] at your house next week I must see him."[46]

As Principal Chief of the Cherokee Nation, Stand Watie and the other chiefs and governors of their respective nations signed peace treaties ending their participation in the Civil War. The specific terms of surrender were negotiated

---

43 S. C. Watie to My [illegible], May 21, 1865, in Cherokee Nation Papers; Dale and Litton, eds., *Cherokee Cavaliers*, 225-226.

44 Ibid., 227-228.

45 A. C. Mathews and Wm. H. Vance to Stand Watie, June 9, 1865, in Cherokee Nation Papers; Franks, *Stand Watie and the Agony of the Cherokee Nation*, 180.

46 Stand to Sallie, June 23, 1865, in Cherokee Nation Papers, microfilm; Dale and Litton, eds., *Cherokee Cavaliers*, 228.

during Reconstruction. Watie, however, had also acted as a Confederate brigadier general commanding the Indian division, and as such on June 23, 1865, was likely the last Confederate general officer to surrender his command.[47]

The Creek and Cherokee Nations were in a horrific state of disarray. During the war years, the population of the Cherokee Nation had fallen from 21,000 to 15,000, or nearly 30 percent.[48] The disruption of the Choctaw Nation was similarly severe. Resolution did not come quickly, and many of the Southern refugee families did not return for years, if they ever did. Some waited until allotment, the process of dividing the lands in severalty among citizens of the Five Tribes, a procedure that began in 1899. The devastation of the loyal full bloods was equally complete.

*   *   *

Watt Gott was born on March 22, 1859. His family had sided with the Confederacy and became refugees during and after the war. They returned to the Cherokee Nation by wagon with the family of George Starr via Fort Smith to the Goingsnake District.

Watt matured during the Reconstruction years and recalled the aftermath of the devastating war in 1938. "The Cherokee Nation was one vast scene of desolation," he began. "Old chimneys, in some instances, marked the sites of what had once been happy homes. The Cherokee Nation had been the No Mans Land between the North and the South, [and] the Cherokees . . . paid dearly for having taken sides in the white man's fight.[49]

---

47 An archivist discovered an original copy of the treaty in the Northeastern State University archives in 2014. There is an additional copy in the Maxey Papers at Gilcrease. Facsimilies are on display at Gilcrease archives and NSU special collections.

48 Thornton, *The Cherokees*, 87, 94.

49 Indian Pioneer History Collection, vol. 84, 250, 258.

Reconstruction in the Nations

The Confederate-aligned factions of the Indian Nations signed armistices with the United States, but resolving the terms of Reconstruction required several months beyond the surrender of the armies.

Recognizing the threat of retaliation from the Federal government, the Confederate factions held a remarkable, if ineffective, council with the southern Plains Indians. The Union and Confederate factions realized they were in real danger of losing their lands and worked together to present as united a front as possible to Federal mediators. The Cherokees, however, remained bitterly divided and refused to cooperate.

The surrender documents signed by Stand Watie and other leaders were to remain in effect only until more detailed terms were addressed at a meeting of the grand council scheduled for September 1, 1865. The Confederate-aligned nations began laying the groundwork in late May for the council meeting to include southern Plains Indians. The idea for the council originated with Col. James E. Harrison of Texas. Harrison discussed the idea some time earlier with President Davis and Secretary of War Seddon as a means of making an alliance with the Comanches. The peace agreement, they believed, might also cut U.S. supply lines with Santé Fe and free Confederate troops garrisoning western Texas for use elsewhere. Kirby Smith communicated with Douglas Cooper on the matter, and the council took place as the war ended, with two non-Indian Confederate officers present. Watie attempted to use the occasion—and the radically changing circumstances—to his advantage. The meeting was held at Camp Napoleon on the Washita River, near the boundary between the Leased District and the Chickasaw Nation. The Five Nations, with Watie and W. P. Adair in attendance, together with

Plains Indian tribes, entered into a treaty of peace and unity in defense of their remaining lands. The compact read in part:

> Whereas the history of the past admonishes the Red man and his once, great and powerful race, is rapidly passing away, as snow beneath the summer sun. . . . We . . . do, for our peace and happiness and the preservation of our race, make and enter unto the following league or compact. . . . Peace and Friendship shall forever exist between all the Tribes and Bands, parties to this Compact.[1]

On June 12, the Grand Council met at Armstrong Academy to determine officially how to treat with the United States. The 37 delegates included: Choctaws Israel Folsom, Sampson Folsom, Peter Folsom, Samuel Garland, and Tandy Walker; Chickasaws Holmes Colbert and Colbert Carter; Creeks D. N. McIntosh, Chilly McIntosh, Samuel Chekota, and Moty Cannard; Seminoles John Jumper and John Brown, Cherokees Stand Watie, William Penn Adair, J. A. Scales, and C. N. Vann; nine Osage representatives, three Caddoes, Osage Chief Black Dog, Caddo Chief George Washington, and Comanche Chiefs Tose-wi and Mar-wa.[2]

Watie outlined the goals of the confederation the following day. "From information I consider to be reliable such of the Trans-Miss armies as have not disbanded, have become so demoralized and paralyzed as to be worthless," began the former Confederate general. "If the Southern states have ceased to exist, our Treaties have also ceased. . . . In your deliberations in the Council the destiny of one Nation should be the destiny of all. . . . We have in our Indian Confederacy some twenty thousand warriors." At that point he softened his tone:

> Peace is always desirable. The sufferings and distresses of our woman and children—and the wasting away of our Nations demand a cessation of hostilities if possible. . . . Let us use the [coming] of peace . . . judiciously and by the blessings of Divine Providence our Indian Confederacy now in its infancy may grow to become a great and powerful Nation.[3]

---

1 Minutes of the Camp Napoleon Grand Council, May 13, 1865, May 20, 1865, May 25, 1865, in Peter Pitchlynn Papers, Gilcrease Museum, Tulsa, Oklahoma; OR 48, pt. 2, 1,266-1,271; Camp Napoleon Compact, May 26, 1865, minutes, May 26, 1865, in Pitchlynn Papers; OR 48, pt. 2, 1,102-1,103; Abel, *The American Indian and the End of the Confederacy, 1863-1866* (Lincoln, NE, 1993), 138-140; Debo, *The Rise and Fall of the Choctaw Republic*, 84.

2 Minutes of the Grand Council at Choctaw Tamaha, June 12, 1865, in Pitchlynn Papers; Baird, *Peter Pitchlynn*, 140, n. #25.

3 Minutes of the Grand Council at Choctaw Tamaha, June 12-13, 1865, in Pitchlynn Papers; Stand Watie to Friends and Brothers of the Grand Council, June 13, 1865, in Pitchlynn Papers.

An agreement was reached and the new Confederation authorized, subject to approval by individual tribal councils. The Five Nations agreed to send five delegates each to Washington to negotiate treaties, also subject to tribal approval, and to negotiate "a cessation of hostilities." The councils asked that the U.S. military provide passports and to refrain from occupying the Indian Nations until the treaties were completed.[4]

As authority passed from the military to the Department of the Interior, however, Federal authorities began dictating the form the negotiations would take. On June 9, Maj. Gen. Francis J. Herron ordered Col. Asa C. Mathews to proceed to the Grand Council with the terms of the surrender and instructions to establish a later meeting somewhere in the Indian Nations to negotiate new treaties. Mathews and his adjutant, William H. Vance, arrived at Armstrong Academy two days after the Grand Council had adjourned. Choctaw chief Peter Pitchlynn, who missed the council because of an illness, met with Mathews and Vance and announced that another Grand Council would meet at Armstrong Academy on September 1 to negotiate new treaties, and that an authorized commissioner from the United States would be present. Pitchlynn also announced that hostilities had officially ceased and ordered soldiers to return to their homes.[5]

At Doaksville the next day, June 19, Chief Pitchlynn signed an armistice identical to the one Watie had signed. It acknowledged that Kirby Smith had surrendered on May 26 and guaranteed protection for Indians and whites loyal to the Union. If the former Rebels abided by these terms, they would also be protected. On June 27, Herron informed Brev. Brig. Gen. James W. Forsyth that the Indians were signing the surrender documents and that Lieutenant Mathews had arranged a meeting to complete the treaties.[6]

To see to the needs of the refugees, Watie dispatched Adair and James Bell to Shreveport, where Brev. Maj. Gen. James C. Veatch received them on July 19. The messengers gave Veatch a copy of the agreements signed at Camp Napoleon and Armstrong and informed him that 4,000 indigent Cherokees, together with 11,500 Creeks, Seminoles, Choctaws, Osages, and Reserve Indians, required immediate

---

4 Ibid.; Debo, *The Rise and Fall of the Choctaw Republic*, 84-85; Abel, *American Indian Under Reconstruction*, 141-143.

5 Proclamation of Peter Pitchlynn, June 18, 1865, in Pitchlynn Papers.

6 OR 48, pt. 2, 1005-1006; Baird, *Peter Pitchlynn*, 139-140. The minutes of this meeting are in the Pitchlynn Papers.

assistance. Veatch passed on this information to the department commander along with his recommendations to provide for the refugees.[7]

Information concerning these activities began to move up the chain of command toward the White House. On July 20, Veatch sent all relevant documents to Maj. Gen. Edward R. Canby, commanding the Department of the Gulf, who sent them, in turn, to Grant. On July 24, Grant approved the next council meeting, but changed its location from Armstrong to Fort Gibson. He also recommended that Col. Ely S. Parker, a Seneca Indian on Grant's staff, attend the council. "The Indian affairs were considered in Cabinet to-day," wrote Secretary of War Stanton to Senator James R. Doolittle of Wisconsin, a member of the committee on Indian affairs. President Andrew Johnson, he continued, "approves the appointment of commissioners to meet the Indian tribes in grand council on the 1st of September at Fort Gibson instead of Armstrong Academy. The Secretary of the Interior will immediately name the commissioners. It is desired that you and your associates should attend the grand council if possible." Stanton moved the location again on August 2, this time to Fort Smith, where better accommodations and telegraph service were available.[8]

Choctaw Chief Pitchlynn protested that it was too late to cancel the Grand Council at Armstrong, and in any event the Choctaw Council would have to meet there by law to appoint delegates to treat with the United States commissioners. There was also concern that the Plains Indians would not be able to fully participate, but General Bussey, commander of the Frontier District with his headquarters at Fort Smith, held firm. Bussey suggested that the Armstrong council meet but elect delegates to Fort Smith, which in the end is what happened. On September 6, the Council approved seven delegates who would be accompanied by a 60-man mounted escort.[9]

John Ross reentered the story at this point in hopes of lending his influence to the loyal Cherokees. He did not arrive in the Cherokee Nation until September 1, but his political influence was already apparent the previous July. At that time, Watie had sent a delegation that included J. A. Scales, Joseph Vann, John Spears, J. T. Davis, Too-noh-volah Foster, and William P. Chambers, with an escort of 50

---

7 *OR* 48, pt. 2, 1,095-1,107.

8 Ibid., 746, 1095-1097, 1099-1,107, 1,100-1,101, 1,102, 1,105-1,106, 1,117-1,118, 1022,.

9 Able, *American Indian under Reconstruction*, 143, 165-171, 167-170, n. #356, #357, #360, #362; Joseph Folsom, *Constitution and Laws of the Choctaw Nation* (New York, NY, 1869), 404-406; Peter Pitchlynn to the Senate of the General Council of the Choctaw Nation, September 1865, in Pitchlynn Papers.

men, to Fort Gibson to treat with the loyal Cherokees. The escort kept south of the Arkansas River but the delegation was allowed into the fort, where it delivered copies of letters from General Herron and the Cherokee surrender document to Colonel Mathews. Colonel John A. Garrett, who was commanding at Fort Gibson, sent copies to General Bussey at Fort Smith. On July 7, Scales requested a meeting with loyal Chief Lewis Downing, and six days later the national council of the loyal Cherokees met at Tahlequah, and, with Downing presiding, passed a law to deal with the Cherokees who had sided with the Confederacy. They would be readmitted to citizenship in the Cherokee Nation "and restored to all rights and privileges enjoyed by other citizens," read its text, "except the right to possess or recover any improvements, or other property, that has or may be sold under provisions of any act confiscating the effects of persons declared to be disloyal to the Cherokee Nation." Those who had fought with a rank higher than captain, or who had participated in the government of the southern Cherokees, were excluded from re-admittance. Everyone else would have to swear a loyalty oath.[10]

It is unlikely Downing and the others would have moved forward with such legislation without the instigation and approval of John Ross. Around July 15, the southern Cherokee delegation met with the loyal Cherokee delegation comprised of Lewis Downing, William P. Ross, Smith Christy, Bud Gritts, Thomas Pegg, Jones C. C. Daniel, White Catcher, James Vann, and Houston Benge. The meeting resolved nothing. Thereafter, the southern Cherokees demanded a physical separation of the two parties within the boundaries of the Cherokee Nation.[11]

When he finally reached the Cherokee Nation, John Ross's steamer was unable to ascend the shoals at Webber's Falls. After waiting two days for the river to rise, he and his son William P. Ross, who was traveling with his family, hired horses to complete the journey to Fort Gibson. They arrived September 3 or 4 and spent the next few days around Tahlequah and Park Hill visiting friends and relatives. "[I] found them well—but overwhelmed with Joy & sorrow at our meeting, joy for

10 Abel, *American Indian under Reconstruction*, 159, n. #345; Phillips wrote Downing earlier on April 24 that "I have learned that persons professing to be Sheriffs; are going over the country, seizing property, [and] selling it . . . under authority of an Act of the National Council." He tried to stop it, predicting it would "lead to bloody feuds and assassinations and endless confusion, as to the rights of property," and asked for a copy of the Act. W. A. Phillips to Liet Col Downing, April 24, 1865, in Fort Gibson Letterbook.

11 The confiscation of Rebel property was informally taking place under the Cherokee council at Fort Gibson as early as December 5, 1863. John F. Cox to W. G. Coffin, December 5, 1863, Letters Received, Cherokee Agency, OIA, microfilm; Abel, *American Indian under Reconstruction*, 156-162, 159-161, n. #s 345, 346; John Ross to Sarah Stapler, August 31, 1865; John Ross to Annie B. Ross, September 18, 1865; Moulton, ed., *The Papers of John Ross*, vol. 2, 649-650.

seeing me & grief for the death of your dear mother," recalled Ross, who witnessed some of the devastation that had visited the land during his absence:

> I then hastened to our once lovely Home and witnessed the ruins and desolation of the premises—the only buildings standing, was Johnny's chicken house—the carriage house & Peggy's Cabbin. We found the old dun mare & the broken leg horse in the garden & riding through the orchard, found a few peaches, other fruits being all gone—from thence we rode up to the Grave yard—the railing & enclosure stand as usual—the grounds full of tall weeds. I cannot express the sadness of my feelings in my rambling over the place.

After eating with friends and relatives, Ross rode on to Fort Gibson for the night. He wanted to meet with Downing, Pegg, and other members of the delegation, but they had already left for Fort Smith. This did not overly concern Ross because he had not authorized them to make a treaty.[12]

The Rebel delegations were delayed at Armstrong when the Fort Smith Council began on September 8. Most of the loyal Indians in attendance thought the purpose of the council was to restore relations between the divided Indian nations, but they soon realized Federal intentions were more ominous.

While he was still in the Senate, James Harlan, who was now Secretary of the Interior, had introduced Senate Bill 459 the previous February to establish a Federal territorial government in the Indian Territory. The bill required the Indian Nations to form a single government that would be subordinate to a Federally appointed governor. The Indians would be entitled to a non-voting delegate in Congress. The bill was debated on February 23 and 24, and March 3. Opponents argued that it was in conflict with the Cherokee treaty of 1835, which conveyed the land in fee simple. Harlan countered that the Indians would agree to the change by treaty. "That is contemplated by this bill," he explained. "It provides distinctly that their rights shall not be interfered with until they agree to it." Senator Lafayette Foster, a Connecticut Republican, thought the bill was nothing short of fraudulent and led the opposition with the support of John Ross. Senator Jim Lane of Kansas strongly supported the bill. With barely a quorum present, Harlan's bill passed the Senate on March 3, but Congress adjourned before it could be considered by the House of Representatives.[13]

12 Moulton, ed., *The Papers of John Ross*, vol. 2, 649-650.

13 Abel, *American Indian under Reconstruction*, 251; ibid., 243-267.

As Secretary of the Interior under President Johnson (he had been nominated by Lincoln but took office after the assassination under Johnson) Harlan appointed the commissioners to the Fort Smith Council and instructed them to use his Senate bill as a model for a single Indian government. Four of the commissioners— Commissioner of Indian Affairs Dennis N. Cooley, head of the southern superintendency Elijah Sells, Pennsylvania Quaker Thomas Wister, and Col. Ely S. Parker—left Fort Leavenworth with an escort of 100 cavalry on August 24, and reached Fort Smith on September 5. General William S. Harney, known for his anti-Indian sentiments, arrived by boat from St. Louis.[14]

The council began on Friday, September 8. Downing said a prayer aloud in Cherokee, after which Commissioner Cooley addressed the gathering of loyal Cherokees, Choctaws, Chickasaws, Creeks, Seminoles, Osages, Shawnees, Senecas, Quapaws, Wynadottes, as well as their agents, interpreters, and representatives of the freed slaves of the Creeks and Euchees. The president, explained Cooley, had sent the commissioners to make new treaties. He wasted no time getting to the point: "Portions of several tribes and nations have attempted to throw off their allegiance with the United States, and have made treaty stipulations with the enemies of the government and have made open war with the United States. All such have rightly forfeited all annuities and interests in the lands in the Indian Territory." However, he continued, the president was willing to forgive and negotiate new treaties. One by one, the shocked representatives protested that they had not known this would be the purpose of this council and requested time to confer amongst themselves. Cooley granted the request and adjourned the council until 4:30 that afternoon. He also reduced the size of the numerous delegations to five members each and insisted on seeing their credentials.[15]

When the council resumed later that afternoon, uncertainty and even chaos reigned. The Cherokees announced that they had been asked by Chief Ross to attend, but had no authorization to make a treaty. The other delegations continued along the same line, saying they believed the council's purpose was to make peace with the disloyal Indians. Someone pointed out that the southern delegates would not even arrive to participate in negotiations until Monday, September 11. An

14 Ibid., 174-176, 178-179, 219-226; *Report of the Commissioner of Indian Affairs, 1865* (Washington D.C., 1866), 296, 353. The two main sources for the Fort Smith Council are the reports of Cooley and Mix therein, in addition to Letters Received by the Office of Indian Affairs.

15 *Report of the Commissioner of Indian Affairs, 1865*, 296-298, 313-315.

exasperated Cooley replied that he would make it clear what the Federal government expected on the following day.[16]

The council reconvened on Saturday at 10:00 a.m. Cooley began by giving the date that each nation and tribe had entered into its alliance with the Confederacy, which abrogated the previous Federal treaties. Even though the present assembly was loyal, he said, it needed to understand the terms Washington wanted in the new treaties. The Commissioner of Indian Affairs expressed the terms in seven points. The first two articles concerned the maintenance of peace, while the third and fourth abolished slavery with citizenship for freedmen or other compensation. The fifth stipulation set aside lands for the settlement of "friendly Indians" under terms yet to be negotiated, and the sixth established one government for the Indian Territory. The final point excluded all unauthorized whites. When Cooley asked for comments, a Creek delegate, speaking on behalf of everyone, announced that the reply would come on Monday. With that, the council adjourned.[17]

On the third day of the council meeting, the commissioners informed the delegates that Winchester Colbert and Peter Pitchlynn had sent word that their southern delegates would be delayed another four days and would not arrive until September 15. Cooley then asked the delegations present for a reaction to his seven points. The delegates from the Creeks remained silent and the Seminoles asked for more time to respond. The small delegation of loyal Chickasaws replied that they did not have the power to negotiate treaties. However, the first two Articles were acceptable, as was the third under the option of making "suitable provisions" rather than incorporating freed blacks into the nation. They did not have the "authority" to rule on Articles Four, Five, and Six. Article Seven, they concluded, needed to be amended so that no outside freed slaves could be brought into the nation.[18]

A Seneca chief testified that former Confederate general Albert Pike had told them they could not live in peace unless they signed the treaty. An interpreter related that the Shawnees agreed with all but the last Article, for the same reason as the Chickasaws and Choctaws, and suggested it be reworded. The Cherokees, probably at John Ross's instruction, and in order to get better terms, went into a lengthy and detailed defense of their wartime actions, including their reluctance to fight at Pea Ridge and their alliance with Opothleyahola. Of the Five Nations, all

16 Ibid., 315-317.

17 Ibid., 298-299, 318-319.

18 Ibid., 319-320.

the loyal elements except the Cherokees were stalling until the remaining southern delegates arrived. They wished to face any threat from the United States with a united front. The Osages, like many of the other delegations, were concerned about Article Seven. "You have prohibited the white man," they said, "why do you say that the negro may come in?" Only the Shawnees, who had been refugees in Kansas, were after a time completely ready to accept the commissioners' offer. At 12:30 p.m., the council adjourned.[19]

The following day the council reconvened. The Seminoles announced their understanding of the need for new treaties. Their objection was that they did not want the Indian Territory to become a colony for freed slaves from the Southern states. Only the freed peoples remaining in Seminole country at the end of the war, they maintained, could stay there. The Seminole delegation wanted to meet with their own council, elect delegates authorized to make a treaty, and meet again with United States commissioners. Thus, the terms negotiated by Harlan's Fort Smith commissioners came to be viewed as preliminary treaties to more complex agreements that would be negotiated the following spring and summer in Washington.[20]

Commissioner Cooley took issue with the previous days' argument by the loyal Cherokees that they were "not guilty" of collaboration with the Rebels. Cooley refused to accept that John Ross had not been an enthusiastic Confederate ally, and produced documents supporting his argument. He insisted the old treaty with the United States was null and void, but conceded President Johnson was willing to restore relations. In return, the commissioners received assurances that the Cherokees would sign these "preliminary" treaties, meet in council, and elect delegates to negotiate the final agreements. Cooley asked all the parties present to be prepared to sign the documents the next day and said that the problems with Articles Three and Seven would be dealt with later. A Creek chief sought sympathy from the commissioners by recounting the suffering of Opothleyahola's band and the subsequent service of the 1st Regiment of Indian Home Guards. Once he had his say, the council adjourned.[21]

The next morning Commissioner Cooley presented a treaty pledging loyalty to the United States and a promise to send delegates to Washington to negotiate the final terms in detail. The treaties would be printed that afternoon, he explained, and

19 Ibid., 322-324.

20 Ibid., 323-325.

21 Ibid., 299-301, 324-325.

he wanted them signed the next day before the Southern delegates arrived. The commissioners were careful to insist that the loyal delegates remain to meet their Rebel counterparts. All the delegates signed the treaties, but the Creeks and Cherokees did so reluctantly and only after two days of delay. The commissioners blamed the delay on the influence of John Ross, who had arrived in Van Buren the previous day. On the day Ross appeared before the commissioners, Watie's nephew and former Confederate officer Elias C. Boudinot, who had been in Van Buren since the council opened, was also present. The commissioners refused to recognize Ross as principal chief of the Cherokees.[22]

Undaunted by the proceedings, Ross asked to speak and Cooley granted his request. Ross denied that he was interfering with the Creek and Cherokee delegations, or that he was the cause of their reluctance to sign the preliminary treaty. "I did no more than express my opinion upon the subject. I did it openly & honorably," he explained. Ross also claimed he had remained loyal to the United States, had been living in Washington and Philadelphia for the past three years, and had been in communication with Presidents Lincoln and Johnson. Ross recounted how he had resisted overtures from the Confederacy until he was forced to sign the Confederate treaty. After Ross spoke, Cooley asked if any other delegates wished to speak, and he recognized Boudinot.

Boudinot stood and started speaking. Only some of the Southern delegates had arrived, he began, and they wanted to wait for all of them before beginning negotiations. They had much to say to the commissioners. Boudinot also wanted them to be aware of the preliminary treaty signed by the Southern delegates at Armstrong Academy. He did not know who had made the allegations against Ross that so concerned Commissioner Cooley, "but, Sir," he explained, "there are serious charges which I will make against him, & I here announce my willingness & intention to make such charges, to state facts & to prove them too, as will prove his duplicity. The fact is the Cherokee Nation has long been rent in twain by dissentions & I here charge these upon this same John Ross." Cooley cut off Boudinot. "The Object of this Council," he interjected, "is not to stir up old feelings. . . . I trust no one may come into this Council and attempt to stir up bad feelings which ought to have been buried years ago." Cooley didn't believe a word he was saying. He did nothing to create an atmosphere of peace and unity at the

22 Ibid., 302-305, 333-336; Abel, *American Indian under Reconstruction*, 199-201, n. #424.

conference, and once back in Washington, sided with the Confederate Cherokees.[23]

On Monday, September 18, the Fort Smith Council met with all the Southern delegates present, who wanted to study the documents and meet again. Boudinot read a statement signed by Adair, Bell, and others, including himself, objecting to Article Three concerning the freedmen issue, and Article Six that required the Indians to form one government. The Cherokees, he explained, intended "no captious [petty] spirit" but on one issue they would hold firm: The Southern Cherokees would never live among the loyal Cherokees again. Boudinot insisted upon a physical separation. The confiscation of Southern Cherokee property complicated the situation.[24]

As the day wore on, Cooley asked the Southern and loyal Cherokees to each form a committee of five delegates, as the Choctaws, Chickasaws, Creeks, and Seminoles had done, and attempt to settle their differences. The loyal Cherokees protested the commissioners' refusal to recognize John Ross as principal chief. The commissioners remained confident in their dismissal of Ross, however, because they had received word that President Johnson had approved their action. Robert Jones and David Birney of the Choctaws announced they could sign this agreement, as it was only a "preliminary" statement of a treaty to be negotiated in Washington. They made it clear that they had not been duped into aligning with the Confederacy, but had done so because it was in their best interest. Having no alternative, they were now willing to resume their relationship with the United States. At that, Stand Watie also signed the preliminary treaty. Commissioner Cooley expressed his hope that the Cherokee committees would resolve their differences and the council adjourned.[25]

---

23 Dialogue between Ross and Dennis N Cooley, September 15, 1865; Moulton, ed., *The Papers of John Ross*, vol. 2, 646-648; Abel, *The American Indian under Reconstruction*, 205, n. #431.

24 John Ross, Annual Message, October 28, 1865; Moulton, ed., *The Papers of John Ross*, 653-657; *Report of the Commissioner of Indian Affairs, 1865*, 306, 338-340; Edwin C. Bearss, "The Civil War in Indian Territory and the Fort Smith Council Transcript of the Keynote Address" in *Proceedings: War and Reconstruction in Indian Territory: A History Conference in Observance of the 130th Anniversary of the Fort Smith Council* (Fort Smith, AR, 1995), 5-10. Once in Washington, Ross used Boudinot's hard and fast position to argue his case that he was loyal to the United States, beginning with his abrogation of the Confederate treaty in February 1863 under Lewis Downing.

25 Jas Harlan to D. N. Cooley, September 18, 1865, Letters Received, Cherokee Agency; *Report of the Commissioner of Indian Affairs, 1865*, 341-347.

The leadership of the Confederate Cherokees coordinated its efforts to make sure the refugees were properly cared for, and the next day Boudinot and Adair addressed the commissioners concerning their fate, as did Adair. Boudinot explained the plight of the people to artillerist Henry J. Hunt, now a brevet major general and the U.S. commander of the district, and contended that the Cherokee Nation had "concluded a treaty of peace" at Fort Smith. The refugees had been sustained by the "so called Confederate States," but were now "in a very destitute condition depend[ing] in a great measure upon the precarious and uncertain charity of the good people of Texas." Hunt, a fair and just officer with a conscience, notified Cooley of his intention to use his military authority, if necessary, to care for the refugees. On November 13, Watie appointed Adair "commissioner with full powers from the Cherokees South . . . [to] assist in entering into full and final negotiations at . . . [Washington] between the Cherokee Nation, 'the United Indian Nations' and the Govt. of the United States."[26]

On October 28, Ross delivered the annual message to the Cherokees at Tahlequah. On November 6, Lewis Downing, with the support of the National Council, appointed Capt. Smith Christy, Capt. White Catcher, Daniel H. Ross, Houston Benge, and John B. Jones to negotiate the new treaty in Washington. The following day, no doubt by Ross's instruction, Downing and the national council recognized Ross as principal chief and asked him to accompany the delegation to the American capital.[27]

26 Mg. Genl. Henry Jackson Hunt to John Levering, October 3, 1865; Stand Watie to Col. W. P. Adair, November 13, 1865, Letters Received, Cherokee Agency; *Report of the Commissioner of Indian Affairs, 1865*, 347, 349, 351, 353.

27 Lewis Downing to Whom it may Concern, November 6, 1865; James Vann, et al. Be it Enacted by the National Council, November 7, 1865, Letters Received, Cherokee Agency; Gary E. Moulton, "Chief John Ross and the Fort Smith Council of 1865," in *Proceedings: War and Reconstruction in Indian Territory: A History Conference in Observance of the 130th Anniversary of the Fort Smith Council* (Fort Smith, AR, 1995), 92-96; Moulton, ed., The *Papers of John Ross*, vol. 2, 652.

Washington

O n November 9, 1865, John Ross left Tahlequah and traveled by boat on the Arkansas, Mississippi, and Ohio rivers to Cincinnati, Ohio. There, he boarded a train for Philadelphia, where he arrived on November 20. The journey was long and hard on Ross, who informed Reverend John B. Jones that ill health had confined him to his room, but he was slowly "improving and gradually gaining strength." Ross told Jones to disregard any reports that the commissioners at Fort Smith had refused to recognize him, and that he was preparing a statement to support their case for President Andrew Johnson. By December 29, 1865, all of the loyal delegation members had gathered in Philadelphia, and by January 10, 1866, they had all taken rooms at a boarding house in Washington.[1]

Two weeks later, on January 24, the loyal delegates published Ross's pamphlet entitled *Memorial of the Delegates of the Cherokee Nation to the President of the United States and the Senate and House of Representatives in Congress*—a powerful response to Harlan's territorial government bill. The delegates regretted that legislation had been introduced "into Congress entitled 'a bill to consolidate the Indian Tribes, and to establish Civil Government in the Indian Territory.' It is our solemn conviction, and the conviction of our people," continued the pamphlet, "that if that bill

---

1 John Ross to John B. Jones, December 16, 1865, and John Ross to J. W. Wright, December 29, 1865, in Moulton, ed., *The Papers of John Ross*, 559-661.

becomes a law, and is carried in execution, it will crush us as a people, and destroy us as a nation."[2]

"Justice," argued the delegates, required the United States to honor the treaty of 1835, which enshrined into law that the Cherokee Nation would never become part of a territory of the United States unless the Cherokees requested it. To support their claims of loyalty, they argued that they were left with few options once Stand Watie raised a battalion, and the U.S. Army abandoned the Indian Nations. "[W]e and Opothleyohola's noble band of Creeks and Seminoles stood alone in our loyalty. . . . As the only means of averting the wholesale slaughter of the loyal Cherokees, a convention was called. At that convention (August 21, 1861) under duress most complete and unmitigated, our people were compelled to empower the authorities of the Nation to treat with the rebels."[3]

The delegates further claimed the mixed-bloods and whites had hidden weapons at Tahlequah during the Cherokee assembly. For their protection, the full-bloods had raised their regiment, but almost all the officers and men had remained loyal to the Union. The *Memorial* went on to recount events leading up to when John Ross joined Col. William Weer's expedition on its way back to Kansas, and copies of the abrogation of the Rebel treaty in February 1863 were appended with a citation of the service of the Union Cherokee regiments. "We boldly claim," concluded the document, "that we have done our duty, to the full extent of our power, as the friends and allies of the Federal Government. . . . We make our earnest appeal to the President of the United States and to Congress."[4]

Ross continued gathering evidence in Washington to present his case. He requested and received a letter from former Commissioner of Indian Affairs William P. Dole stating that he had been present at a meeting with President Lincoln and Ross in 1863, and that Lincoln "appeared to be satisfied that . . . [the alliance with the Confederacy] was done under coercion and was only meant for you to save the lives and property of your people." On January 30, the loyal

---

2 This was but the first of six pamphlets to be published concerning the Cherokee treaty negotiations: three by the loyal Cherokees, two by the southern Cherokees, and one by the Commissioner of Indian Affairs. Smith Christie et al., *Memorial of the Delegates of the Cherokee Nation to the President of the United States and the Senate and House of Representatives in Congress*, 12, in *Pamphlets in American History* (Sanford, NC, 1979); Abel, *The American Indian under Reconstruction*, 346; Franks, *Stand Watie and the Agony of the Cherokee Nation*, 189.

3 Christie et al., *Memorial of the Delegates of the Cherokee Nation*, 4.

4 Ibid., vol. 8, 3-8.

Cherokee delegation presented their credentials to Commissioner of Indian Affairs D. N. Cooley. On January 31, they published a second pamphlet.[5]

The 48 pages of *Communication of the Delegates of the Delegation of the Cherokee Nation to the President of the United States Submitting the Memorial of the National Council, with the Correspondence between John Ross, Principal Chief, and Certain Officers of the Rebellious States*, including enclosures, was a memorial to Ross. The publication explained that he had resisted Confederate agents and maintained neutrality as long as it had been safe to do so. Among the letters Ross appended as evidence of his reluctance to align with the Confederacy were many of his own to Chickasaw Governor Cyrus Harris, Creek and Choctaw leaders, Arkansas Governor Henry M. Rector, Ben McCulloch, and Albert Pike. The pamphlet protested Ross's treatment at Fort Smith and enclosed copies of the national council's recognition of Ross as principal chief, and the council's request that Ross accompany the delegation to Washington.[6]

Elias C. Boudinot and William Penn Adair, the only Southern Cherokee delegates yet to arrive in Washington, countered with a pamphlet of their own entitled *Reply of the Southern Delegates to the Memorial of Certain Delegates from the Cherokee Nation, together with the Message of John Ross, Ex Chief of the Cherokees, and the Proceedings of the "Loyal Cherokees" Relative to the Alliance with the So-Called Confederate States*. Its purposes were to challenge Ross's claim of loyalty and to argue that the two Cherokee parties were so divided that they could no longer live together. "The bitterness of feeling between these rival factions has ever been, and still is, intense and unappeasable," they argued. "It was proven in the brutal assassination of the Ridges and Boudinot in 1839, and the reign of terror that followed." The reconciliation treaty of 1846 was a hollow failure, they continued. "The 'Pin Society' was organized five years before the war, when the words 'loyal' and 'disloyal,' now so common, were unknown."[7] The society's sole purpose was to

---

5 W. P. Dole to John Ross, January 26, 1866; Smith Christy, et al. to D. N. Cooley, January 30, 1866, Letters Received, Cherokee Agency, OIA; John Ross to Sara F. Stapler, November 12, 1865; John Ross to John B. Jones, December 16, 1865; John Ross to J. W. Wright, December 29, 1865; Moulton, ed., *The Papers of John Ross*, 660-661; *Communication of the Delegation of the Cherokee Nation to the President of the United States Submitting the Memorial of the National Council, with the Correspondence between John Ross, Principle Chief, and Certain Officers of the Rebellious States* (Washington D.C., 1866), 3, in *Western Americana: Frontier History of the Trans-Mississippi West, 1550–1900*, microfilm, reel 105.

6 *Communication of the Delegation of the Cherokee Nation to the President*, 22-25, 35-37, 42-43, 48.

7 *Reply of the Southern Cherokees to the Memorial of Certain Delegates from the Cherokee Nation, together with the Message of John Ross, Ex-Chief of the Cherokees, and Proceedings of the Council of the 'Loyal*

organize the full bloods and keep Ross in power against the outnumbered mixed bloods. "The great injustice and wrong we have endured at the hands of the pretended loyal party have utterly destroyed all sentiments of brotherhood between us," continued the pamphlet. "Let us be sundered by territorial boundaries, within which each people may possess their own laws, regulations and customs, distinct from each other, free to follow the pursuits of life and happiness in security." They attached Ross's speech to the full bloods at Tahlequah and a declaration by the Cherokee government, signed by Ross and others, that recounted the circumstances of the severance of relations with the United States.[8]

On February 15, Ross and the loyal Cherokee delegates, accompanied by Secretary of the Interior James Harlan and Commissioner of Indian Affairs Dennis N. Cooley, met with President Johnson at the White House. Johnson assured them that they would be treated fairly. Ross was justifiably concerned because Cooley was so closely associated with the Southern Cherokees. He had met privately with Harlan the day before, only to be assured they could negotiate directly through him. The meeting encouraged Ross, who had no inkling of Harlan's ability for duplicity, for his true loyalty was with Boudinot, Adair, and the Southern Cherokees. Harlan suggested Ross prepare a draft treaty. Referring to himself as principal chief, Ross kept Harlan apprised of their progress and presented a draft to the commissioners on March 15.[9]

The treaty provided for land, property rights, and education for the freed slaves and their heirs. It pardoned the Southern Cherokees and required they swear a loyalty oath. Unclaimed pay for deceased solders without heirs of the Union Indian Brigade were to be transferred to an orphan fund. The treaty agreed to settle other tribes, including the Eastern Cherokees, inside the Cherokee Nation. Although the Cherokee Outlet was not mentioned, it was understood that it would involve the resettlement of other tribes, which Ross would concede later. Criminal and civil trials involving U.S. citizens residing illegally in the Cherokee Nation

---

Cherokees' Relative to the Alliance with the So-Called Confederate States. To the President, Senate, and House of Representatives (Washington D.C.: McGill & Witherow, 1866), 3-4, in *Pamphlets in American History*.

8 Ibid., 3, 8-10, 12-19.

9 John Ross and Others to James Harlan, March 7, 1866; John Ross, et al., to James Harlan, March 22, 1866, Letters Received, Cherokee Agency, Office of Indian Affairs, National Archives, microfilm; John Ross to Sarah Stapler, February 22, 1866; John Ross, et. al., to James Harlan, March 15, 1866; Moulton, ed., *The Papers of John Ross*, 665-667; Moulton, *John Ross*, 191-192.

would be tried in Cherokee courts, while those residing legally in the nation would be tried in U.S. courts with mixed juries and the participation of Cherokee attorneys. The treaty also granted a 200-foot easement for a railroad running between Lawrence and Galveston, regulated the employees of railroads, and provided for the general regulation of trade. There was also a provision allowing loyal Cherokees to make damage claims. The treaty agreed to sell the Cherokee Neutral Lands in Kansas for an appraised value of not less than $1.25 per acre. The Nation would be re-surveyed, and there would be a periodic auditing of Cherokee accounts. All things considered, the draft was a reasonable first step. What Ross did not know, however, was that Harlan and Cooley were in earnest negotiation with the Southern Cherokees to support Harlan's Indian Territory bill, which called for the physical separation of the two Cherokee factions.[10]

By the first week of March, Stand Watie, John R. Ridge, Richard Fields, Joseph A. Scales, and J. Woodward Washbourne had joined Adair and Boudinot in Washington. On March 6, Watie requested that Commissioner of Indian Affairs Cooley produce an accurate map of the Cherokee Nation based on the treaty of 1835. The map, explained Watie, would be of "great importance to us in the cession of land contemplated to be made, and the grants of land for Rail roads, which we and the tribe desire to make." On April 10, the delegation told Cooley they wanted to separate the two factions, with the mixed bloods taking the Canadian district and the rest of the Nation west of the Grand River, which left the wooded hill country east of the river. (This was, in fact, the natural division that had taken place over the years, but with exceptions on both sides.)[11]

Working with Cooley, Elijah Sells, who had replaced Coffin as head of the Southern Superintendency, and Cherokee agent Justin Harlan (not to be confused with Secretary of the Interior James Harlan), the Southern Cherokee delegates produced a counter proposal to the Ross March 15 draft. They wanted to give every man, woman, and child in the Ross party 320 acres east of the Grand River and north of the Arkansas River, while reserving 160 acres for each member of the Watie faction in the Canadian district and in the area west of the Grand and north

10 The Cherokee Outlet (or Cherokee Strip) in what is now Oklahoma was a 60-mile wide piece of land south of the Oklahoma-Kansas border created in 1836. Project of a Treaty Submitted to the Hon Jas Harlan, Secretary of the Interior by the Delegation of the Cherokee Nation, March 15, 1866, Special Files of the Office of Indian Affairs, National Archives, microcopy No. 574, roll 24, file 125.

11 Stand Watie to D. N. Cooley, March 6, 1866, and Stand Watie, et. al., to D. N. Cooley, April 10, 1866, Letters Received, Cherokee Agency; Douglas H. Cooper to D. N. Cooley, May 16, 1866; Thoburn, ed., "The Cherokee Question," 216.

Confederate Cherokee Delegation: William Penn Adair (seated right), Elias Cornelius Boudinot (standing right), Saladin Watie (standing left). *Gilcrease Museum Archives, University of Tulsa*

of the Arkansas. Freed slaves would receive 40 acres. School and orphan funds would be prorated, and the Watie faction would be guaranteed access to the two seminaries, both of which were located east of the Grand River. Each party would have political control over its own district, but in relations with the United States, the two would act as one nation. The confiscation laws were nullified. Importantly, there was a provision to survey the Southern Cherokee district into townships and sections so that fee simple land ownership could be taken by individuals, ending the tradition of communal ownership of Cherokee lands. They also agreed to allow for territorial status according to the terms of the Harlan bill.[12]

In addition, the proposed treaty called for the sale of land and railroad rights to be prorated. The Southern Cherokees proposed to give alternate sections in a 10-mile-wide strip in return for property damages and railroad stock. They agreed to

12 John Ross, et al. to James Harlan, March 22, 1866; Moulton, ed., *The Papers of John Ross*, 670; "Whereas the political connection heretofore existing . . ." Unsigned and undated draft in Special Files of the Office of Indian Affairs, 1807–1904 (microcopy no. 574, roll 24, National Archives, microfilm).

sell to the United States their interest in the Neutral Lands for $150,000, and their interest in all other Cherokee lands for $1,100,000. Of these funds, $500,000 would be distributed among the Southern Cherokees for rebuilding, the remainder to be placed in trust with the United States at five percent interest.[13]

The Watie party took their apparent agreement with Federal officials as a victory and asked for funds to send Watie and Scales back to the Cherokee Nation, some time after April 25, to explain the plan to the people and have them moved in time for spring planting. They repeatedly requested military protection. Perhaps anticipating a construction boom, Watie requested that his steam sawmill be moved from the Delaware district, east of Grand River, to the Canadian district. He arrived in Fort Smith by steamer on May 10. On May 12, he informed Saladin in Washington, "Everyone that I have seen agrees to [illegible] has been done by their delegates. Our people are settled from Little Boggy to the Canadian & Arks. Rivers." Watie continued to Boggy Depot. J. W. Washbourne encouraged J. A. Scales "to have the Southern Cherokee Government organized immediately. Have it done by all means, even should General Watie's Proclamation not be able, in time, to collect a thousand voters, organize it with a few hundred votes . . . and afterward we will settle elections again."[14]

On March 22, the day after he became aware of the Southern Cherokee treaty and Secretary Harlan's perfidy, John Ross and the loyal delegation met with the cabinet official. Just seven days earlier, they complained, they had presented him with the draft treaty he asked them to prepare. As to the Southern Cherokee proposal, they were indignant: "As a whole it is unacceptable to us. . . . We respectfully suggest as the draft we submitted to you was prepared at your request as a basis for negotiations, that it be so received . . . and that any modifications . . . be proposed as 'amendments' to the draft we presented." The Ross delegation, by way of negotiation, accepted the return of confiscated property, amnesty, cession of the Neutral Lands, freedmen's rights, acceptance of the Eastern Cherokees, and Southern Cherokee participation in government. The rest, however, was so objectionable that the delegation published a third pamphlet, *Reply of the Delegates of*

---

13 Ibid.

14 John Ross, et. al., to James Harlan, March 22, 1866; J. W. Washboure to D. N. Cooley, April 10, 1866; R. Fields and Others to D. N. Cooley, April 18, 1866; Stand Watie to D. N. Cooley, April 23, 1866; Stand Watie to D. N. Cooley, April 25, 1866, Letters Received, Cherokee Agency; Stand Watie to Saladin Watie, May 12, 1866, in Cherokee Nation Papers; Dale and Litton, eds., *Cherokee Cavaliers*, 242-243; J. W. Washbourne to J. A. Scales, June 1, 1866, in Cherokee Nation Papers; Dale and Litton, eds., *Cherokee Cavaliers*, 243-245.

the Cherokee Nation to the Demands of the Commissioner of Indian Affairs, to explain its objections.[15]

The Ross faction strongly disagreed with the proposal to form a territorial government and the geographical division of the nation and its assets, and accused the Southern Cherokees of attempting to hold onto power even though they had lost the Civil War. "It is not peace, security, and fraternity, these lately disloyal leaders want—it is political power," they argued. "They know . . . that the men who organized the Knights of the Golden Circle in 1859 . . . will not soon again be honored with public confidence in the nation." Ross's people also complained to President Johnson that the proposed treaty would "destroy" their nation, and asked for an audience with him.[16]

The Southern Cherokees responded with a pamphlet of their own: *Comments on the Objections of Certain Cherokee Delegates to the Proposition of the Government to Separate the Hostile Parties of the Cherokee Nation*. The Southern delegates argued "that the Government is solemnly bound by former treaties to divide us; for in no other way can the United States 'protect the Cherokees from domestic strife,'" a reference to the 1835 treaty. They strongly denied that they could live in peace with the full bloods, citing "Pin" activity before the war and giving examples of several recent murders: "Mr. Ross and his party . . . are interested in holding the entire control of the public funds and in destroying and murdering all honest men opposed to them."[17] These issues would not be decided until mid-July.

While the Cherokee delegations remained divided, the other nations put aside their differences, hired lawyers, and negotiated in turn with Commissioner Cooley and Secretary Harlan. The parties signed the Seminole treaty on March 21, the

---

15 John Ross and Others to James Harlan, March 22, 1866; ibid; John Ross and Others to Andrew Johnson, May 13, 1866; Moulton, ed., *The Papers of John Ross*, 676-677; *Reply of the Delegates of the Cherokee Nation to the Demands of the Commissioner of Indian Affairs* (Washington D.C., 1866), 3, in *Western Americana: Frontier History of the Trans-Mississippi West*, reel 105.

16 *Reply of the Delegates of the Cherokee Nation to the Demands of the Commissioner of Indian Affairs* (Washington D.C., 1866), 3, in *Western Americana: Frontier History of the Trans-Mississippi West*, reel 105, 10-11, 3-10, 13; John Ross, et. al., to Andrew Johnson, May 13, 1866; Moulton, ed., *The Papers of John Ross*, 676-677.

17 *Reply of the Delegates*, 7; *Comments on the Objections of Certain Cherokee Delegates to the Proposition of the Government to Separate the Hostile Parties of the Cherokee Nation* (Washington D.C., 1866), vol. 11, 3-4, 6, 10-15, in *Pamphlets in American History*.

Choctaw-Chickasaw treaty on April 28, and the Creek treaty on June 4. The treaties were not identical, but they contained similar clauses to address the issues.[18]

Cooley failed to obtain either a single tribal government or a request for territorial status, but there was a similarly worded compromise in all the treaties. The Indian Nations agreed to a "general council," the first session to be called by the superintendent of Indian Affairs. Subsequent sessions would be called by the general council, although the Superintendent, who would preside over the council, could call special sessions. Each nation was entitled to one delegate plus one for every 1,000 citizens.

The treaties created councils with influence, but with no authority over tribal sovereignty:

> [The] general council shall have the power to legislate upon all rightful subjects and matters pertaining to the intercourse and relations of the Indian tribes and nations resident in said Territory neither in conflict with the United States nor treaty provision, [but] no law shall be enacted inconsistent with the Constitution of the United States, of the laws of Congress, or existing treaty stipulations with the United States, nor shall said council legislate upon matters pertaining to the organization, laws, or customs of the several tribes, except as herein provided for.

This was hardly a territorial government, nor a victory for Harlan. Rather, it reflected the government's attempt to weaken the sovereignty of the Indian Nations after the Civil War. Harlan had detailed in the Choctaw-Chickasaw treaty how territorial government could be created in the future, but it was contingent upon the approval of the tribal council, which was not forthcoming.[19]

All of the nations were forced to make significant land cessions, although they were compensated and the lands were generally west of those occupied by the Five Nations. The Choctaws and Chickasaws ceded the "Leased District" for $300,000. The Creeks ceded 3,250,500 acres in the west for $975,168. The Seminoles ceded all their land—2,169,080 acres—for $325,362 and received in return 200,000 acres west of the Creek Nation between the Canadian River and its North Fork. Some of the monies were earmarked for individual awards to refugees and soldiers, or for

---

18 Kappler, ed., *Indian Affairs*, 910, 918, 931; Harry Henslick, "The Seminole Treaty of 1866," in *Chronicles of Oklahoma* (Autumn 1970), Issue 48, 280-294; Marion Ray McCullar, "The Choctaw-Chickasaw Reconstruction Treaty of 1866," in *Journal of the West* (July 1973), Issue 12, 462-470; Gail Balman, "The Creek Treaty of 1866," in *Chronicles of Oklahoma* (Autumn 1970), Issue 48, 184-196.

19 Kappler, ed., *Indian Affairs*, 913-914, 921-922, 923, 934-936.

property repair, stock and seed purchase, mill construction, and school funds. Some was distributed per capita, but most was kept in trust by the U.S. government, which distributed the interest to the individual nations on a regular basis.[20]

Concerning the construction of railroads through these lands, the Choctaws and Chickasaws agreed to both north-south and east-west lines and to give "alternate" sections of land for six miles on each side of the line in exchange for stock in the railroad company. The Creeks and Seminoles agreed to two lines, and to sell not alternate sections, but all land for three miles on either side of the lines. Each treaty contained a clause concerning the treatment of freed slaves. The Seminoles and Creeks gave them full citizenship while the Choctaws and Chickasaws made them equal under the law and allowed them to occupy all the land they could farm.[21]

With John Ross refusing to cooperate, Cooley and the Southern Cherokee delegates decided to formalize their collaborative draft. The final document differed somewhat from the original. It omitted settlement terms for the loyal Cherokees and agreed to cede lands beyond their own 160-acre holdings at appraised values, rather than at a set price. It continued to promote territorial status, but omitted any mention of fee simple ownership. On June 13, all the Southern delegates signed it, as did Cooley, Sells, and Special Commissioner Ely S. Parker. Cooley gave the treaty to Secretary Harlan, who passed it to President Johnson with the belief that he would sign the document and make it law.[22]

To gain support for his treaty, Cooley had made inquiries among prominent figures in the region as to whether the Ross and Watie parties could live together peacefully. He anticipated negative responses, and he got them. The replies arrived from February 7 through May 25, 1866. Testimony came from Albert Pike, Douglas Cooper, Justin Harlan, and longtime residents J. M. Tebbetts, Charles B. Johnson, R. T. Van Horn, and J. B. Luce. Cooley appended copies of the letters to a

---

20 Ibid., 911-912, 919, 933-934.

21 Ibid., 912-913, 919-920, 934; Daniel F. Littlefield, "The Treaties of 1866: Reconstruction or Re-Destruction?", in *Proceedings: War and Reconstruction in Indian Territory: A History Conference in Observance of the 130th Anniversary of the Fort Smith Council* (Fort Smith, AR, 1995), 97-109. Littlefield argues that the clauses concerning the freed slaves were intended to break down tribal sovereignty.

22 Articles of Agreement, made and concluded at Washington City, D.C., on the 13th day of June, A.D. 1866, file 125, Special Files of the Office of Indian Affairs, National Archives, microfilm #574, roll 24.

pamphlet of his own entitled *The Cherokee Question* and addressed to President Johnson in support of the treaty with the Southern Cherokees.[23]

Cooley attempted to convince the president that Ross had not been forced into the Confederate treaty but had willingly thrown his lot in with the South. He also noted that the Southern Cherokees were offering better treaty terms than the loyal Cherokees, and that his original instructions from Secretary Harlan held out the possibility of separate negotiations. Addressing the president, Cooley concluded, "[T]his document is laid before you for your constitutional action. If it shall meet with your approval and be ratified, and go into full effect, we may reasonably hope for a cessation of the long continued troubles of the Cherokee people."[24]

In March, Ross asked Evan Jones to seek help for their cause from Colonel Phillips. On May 21, the *New York Tribune* ran a front-page article by Phillips condemning the treaty. The article recounted the history of the Cherokees, praised their civilization, and defended the Ross party. "A proposition is deliberately made by the Commissioners of Indian Affairs to disrupt the Cherokee nation and give the Rebels a separate Government, and divide their lands and their funds," explained the editorial. "The department may indeed make a treaty with the irresponsible, self-constituted Rebel leaders, rejecting the loyal masses of the Cherokee Nation, but can corrupt money-power bring an influence on Congress [for ratification] sufficient to destroy claims so just? I do not believe it."[25]

Phillips also used the article to continue his exposure of the financial irregularities and general corruption surrounding James Blunt and Jim Lane. "A company possessing no small degree of enterprise was organized," he explained, "their written articles of agreement setting forth specifically that a portion of the profits were designed for 'parties not named in the articles.' Those who could

---

23 Thoburn, ed., "The Cherokee Question," 172-180, 193-194, 205-207, 212-219.

24 Ibid., 167, 146-172, 180-198; Hans L. Trefousse, *Andrew Johnson: A Biography* (New York, NY, 1989), 31; Dale and Litton, eds., *Cherokee Cavaliers*, 242-245. Trefousse, *Andrew Johnson*, 208, 257; David Herbert Donald, *Lincoln* (New York, NY, 1995), 551; Katherine Helm, *The True Story of Mary, Wife of Lincoln* (New York, NY, 1928), 252-253; Benjamin P. Thomas and Harold M. Hyman, *Stanton: the Life and Times of Lincoln's Secretary of War* (New York, NY, 1962), 469; Patrick W. Riddleberger, *1866: The Critical Year Revisited* (London, UK, 1979), 204-206; Paul H. Bergeron, ed., *The Papers of Andrew Johnson*, 10 vols. (Knoxville, TN, 1979), vol. 10, 689, 741.

25 John Ross to Evan Jones, March 22, 1866; Moulton, ed., *The Papers of John Ross*, 671; *New York Tribune*, May 21, 1866; John Ross to Evan Jones, March 22, 1866; Moulton, ed., *The Papers of John Ross*, 671.

afford to pay a high official [Blunt] and a United States Senator [Lane] $20,000 each on a single six months contract no doubt find plenty of men they can buy."[26]

The *Boston Commonwealth* commented on Phillips' article five days later on May 26: "The writer says that he can prove this charge, but he does not give the Senator's name. I propose to fill up the hiatus, and let the public know that the aforesaid charge refers to Senator James H. Lane." Lane denied the charge on the Senate floor. "Mr. President," he began, "[f]rom 1855 till now I have been the subject of constant assault from the Democratic papers throughout the country from one extreme to the other. For the last month I have been the subject of assault from the papers of my own party. . . . [T]he imputation contained in that paper is without the slightest foundation; it is a baseless calumny."[27]

The *Commonwealth* shot back at Lane on June 2. "In place of being grateful to your correspondent for placing before him an opportunity of courting an investigation, which Senators usually desire when such damaging rumors are circulated," charged the Boston paper, "General Lane took occasion to-day in the Senate to express anger, not only at the charge, but at the incident which gave him the opportunity of denial." In the midst of the Cherokee treaty negotiations, Lane was finally vulnerable. A month later, having returned to Kansas, a distraught Jim Lane shot himself as he left his carriage in Leavenworth. He died ten days later.[28]

Following his doctor's advice, Ross sent for his sister-in-law, Sara Stapler, and his daughter, Annie Ross, to join him in April. On June 28, Ross dictated to his daughters Jane Nave and Annie his last letter, an appeal to President Johnson to confirm the loyal Cherokee treaty. Ross deeply resented his treatment by Secretary Harlan and Commissioner Cooley. Ross assured Johnson that "it has been agreed upon that all Southern Cherokees shall have the right to come into the Country and occupy their Places at once, and as there are a great many who have left valuable improvements scattered over the Country and they all desire to come in and occupy them at once, and to enjoy equal privileges."[29]

26 *New York Tribune*, May 21, 1866.

27 *Boston Commonwealth*, May 26, 1866; F. and J. Rives, eds., *The Congressional Globe: Containing the Debates and Proceedings of the First Session of the Thirty-Ninth Congress* (Washington D.C., 1866), vol. 36, part 3, 286.

28 *Boston Commonwealth*, June 2, 1866; John Spear, *Life of General James H. Lane: "The Liberator of Kansas,"* 2nd ed. (Garden City, KS, 1897), 313-316.

29 John Ross to Sarah Stapler, March 30, 1866; John Ross to Sara Stapler, April 4, 1866; John Ross to Andrew Johnson, June 28, 1866; Moulton, ed., *The Papers of John Ross*, 672, 672-673, 678-680.

The political atmosphere in Washington almost certainly influenced Johnson's decision regarding whether he should sign the Southern Cherokee treaty. Harlan, the prime facilitator with the Watie faction, had been nominated for his cabinet position by Lincoln, and the deceased president and Harlan had been good friends. In addition, Harlan's daughter was engaged to marry Lincoln's son, Robert. Johnson had let the Harlan confirmation go forward, but according to a recent biographer, the new president merely "tolerated" the new cabinet secretary. In June and July, Johnson attempted to form a third party of conservative Democrats and Republicans to oppose a movement for black male suffrage by Radical Republicans in Congress. Johnson was aware that Harlan disagreed with him on this subject. When the president asked his cabinet to write letters condemning black suffrage, three members, including Harlan, resigned on July 27.[30]

A few weeks earlier on July 2, the day after Lane had shot himself, Boudinot had written to his brother William the distressing news that President Johnson had rejected the Southern Cherokee treaty and had instructed Harlan to write another one. On July 19, the delegates of the loyal Cherokees signed their new treaty with Commissioner Cooley, and the president returned the proposed treaty with the Southern Cherokees without his signature. The Ross party had pleased Johnson by removing the laws of confiscation and by ceding the Cherokee Outlet and Neutral Lands for appraised value. The loyal Cherokees allowed the railroads only a 200-foot easement and gave ex-slaves "all the rights of native Cherokees" provided they claimed them within six months of the date of the treaty. There was even a clause for allotment should the Cherokee government request it.[31]

Ross's daughters may have influenced Johnson's decision. They had sent him a note on July 14, originally meant to be included with Ross's letter of June 28. "[H]is [Ross's] mind dwells on the unjust and outrageous treatment inflicted on him by the Commission at Fort Smith in September last," they explained. "He has been placed by it, in a false and unjust position before the world—and before the world he craves to have his honor vindicated and exonerated." They continued: "The verbal assurances given by your honor, to our Delegation,

30 Trefousse, *Andrew Johnson*, 208, 257; Bergeron, ed., *The Papers of Andrew Johnson*, 689, 741. Riddleberger, *1866: The Critical Year*, 204-206; Donald, *Lincoln*, 551; Thomas and Hyman, *Stanton*, 469.

31 Bergeron, ed., *The Papers of Andrew Johnson*, 696-697, note; Dale and Litton, eds., *Cherokee Cavaliers*, 246; Jas Harlan to D. N. Cooley, July 10, 1866, Letter Received, Cherokee Agency, OIA; Spear, *Life of Lane*, 313-316; Paul F. Lambert, "The Cherokee Reconstruction Treaty of 1866," in *Journal of the West* (July 1973), Issue 12, 471-489; Kappler, *Indian Affairs*, 943-948.

as well as to myself (altho' he is still unapprised of my visits to you) was very gratifying to him and has been a source of relief as he lays on his bed of suffering and anything Official from you would indeed remove every thorn from his pillow. . . . [He has] unshaken confidence in the President, and his firm belief that you will see him righted.[32]

Johnson, whose first public political act was a debate against the Tennessee Legislature's effort to extend state law over the Cherokees in the 1820s, may have been moved by the letter. He marked it "for special attention" and directed it to Secretary Harlan, who passed it on to Cooley.[33]

Saladin Watie informed his father on July 25 that President Johnson had signed the Ross treaty and that the Senate would ratify it. Boudinot did his best to console his uncle. Although Adair and the rest of the delegates wanted to fight the new treaty, Boudinot believed they would be better served working under its terms. The United States Senate ratified the treaty on July 27, 1866.

John Ross died five days later on August 1.

At the next election Lewis Downing, representing the full bloods, ran against John Ross's son William for principal chief. The Watie faction, led by fluent Cherokee speaker William Penn Adair, backed Downing. In return, Adair asked that he and other mixed bloods be included in the Cherokee delegation in Washington, thus presenting unified opposition to territorial government and statehood.

Downing won the election. A relative peace followed in the Cherokee Nation, and in the Indian Nations generally, the lands dominated by the range cattle industry, railroads, and railroad towns.[34]

32 Jane Nave and Annie B. Ross to Andrew Johnson, n.d., Letters Received, Cherokee Agency.

33 Bergeron, ed., *The Papers of Andrew Johnson*, 696-697, n. #6. *Greeneville* (Tennessee) *Intelligencer*, (Tennessee) August 6, 1875. Johnson's son, Andrew Johnson, Jr. was one of the editors of the newspaper. The story is recounted in Johnson's obituary. Trefousse, *Andrew Johnson*, 31; John Savage, *Life and Public Services of Andrew Johnson, Seventeenth President of the United States* (New York, NY, 1866), 20-21; Richard Harrison Doughty, *Greenville: One Hundred Year Portrait, 1775–1875* (Greeneville, TN, 1975), 61-62.

34 *Reply of the Delegates of the Cherokee Nation to the Pamphlet of the Commissioner of Indian Affairs*, 3-6, in *Western Americana: Frontier History of the Trans-Mississippi West, 1550–1900* (New Haven, CT, 1975), microfilm, reel 105; Saladin Watie to Stand Watie, July 24, 1866; Dale and Litton, eds., *Cherokee Cavaliers*, 246-247; Wardell, *A Political History of the Cherokee Nation*, 206.

Bibliography

Primary Sources

Abilene Christian University
    Gano, William. Papers
American Baptist Historical Society, Rochester, New York.
    Jones, Evan Papers, microfilm
American Baptist Historical Society, Rochester, New York
    Jones, John Papers
Arkansas History Commission
    Avera, William Franklin and E. H. Cathey, Jr., Six Generations: Avera-Cathey
Center for American History, University of Texas, Austin
    Maxey, Samuel Bell Papers
Gilcrease Museum. Tulsa, Oklahoma
    Maxey, Samuel Bell Collection
Gilcrease Museum, Tulsa, Oklahoma
    Pitchlynn, Peter Papers
Gilcrease Museum, Tulsa, Oklahoma
    Ross, John Papers
Library of Congress, Washington, D.C.
    Schofield, John M. Papers.
National Archives, Washington, D.C.
    Fort Gibson Letterbook. Record Group 393, vol. 92
    Department of Arkansas, Letters and Orders
    Letters Received by the Office of AG, 1861-1870
    Letters Received by the Office of Indian Affairs. Cherokee Agency, 1865-66
    Letters Received by the Office of Indian Affairs. Choctaw Agency, 1867-68
Southern Baptist Convention Archives, Nashville, Tennessee
    Compere, E. L. Papers
Southwest Arkansas Regional Archives, Washington, Arkansas
    "History of J. T. Kidd, from March 18, 1862, until May 28th, 1865"
State Historical Society of Iowa, Des Moines
    Curtis, Samuel R. Papers
University of Arkansas, Fayetteville, Special Collections
    Braly, Amanda Malvina Fetzallen McClellan Papers
University of Oklahoma, Norman
    Cherokee Nation Papers. Western History Collection, microfilm
    Foreman, Stephen. "Journal and Letters of Stephen Foreman," typescript

Government Documents

Journal of the Congress of the Confederate States of America. 7 vols. Washington: Government Printing Office, 1904-05, microfilm.

Kappler, Charles J., ed. *Indian Affairs, Laws and Treaties.* Vol. 2. Washington: Government Printing Office, 1904.

Letters Received by the Office of Indian Affairs, Creek Agency. Microfilm.

Report of the Commissioner of Indian Affairs for the Years 1854-1866. Washington: Government Printing Office, 1855-1866.[Separate vols. each year]

Special Confederate Documents. Oklahoma City Civil War Commission, 1961-65. Oklahoma Civil War Round Table, Organized 1961. Microfilm.

Special Files of the Office of Indian Affairs, National Archives, Microfilm.

United States War Department, *War of the Rebellion: A Compilation of the Official Records of the Union and Confederate Armies.* 128 vols. Washington, D.C., 1880-1901.

U. S. Congress. Senate. Committee on Claims. Report #113. 41st Cong., 2d Sess., 1870.

Published Sources

Ashcraft, Allen C. "Confederate Indian Department Conditions in August, 1864." *Chronicles of Oklahoma,* 41 (Autumn, 1963): 442-49.

Basler, Roy P., ed. *The Collected Works of Abraham Lincoln.* New Brunswick: Rutgers University Press, 1955.

Blunt, James G. "General Blunt's Account of His Civil War Experiences." *Kansas Historical Quarterly,* 1 (May, 1932): 211-265.

Britton, Willey. *The Union Indian Brigade in the Civil War.* Kansas City, Franklin Hudson, 1922.

———. *Memoirs of the Rebellion on the Border, 1863.* Chicago: Thomas & Co., 1882.

Carrigan, Alfred Holt and Jesse N. Cypert. "Reminiscences of the Secession Convention." *Publications of the Arkansas Historical Association,* 1 (1906): 305-23.

"Comments on the Objections of Certain Cherokee Delegates to the Proposition of the Government to Separate the Hostile Parties of the Cherokee Nation." *Pamphlets in American History.* Sanford, North Carolina: Microfilming Corp of America, 1979.

"Communication of the Delegation of the Cherokee Nation to the President of the United States Submitting the Memorial of the National Council, with Correspondence between John Ross, Principle Chief, and Certain Officers of the Rebellious States. *Western Americana: Frontier History of the Trans-Mississippi West, 1550-1900.* New Haven, CT: Research Publications, 1975. Microfilm.

Christie, Smith, James McDaniel, Thomas Pegg, White Catcher, Daniel H. Ross, J. B. Jones, S. H. Benge. "Memorial of the Delegates of the Cherokee Nation to the President of the United States, and the Senate and House of Representatives in Congress." Washington, D.C.: Washington Chronicle Print, 1866. *Pamphlets in American History.* New Haven: Research Publications, #190.

Davis, Jefferson. *Papers of Jefferson Davis,* 14 vols. Baton Rouge: Louisiana State University, 1999.

Edwards, John N. *Shelby and His Men; or, The War in the West.* Cincinnati: Miami Printing, 1867.

Folsom, Joseph P. *Constitution and Laws of the Choctaw Nation with the Treaties of 1855, 1865, and 1866.* New York, NY, 1869.

Grayson, G. W. *A Creek Warrior for the Confederacy.* W. David Baird, ed. Norman: University of Oklahoma Press, 1988.

Greeley, Horace. *The American Conflict: A History of the Great Rebellion in the United States of America, 1860-65.* Hartford: O. D. Case, 1885.

Griscom, George L. *Fighting with Ross' Texas Cavalry C.S.A.: The Diary of George L. Griscom, Adjutant, 9th Texas Cavalry Regiment.* Homer Kerr, ed. Hillsboro, Texas: Hill Junior College Press, 1976.

Hampton, David Keith. *Cherokee Mixed Bloods: Additions and Corrections to Family Genealogies of Dr. Emmet Starr, Vol. 1: Cordery, Ghigau, Ridge-Watie, Ross, Sanders and Ward.* Lincoln, Arkansas: ARC Press of Cane Hill, 2005.

Jefferson, Thomas. *Thomas Jefferson: Writings.* Merrill Peterson, ed. New York: Library of America, 1984.

Laws of the Cherokee Nation: Adopted by the Council at Various Periods. Tahlequah, Cherokee Nation: Cherokee Nation, 1852; *The Constitutions and Laws of the American Indian Tribes.* Vol. 5. Wilmington, Delaware and London: Scholarly Resources, 1973.

Lothrop, Charles H. *A History of the First Regiment Iowa Cavalry Veteran Volunteers: From Its Organization in 1861 to Its Muster Out of the United States Service in 1866.* Lyons, Iowa: 1890.

MacGowan, D. J. "Indian Secret Societies." *Historical Magazine,* 10 (May, 1866).

Mooney, James. *Myths of the Cherokee and Sacred Formulas of the Cherokees from 19th and 7th Annual Reports Bureau of Ethnology.* Nashville: Charles Elder, 1972.

Memorial of the Delegates of the Cherokee Nation to the President of the United States and the Senate and House of Representatives in Congress. Washington D.C.: Washington Chronicle Print, 1866. *Pamphlets in American History.* Sanford, NC: Microfilming Corp of America, 1979.

Missionary Herald. Vol. 29. (May, 1833), Boston: Clocker and Brewster. Microfilm.

Official Military History of Kansas Regiments During the War for the Suppression of the Great Rebellion. Leavenworth: 1870.

Peters, Richard. *Reports of Cases Argued and Adjudged in the Supreme Court of the United States.* Vol. 5. (January term, 1831) Philadelphia: John Grigg, 1831.

Reply of the Delegates of the Cherokee Nation to the Demands of the Commissioner of Indian Affairs. Woodbridge, CT: Research Publications, Inc., 1976. Microfilm.

Reply of the Delegates of the Cherokee Nation to the Pamphlet of the Commissioner of Indian Affairs. New Haven, CT: Research Publications, 1975

"Reply of the Southern Delegates to the Memorial of Certain Delegates from the Cherokee Nation, together with the Message of John Ross, Ex Chief of the Cherokees, and the Proceedings of the 'Loyal Cherokees' Relative to the Alliance with the So-Called Confederate States." Pamphlets in American History. Sanford, North Carolina: Microfilming Corp of America, 1979.

Schofield, John M. *Forty-Six Years in the Army.* New York, 1897.

Thoburn, Joseph B., ed. "The Cherokee Question." *Chronicles of Oklahoma,* 2 (March, 1924).

US Indian Territory Freedmen Commission, Circulars Nos. 1-4. Fort Smith. Fort Smith New Era, 1866.

Newspapers

Atlanta Baptist Banner
Boston Commonwealth
Greeneville (Tennessee) *Intelligencer*
Lawrence Kansas State Journal
Macon Christian Index
New York Tribune
Washington (Arkansas) *Telegraph*
White Cloud (Kansas) *Chief*

Books and Articles

Abel, Annie Heloise. *The American Indian as Slaveholder and Secessionist*. Lincoln: University of Nebraska Press, 1992.

————. *The American Indian in the Civil War, 1862-1865*. University of Nebraska Press, 1993.

————. *The American Indian and the End of the Confederacy, 1863-1866*. Lincoln: University of Nebraska Press, 1994.

Adair, James. *History of the American Indians*. New York: Promontory Press, n.d.

Agnew, Brad. *Fort Gibson: Terminal on the Trail of Tears*. University of Oklahoma Press, 1981.

————. "War Against the Comanches." *Chronicles of Oklahoma*, 49 (Summer, 1971): 211-29.

————. "Indian Territory" in *Abraham Lincoln and the Western Territories*, Ralph Y. McGinnis, ed. Chicago: Nelson-Hall, 1994, 191-206.

————. "Indian Territory on the Eve of the Civil War." *Proceedings: War and Reconstruction in Indian Territory: A History Conference in Observation of the 130th Anniversary of the Fort Smith Council*. National Park Service, Oklahoma Historical Society, and Arkansas Historical Association, 1995.

Allsopp, Fred W. *History of the Arkansas Press for a Hundred Years and More*. Little Rock, Arkansas, 1922.

Bahos, Charles. "On Opothleyahola's Trail: Locating the Battle of Round Mountains." *Chronicles of Oklahoma*, 63 (Spring, 1985), 58-89.

Baird, David. *Peter Pitchlynn: Chief of the Choctaws*. Norman: University of Oklahoma Press, 1972.

————. *The Quapaw Indians: A History of the Downstream People*. Norman: University of Oklahoma Press, 1980.

Balman, Gail. "The Creek Treaty of 1866." *Chronicles of Oklahoma*, 48 (Autumn, 1970), 184-96.

Barton, O. S. *Three Years with Quantrill: A True Story Told by His Scout John McCorkle*. Norman: University of Oklahoma Press, 1992.

Bass, Althea. *Cherokee Messenger*. Norman: University of Oklahoma Press, 1968.

Bearss, Edwin C. "The Army of the Frontier's First Campaign: The Confederates Win at Newtonia." *Missouri Historical Review*, 60 (October, 1965), 283-319.

Bearss, Edwin C. and Arrell M. Gibson. *Fort Smith: Little Gibraltar on the Arkansas*. Norman: University of Oklahoma Press, 1969.

————. *The Battle of Wilson's Creek*. Cassville, MO: Wilson's Creek National Battlefield Foundation, 1992.

Beringer, Richard E., Herman Hattaway, Archer Jones, William N. Still, Jr. *Why the South Lost the Civil War*. Athens: University of Georgia Press, 1986.

Berlin, Ira, ed. *Freedom: A Documentary History of Emancipation 1861-1867, Series II, The Black Military Experience*. Cambridge, UK: Cambridge University Press, 1982.

Berwanger, Eugene H. *The Frontier Against Slavery: Western Anti-Negro Prejudice and the Slavery Extension Controversy*. Urbana: University of Illinois Press, 1967.

Billington, Ray Allen. *Westward Expansion: A History of the American Frontier*. New York: Macmillan, 1960.

Boatner, Mark M. *The Civil War Dictionary*. New York: Vintage, 1991.

Bridges, C. A. "The Knights of the Golden Circle: Filibustering Fantasy." *Southwestern Historical Quarterly*, 44 (January, 1941), 287-302.

Brown, Walter Lee. *A Life of Albert Pike*. Fayetteville: University of Arkansas Press, 1997.

Castel, Albert. *General Sterling Price and the Civil War in the West*. Baton Rouge: Louisiana State University Press. 1968.

————. *A Frontier State at War*. 1958. Lawrence: Kansas Heritage Press, 1992.

————. *William Clarke Quantrill: His Life and Times*. University of Oklahoma Press, 1999.

Channing, Stephen A. *Crisis of Fear: Secession in South Carolina*. New York: Norton, 1974.

Christ, Mark K., ed. *"All Cut to Pieces and Gone to Hell:" The Civil War, Race Relations, and the Battle of Honey Springs*. Little Rock: August House, 2003.

Confer, Clarissa W. *The Cherokee Nation in the Civil War*. University of Oklahoma Press, 2007.

Connelley, William Elsie. *Quantrill and the Border Wars*. New York: Pageant, 1956.

————. *A Standard History of Kansas and Kansans*. Chicago: Lewis, 1918.

Cornish, Dudley Cornish. "Kansas Negro Regiments in the Civil War." *Kansas Historical Quarterly*, 20 (May, 1953), 417-29.

————. *The Sable Arm: Negro Troops in the Union Army, 1861-1865*. New York: Longmans, 1956.

Cotterill, R. S. *The Southern Indians: The Story of the Civilized Tribes before Removal*. Norman: University of Oklahoma Press, 1966.

Crenshaw, Ollinger. "The Knights of the Golden Circle." *American Historical Review*, 37 (October 1941 to July 1942), 23-50.

Cutrer, Thomas W. *Ben McCulloch and the Frontier Military Tradition*. Chapel Hill and London: University of North Carolina Press, 1993.

Dale, Edward Everett and Gaston Litton, eds. *Cherokee Cavaliers*. Norman: University of Oklahoma Press, 1939.

Danziger, Edmund J., Jr. "The Office of Indian Affairs and the Problem of Civil War Indian Refugees in Kansas." *Kansas Historical Quarterly*, 35 (Autumn, 1969), 257-75.

Debo, Angie. *The Road to Disappearance: A History of the Creek Indians*. Norman: University of Oklahoma Press, 1941.

————. *A History of the Indians of the United States*. Norman: University of Oklahoma Press, 1979.

————. *The Rise and Fall of the Choctaw Republic*. Norman: University of Oklahoma Press, 1982.

————. "The Location of the Battle of Round Mountains." *Chronicles of Oklahoma*, 41 (Spring, 1963), 70-104.

Dougan, Michael. *Confederate Arkansas: The People and Policies of a Frontier State in Wartime*. Tuscaloosa: University of Alabama Press, 1976.

————. "A Look at the 'Family' in Arkansas Politics, 1858-1865." *Arkansas Historical Quarterly*, 22 (Spring-Winter, 1970), 97-111.

Doughty, Richard Harrison. *Greenville: One Hundred Year Portrait, 1775-1875*. Greenville: Doughty, 1975.

Duncan, Robert Lipscomb. *Reluctant General: The Life and Times of Albert Pike*. New York: E. P. Dutton & Co., 1961.

Dunn, Roy Sylvan. "The KGC in Texas, 1860-1861." *Southwestern Historical Quarterly*, 70 (April, 1967), 544-73.

Eaton, Clement. *A History of the Old South: The Emergence of a Reluctant Nation*. New York: Macmillan, 1975.

Eicher, David. *The Longest Night: A Military History of the Civil War*. New York: Simon and Schuster, 2001.

Eison, James R,. ed. "'Stand We in Jeopardy Every Hour,' A Confederate Letter, 1864." *Pulaski County Historical Review*, 33 (Fall, 1983), 50-54.

Faust, Drew Gilpin. *James Henry Hammond and the Old South: A Design for Mastery*. Baton Rouge: Louisiana State University Press, 1982.

Fisher, Leroy H. and William R. McMurry. "Confederate Refugees from Indian Territory." *Chronicles of Oklahoma*, 57 (Winter, 1979-80), 450-62.

Foner, Eric. *Reconstruction: America's Unfinished Revolution, 1863-1877*. Harper & Row, 1988.

Foote, Shelby. *The Civil War, A Narrative*, 3 vols. New York: Random House, 1974.

Foreman, Carolyn Thomas. *Park Hill*. Muskogee, Oklahoma: Star Printery, 1948.

Foreman, Grant. *The Last Trek of the Indians*. New York: Russell & Russell, 1946.

———. "Early Post Offices of Oklahoma." *Chronicles of Oklahoma*, 6 (March, 1928): 4-25.

Ford, Lacy K., Jr. *Origins of Southern Radicalism: The South Carolina Upcountry, 1800-1860*. New York: University of Oxford Press, 1988.

Franks, Kenny A. *Stand Watie and the Agony of the Cherokee Nation*. Memphis: Memphis State University Press, 1979.

Frazer, Robert W. *Forts of the West: Military Forts and Presidios and Posts Commonly Called Forts West of the Mississippi River to 1898*. Norman: University of Oklahoma Press, 1965.

Friend, Llerena. *Sam Houston: The Great Designer*. Austin: University of Texas Press, 1954.

Gaines, W. Craig. *The Confederate Cherokees: John Drew's Regiment of Mounted Rifles*. Baton Rouge: Louisiana State University Press, 1989.

Gardner, Robert G. "Missionary Chaplain to the Cherokees: Ebenezer Lee Compere." *Oklahoma Baptist Chronicle*, 18 (Spring, 1975), 5-32.

———. "Ebenezer Lee Compere, Cherokee Georgia Baptist Missionary." *Viewpoints: Georgia Baptist History*, 5 (1976), 91-102.

———. "Ebenezer Lee Compere and Problems of the Civil War." *The Quarterly Review: A Survey of the Southern Baptist Progress*, 37 (January-February-March, 1977), 23-31.

Gibson, Arrell M. *The Chickasaws*. Norman: University of Oklahoma Press, 1971.

———. *Oklahoma: A History of Five Centuries*. Norman: University of Oklahoma Press, 1981.

Goebel, Dorothy Burne. *William Henry Harrison: A Political Biography*. Philadelphia: Porcupine Press, 1974.

Green, Michael D. *The Politics of Indian Removal: Creek Government and Society in Crisis*. Lincoln and London: University of Nebraska Press, 1982.

Griffith, Benjamin W., Jr. *McIntosh and Weatherford: Creek Indian Leaders*. Tuscaloosa: University of Alabama Press, 1988.

Hagan, Horace Henry. *Eight Great Lawyers*. Oklahoma City: Harlow, 1923.

Hale, Douglas. "Rehearsal for Civil War." *Chronicles of Oklahoma*, 68 (Fall, 1990), 228-65.

———. "The Location of the Battle of Round Mountains." *Chronicles of Oklahoma*, 41 (Spring, 1963), 70-104.

———. *The Third Texas Cavalry*. Norman: University of Oklahoma Press, 1993.

Halliburton, R., Jr. *Red over Black: Black Slavery among the Cherokee Indians*. Westport, Connecticut and London: Greenwood, 1977.

Hall, Kermit L., ed. *Oxford Companion to the Supreme Court of the United States*. New York: Oxford University Press, 1992.

Hartje, Robert G. *Van Dorn: The Life and Times of a Confederate General*. Nashville: Vanderbilt University Press, 1967.

Heath, Gary N. "The First Federal Invasion of the Indian Territory." *Chronicles of Oklahoma*, 44 (Winter, 1966-67), 409-19.

Hendrix, Janey B. "Redbird Smith and the Nighthawk Keetoowahs." *Journal of Cherokee Studies*, 8 (Fall, 1983), 22-39.

Henslick, Harry. "The Seminole Treaty of 1866." *Chronicles of Oklahoma*, 48 (Autumn, 1970): 280-94.

Hill, Samuel S., Jr. *The South and the North in American Religion*. Athens: University of Georgia Press, 1980.

Howard, James Henri. *Shawnee! The Ceremonialism of a Native Indian Tribe and Its Culture*. Athens: Ohio University Press, 1981.

Kerby, Robert L. *Kirby Smith's Confederacy: The Trans-Mississippi South*. New York: Columbia University Press, 1972.

Knight, Wilfred. *Red Fox: Stand Watie and the Confederate Indian Nations during the Civil War Years in Indian Territory*. Glendale, California: Clark, 1988.

Lambert, Paul F. "The Cherokee Reconstruction Treaty of 1866." *Journal of the West*, 12 (July, 1973), 471-89.

Leslie, Edward E. *The Devil Knows How to Ride: The True Story of William Clarke Quantrill and his Confederate Raiders*. New York: Random House, 1996.

Lewis, Elsie M. "Robert Ward Johnson: Militant Spokesman of the Old-South-West." *Arkansas Historical Quarterly*, 13 (1954), 16-30.

Littlefield, Daniel F., Jr. *Africans and Seminoles: From Removal to Emancipation*. Westport: Greenwood, 1977.

———. *Africans and Creeks from the Colonial Period to the Civil War*. Westport: Greenwood, 1979.

Lothrop, Charles H. *A History of the First Regiment Iowa Cavalry Veteran Volunteers, from Its Organization in 1861 to Its Muster Out of the United States Service in 1866*. Lyons, Iowa: Beers and Eaton Printers, 1890.

McCardell, John. *The Idea of a Southern Nation: Southern Nationalists and Southern Nationalism*. New York: Norton, 1974.

McCullar, Marion Ray. "The Choctaw-Chickasaw Reconstruction Treaty of 1866." *Journal of the West*, 12 (July, 1973): 462-70.

McLoughlin, William G. *Champions of the Cherokees: Evan and John B. Jones*. Princeton: Princeton University Press, 1990.

———. *After the Trail of Tears: The Cherokees' Struggle for Sovereignty, 1839-1880*. Chapel Hill: University of North Carolina Press, 1993.

McPherson, James M. *Battle Cry of Freedom: The Civil War Era*. New York and Oxford: Oxford University Press, 1988.

McReynolds, Edwin C. *The Seminoles*. Norman: University of Oklahoma Press, 1972.

McCurry, Stephanie. *Masters of Small Worlds: Yeoman Households, Gender Relations, and the Political Culture of the Antebellum South Carolina Low Country*. New York: Oxford University Press, 1995.

McWhiney, Grady. *Cracker Culture: Celtic Ways in the Old South*. Tuscaloosa and London: University of Alabama Press, 1990.

Mails, Thomas E. *The Cherokee People: The Story of the Cherokees from Earliest Origins to Contemporary Times*. Tulsa: Council Oak Books, 1992.

May, Robert E. *The Southern Dream of a Caribbean Empire: 1854-1861*. Athens and London: University of Georgia Press, 1989.

Merrell, Henry. *The Autobiography of Henry Merrell: Industrial Missionary to the South*. James L. Skinner, III, ed. Athens: University of Georgia Press, 1991.

Meserve, John Bartlett. "Chief Opothleyahola." *Chronicles of Oklahoma*, 9 (December, 1931), 439-53.

Mihesuah, Devon A. *Cultivating the Rosebuds: The Education of Women at the Cherokee Female Seminary, 1851-1909*. Urbana. University of Illinois Press, 1993.

Miles, Edwin A. "After John Marshall's Decision: Worcester v. Georgia and the Nullification Crisis." *Journal of Southern History*, 39 (November, 1973), 519-44.

Morris, John W., Charles R. Goins, and Edwin C. McReynolds. *Historical Atlas of Oklahoma*. Norman: University of Oklahoma Press, 1986.

Moulton, Gary E. "Chief John Ross during the Civil War." *Civil War History*, 19 (December, 1973).

———. *John Ross: Cherokee Chief*. Athens: University of Georgia Press, 1978.

————., ed. *The Papers of John Ross: 1840-1866*, 2 vols. Norman: University of Oklahoma Press, 1985.

Oaks, James. *The Ruling Race: A History of American Slaveholders*. New York: Knopf, 1982.

Oats, Stephen B. *Confederate Cavalry West of the River*. Austin: University of Texas Press, 1961.

O'Flaherty, Daniel. *General Joe Shelby: Undefeated Rebel*. Chapel Hill: University of North Carolina Press, 1954.

Parins, James W. *Elias Cornelius Boudinot: A Life on the Cherokee Border*. Lincoln: University of Nebraska Press, 2006.

————. *The Great Triumvirate: Webster, Clay, and Calhoun*. Oxford University Press, 1987.

Perdue, Theda. *Slavery and the Evolution of Cherokee Society*. Knoxville: University of Tennessee Press, 1979.

————. "Cherokee Planters: The Development of Plantation Slavery Before Removal." Duane H. King, ed. *The Cherokee Indian Nation: A Troubled History*. Knoxville: University of Tennessee Press, 1979.

————. "The Conflict Within: Cherokees and Removal," William Anderson, ed. *Cherokee Removal: Before and After*. Athens: University of Georgia Press, 1991.

————. *"Mixed Blood" Indians: Racial Construction in the Early South*. Athens: University of Georgia Press, 2003.

Perdue, Theda and Michael D. Green. *The Cherokee Nation and the Trail of Tears*. New York: Penguin, 2007.

Phillips, Christopher. *Damned Yankee: The Life of General Nathaniel Lyon*. Columbia: University of Missouri Press, 1990.

Piston, William Garrett and Richard W. Hatcher III. *Wilson's Creek: The Second Battle of the Civil War and the Men Who Fought It*. Chapel Hill: University of North Carolina Press, 2000.

Proceedings: War and Reconstruction in Indian Territory: A History Conference in Observance of the 130th Anniversary of the Fort Smith Council. National Park Service, Oklahoma Historical Society, and Arkansas Historical Association (Fort Smith, AR, 1995).

Prucha, Francis Paul. *The Great Father: the United States Government and the American Indians*. Vol. 1. Lincoln and London: University of Nebraska Press, 1984.

————. "Andrew Jackson's Indian Policy: A Reassessment." *Journal of American History*, 56 (December, 1969), 527-39.

"Poison Springs Battle Recalled by 1864 Letter." *Ouachita County Historical Quarterly*, 19 (September, 1987), 13-14.

Rampp, Donald and Larry Rampp. *The Civil War in the Indian Territory*. Austin: Presidial, 1975.

Reed, Gerard. "Postremoval Factionalism in the Cherokee Nation." Duane H. King, ed. *The Cherokee Indian Nation: A Troubled History*. Knoxville: University of Georgia Press, 1991.

Remini, Robert V. *The Jacksonian Era*. Arlington Heights, Illinois: Harlan Davidson, 1989.

————. *Henry Clay: Statesman for the Union*. New York: Norton, 1991.

————. *Andrew Jackson and the Course of American Freedom, 1822-1832*. Vol. 2. New York: Harper and Row, 1981.

Satz, Ronald N. *American Indian Policy in the Jacksonian Period*. Lincoln: University of Nebraska Press, 1978.

Savage, John. *The Life and Services of Andrew Johnson Seventeenth President of the United States*. New York: Derby and Miller, 1866.

Scroggs, Jack B. "Arkansas in the Secession Crisis." *Arkansas Historical Quarterly*, 12 (Autumn, 1953), 179-224.

Shea, William L. and Earl J. Hess. *Pea Ridge: Civil War Campaign in the West*. Chapel Hill: University of North Carolina Press, 1992.

Shea, William L. *War in the West: Pea Ridge and Prairie Grove*. Ryan Place Publishers, 1996.

———. *Fields of Blood: The Prairie Grove Campaign*. Chapel Hill: University of North Carolina Press, 2009.

Spear, John. *Life of General James H. Lane: "The Liberator of Kansas."* Garden City, Kansas: Spear, 1897.

Spring, Leverett W. *Kansas: The Prelude to the War for the Union*. Boston: Houghton Mifflin, 1885.

———. "The Career of a Kansas Politician." *American Historical Review*, 4 (October, 1898), 80-104.

Starr, Emmet. *History of the Cherokee Indians and Their Legends and Folk Lore*. Oklahoma City: Warden, 1921.

Sutherland, Daniel. "1864: 'A Strange Wild Time.'" *Rugged and Sublime: The Civil War in Arkansas*, Mark K. Smith, ed., 105-44. Fayetteville: University of Arkansas Press, 2003.

Taylor, Lenette Sengle. "Polemics and Partisanship: The Arkansas Press in the 1860 Election." *Arkansas Historical Quarterly*, 44 (Spring, 1985), 314-35.

Thoburn, Joseph B. and Muriel H. Wright. *Oklahoma: A History of a State and Its People*. New York: Lewis Historical Publishing, 1929.

Thornton, J. Mills, III. *Politics and Power in a Slave Society: Alabama, 1800-1860*. Baton Rouge: Louisiana State University Press, 1977.

Thornton, Russell. *The Cherokees: A Population History*. Lincoln: University of Nebraska Press, 1990.

Trefouse, Hans L. *Andrew Johnson: A Biography*. New York: Norton, 1989.

Tricket, Dean. "The Civil War in the Indian Territory: 1861." *The Chronicles of Oklahoma*, 18 (June, 1940), 142-53.

———. "The Civil War in Indian Territory: 1862." *The Chronicles of Oklahoma*, 18 (September, 1940), 266-80.

Urwin, Gregory J. W., ed. *Black Flag over Dixie: Racial Atrocities and Reprisals in the Civil War*. Carbondale: Southern Illinois University Press, 2004.

Warde, Mary Jane. *George Washington Greyson and the Creek Nation, 1843-1920*. Norman: University of Oklahoma Press, 1999.

———. *When the Wolf Came: The Civil War and the Indian Territory*. Fayetteville: University of Arkansas Press, 2013.

Wardell, Morris L. *A Political History of the Cherokee Nation*. Norman: University of Oklahoma Press, 1938.

Wilkins, Thurman. *Cherokee Tragedy: The Ridge Family and the Decimation of a People*. Norman: University of Oklahoma Press, 1986.

Williams, T. Harry. *P. G. T. Beauregard: Napoleon in Gray*. Baton Rouge: Louisiana State University Press, 1991.

Wilson, T. Paul. "Delegates of the Five Civilized Tribes to the Confederate Congress." *Chronicles of Oklahoma*, 53 (Fall, 1975), 353-366.

Winters, John D. *The Civil War in Louisiana*. Baton Rouge: Louisiana State University, 1963.

Woods, James M. *Rebellion and Realignment: Arkansas's Road to Secession*. Fayetteville: University of Arkansas Press, 1987.

Woodward, Grace Steele. *The Cherokees*. Norman: University of Oklahoma Press, 1978.

Wooster, Ralph. *The Secession Conventions of the South*. Greenwood Press, 1962.

Wright, John C. *Memoirs of Colonel John C. Wright*. Rare Book Publishers, 1982.

Wright, J. Leitch. *Creeks and Seminoles: Destruction and Regeneration of the Muscogulge People*. University of Nebraska Press, 1986.

Wright, Muriel H. *A Guide to the Indian Tribes of Oklahoma*. Norman: University of Oklahoma Press, 1951.

———.. "Early Navigation along the Arkansas and Red Rivers in Oklahoma." *Chronicles of Oklahoma*, 8 (March, 1930), 65-88.

———. "Colonel Cooper's Civil War Report on the Battle of Round Mountain." *Chronicles of Oklahoma*, 39 (Winter, 1961-62), 352-97.

Wright, Muriel H. and LeRoy H. Fischer. "Civil War Sites in Oklahoma." *Chronicles of Oklahoma*, 44 (Summer, 1966), 158-215.

Wyatt-Brown, Bertram. *Honor and Violence in the Old South*. New York: Oxford University Press, 1986.

Zellar, Gary. *African Creeks: Estelvste and the Creek Nation*. Norman: University of Oklahoma Press, 2007.

Zorn, Roman J., ed. "Campaigning in Southern Arkansas: A Memoir by C. T. Anderson." *Arkansas Historical Quarterly*, 8 (Autumn, 1949), 240-44.

Zornow, William Frank. "The Kansas Senators and the Re-election of Lincoln." *Kansas Historical Quarterly*, 19 (May, 1951), 133-44.

———. *Lincoln and the Party Divided*. Norman: University of Oklahoma Press, 1954.

Theses and Dissertations

Buice, David S. "The Civil War and the Five Civilized Tribes: A Study in Federal-Indian Relations." Ph.D. diss., University of Oklahoma, 1970.

Colbert, Thomas Burnell. "Prophet of Progress: The Life and Times of Elias Cornelius Boudinot." Ph.D. diss., Oklahoma State University, 1982.

Corbett, William Paul. "Oklahoma's Highways: Indian Trails to Urban Expressways." Ph.D. diss., Oklahoma State University, 1982.

Crowe, Clinton S. "A Civil War within the Civil War: The Division in the Indian Nations." Master's thesis, Northeastern Oklahoma State University, 1995.

Fink, Kenneth Ernst. "A Cherokee Nation of Development." Ph.D. diss., Union Graduate School, 1978.

Fullerton, Eula. "Some Social Institutions of the Cherokees." Master's thesis, University of Oklahoma, 1931.

Gill, Jerry Leon. "Federal Refugees from Indian Territory, 1861-1867." Master's thesis, Oklahoma State University, 1967.

Jones, Steven. "General James G. Blunt and the Civil War in the Trans-Mississippi West." Master's thesis, Oklahoma State University, 1990.

Jordon, Janet Etheridge. "Politics and Religion in a Western Cherokee Community: A Century of Struggle in a White Man's World." Ph.D. diss., University of Connecticut, 1975.

Le Bahos, Charles. "John Ross: Unionist or Secessionist in 1861." Master's thesis, University of Tulsa, 1968.

Thomas, Robert K. "Origin and Development of the Redbird Smith Movement." Master's thesis, University of Arizona, 1983.

Tyner, Howard. "The Keetoowah Society in Cherokee History." Master's thesis, University of Tulsa, 1949.

Wyant, Sharon Dixon. "William A. Phillips and the Civil War in the Indian Territory." Master's thesis, Oklahoma State University, 1964.

Index

Abel, Dr. Annie, 67, 87n

Ad Hine (steamer), 212

Adair, Col. William Penn, Cherokee Nation
attorney, 47, 169-170, 184, 190, 203, 208, 215,
218-220, 228-229, 232-234, 243, 235; *photo*, 169

Adams, Cpt. M. S., 184

African Creek Indians, 58

Alexander, Col. A. M., 88

Alexander, Lee, 214

Allen, Gen. Robert, 141

American Board Mission, 22

American Board of Commissioners for Foreign
Missionaries, 4n

Anderson, Cpt. H. S., 155

Anderson, Col. S. S., 169-170, 214

Anderson, Cpt. Thomas F., 132n, 207, 209- 209n,
210

Arkansas True Democrat, 13

Arkansas Military Units: 1st Mounted Rifles, 68;
2nd Rifles (dismounted), 68; 10th Cavalry, 179;
16th Cavalry, 68; 17th Cavalry, 68

Arkansas, Department of, 210, 215

Armstrong Academy, 129, 163, 166, 192, 203,
215-216, 219-221, 223, 227

Armstrong Council, 169

Atchison Champion, 156

Averell, Lt. William W., 28-29

Banks, Gen. Nathaniel, 173-173n, 174, 180, 192n

Baptist Banner, 131-132

Baptist Missionary Magazine, 23

Baptist Home Mission Board, 21

Baptist Mission, 23

Barker, Cpt. Edgar A., 196

Barker, Edgar A., 197-197n

Bayou Manard, 117-117n

Beattie's Prairie, 96n

Beauregard, Gen. Pierre G. T., 25, 71-71n, 72n

Bell, Caroline, 163

Bell, Lt. Col. James M., 163, 183, 190, 220, 228

Bell, M. L., 214

Benge, Houston, 222, 229

Benham, Cpt. S. C., 142, 144

Benjamin, Judah P., 60

Bentonville Detour, 63-64

Bickley, George W., 11-13, 15

Bird Creek, Battle of, 79

Birney, David, 228

Bishop, Gilbert, 80

Black Dog, Osage Chief, 219

Blair, Francis P. Jr., 37

Blair, Maj. W. B., 101, 104

Bledsoe, Cpt. Joseph, 88, 91

Bloomfield Academy, (Chickasaw Nation), 120

Blunt, James, 240-241

Blunt, Gen. James G., 76, 80, 84, 86, 87-87n, 91, 94,
96-96n, 98, 102-102n, 103-104, 106-108,
134-135, 137-151, 154-156, 172- 173, 206, 210,
215; *photo*, 103

Boggs, Gen. William R., 101, 186n, 192n, 202, 204,
206

Boston Evening Transcript, 70

Boudinot, Elias, 5, 8, 20

Boudinot, Lt. Col. Elias C., 15-16, 31, 42n, 57, 68,
133, 134n, 163-164, 182, 194, 204n, 207-208,
215-216, 227-229, 232- 234, 242-243; *photo*, 235

Boudinot, William, 242

Bowlegs, Billy, Seminole Chief, 46

Boyal, James, 66n

Bragg, Gen. Braxton, 60, 61-61n

Braly, W. C., 180

Breckinridge, Gen. John C., 15

Brewer, Mrs. Perry V., 119

Briartown, 113n, 120, 184

Brown, James, 39

Brown, John, 219

Bryan, Maj. J. M., 86, 88

Buckner, Gen. Simon, 209

Buell, Gen. Don Carlos, 202

Buffalo Hump's Comanche band, 61

Bureau of Indian Affairs, 34

Bussey, Cyrus I., Col., 64, 71, 211, 221-222

Buster, Col. M. W., 87, 94

Butler, George, 21

Cabell, Gen. William L., 97-99, 101-102, 106, 108,
166, 174-175, 206

Cabin Creek, Battle of, 100, 139

Camden Expedition, 173n, 180-181, 183

Camp Dry Wood, (Cherokee refugee camp), 135

Camp Napoleon, 218, 220

Camp Pike, 195

Camp Stephens, 68

Campbell, Lt. Col. William T., 81, 104, 185

Canadian district, 234-236

Canard, Chief Motey, 27, 35-36, 44, 50-51, 219

Canby, Gen. Edward R. S., 158, 159-160, 221

Cane Hill, Battle of, 96, 141

Carney, Gov. Thomas, 141-143

Carr, Gen. Eugene A., 69

Carruth, Edwin H., 12, 46, 79

Carter, Colbert, 219

Caving Banks, 54

Chambers, William P., 221

Chase, Salmon P., 143

Chekote, Lt. Col. Samuel, 195, 216, 219

Cherokee Battalion, 93

Cherokee Convention, 133

Cherokee Council, 21, 136-137, 208, 222n

Cherokee (Eastern Indian) Tribe, 2, 3-3n, 5, 8- 9, 16n, 21, 26-27, 29, 31, 41-42, 48, 50-52, 54, 64, 67, 82, 86, 91, 110, 113n, 114, 122, 124-125, 127, 130, 132-134, 139-140, 152, 155-156, 162-163, 197-199, 207-208, 210, 215, 218-220, 224-229, 231-231n, 233-234, 236, 240-241, 243

Cherokee Male Seminary, 137

Cherokee Military Units: 1st Regiment, 96, 102, 105, 113; 2nd Mounted Rifles, 41; 2nd Regiment, 96, 102-105, 130; 3rd Regiment, 99; Cherokee Mounted Rifles, 18

Cherokee Nation, 3-8, 10, 12, 16, 18-20, 22- 24, 27, 34, 39, 43, 46, 48-48n, 50-51, 58, 70, 73-75, 77, 79-81, 84-85, 87n, 91-94, 96-98, 109-110, 112-113, 114n, 115-116, 117-117n, 118n, 119n, 124, 126, 130, 133, 135-137, 139-140, 147, 151-152, 154, 169, 187, 217, 221-222, 229, 231, 233-234, 236, 243

Cherokee Orphan fund, 154

Cherokee Outlet, 233-234, 242

Cherokee Strip, 234

Cherokee Tomahawk, 153

Cherokee Treaty, 47

Cherokee Treaty of 1835, 223

Cherokee Treaty of 1846, 8

Cherokee, Georgia, Baptist Convention, 130-131

Chickasaw Indian Tribe, 2, 6-7, 25, 27, 30, 32, 34-36, 49, 54, 120, 125, 128, 133, 162-163, 166-168, 185, 216, 219, 224- 225, 228, 232, 238-239

Chickasaw Nation, 26, 28n, 123, 162, 167, 170, 218

Choctaw capital, 203-204

Choctaw General Council, 26, 221

Choctaw Indian Tribe, 2, 4, 25, 27, 30, 34, 35-35n, 36, 49, 52, 54, 90, 93, 108, 120, 125-129, 133, 139, 162-163, 164n, 166- 168, 179-180, 216, 219-220, 224-225, 228, 232, 238-239

Choctaw Nation, 6-7, 16, 26, 28n, 32, 96, 108, 114n, 116, 121, 124, 126, 162, 166, 170, 183, 217

Choctaw-Chickasaw Regiment, 47, 51

Choctaw-Chickasaw treaty, 238

Choska, 56, 148, 195

Christy, Cpt. Smith, 152, 222, 229

Chuppco, Chief John, 46

Chustanala, Battle of, 56-56n, 66n

Chusto Talasah, 51, 54

Chusto Talasah, battle of, 52, 54

Clark, Gov. William, 27

Clarkson, Col. J. J., 78

Clay, Henry, 4

Clear Boggy River, 125, 167

Cloud, Col. William S., 79n, 84, 86, 96, 107, 183, 187

Cloud's Kansas cavalry, 107-108

Coffee, Col. John T., 78, 86

Coffin, William G., 78, 85, 135-137, 139-141, 151, 154, 156, 160, 234

Colbert, Holmes, 219

Colbert, Winchester, 122, 216, 225

Colbert's Ferry, 120, 122, 148, 165

Colorado Military Units: 2nd Volunteer Infantry, 99, 102n, 105, 144

Comanche Indian Tribes, 7, 36, 42, 67, 218- 219

Commissioner of Indian Affairs, 34, 208, 211, 225, 231n

The Compact, 219

Compere, Rev. Ebenezer Lee, 130-130n, 131, 132n, 209n

Confederate Cherokee Delegation, 235

Confederate Cherokee Regiment, 50, 229

Confederate Congress, 32, 36, 59, 109, 128, 133-134, 182, 208

Confederate Indian forces, 47, 92-93

Confederate Trans-Mississippi Department, 215

Confederate Treaty, 137

Coody, Elizabeth, 118-119

Coody, Ella F., 117-120, 121n, 123

Coody, William Shorey, 117-120

Cook, Lt. Horace, 184-185

Cooley, Dennis N., 224-229, 232-234, 237-243

Cooper, Gen. Douglas H., 36, 47-49, 50-50n, 51-52, 54-57, 59, 64n, 81-82, 86, 88-91, 93- 94, 96-96n, 97-97n, 98, 100-108, 113, 129, 139,

148, 163, 164-164n, 165-166, 169, 181-182, 183n, 185, 186-186n, 187-190, 192, 200, 202, 204-204n, 205, 213-215, 218, 239
Cooper, Gen. Samuel, 164, 181; *photo*, 90
Cooper's Choctaws, Chickasaws, and Creeks, 82, 101
Copper's Artillery, 106
Corps d'Afrique, 192n
Cower, R. J., 30
Cowert, Robert, 23
Cowskin Prairie, 77, 136
Crawford, Col. Samuel J., 185
Creek Agency, 34-35, 104, 112, 114, 167, 195
Creek Council ground, 167, 200
Creek Council Grounds, 30
Creek Indian Tribe, 2, 26-27, 30, 36n, 42, 46- 52, 54, 56, 58, 75, 96, 108, 112, 122-123, 125-127, 134-135, 138-140, 148, 152, 155-156, 162-163, 168, 170, 183, 194, 197-199, 210-211, 216, 219-220, 224-228, 232, 238-239
Creek Military Units: Creek Regiment, 51, 99; 1st Regiment, 102, 105; 2nd Regiment, 102, 105; Creek Battalion, 93
Creek Nation, 6-7, 9, 10-10n, 16, 22, 27, 32, 36, 44, 50, 83, 93, 98, 109, 117n, 124, 165, 184, 211, 217, 238
Creek treaty, 238
Cross Timbers, 7, 48n, 49-49n
Curtis, Gen. Samuel R., 62-63, 68-71, 87, 136-137, 140, 145-147, 149, 152-153, 157, 172-173, 206; photo, 64
Cutler, George A., 140
Daily Missouri Democrat, 66n
Daniel, Jones C. C., 222
Dardanelle, Arkansas, 183, 194
Davis, Charles, 145
Davis, J. T., 221
Davis, Jefferson, 25, 27, 32, 34-34n, 61, 72, 74, 82, 133, 163-164, 181, 182-182n, 193, 203, 208, 215, 218
Debo, Dr. Angie, 48n
Deer, Bob, 44
Delaware Indians, 19, 29, 47, 58, 236
DeMorse, Col. Charles, 175, 179
Devil's Backbone, 108
Devil's Backbone Mountain, 189
District of Indian Territory, 163, 171, 174, 213
Doaksville, Oklahoma, 207, 216, 220
Dole, William P., 50, 75, 85, 91, 136, 139- 140, 149, 154-155, 160, 231
Doolittle, James R., 221
Doubleday, Col. Charles D., 77

Downing, Lewis, 222-223, 228-229, 243
Drew, Col. John and his regiment, 39, 41, 48, 50-52, 67, 73, 79-80, 82, 87, 118
Drowning Bear, Lt. Noah, 51-51n
DuBois, Col. J. V., 142-143, 171
Dwight Mission, 70
Eastern Cherokees, 233, 236
Easton, Maj. L. C., 141
Elements of Military Arts and Science, 62,
Elk Creek, 97, 104, 106, 112
Elkhorn Tavern, 62, 64, 69
Ellis, Joseph, 44
Emory, Lt. Col. William H., 27, 28-28n
Ewing, Gen. Thomas, 143n, 148, 206
Fayetteville Arkansan, 15
Female Seminary, 9, 80, 154
Fields, Elizabeth, 117
Fields, Richard, 234
First Christian Church (Disciples of Christ), 165
Five Nations, 18, 24, 26-27, 30-32, 218, 220, 225, 238
Five Tribes, 7, 26, 217
Floyd, John B., 11, 12n
Folsom, Israel, 219
Folsom, Peter, 219
Folsom, Col. Sampson, 90, 219
Foreman, Grant, 78n
Foreman, Maj. John A., 98-99, 123, 139
Foreman, Rev. Stephen, 22, 80-81, 110, 112- 113, 114-114n, 117, 121-123
Foreman, Suzie, 121
Forsyth, Gen. James W., 220
Fort Arbuckle, 28, 42, 55, 61, 167
Fort Baxter (also known as Fort Blair), 145- 145n, 146-147
Fort Blunt (see Fort Gibson)
Fort Cobb, 27-29, 55
Fort Davidson, 206
Fort Davis, 59, 63-64, 73, 81-82, 112
Fort Gibson (renamed Fort Blunt, 7, 28n, 32, 42, 54, 56, 59, 73, 81-83, 85, 96-98, 100- 101, 102-102n, 103-104, 106-107, 112-113, 117-118, 135-139, 142, 144-145, 147-148, 151-154, 156-159, 166-167, 169, 171-172, 183-184, 186-187, 190-191, 193-197, 200-201, 203-206, 210, 212-213, 215, 221, 222-222n, 223
Fort Leavenworth, 28-29, 141, 150, 224
Fort McCulloch, 73

Fort Scott, 46, 75, 83, 87, 93, 98, 103, 138, 141, 144-145, 147-148, 152, 155, 160-161, 184, 186, 191n, 194-195, 201, 203, 212-213

Fort Smith, 7, 28-28n, 29-30, 34-35, 55, 63, 74, 96-97, 101, 106, 108, 116, 118, 130, 137, 145, 148-149, 154-159, 161, 165- 166, 169-170, 174, 183-193, 203, 205-206, 210-212, 214, 217, 221-224, 226, 229-230, 232, 236

Fort Smith Council, 223-224, 228

Fort Sumter, 25, 31, 37

Fort Towson, 7, 126-127, 166, 169-171, 204- 205, 207, 210

Fort Washita, 27-28, 123, 126, 134, 170, 202, 204, 210, 215

Fort Wayne, 96

Foster, Senator Lafayette, 223

Franklin, battle of, 150n

Frémont, Gen. John C., Gen., 50-51, 62, 75

Frozen Rock Landing, 118

Furnas, Col. Robert W., 83

Gains, Lt. Col. J. J., 29-30

Gamble, Hamilton R., 140-142

Gano, Mattie, 165

Gano, Col. Richard M., 165

Gano, Richard M., 166, 174-175, 179, 189- 190, 193-196, 197-197n, 198, 199-199n, 200-200n, 201, 203-205, 214

Garland, Samuel, 219

Garrett, Col. John A., 222

Gaylord, Col. George L., 158-159, 184

General Ground Council, 181

General Orders No. 164, 150

Gibbons, Lt. William, 177

Gillpatrick, Dr. Rufus, 79-79n

Good's Texas Battery, 68

Gott, Watt, 217

Grand Council, 163-164, 166-167, 203-204, 208, 215, 219-221

Grand Council, November 1863, 42, 56, 58, 77-78, 82-84, 98-100, 104, 117n, 118, 139, 148, 154-155, 161, 172, 194-195, 197, 212, 234-236

Grant, Gen. Ulysses S., 61, 98, 131, 132-132n, 138-138n, 149, 150-150n, 182, 210-221

Grayson, George Washington (Tulwa Tustunugge, Wolf Warrior), 184-185, 197

Green, Gen. Martin E., 70

Greeno, Cpt. Harris S., 81-82

Griscom, Adjutant George L., 49

Gritts, Bud, 18-22, 222

Halleck, Gen. Henry W., 62, 76, 98, 136, 141- 143, 149, 150n, 155, 173, 210

Harjo, Icho, 35, 44, 50-51

Harlan, James, 223-224, 226, 233-234, 236-243

Harlan, Justin J., 135-137, 139-140, 151-152, 154, 160, 234, 239

Harlan's Indian Territory bill, 223, 230, 234- 235

Harney, Gen. William S., 28, 224

Harris, Cyrus, 232

Harrison, Col. James E., 26-27, 218

Harrison, William H., 1

Hawpe, Col. Trezevant C., 88

Hearn, Alfred, 179

Hebert, Col. Louis, 67-68

Hemp Bales, battle of the, 60

Herron, Gen. Francis J., 96, 138n, 157-158, 216, 220, 222

Hindman, Gen. Thomas C., 15, 72-74, 81-82, 86, 96

Hoffmann's battery, 64

Honey Springs, 67, 97, 101, 104, 106-107, 115, 117, 119-120

Honey Springs, Battle of, 93, 102n, 106, 109, 119n, 121, 130, 139-142, 162, 175, 192

Hood, Gen. John B., 150n

Hopkins, Maj. Henry, 103n, 105, 195, 197-199, 200-200n

Horse Creek, 83

Houston, Sam, 11-12, 26-27

Howard, Cpt. R. A., 142, 144

Howell, Cpt. Sylvanus, 88, 91, 96

Hoyt, Esther, 80

Hubbard, David, 29, 34

Hudson's Ford, 98, 161

Hump, War Chief Buffalo, 36

Hunt, Henry J., 229

Huston, Lt. George, 184-185

Hutkee, Mikko, 44, 46

Illinois Military Units: 36th Infantry, 64, 68

Indian Battalion, 94

Indian Brigade, 135, 139, 166

Indian Home Guard; Cherokee brigade, 190; 1st Cherokee, 194-195; 1st Creek, 96; 1st Regiment, 58, 77-78, 83, 102, 226; 2nd Cherokee, 194; Choctaw Brigade, 189, 215, 2nd Choctaw, 189; 2nd Creek Mounted Volunteers, 184; 2nd Regiment, 58, 77-78, 83, 91, 102, 185; 3rd Choctaw, 183; 3rd Regiment, (known as the Union Indian Brigade), 58, 80, 83, 85, 87-87n, 88, 91, 94, 96, 98, 139, 198; Creek brigade, 184; Grayson's Creeks, 185; Indian Brigade, 152-153, 155, 160, 172; Phillips Indian Brigade, 166; Tandy Walker's Choctaws, 174-175; Union Cherokees, 198-Union Indian Brigade, 158; 233; Walker's Choctaws, 171, 180; Watie's Creeks, 199; Watie's Indian Brigade, 198

Indian Nations, 7, 9, 12-12n, 16, 25-26, 28- 29, 31-32, 34, 60, 63, 70, 73-74, 79, 92, 128, 132-133, 144, 166, 168, 172, 186n, 192-193, 202, 205-206, 208, 214-215, 218, 220, 223, 231, 238, 243

Indian Nations, War for the, 108

Indian Removal Act, 1, 4

Indian Territory, 2, 27, 36, 46, 74, 136, 149, 158, 166, 172, 213, 215, 223, 225-226

Indiana battery, 77

Indiana Military Units: 22nd Infantry, 64

Insley, Cpt. M. H., 172

Iowa Military Units: 3rd Cavalry, 64; 18th Infantry, 174, 177

J. R. Williams (steamer), 184-186, 192, 197

Jackson, Andrew, 1, 4, 5-5n

Jackson, Governor Clayborn F., 37-38

Jeans' Missourians, 88, 90

Jeans, Col. Beal G., 88

Jessie Chisholm's trading post, 46

Jim Lane's Jayhawkers, 60, 65, 147-148

Johnson, President Andrew, 221, 224, 226- 228, 230, 233, 237, 239-243

Johnson, Charles B., 36, 239

Johnson, J. R., 202

Johnson, Richard H., 13, 15

Johnson, Sen., Robert Ward, 13, 32, 34, 59, 182

Johnson's Station, 126

Johnston, Gen. Albert Sidney, Gen., 71-71n, 72n

Johnston, Gen. Joseph E., 183, 214

Joint Committee on the Conduct of the War, 71

Jones, Rev. Evan, 19-19n, 21-24, 46, 50, 51n, 78, 79-79n, 81, 240

Jones, Rev. John B., 19-24, 51n, 110, 229-230

Jones, Robert M., 116, 128, 133, 216, 228

Judson, Col. William R., 94, 105, 149

Jumper, Principal Chief and Col. John, 36, 195, 208, 216, 219

Kanard, Moty, 169

Kansas State Journal, 156

Kansas Cavalry, 99, 167

Kansas Colored Volunteers, 98

Kansas Jayhawkers, 41, 60, 75, 147-148

Kansas Military Units: 1st Colored Infantry, 98-99, 101-102, 104, 106, 138, 144, 174- 178, 189, 192, 195; 2nd Cavalry, 94, 108, 174, 177, 195; 2nd Colored Infantry, 146, 185; 6th Cavalry, 81, 88, 94, 103-106, 174, 177, 189, 195; 9th Cavalry, 77-78, 88, 187; 10th Cavalry, 77, 90, 96; 13th Infantry, 143; 14th Cavalry, 145, 167, 174, 195

Kansas-Nebraska Act, 11

Keetoowah Constitution, 19

Keetoowah regiment, 58

Keetoowah Society, 10n, 18-22, 24, 41, 50, 52, 67, 78-80, 81-81n, 87n, 109, 110n, 112, 113n, 114-115, 237

Keys, Riley, 91

Kimball, Gen. Nathan, 149

Knights of the Columbian Star, 11

Knights of the Golden Circle (KGC), 11-13, 15, 24

Knights of the Iron Fist, 11

Knights of the True Faith, 11

Landmark Banner and Cherokee Baptist, 130

Lane, Senator and Gen. James H., 46-46n, 75-76, 79, 98, 135, 137n, 140, 142-143, 154-157, 223, 240-242; *photo*, 76

Leased District, 27, 35-36, 218, 238

Leavenworth, 135, 139, 143-144, 148, 241

Lee, Col., R. W., 125-128, 134, 171, 214

Lee, Col. Robert E., 12, 183, 214

Lee's light battery, 102, 106

Leetown, Battle of, 64, 68-69

LeFlore, Cpt. Campbell, 164, 182

Lennex Mission, 166

Leslie's Weekly, 145, 147

Lexington Campaign, 75

Lexington, battle of, 60

Limestone Prairie, 190, 192

Lincoln, Abraham, 12, 25, 29n, 31-32, 44, 46n, 62, 75, 84, 91, 138, 140, 142-143, 149, 150n, 153, 157, 167, 168n, 173, 224, 227, 231, 242

Lincoln, Robert, 242

Lotus (steamer), 213

Louisiana Military Units: 3rd Cavalry, 62

Lower Creeks, 2-3, 7-8, 35, 44

Loyal Cherokee Delegation, 58, 222, 228, 231n, 232-234, 239-240, 242

Loyal Cherokee Treaty, 241

Lubbock, Governor Francis R., 61

Luce, J. B., 239

Lynde, Col. E., 88

Lyon, Gen. Nathaniel, 37-38

MacGowan, D. J., 12

Macon (Georgia) *Christian Index*, 130

Magruder, Gen. John B., 203-206, 215

Male Seminary (Cherokee School), 9, 80

Marmaduke, Gen. John S., 173-178, 206

Marshall, John J., 4-5

Martin, H. W., 79

Martin, Joseph, 121, 124-125

Mar-wa, Comanche Chief, 219

Masonic Blue Lodges, 12, 23

Mathews, Col. Asa C., 216, 220, 222

Maxey, Marilda, 126, 164, 166

Maxey, Gen. Samuel Bell, 126-126n, 127-129, 162-166, 169, 171-178, 180-181, 182-182n, 183-183n, 186-186n, 187-191, 192-192n, 193-194, 201-203, 204-204n, 205, 207-209, 213-214; *photo*, 164

Maysville, Battle of, 94, 96n, 139

McCulloch, Ben, 11-12, 16, 18, 34-35, 37-38, 41, 50-51, 54, 56n, 60-64, 66-69, 71, 73, 232; *photo*, 35

McCulloch, Gen. Henry E., 214

McCurtain, Col. Jackson, 183

McDaniel, Cpt. James, 51, 79

McDonald and Company, 140, 148, 155-156, 160-161

McIntosh, Chilly, 36, 219

McIntosh, Col., James, 54

McIntosh, Col. Daniel N., 44, 47-48, 64n, 66- 69, 71, 108, 112, 148, 203, 204n, 208, 219

McIntosh, Gen. James, 56-57, 63

McIntosh, Lewis, 112

McIntosh, Roley, 8

McIntosh, Suzie, 112

McIntosh, William, 2, 204n

McLendon, Lt. S. G., 132

McLoughlin, William, 79n

McNeil, Gen. John, 148-149

Mead, Elizabeth Kemp, 122

Meade, Gen. George G., 182

Medal of Honor, 146

Merrell, Henry, 179

Miller, Robert C., 128-129

Mississippi River, 118n, 186, 209-210, 214, 230

Missouri Military Units: 1st Cavalry, 64; 2nd Division Missouri State Guard, 70; 5th Cavalry, 64; 12th Infantry, 64

Mitchell, Charles, 182

Mix, Charles, 139

Mooney, James, 19-19n, 50

Moore, Andrew B., 29

Moravian Mission, 87, 96

Morgan, Gen. John Hunt, 165

Mounted Cherokee Rifles, 18

National Committee and Council of the Cherokee Nation, 3, 190

National Council of the Loyal Cherokees, 3, 154, 222, 229

Nave, Jane, 241

Neutral Lands, 16-16n, 18, 42, 236, 242

New York Daily Tribune, 70, 80, 240

New Echota Treaty, 20

New England Congregationalists, 4n

Newtonia, Missouri, 67, 85-88, 93-94, 102

Noble, John W., 71

North Canadian River, 148

North Fork of the Canadian River, 121, 167, 238

North Fork Town, 27, 35, 47, 113, 121-122, 167, 200

Office of Indian Affairs, 156

Ohio Military Units: 2nd Cavalry, 77

Old Fort Wayne, 18, 93-94, 96n, 99, 102, 135

Old Fort Wayne, battle of, 93, 102, 136

Old Settlers, 8, 117

Opothleyahola (Chief), 4, 8, 35-36, 44, 46- 48, 49n, 50-50n, 51-52, 54, 56-57, 70, 200, 225-226; *photo*, 45

The Opothleyahola Affair, 59

Opothleyahola's revolt, 138

Osage Tribe, 42, 58, 126, 155-156, 219-220, 224, 226

Osterhaus, Col. Peter J., 64, 66-66n, 67-68

Ouachita Mountains, 7, 183, 205

Park Hill, 22, 34, 42, 79-79n, 81-82, 84, 110, 114, 117, 136-138, 154, 163, 222

Parker, Col. Ely S., 221, 224

Parker, Ely S., 239

Parks, Lt. Col. R. C., 113

Pea Ridge, 69, 71-73, 86, 90, 119, 225

Pea Ridge, battle of, 63, 67, 75, 77, 103

Pearce, Gen. N. Bart, 32, 38, 73

Peck, Cpt. S. S., 158-159

Pegg, Maj. Thomas, 52, 82, 161, 222-223

Pemberton, Gen. John C., 131

Perdue, Theda, 3

Perryville, 96, 108, 122, 170, 194

Phillips, Col. William A., 79-80, 82n, 83-84, 87-87n, 90-91, 94, 96, 98-99, 101, 102- 102n, 103, 105, 110n, 112, 119-119n, 136-140, 148, 152-159, 160-160n, 161, 166, 170-173, 184, 186, 191n, 210-213, 215, 240-241

Pike, Gen. Albert, 16, 26, 31-31n, 32-32n, 33-36, 42, 44, 47, 48n, 59-60, 63, 66-66n, 67-68, 70-74, 79-79n, 81-82, 90, 225, 232, 239, 206

Pin Indians, see Keetoowahs, 112

Pitchlynn, Peter P., 126-127, 129, 208, 216, 220-221, 225

Plains Indians, 35n, 218-219, 221

Pleasonton, Alfred, 206

Poison Spring, Battle of, 174-175, 189

Pomeroy, Samuel, 137n, 143

Pond, James, Lt., 145, 147

Pope, Gen. John, 160

Prairie Grove, Battle of, 96, 103, 141

Price, Gen. Sterling, 37-38, 56n, 60, 62, 64, 69, 71, 72n, 75, 98, 108, 173-174, 180, 191, 194, 203-207
Price's Missouri Expedition, 194
Proclamation of Amnesty and Reconstruction, 167
Proctor, A. G., 135-136, 140
Provisional Congress of the Confederacy, 34
Quantrill, William Clarke, 145-148, 186n
Quapaw, 42, 46, 58, 137, 224
Quayle, William, 66n
Rains, Gen. James S., 77-78, 86, 93-94
Rector, Elias, 30
Rector, Henry M., 29-31, 72, 232
"Red Legs" (Jayhawkers), 147
Red River Campaign, 173n, 180
"Reserve" Indians, 126, 220
Reynolds, Gen. Joseph J., 159, 210-211, 215
Rich, Houston, 107
Ridge Faction (Cherokee Treaty Party), 5, 8-8n, 9, 15
Ridge, John R., 5, 8, 234
Ridge, Major, 5, 8
Riley, Lt. Col. James, 166
Ritchie, Col. John, 185
Robb, Lt. A. W., 159, 161
Robinson, Ella Coody, 117n
Robinson, J. C., 125
Robinson, Lt. Joe, 120
Robinson's Academy, 125
Rose Cottage, 42, 83, 110; *photo*, 43
Rosecrans, Gen. William S., 149, 206
Ross Treaty, 243
Ross, Annie, 241
Ross, Daniel H., 85, 229
Ross, John, 3, 6, 8-n, 13, 16, 18, 20, 22-24, 26-27, 29-31, 34-35, 37, 39, 41, 42-42n, 43, 46, 50-51, 77-79, 81, 82-82n, 83-85, 91, 109-110, 115n, 191, 221-236, 237, 239-243; *photo*, 17
Ross, Maj. Lawrence, 67
Ross, Lewis, 154
Ross, Col. William P., 39, 82, 115n, 153, 222, 243
Round Mountain, battle of, 48-48n, 50
Sac and Fox Reservation, 135
Salomon, Gen. Frederick S., 77-78, 83, 86, 87-87n, 88-89, 91
San Bois Creek, 120, 121n, 183, 185, 190
Sands, Creek Chief, 46, 211
Scales, Joseph A., 121, 219, 221-222, 234, 236
Schofield, Gen. John M., 87, 94, 98, 107, 138-138n, 140-142, 143-143n, 145, 148, 150-150n
Scott, Sutton S., 124, 128-129, 133-134, 192-193, 207
Scott, Gen. Winfield, 6
Scottish Rite, 31n

Seddon, James, 97, 192n,218
Sells, Elijah, 224, 234, 239
Seminole Agency, 36
Seminole Nation, 2, 6, 25, 27, 30, 34, 36-36n, 46, 47, 49-50, 51, 56, 58, 126-127, 139, 152, 163, 167-168, 170, 195, 199, 216, 219-220, 224-226, 228, 237-239
Senate Bill 459, 223-224
Seneca Nation, 42, 58, 137, 221, 224-225
Sequoyah, 3n, 152
Seward, William H., 29
Shawnee Nation, 42, 58, 137, 224-226
Shelby, Gen. Joseph O., 86-86n, 88, 173, 183, 186-187, 189, 206
Sherman, Gen. William T., 150n, 183, 209n
Sigel, Gen. Franz, 38, 60, 62-63, 69
Sims, Col., William B., 51, 54, 66n
Slack, William, 71
Smith, Cpt. Edward A., 103n
Smith, Gen. Edmund Kirby, 101, 126n, 127-127n, 129, 133, 162-164, 166, 169-171, 173-174, 178, 180-181, 182-182n, 186-186n, 191, 192-192n, 193, 201-204, 207-209, 213-215, 218, 220
Smith, Henry, 139
Smith, Sam, 19
Southern Baptists, 21n, 109, 130
Southern Cherokee Delegation, 222
Southern Cherokee District, 235
Southern Cherokee Nation, 86, 109, 228, 231n, 232-234, 236-237
Southern Plains Indians, 28n, 218
Spears, Cpt. John, 167, 221
Stand Watie Faction, 34
Stanton, Edwin M., 84, 91, 98, 141, 148, 210, 221
Stapler, Sara, 241
Starr, Emmet, 19-19n
Starr, George, 217
Starr, Tom, 113n, 184
Steele, Gen. Frederick, 108, 149, 155, 173-173n, 174, 180-181, 203-204
Steele, Gen. William, 96-97, 99, 101, 106-108, 124, 126, 164-164n
Stevens, Col. J. G., 88
Stockton, Cpt. Job B., 90
Stone, Col. B. Warren, 68, 70
Stop, Lt. Watt, 51
Strayhorn, Cpt. (-), 195-196
Sturgis, Maj. Samuel D., 28n, 29, 38
Sumner, Charles, 71
Superintendent of Issues, 127-128
Tahlequah, Oklahoma, 9, 22, 39, 42, 80-81, 86-87, 96, 137-139, 152, 163, 191, 222, 229, 231, 233

Tandy Walker's Choctaws, 86, 88, 106

Taylor, Gen. Richard, 173-173n, 180, 192n

Taylor, Lt. Col. Thomas F., 83

Taylor, Zachary, 67

Tebbetts, J. M., 239

Texas Military Units: 3rd Cavalry, 69; 4th Cavalry, 68; 5th Texas Partisan Rangers, 99, 102; 6th Cavalry, 67, 9th Cavalry, 49, 51, 54, 66n; 9th Infantry, 126; 20th Cavalry (dismounted), 102, 106; 29th Cavalry, 99, 102, 106, 175; 30th Cavalry, 195; 31st Cavalry, 88; Gano's brigade, 175, 179, 196, 200, 205; Howell's Battery, 93, 189, 195-196, 198

Thayer, Gen. John M., 155, 158, 160n, 161, 173, 183-185, 190, 205, 211-212

Thoburn, Joseph, 107

Thomas, Lydia, 147

Three Forks, 7, 104, 117n, 155

Tishomingo, 125, 183

Todd, George, 147

Toombs, Robert A., 32, 34

Tose-wi, (Comanche Chief), 219

Trail of Blood on Ice Campaign, 48, 54, 56

Trail of Tears, 6, 8

Treaty of 1835, 231, 234, 237

Treaty of 1846, 232

Treaty of Doaksville, 6

Treaty of New Echota, 6, 117

Treaty Party, Cherokee (Ridge Faction), 5-6, 8, 13

True Democrat, 15

Tullahassee Mission, 211

Tustenuggee, Chief Halleck, 46, 56

Union Indian Brigade (3rd Regiment Indian Home Guard); 58, 67, 78, 86, 87n, 92-93, 110n

United States Military Units: 1st Cavalry, 27, 55

Upper Creek Indians, 2-4, 7-8, 35, 44

United States Military Academy at West Point, 126

Usher, John P., 153

Van Buren, Arkansas, 55, 69, 101, 116, 118, 138, 152, 227

Van Dorn, Gen. Earl, 61-64, 68-69, 70-71, 72-72n, 73-74, 78; photo, 61

Van Horn, R. T., 239

Vance, William H., 216, 220

Vann, Lt. Col. Clement Neeley, 194-196, 198-199, 219

Vann, Elizabeth, 120

Vann, James, 222

Vann, Maj. John, 118-120, 121n, 194-195

Vann, Joseph "Rich Joe," 39, 118-118n, 221

Veatch, Gen. James C., 220-221

Virginia Barton (steamer), 212-213

Walker, David, 31

Walker, Sgt. John, 132n, 171, 177, 180, 209

Walker, Leroy Pope, 16, 34, 41

Walker, Tandy, 90, 102, 215, 219

Ward, James, 80

Ward, Maj. Richard G., 176-177

Washbourne, J. Woodward, 234, 236

Washington (Arkansas) *Telegraph*, 79n, 179

Watie Faction, 24, 35, 82

Watie, Charlotte, 115

Watie, Eugene Cumiskey, 115

Watie, Josephine, 115

Watie, Cpt. Saladin, 115, 236, 243; photo, 235

Watie, Sarah, 100, 114-114n, 115, 117, 123, 163, 194, 201, 207, 213, 215-216

Watie, Solon, 115

Watie, Gen. Stand, 5, 8, 13, 15, 18, 31, 41, 56- 57, 66-70, 73, 77-78, 83, 86, 88, 93-94, 96- 97, 99-100, 102, 107-108, 110-110n, 113- 113n, 114-114n, 115, 117-118, 119n, 121, 123-125, 130, 132-133, 138-139, 162-167, 169-171, 174, 182-185, 186-186n, 188-191, 192-192n, 194-198, 199-199n, 200, 204n, 207-208, 209-209n, 210, 213, 215-221, 227- 229, 231, 234-236, 239, 242; photo, 14

Watie, Watica, 117

Wattles, Lt. Col. Stephen H., 96, 197-198, 205

Watts, Elizabeth, 180

Webster, Daniel, 4

Weer, Col. William, 77, 78-78n, 79-83, 86, 87- 87n, 91, 148, 231

Welfley's battery, 64

Wells, Col. J. W., 189

Western Creek Nation, 46-47

Westport, Battle of, 206

Wharton, Gen. John, 205-206

White Cloud Kansas Chief,, 156

White Cpt. Catcher, 222, 229

White Chief, 44

Whitlow, Lt. B. H., 198

Wichita Agency, 36, 156

Williams, Col. James M., 98-99, 101, 174-178

Williamson, Maj. George, 181

Wilson's Creek, Battle of, 37-39, 77

Wisconsin Military Units: 3rd Cavalry, 88, 99, 103-104, 145, 160; 9th Cavalry, 77

Wister, Thomas, 224

Worcester, Rev. Samuel A., 4, 5-5n, 22, 80, 110

Wright, Col. John C., 180

Wright, Muriel, 48n

Johnsonville

Union Supply Operations on the Tennessee River
and the Battle of Johnsonville, November 4–5, 1864

J E R R Y T. W O O T E N

"Deftly fills an important void in the story of the Civil War's Western Theater."
— A. Wilson Greene, author of *A Campaign of Giants: The Battle for Petersburg*

Read on for an exclusive excerpt from
this new study from Savas Beatie!

November 2019

CHAPTER 6

— EXCLUSIVE EXCERPT —

Protecting Johnsonville:
Union Defense of the Supply Depot

DURING the height of Johnsonville's operation as a supply depot from May to November 1864, a garrison of both white and United States Colored Troops protected the logistics center. Johnsonville's garrison included artillerists, infantrymen (both foot and mounted), cavalrymen, and armed civilian laborers from the Quartermaster's Department in Nashville. The unique supply depot and railroad terminus also had two commanders, an army officer and a naval officer.[1]

Johnsonville's Commanders

Col. Charles R. Thompson of the 12th USCT commanded the U.S. Army forces, or "the troops," as one 1865 report put it, while Acting Volunteer Lt. Edward M. King served as the ranking officer for "the gunboats." As correspondence between Thompson and King demonstrates, neither officer liked the other, and the records remain silent as to whether one served under the overall command of the other while at Johnsonville. Each man made important command decisions that impacted operations at Johnsonville, and both regularly communicated directly with the

---

1 *OR Supplement*, vol. 77, 473, 477; *OR* 52, pt. 1, 655-59.

Colonel Charles R. Thompson, Commander of the 12th U.S.C.T Regiment, ca. 1862. *Dayton Metro Library, Dayton, Ohio*

commander of the Department of the Cumberland, Maj. Gen. George H. Thomas in Nashville.[2]

Charles R. Thompson was born in 1840 in Bath, Maine, and was a resident of St. Louis, Missouri, by the age of nineteen. He was engaged in the mercantile trade there when the Civil War broke out in 1861. Thompson enlisted as a private in the Engineer Regiment of the West, Missouri Volunteers, and served under Brig. Gen. John C. Fremont. In March 1862, Thompson was promoted to 1st lieutenant and participated in the Battle of New Madrid, Missouri, and the Siege of Island No. 10, where, according to one writer, he assisted in building "the famous canal which led to the capture of the entire rebel force."[3]

That June, Thompson received an appointment as Post Quartermaster at Hamburg, Tennessee, and later as Ordnance Officer in the Army of the Mississippi under Maj. Gen. William S. Rosecrans. He was a young man on the rise, and Thompson's fellow officers in the Department of the Cumberland held him in high esteem. At the October 3-4, 1862, Battle of Corinth, Mississippi, Thompson served as Rosecrans' aide-de-camp and

---

2 *Official Records of the Union and Confederate Navies in the War of the Rebellion*, 30 Vols. (Government Printing Office, Washington, D.C., 1894-1927), vol. 26, Series I, 615, hereafter cited as *ORN*. All references are to Series 1 unless otherwise noted; *OR* 39, pt. 1, 861.

3 John Fitch, *Annals of the Army of the Cumberland: Comprising Biographies, Descriptions of Departments, Accounts of Expeditions, Skirmishes, and Battles* (Philadelphia, 1864), 53.

Major General George H. Thomas, commander, U.S. Army of the Cumberland, 1864. *Library of Congress*

turned in a fine performance. The army commander so revered Thompson that he awarded him with the "red ribbon of the Roll of Honor for his organization of the First Regiment of Colored Troops in the Department of the Cumberland, and for his meritorious services and gallantry as aide-de-camp to the general commanding at the battles of Corinth and Stone's River." Rosecrans also expressed his admiration "for the qualities which have raised Colonel Thompson from the position of private, in which he entered the service at the commencement of the rebellion, to his present rank, which has been attained solely by his own merit and attention to duty."[4]

In August 1863, Thompson was promoted to colonel and given command of the 12th USCT. His regiment was stationed at various locations in Tennessee and at practically every section along the Nashville and Northwestern Railroad from Kingston Springs westward to Johnsonville. Though Thompson's command performed primarily guard duty at these posts, the 12th USCT, along with the 13th and 100th USCT regiments, participated in their fair share of engagements with bands of marauding guerillas.[5]

It is unclear when Thompson arrived at Johnsonville, but various accounts point to reaching the depot in mid-October 1864. By that time Johnsonville was well-established with buildings, loading platforms, corrals, and barracks. How, exactly, he came to be there, and whether he was

4 Ibid, 54; *OR* 30, pt. 3, 298.

5 *OR* 77, Supplement, Records of Events, 470-77.

at some point supposed to command the entire facility is something of a mystery. "I was in command of all troops on line of the N. and N. W. Rail Road, and went to Johnsonville when the place was threatened by [Gen. Nathan Bedford] Forrest early in October with about 600 Col'd Troops from the 12th, 13th and 100th U.S.C. and 43rd Wis.," Thompson confirmed in an affidavit later that year. "I was not ordered there but took my Head Quarters and all the men that could be spared from the defence of the Rail Road. My Quarters were about four hundred yards from the Levee in the beginning of the fight," he added, "when I moved on the hill."[6]

Thompson's statement makes it clear he was not ordered to move to Johnsonville to assume command. As he explained it, Thompson never received orders from Gen. Thomas, Governor Johnson, or any other superior officer assigning him to that effect. Instead, as colonel of the 12th USCT, he took it upon himself to move his command there to protect the vital logistics center. As one of the ranking officers present, Thompson established his headquarters at Johnsonville and awaited for new orders.

The 43rd Wisconsin's Cpl. Atwood provided a clue about this command confusion when he failed to mention anything about Col. Thompson being in charge of the post. Atwood and his Wisconsin regiment comrades arrived at Johnsonville in mid-October, and a short time later Atwood wrote home that "Colonel Cobb has received the command of this post and Lieu Paine has the com. of the Reg." The "Colonel Cobb" to whom he referred was Amasa Cobb, a seasoned veteran and former commander of the 5th Wisconsin Infantry in the Army of the Potomac. The Illinois native who had spent most of his life in Wisconsin was also a sitting member of Congress and had only just weeks earlier resumed his military career by taking command of the newly formed 43rd Wisconsin.[7]

The 43rd Wisconsin arrived at Johnsonville on October 15, and Atwood's reference to Cobb being in command was penned just four days later. Perhaps Cobb commanded at Johnsonville for a short period before

---

6 Affidavit account provided by Colonel Charles R. Thompson regarding the actions of the U.S. forces at Johnsonville, Tennessee, that resulted in the destruction of government property on November 4, 1864, for the Board of Survey at Nashville, Tennessee, in the Court Martial case of Acting Volunteer Lt. Commander, Edward M. King, December 29, 1864, *U.S. Navy Records 1864-65, Courts Martial*, RG 11-86, U.S. Navy Department Records, National Archives, Washington, D.C., page # not provided.

7 Atwood, October 19, 1864.

Colonel Amasa Cobb (center, seated) with staff officers of the 43rd Wisconsin
Volunteer Infantry Regiment, Nashville, Tennessee, 1865. *Wisconsin Historical Society*

Thompson's arrival. It appears that Thompson became the overall
commander simply because he got there and began making decisions before
Col. Cobb and his 43rd Wisconsin arrived.

Cobb verified his subordination to Thompson's authority on November
4 when he reported, "I was ordered by Colonel Thompson to remain in the
fort with my regiment. My orders from Colonel Thompson were to keep my
men in the intrenchments." However it came to be, Col. Thompson was in
command of the land forces at Johnsonville.[8]

Early that same November, Acting Volunteer Lieutenant Edward M.
King was at "the town of Johnsonville, Tennessee as the senior naval officer
present." King commanded the "USS *Key West* (Gunboat No. 32) in
company with the USS *Tawah* (Gunboat No. 29) and the USS *Elfin*
(Gunboat No. 52), all part of the United States Navy's Mississippi
Squadron." Why he was sent to Johnsonville, or by whom, remains unclear.
Very little is known about Johnsonville's ranking naval officer. King hailed
from Massachusetts and enlisted in the U. S. Navy on October 31, 1863.

8 *OR* 39, pt. 1, 866.

Private Ralph Bushnell,
43rd Wisconsin Volunteer
Infantry Regiment, 1864.
Courtesy of Mr. Don McFall and Family

Apparently, he shared dual-command responsibility with Thompson at Johnsonville, but there is no evidence to suggest that either officer understood his official capacity.[9]

Johnsonville's Defense Forces

Although Cpl. Atwood wrote home that Johnsonville's garrison included "nearly 4,000 men," the number of troops present prior to the arrival of reinforcements on November 5 was only about 2,200. No other site in Tennessee hosted such a convoluted array of U.S. Army and Navy forces assisted by armed civilian employees, all within a 90-acre perimeter whose duty it was to protect one of the country's most important military supply depots and railroads.[10]

It is difficult to calculate the exact number of troops stationed at Johnsonville prior to October 1864 because the place was a rotating door of

9 Jack B. Irion and David V. Beard, *Underwater Archaeological Assessment of Civil War Shipwrecks in Kentucky Lake, Benton and Humphries Counties, Tennessee. Study for Tennessee Dept. of Archaeology, Department of Environment and Conservation* (Nashville, 1993), 35, 39. There is very little biographical information on Edward King, other than a handful of thin references in the *Official Records*. It appears he was honorably discharged from the Navy on July 18, 1867. Acting Volunteer Lieutenant Edward M. King to Capt. Henry Howland, November 3, 1864, RG 94, Carded Records Relating to Civil War Staff Officers, National Archives, Washington, D.C; *ORN* 26, 607, 615.

10 Atwood, November 8, 1864; David W. Higgs, *Nathan Bedford Forrest and the Battle of Johnsonville* (Nashville, 1976), 59-62.

Unidentified Union private, United States Colored Troops, ca. 1863.
Library of Congress

troops who were present one week, but ordered away the next to fill outposts at various sections along the vital Nashville and Northwestern Railroad. Tabulating the forces there for October and November is much easier because when it became known that Nathan Bedford Forrest's Confederate cavalry had entered the region, the exact number of troops and where they were located was reported, and various regiments or companies of regiments received orders to move to Johnsonville to defend it.

As a variety of Union officers stationed at Johnsonville in early November 1864 reported, the garrison included 700 men from the 43rd Wisconsin Infantry, various companies of the 12th,13th, and 100th USCT totaling 400 men, and another 800 armed Quartermaster's Department employees (300 civilians who had been working there since May 1864, and some 500 employees who arrived on November 3 from the Nashville Depot). Other troops included 20 men of the 11th Tennessee Mounted Infantry, and 100 men of the 2nd Tennessee Mounted Infantry (which was operating in the vicinity of Johnsonville, but who were not assigned to the post.)[11]

---

11 The *Official Records* offers no evidence the 13th, 40th, 100th, and 101st USCT were present at Johnsonville after October 1864. Only two companies of the 12th USCT

Unidentified Union corporal, 2nd Tennessee Mounted Infantry Regiment. *Courtesy of Scott W. Gilmer*

The artillery forces present at Johnsonville from September to November 1864 included six 10-pounder Parrott Rifles of the 1st Kansas Battery (80 men), two 12-pounder Napoleons of Battery A, 2nd U.S. Colored Light Artillery (40 men), two 12-pounder bronze Napoleons belonging to a battery operated by the Quartermaster's Department from Nashville (about 30 men), and a pair of 20-pounder Parrott Rifles captured from the Confederates aboard the transport USS *Venus* "mounted on a hill north of the battery of 10-pdrs" (manned by 30 artillerists who were likely Quartermaster's Department employees).[12]

(Companies C and I) seem to have been at the supply depot during the battle of November 4-5, 1864. However, an after-action report by Lt. Col. William Sinclair, assistant inspector General, U.S. Army, on January 7, 1865, in *OR* 39, pt. 1, 861, claims that "detachments of the Twelfth, Thirteenth, and One hundredth U.S. Colored Infantry" were present at Johnsonville on November 4, 1864. Sinclair also mentioned in his report that Col. Thompson stated "the 400 colored troops were the only ones that were drilled." *OR* 39, pt. 1, 865. It is my conclusion that "the 400 colored troops" were "detachments" of the 12th, 13th, and 100th USCT regiments, and they were present at the post on November 4-5 and were engaged with the Confederates.

12 U.S. Navy Department, testimony of Acting 1st Assistant Engineer for the USS *Key West*, Peter Wagner, regarding the destruction of government property at Johnsonville, Tennessee, on November 4, 1864, for the Court of Inquiry at Mound City, Illinois, for the Court Martial case of Acting Volunteer Lt. Commander Edward M. King, May 15, 1865, *U.S. Navy Records 1864-65, Courts Martial*, RG 11-86, 75.

U.S. Navy and Quartermaster's Department

In addition to the land forces, Johnsonville had a thriving river front and served as a docking point for gunboats and privately owned transports leased to the U.S. Navy. The Quartermaster's Department operated the wharf, a macadamized surface (compacted layers of broken stone) at which riverine vessels regularly moored for unloading. Quartermaster employees ran wharf operations, and the Navy, garrison troops, and armed Quartermaster's Department civilian employees helped defend it.[13]

Johnsonville's riverfront was a hive of activity from dawn to dusk every day. Fifteen to as many as thirty boats and barges could be seen moored at the massive wharf at any given time. Sailors served primarily as deck hands, cooks, engineers, mechanics, and gunners aboard their assigned vessels, and assisted with the loading and unloading of supplies, and, at times, even helped haul them inside warehouses alongside employees.

When sailors were not performing the heavy manual labor associated with a busy supply depot, they were participating in gunnery drills or working on repairs and other associated naval matters. Most sailors on the gunboats at Johnsonville's wharf were not stationed there. Instead, they served as crew members aboard transports and other gunboats that frequently docked at the long wharf during their patrols of the 257 miles of the winding Tennessee River between Paducah, Kentucky, and Muscle Shoals, Alabama. In early November 1864, the U.S. Navy could count some 400 sailors and officers aboard the various gunboats and transports docked at the wharf.[14]

---

13 Affidavits from representatives of the states of Ohio, Tennessee, Kentucky, Illinois, and Iowa regarding the destruction of privately owned transports destroyed at Johnsonville, Tennessee, on November 4, 1864. Affidavits sworn and subscribed from January to February, 1865, at Nashville, Tennessee, *U.S. Navy Records 1864-65, Courts Martial*, RG 11-86, U.S. Navy Department, National Archives, Washington, D.C.; *OR* 52, pt.1, 659.

14 *Muscle Shoals Hearings, Before the Committee on Agriculture and Forestry, United States Senate, Sixty-Seventh Congress, Second Session* (Washington, 1922), 901; Charles Dana Gibson and E. Kay Gibson, *The Army's Navy Series, Volume II, Assault and Logistics: Union Army Coastal and River Operations 1861-1866* (Camden, 1995), 385; *ORN* 26, 589; Roscoe C. Martin, "The Tennessee Valley Authority: A Study of Federal Control," *Law and Contemporary Problems* 22 (Summer 1957): 351-377.

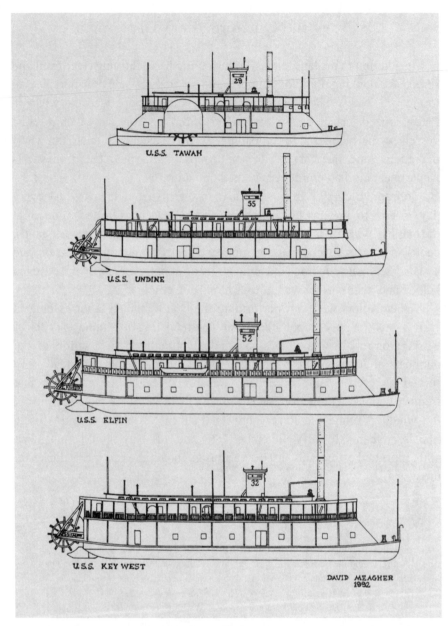

Original profile drawings of Johnsonville's U.S. Navy "Tinclad" Gunboats: U.S.S. *Tawah*, U.S.S. *Elfin*, U.S.S. *Undine*, and U.S.S. *Key West*, 1992. *David J. Meagher*

Johnsonville's gunboats, called "tinclads," were civilian packet boats converted to military use by adding guns and light armor to the front and sides. A gunboat's armor "was intended to deflect light arms fire and not much more, hence its name "tinclad" instead of the more heavily shielded "ironclads." Four gunboats regularly operated out of Johnsonville: USS *Tawah* (Gunboat No. 29), USS *Undine* (Gunboat No. 55), USS *Elfin* (Gunboat No. 52), and USS *Key West* (Gunboat No. 32). The latter was the flagship of Johnsonville's naval commander, Acting Volunteer Lt. Edward M. King. The gunboats at Johnsonville were all stern-wheels except for the side-wheeler USS *Tawah*.[15]

Drill and Quarters

Officers drilled infantry in the open areas of Trace Creek and along the Tennessee River on the clear-cut bank north of the supply depot's central area. Brothers Henry and Walter Howland shared quarters at the supply depot, along with other officers and enlisted men permanently assigned to Johnsonville. On September 23, 1864, Walter described a brief sojourn outside the depot and discovered just how dangerous it was there. "I went with two others some eight miles into the country to attend a meeting," he began,

> It was a little exciting too as a guerrilla band stopped there the night before and interrupted a meeting which was then going on. We are hearing reports constantly of guerrillas abroad and I suppose it is not quite safe to venture out. Rumors are afloat of an anticipated attack from Forrest and the men are today out drilling.[16]

Captain McConnell of the 71st Ohio Infantry (who was also acting assistant-inspector general for the District of Tennessee), filed an informative report about the lack of military drill and training by infantry forces at Johnsonville. "None of the troops, except the men of the First Kansas Battery, had ever been under fire," he complained, and "the 400

---

15 Stephen R. James, Jr., "Additional Archaeological Investigations of Two Battle of Johnsonville Troop Transports Site 40HS338, Tennessee River, Humphries County, Tennessee," Pan-American Consultants, Inc., Memphis, Tennessee (February 2011): 11; *ORN* 26, 605-18.

16 Walter Howland, September 23, 1864; *OR* 39, pt. 1, 865.

Original Sketch of Johnsonville's
Interior by Corporal Lorenzo D.
Atwood, 43rd Wisconsin Volunteer
Infantry, October 19, 1864.
Courtesy of Warren, Robin, and Leon Atwood

colored troops were the only ones that were drilled." The infantry "were posted in rifle pits that had been dug on the flat just north of the railroad—the remainder of the troops were stationed in and around the fortifications."[17]

When not serving on picket duty or drilling the men did all the things soldiers have been doing for centuries: sleeping, resting, telling stories, writing letters, or playing games. They were housed in a variety of shelters, including 30x60 clapboard barracks with bunks along the walls and a stove at each end. The 43rd Wisconsin built small wooden huts with chimneys in anticipation of a long winter. Generally speaking, garrison troops had it easy, and certainly much easier than soldiers at the front. They went to sleep each night in roofed quarters and usually prepared their own meals or were served hot meals by regimental cooks. Cpl. Atwood seemed content with the posting and even wrote home that his friend "Jairus" was "a good bunk mate."

In one of his letters to his wife Cordelia, Atwood enclosed a remarkable sketch showing the perimeter of Johnsonville that included many interior details of the depot. The young corporal sketched the barracks in which he lived, how they were arranged like row houses, and even identified them by their company letter. (It is interesting to note that the sequence of company letters did not match military alphabetical sequence.) Atwood's sketch also identified specific postings, such as "No. 1 is a battery of 6, guns," and "No 2. Reg. of Cavelry." Another important detail found no where else was his semi-circular sketch identifying a "picket line five miles long."

Atwood's drawing is an extremely important contribution to Johnsonville's Civil War history because it identifies details, including the

17 *ORN* 26, 641.

existence of eleven wooden barracks, the location of a second corral at the position of ("No.2 Reg. of Cavelry), and possibly the position of Redoubt No. 2 (described in the sketch as "No. 3, Company Battr'y of our Reg. on a high hill 100 rods.")[18]

Land Defenses at the Supply Depot

When a train from Nashville arrived at the entrance of the supply depot, a combination of USCT troops, various mounted infantry and cavalry, and men from the 43rd Wisconsin searched the cars for any unauthorized persons. Cpl. Atwood told his wife about how he served as "Corparel of the guard" that conducted some of these searches, and, on occasion, helped "keep out a picket guard in the edge of the woods."[19]

A wagon road sixteen feet wide ran along the left side of the railroad directly into the central area of the depot. The rutted dirt route accommodated regular trains of supply wagons, trotting cavalry, tramping infantry, civilians, and every individual who entered the supply depot who wasn't aboard a train.

No records or correspondence indicate whether the post had a formal entrance gate. Other similar posts and forts, including Fort Donelson in Dover, Tennessee, and Fortress Rosecrans in Murfreesboro, Tennessee, did have such designated entrances, meaning Johnsonville almost certainly did as well. An entry gate is visible in one of Coonley's photographs of Fort Johnson Redoubt No. 1 (i.e., the lower redoubt), so it makes sense that something similar or identical would have been constructed at the depot's main entrance, especially since there were "reports constantly of guerrillas abroad." Soldiers stationed at Johnsonville quickly learned it was dangerous outside the depot. Lt. Walter Howland, who rode the rails with a satchel holding $20,000 in pay for the men inside the entrenchments, fully acknowledged that it "was not quite safe to venture out."[20]

18 Atwood, October 31, 1864.

19 Atwood, October 19, 1864.

20 Samuel D. Smith, Benjamin C. Nance, and Fred M. Prouty, *A Survey of Civil War Era Military Sites in Tennessee* (Nashville, 2003), 133. Detail from Jacob Coonley's photographic image of Johnsonville's south view of the supply depot and Fort Johnson

Trace Creek Trestle and Blockhouse, Nashville and Northwestern Railroad near Denver, Tennessee, 1864. *Tennessee State Library & Archives*

The Blockhouse

Trains could not enter Johnsonville's 90-acre compound without passing a small blockhouse sitting atop a steep knob on the left side of the tracks. Richard Wagner, acting first assistant engineer aboard the gunboat USS *Key West*, remembered the fortification as "a small blockhouse, unfinished and unmanned."[21]

By 1864, blockhouses had replaced the more popular spike-topped military log stockades. Johnsonville's blockhouse would have followed

taken in November 1864, at Johnsonville, Tennessee; Walter Howland, September 23, 1864.

21 *The Official Atlas of the Civil War*, Plate XIV; Testimony of Acting 1st Assistant Engineer for the USS *Key West*, Peter Wagner, regarding the destruction of government property at Johnsonville, Tennessee on November 4, 1864, for the Court of Inquiry at Mound City, Illinois, for the Court Martial case of Acting Volunteer Lt. Commander Edward M. King, May 15, 1865, *U.S. Navy Records 1864-65, Courts Martial*, RG 11-86, U.S. Navy Department, 75.

military specifications of "30 feet square and designed to hold about 30 men: a sufficient guard for the less important railroad bridges," but no details seem to exist describing it other than it looked "small." Almost certainly the square log stronghold boasted shuttered windows and loop holes—small openings in the walls that allowed soldiers inside to slide their rifle barrels out and fire while protected from the enemy.

The blockhouse roof consisted of a "layer of logs laid side by side and covered with earth. On top of that was a roof of shingles or boards and battens. It was very important to keep the block house dry so the garrison could live comfortably inside. Blockhouses were supplied with ventilators, cellars, water tanks, and bunks." Blockhouse guards had a clear view of anyone traveling on the road within a mile of the post, and could spot incoming trains from about the same distance.[22]

It is clear that Johnsonville boasted fairly significant defensive lines, but a report by Henry Howland, captain and assistant quartermaster, indicated otherwise. "I should here remark that at this time," he later wrote, "that we had nothing worthy [of] the name of fortifications, only one small block-house and a little earthwork thrown up on two hills overlooking the town and river, where were mounted the six 10-pounder Parrotts of the First Kansas Battery, the only guns then here." As we will see, the "little earthwork thrown up on two hills" was in fact two strong redoubts that helped anchor a long line of entrenchments.[23]

Fort Johnson (Redoubts No.1 and No. 2)

Johnsonville's land defenses were anchored by two earthen redoubts collectively called Fort Johnson, after Gov. Andrew Johnson. For reasons that remain unexplained, the Federals often referred to both forts collectively as "Fort Johnson," even though many references to "Fort Johnson" are actually a reference to the lower redoubt closer to the Tennessee River. Unfortunately, very little information exists regarding the upper redoubt.

End of Excerpt

---

22 *OR* 16, pt. 2, 178; Smith, Nance, and Prouty, *A Survey of Civil War Era Military Sites in Tennessee*, 144-48. Battens are cut boards that provide the fixing point for other roofing materials, such as shingles.

23 *ORN* 26, 621.

© Cornelius - Tulsa

Dr. Clint Crowe is Assistant Professor of History and Political Science at Tulsa Community College. He was Dr. Daniel Sutherland's student at the University of Arkansas. *Caught in the Maelstrom* is based on his dissertation. Dr. Crowe began this study with a Master's Thesis under Dr. Brad Agnew at Northeastern State University at Tahlequah, OK.